THE JOURNEY SO FAR

PHILOSOPHY THROUGH THE AGES

PETER HICKS

ZONDERVAN™

GRAND RAPIDS, MICHIGAN 49530 USA

ZONDERVAN™

The Journey So Far
Copyright © 2003 by Peter Hicks

Requests for information should be addressed to:

Zondervan, *Grand Rapids, Michigan 49530*

Library of Congress Cataloging-in-Publication Data
Hicks, Peter, 1940–
    The journey so far : philosophy through the ages / Peter Hicks. —1st ed.
        p. cm.
Includes bibliographical references and index.
    ISBN 0-310-24003-4
    1. Christianity—Philosophy—History.   2. Philosophy and religion—History.
3. History—Philosophy.   I. Title.
BR100.H45   2003
190—dc21   2003009512

This edition printed on acid-free paper.

Interior design by Todd Sprague

Printed in the United States of America

03 04 05 06 07 08 09 /❖ DC/ 10 9 8 7 6 5 4 3 2 1

CONTENTS

PART 1: GETTING GOING

PART 2: CHRISTIANITY

PART 3: THE NOT-SO-DARK AGE: THE MEDIEVAL SYSTEM

PART 6: THE DEATH OF PHILOSOPHY

LIST OF ICONS

 Aesthetics

 Cause, causality, explanation

 Empirical observation, perception

 Evil, suffering

 Freedom, will

 God

 Language, communication

 Logic

 Meaning, hermeneutics

 Morality, ethics, virtue, goodness, right living, value

 Persons, soul, immortality, humanity

 Reality, existence, ontology, being

 Reason, rationalism

 Revelation, illumination

 Science, the scientific worldview

 Society, community, political philosophy

 Time, history

 Truth, knowledge, epistemology, objectivity, subjectivity

 World

PREFACE

THE HISTORY OF PHILOSOPHY SHOWS, REGRETTABLY, THAT it is a male-dominated subject. Almost all of the early philosophers, for all their wisdom, shared the extraordinary blindness of their cultures toward women. Christianity liberated women, but the church made sure their liberty was limited. The Age of Reason and freethinking appears to have assumed for the most part that women can neither reason nor think. Things improved in the twentieth century, but the discipline is still male dominated.

For this reason I want to start with Catherine, the woman who has given her name to a pinwheel firework that we in England call a Catherine wheel. Throughout the Middle Ages she was accepted as the patron saint of philosophers.

Her story is an exemplary one. Catherine was a Christian who lived in Alexandria in the early fourth century. The Roman emperor Maxentius admired her and wished to marry her, but he was not a Christian. So he found fifty philosophers who set out to convince her that Christianity was not true. They failed. Catherine replied to and defeated every one of their arguments.

In response the furious emperor tortured and killed her on the wheel.

She makes a worthy patron saint.

In planning this book it has been hard to decide what to include and what to leave out. In an ideal world a history of philosophy should cover all philosophies from all ages and all cultures. In practice most histories have limited themselves to highlights of Western thought from the Presocratics to the twentieth century. This is both parochial and unhelpful to the student who wants to find out something about lesser known thinkers, such as Amo, an eighteenth-century African philosopher, or Hipparchia the Cynic, a noteworthy woman philosopher who lived round about 300 B.C.

The main difficulty with an inclusive survey, however, is the fragmenting effect it has. Of the thousands of philosophers, each is different. And many have the bad habit of dismissing the work of their predecessors as inadequate and starting from scratch in producing their own systems. That doubtless helped make their names, but it makes it very difficult to make the history of philosophy sound like a developing story.

In fact, this book does claim that the history of philosophy, for all its fragmentation, is a developing story and even that it has a significant plot. So I've resisted the pressure to turn it into a chronological dictionary of all the philosophers who have ever lived. Instead, I've tried to trace the main trends and make sure I cover the most significant thinkers.

And, in any case, the world is not ideal. Space is limited, and any attempt to include more than the better known thinkers would mean that no one would get adequate treatment. I've found it virtually impossible, as it is, to reduce the life work of a complex and detailed thinker to a page or two of intelligible summary. If it took Aristotle or Kant or Heidegger hundreds of thousands of words to say it, how can I say it in a few hundred? And haven't many eminent philosophers professed themselves baffled by the complexities (or absurdities!) of the views of other philosophers? Who, after all, would dare to reduce a Mahler symphony to a few simple bars? But it has had to be done, with all the risk of oversimplification and misrepresentation that goes with it.

But there's another factor. I would have loved to include the story of, say, sub-Saharan African philosophy. But it has been a living story that has developed through oral transmission. We have no records of what Africans were thinking a thousand or two thousand years ago. We only have what they're thinking now. Even where cultures and civilizations of the past have kept records of their beliefs and practices, in many cases these have been lost or have come down to us in such a fragmented form that scholars are unable to build up an agreed picture of their total philosophies.

So, to a large extent, I've had to give way and spend almost all the time on the story of Western philosophy, consoling myself with the thought that most of the people who will read this book will themselves be part of the Western tradition, seeking to know how we have got into the mess we are currently in and determined, hopefully, to find a positive way out.

Somewhere toward the end of the book, we will come across the concept, accepted by just about everyone these days, that no interpretation of a text or a story can be, or even should be, totally objective. The myth that the historian and storyteller can produce something that contains nothing of themselves has been exploded. Every book you read is biased. All writers and teachers and friends you discuss things with start with a set of presuppositions, and those presuppositions affect how they see and say things.

And I am no exception. Years ago I greatly enjoyed reading Bertrand Russell's *History of Western Philosophy*. I still enjoy it. But then and now I gasp at Russell's powerful bias, something less excusable in the 1940s than it would be today. But that bias hasn't lessened the value of his book. In many ways, for me as a Christian, the strength of his atheism has provoked me to creative and productive responses. As you go through this book you will doubtless pick up my bias. I hope you will enjoy it. You don't have to agree with it. But I will be disappointed if it doesn't provoke you to some creative and productive thinking. After all, as I point out at the start, I have not written this book just to tell the history of philosophy; I have written it so that you can write the next chapter and change the world.

WELCOME

YOU ARE STUDYING PHILOSOPHY AT THE MOST EXCITING and potentially most fruitful moment in all its history. This is the key moment. All past philosophy has led to this moment. Decisions made at this moment will shape the whole future of philosophy and so the whole history of humanity.

In the last five hundred years, Western thinkers have attempted the greatest task ever undertaken by the human intellect. Dissatisfied with the God-centered understanding of the world and way of living in the world that had been followed for the previous thousand years and more, they set out to establish a whole new approach built on human reason. For a time there was a tremendous optimism that this could be done, and plenty of philosophers claimed they had actually done it.

But the sad fact was that none of their proposed systems was satisfactory. Every system had flaws that ultimately made it unworkable. As the years went by, the initial optimism began to wane. From talking confidently about the conquests of human reason, thinkers started talking about the limits of human reason and then about the inadequacy and failure of human reason. By the end of the twentieth century it was universally acknowledged that the project had failed.

Putting it very simply, you could think of the story of philosophy, at any rate in the West, in terms of blocks of roughly half a millennium each. The half millennium before Christ posed the big questions and offered plenty of answers. None of the answers won universal acceptance; lots of them were pretty short lived. So, by the time of Christ, there was quite a range of available philosophies or worldviews, ways of understanding the world and living in the world. In other words, relativism ruled. But relativism was livable at that time because it wasn't total. Though people disagreed over how to define things like virtue and truth, they still believed that virtue and truth existed, at least in some sense. Meanings and interpretations varied, but all believed meaning was possible.

The next half-millennium saw the coming of Christianity and the permeation of its worldview, which provided the firmest of foundations for goodness, value, truth, meaning, and purpose. Other worldviews remained during this period and fought hard to destroy Christianity, either by showing its inadequacy or simply by using force. But they failed, and Christianity became established as a comprehensive worldview that united Western thought on a secure basis for the next two half-millennium blocks. The reason for its effectiveness was that it provided a philosophy or worldview that worked. Christianity as a worldview supplied an explanatory system and way of living that was comprehensive, that answered all the big questions, that was internally coherent, and that was accepted throughout the West.

But the fifth half-millennium, the era of modernism from which we have just emerged, destroyed that unitary worldview. It did so not so much by showing that it was false, but by pushing it to one side in favor of an exciting new alternative, a philosophy that explained everything in terms of humanity.

So at the start of the sixth block, we are confronted with the failure and rejection of the quest of the last half-millennium. Modernism has drawn a blank. The attempt to establish a worldview based on human reason, in place of the God-centered worldview of the medieval period, has failed. Instead of offering a way of understanding and living in the world, the current philosophical scene is strewn with negatives such as irrationalism, postmodernism, and anarchy. And the issue is, where do we go from here?

A lot of people would say there is nowhere to go. We have pushed on every door, and the last one is "No Exit." So we give up. There are no answers, no truth, no meaning, no values—only despair, nihilism, chaos, and suicide.

They are wrong. There are a lot of answers. That's what this book is about: the answers people have put forward to the big questions. Some of them may be pretty poor answers, and many of them may be out of fashion. But that doesn't stop them from being answers.

What's more, those who go for relativism and despair know that we can't live without answers. It is okay being a relativist in a philosophical discussion: "It may be true for you, but it's not true for me." "You say it's wrong, but I say it's right; and there's no way of deciding between us." But when it comes to anything in real life, the relativists have to drop their relativism. They have to walk out through the door and not through the brick wall. They have to accept that when human life cries out for love and justice and meaning, it has to be given something real. To live in the real world you have to have answers.

Others say that, faced with the collapse of modernism, we can return to the sort of relativism that was around before the coming of Christianity; but for two hugely significant reasons, this can't be done. The first is the global village. If human life is going to continue to exist in any acceptable form in our shrinking world, we all must share at least some basic principles and beliefs. We can't all hide away in our little corners by ourselves.

The second, more profound reason why we can't return to pre-Christian relativism is that the version of relativism that is being offered today is much more radical than what was on offer then. Then there was disagreement over what is good but almost universal agreement over the fact that there is such a thing as goodness and that we ought to do what is good. There was disagreement over aspects of the truth, but practically everyone believed there was such a thing as truth. Granted, there were the occasional thinkers even then who realized that such partial relativism was ultimately impossible. But they were in the minority and were able to go on living on the backs of those who had at least some positive beliefs. But today no agreement exists in these areas. The form of relativism we are offered has dispensed even with these elements. It isn't telling us we can choose to disagree over what is true or good or of value. It is saying there are no such things as truth or goodness or value. It isn't giving us permission to choose our own worldview. It is telling us that it has abolished all worldviews. Such extreme relativism is indistinguishable from total despair, chaos, and suicide.

So the choice is to accept the despair or to start again. Since you have chosen to study philosophy, I guess it is reasonable to assume that you have not given way to total despair or committed suicide. I also guess that you are the sort of person who is going to have the opportunity to shape the thinking of many people in years to come. So you have a big responsibility to offer them a philosophy that works. They need a worldview that has an answer to meaninglessness and despair and chaos. They have to have a set of beliefs that can be the foundation for justice and goodness and the basis on which we all set about building a society in which people can find love, truth, security, purpose, meaning, value, and all the other things that go into making up the wholeness of human life.

That in turn gives us two choices: to find a brand new worldview that is such that everyone can accept or to reestablish and reauthenticate the Christian worldview, which, in theory at least, already permeates much of our society and is, according to statistics, accepted by one-third of the world's population.

If the first of these two options looks immense, the second isn't easy either. There is no way we could simply write off the modern experiment as a dead loss and return to the medieval Christian worldview. If we believe that a God-centered worldview can provide a basis for life in the twenty-first century, we need to show how making God the basis for meaning and truth and value answers the questions and needs of women and men in the twenty-first century. But to do that we need to look at those questions and at the various answers that have been offered in the past. We need to work through the differences between a philosophy that is based on God and one that is based on human beings. We need to know why, after more than two thousand years, when just about every philosophy gave God a key role, people in the last couple of hundred years or so have started trying to produce worldviews that exclude him, with such shattering results. And to do this we need to study the story of philosophy.

GETTING GOING

PART ONE

ONE

DAWN IN THE EAST

WORLDVIEWS BEFORE THE RISE OF GREEK THOUGHT

> In this chapter we look at two ancient world-views, the Hebrew and the Hindu. Both were strongly God-centered.

PEOPLE HAVE ALWAYS HAD BELIEFS. GENERALLY, WE MAY guess, their beliefs fitted together to make up some sort of worldview or philosophy. For the most part they shared these beliefs and worldview with others in their community or culture and passed them on from one generation to the next. Probably these sets of beliefs developed and changed only slowly. Every now and then someone would come up with a new idea, but even then it would be fairly safe to assume that it would have taken some time for anything new to be generally accepted and absorbed into the overall worldview of the community. So, for the most part, sets of beliefs would have been handed down without a great deal of change from one generation to another.

The most common way for a philosophy or set of beliefs to be abandoned or changed radically was defeat in war. One community, with its beliefs, would be overwhelmed by another with a different set of beliefs. Perhaps the conquerors would force their views on the conquered. But, additionally, the conquered might readily choose to change their beliefs. After all, the conquerors' beliefs or worldview had shown themselves to be superior in that they had won the battle.

Many of the earliest philosophies or worldviews have been lost or have come down to us in a very limited or fragmented form. So we have no means of discovering the beliefs of many of the earliest communities and civilizations. There are, for example, virtually no records of the cultures and beliefs of Africa south of the Sahara until comparatively recent times. At best we can make a few guesses about them. But it is important to accept that guesses are only guesses. The very limited information we have is always open to more than one interpretation.

The earliest collection of material that can justifiably be called a coherent worldview is that of the ancient Hebrews. Other cultures and civilizations predated them, but we know little about their worldview compared with that expressed in the earliest parts of the Old Testament.

Writing was in use in the Middle East from before 3000 B.C., and something of these other cultures can be gleaned from very early inscriptions and from other archaeological discoveries. Perhaps the earliest writings so far discovered that might be called philosophical date back to about 1500 B.C. These are the religious and mythological texts from Ugarit (Ras Shamra) in north Syria. Ugaritic is a language cognate to ancient Hebrew, and the texts have parallels with Hebrew poetry, some of which could well date from the same era. At about the same time, religious poems were being composed further east in India. These were handed down orally for a thousand years and formed the basis for the various schools of what we now call Hindu thought.

The fact that these Middle Eastern and Indian poems were basically religious and were for the most part orally transmitted may suggest that they are irrelevant to philosophy or that they are an unreliable guide to what people actually believed. But almost all early philosophy was essentially religious. Indeed, as we shall see, almost all philosophy until the last couple of centuries has been essentially religious. And oral transmission of poetry in an age when few people could write was in fact tremendously reliable. This was especially so where that poetry was used in ritual and worship, as appears to be the case with the Ras Shamra texts, the Hebrew Psalms and other poetry, and the Indian Vedas. There is little reason to doubt that at least some of the Hebrew oral tradition goes back to the era of Ras Shamra and even earlier to the patriarchal period before the eighteenth century B.C. Similarly, in the Hindu tradition, although it lacks the anchor points in historical figures and events that the Hebrew tradition has, there is no reason to doubt that the oral tradition could go back to about 1500 B.C. In each case, despite the skepticism of some scholars, it seems reasonable to assume that the tradition they embody is reliable.

We start our survey of the story of philosophy with a look at these two great worldviews, each of which has had a profound effect on the development of subsequent thought. This means we will not explore the rather tenuous speculations of those who have tried to piece together the philosophies of earlier cultures, whose influence has been less marked, such as those of ancient Egypt and Babylonia and the Minoan civilization of Crete, except to say that religion played a major part in their worldviews, which were essentially polytheistic but with a tendency to make one god supreme.

TO THINK THROUGH

Until fairly recently it was standard to assume that early beliefs and worldviews were necessarily false, or, at the very least, very inferior to our contemporary way of seeing things. Commentators used words like "primitive" to imply that the beliefs of these early worldviews were crude, poorly thought out, illogical, and not worthy of our attention. Perhaps this tells us more about the attitude of the commentators than about the worldviews. Why do you think commentators adopted this attitude? Why do people still tend to assume the latest ideas are necessarily better than the earlier ones?

THE HEBREW WORLDVIEW

About 300 B.C. Theophrastus, a disciple of Aristotle, wrote of the Jews that "being philosophers by race, they converse with each other about 'the Divine.'" Though the Old Testament is rightly looked on as a collection of religious writings, it also provides us with the earliest, most detailed, and most complete worldview or set of philosophical beliefs we possess.

How old is old? The dating of Old Testament material has been a matter of vigorous debate between scholars. Some are prepared to accept the early Hebrew writings more or less at their face value and believe, for example, that the material preserved in the Pentateuch, the first five books of the Old Testament, goes back to the time of Moses in the thirteenth century B.C., and that a substantial amount of the poetic and Wisdom literature was in circulation by the time of David (about 1000 B.C.). Others seek to date the material a lot later. Many would compromise and suggest that the documents as we have them may be as late as, say, the fifth century B.C., but they are based on documents or oral tradition that go back much earlier.

It is hard to avoid the conclusion that differing presuppositions have had considerable influence on the way differing scholars approach and interpret the evidence. In particular, those who believe that anything as "advanced" as the worldview they contain can't have arisen early, feel it necessary to seek to date the material as late as possible. It is worth noting, however, that even the most skeptical of scholars has to admit that a substantial amount of the early Old Testament material we now have reached the form in which we have it well before the time of Plato.

My own view is that the basic principles of the Hebrew worldview, such as the nature of God and its implications, go back a very long way, through a variety of written forms, often to earlier oral forms. Skeptical presuppositions apart, there are no compelling reasons to reject the historicity of Moses or, indeed, of Abraham, some seven hundred years earlier, or to question the basic worldview and beliefs attributed to them, even though, inevitably, Jewish thought developed substantially in detail in the two millennia between Abraham and Christ.

Moses. Egypt (thirteenth century B.C.). Brought up in the court of the pharaoh of Egypt, Moses was "educated in all the wisdom of the Egyptians" (Acts 7:22), not least in their philosophy and religion. After murdering an Egyptian and fleeing to Midian, he was met by God, who called him to lead the captive Israelites out of Egypt. This entailed considerable confrontation with Pharaoh (probably Rameses II). The people escaped through the miraculous parting of the sea of reeds. God met with Moses on Sinai and gave him the Ten Commandments and the terms of the covenant, outlining the basis of the relationship between God and his people. Instead of traveling straight to Canaan, the Promised Land, the people rebelled, and Moses led them in forty years of wilderness wanderings before dying just before the people entered Canaan.

Though widely viewed as the most significant person in the development of Hebrew thought and culture, Moses is in fact presented in the Old Testament as a paradoxical figure. On the one hand, he was chosen and protected by God at birth. He led the Hebrews out of slavery in Egypt, received the covenant of God on Sinai, and led them through the desert. He was rewarded with the verdict "No prophet has risen in Israel like Moses, whom the LORD knew face to face. . . . No one has ever shown the mighty power or performed the awesome deeds that Moses did in the sight of all Israel" (Deut. 34:10–12).

Yet Moses started his mission with a disastrous murder and then ran and hid. He virtually refused to respond to God's call. And he was not allowed to enter the Promised Land because of his disobedience. The Old Testament accounts are less interested in focusing attention on Moses than on the God who is speaking and working through Moses.

Poetry and Wisdom literature.

In the days before books, even uneducated people were able to remember and pass on to subsequent generations large quantities of material they had learned by heart. The accuracy of such oral transmission was very high, especially when the material had been widely disseminated and frequently used, as, for instance, with the Psalms. The poetic form of the five Hebrew books Job, Psalms, Proverbs, Ecclesiastes, and Song of Songs made them all the easier to learn by heart and pass on accurately. Thus it is very possible that though the written form of these books may be later, much of the content goes back at least to the time of David and Solomon, perhaps half a millennium before Zarathustra, Buddha, Confucius, and the earliest Greek philosophers.

The poetry and Wisdom literature of the Old Testament provide a rich source of the early Hebrew worldview in action. They show us people worshiping and praying, struggling with the problems of life, celebrating the good things of life, and expressing the accumulated wisdom of their community on how we should live. Though it is important to remember that poetry and hymns and even the generalized sayings of the wise are not primarily designed to give us philosophical truths, we still can use them to help build up our understanding of the worldview of the early Hebrews and supplement the other Old Testament writings. Indeed, such poetry and hymns make up the only sources of information we have about the teaching of Zarathustra, Buddha, Confucius, and several of the early Greek philosophers. Thus we can find in the Psalms, for example, clear indications about the nature of God or the centrality of our personal relationship with him and our dependence on him. In the book of Job we are faced with the agonizing issues of the problem of evil. And in Proverbs we see again and again the inseparability of the three key features—a right relationship with God, true wisdom, and right living.

The nature of God.

Theophrastus was right. At the heart of the ancient Hebrews' philosophy is a radical concept of God. Every other part of the Hebrew worldview derives from this. Perhaps there are five main elements in their concept of God.

- God is one (monotheism). There are other supernatural beings, both good and evil, but Yahweh alone is the one true God and alone is to be worshiped.
- God is Creator. The world had a beginning; it was planned and called into being by God's powerful creative word. Everything depends on him for its continuing existence. All powerful, he rules over everything.
- God relates to his creation. Not only does he hold everything in being; he communicates with and acts in the world. He reveals his name and his nature; he calls people to worship him and join in covenant relationship with him. He shows compassion, grace, and love; he cares for his creation and for his people and demonstrates his goodness and love to them. He is a protector and a savior. Both individuals and God's people as a whole can experience a relationship with him, expressed in worship, prayer, obedience, love, and right living.
- God is holy. His moral standards and demands are the highest, high enough to terrify those who do wrong. Because he is holy, he is also judge. His judgments are universal, extending to those who do not acknowledge him, but always just and with the goal of eliminating evil and establishing goodness on the earth.
- God is true. He is faithful, dependable. What he says can be trusted. All that he does is fair and just.

The world. The world is God's creation and can be understood only in relationship to him. He made it in the first place, and he holds it in being; without his power it would cease to exist. His power is sovereign over nature and all the creatures he has made. The act of creation and his continuing involvement with the world is planned and meaningful; there is a divine purpose in all things.

Meaning. A key saying of the wise is "The fear of the LORD is the beginning of wisdom" (Prov. 1:7). To understand anything in the world we need to start with God. Apart from God there is only chaos and meaninglessness. Wisdom isn't just cerebral; it is right living, and right living is living according to the revelations and character of God. Understanding, similarly, is more than cognitive; it is putting into practice what we have apprehended.

Truth. Again, truth is an essentially God-centered concept. Truth exists because God is true. What he says is true; in his nature he is dependable; his acts demonstrate his faithfulness. Truth is much richer than detached propositions. It has powerful moral implications. What is true is right. If we say "Amen" (one of the Hebrew words for truth) to a proposition, we are committing ourselves to live by it. God's commands are true, not just because they reflect reality, but because obeying them enables us to live reality. Truth cannot be divorced from goodness, rightness, and justice; truth that is not lived out ceases to be truth.

Humanity.

Like the rest of creation, we gain our significance because we are planned and created by God. But in our case the significance is much greater because we are capable of moral choice and a personal relationship with him. Compared with that of God, our being is limited and tenuous; but his power and covenant love offer us security. We are but dust or clay, but into that dust God has breathed his breath, implanted his image. As complex creatures, we can be described in a variety of ways—as spirit, soul, heart, body, and flesh. Each description has its own nuance, but they all tend to overlap with each other, emphasizing the unity, rather than the fragmentation, of the human person.

Morality.

Goodness or holiness is a key issue because holiness is a key feature of the nature of God. He is the standard for our morality and the judge of our failure. A substantial part of the law code of Moses is taken up with the need for ceremonial holiness and right living. Goodness or holiness is both a matter of being in a right relationship with God (and so with others) and of doing the right things. As creatures we are morally responsible to God. We have freedom to choose to obey or disobey him, and he will judge our actions and reward or punish us accordingly.

Time and history.

Time has its beginning in God, and history is the story of his purposes. Time is linear, an unfolding and purposive story, not cyclical, as, for example, in Egyptian thought, where everything goes in a circle, back to where it started.

In the Old Testament, then, we have a very rich supply of material from which we can build up a picture of the philosophical principles of the early Hebrews. The quantity, richness, and diversity of the material means that we can be very confident that our picture is an accurate one. The debate continues about the dating of much of the material, but even if we play safe and go for the later dates that some scholars propose, the material is still much earlier than anything else comparable in the ancient world.

The picture drawn is of a well-developed coherent worldview that is radically theocentric, that is, putting God at the center. Everything else draws its significance from him and his nature. The picture given of God is itself radical. It is strongly monotheistic and entails a close involvement and relationship between God and his world and, in particular, with his people.

TO THINK THROUGH

Many of us are so familiar with the Hebrews' worldview that we find it hard to appreciate how radical it was. Try to imagine how their concept of God must have appeared to their contemporaries, most of whom believed in many gods, each limited in power and often confined to a specific locality or people group. Try to picture, too, the impact of a belief in God, who is both holy (and so in many ways terrifying) and loving and is involved in personal relationships with his people.

The philosophy of the Hebrews had enormous impact on the development of Christianity and so on the story of all Western thought. Do you feel there are any useful elements of it that seem to have got lost on the way? What do you think are the most significant insights of the Hebrew worldview that could have particular relevance today?

EARLY HINDU PHILOSOPHY

The Vedas. Early Hebrew thought formed a coherent system with accepted beliefs and clear principles for living. By contrast, the earliest expression of what has come to be known as Hindu thought is widely varied, even more varied than that of the Presocratics. The term *Hinduism* was attached comparatively late to what originated as a collection of grassroots religious practices and beliefs. Its earliest hymns, or *Vedas*, were probably composed independently of each other and reflect differing attitudes and situations. Their composition was spread over a period of a thousand years; some of them go back to the period when the Hebrews were slaves in Egypt. No attempt was made in the early period to systematize them or to make them agree with each other. Even when, later, the Vedas were collected and some such attempt was made, Hinduism split into several schools, each emphasizing differing aspects of its approach and teaching.

So it isn't possible to summarize the main points of the Vedic worldview in the way that we summarized the main points of the Hebrew worldview. Rather, each poem or collection of poems is to be seen as the product of a specific ritual or the wisdom of a specific seer. They address a range of nature deities, such as Fire, the Atmosphere, and Soma, an intoxicating drink. They include ritual chants and mantras to accompany rites and sacrifices, and spells to ward off evil. They express an overall worldview in which the supernatural and the natural merge and in which gods lack both the ontological transcendence and loving involvement of the God of the Hebrews.

The Upanishads. But from about 800 B.C. collections of the Vedas were supplemented by teaching in the form of story, parable, and dialogue, known as the *Upanishads*. The name, which means "to sit down near," comes from the reverent and confidential setting of the students learning from their teacher. The wisdom of the Upanishads soon became authoritative in the development of Hindu thought. Though there are over a hundred of them, only a small proportion actually date back to the early period. The key ones were probably composed between 600 and 400 B.C.

Monism. The Upanishads presented themselves as explaining the inner meaning of the Vedas. In fact, they marked a radical shift from the nature-worshiping polytheism of the Vedas to a focus on something much more monistic, the One, the Absolute. Additionally, they called for a rejection of the Vedas' belief in the validity of external rituals and sacrifices as the key to salvation and proposed instead that the seeker after truth and salvation turn inward and find Brahman there.

Brahman. Brahman is seen by the Upanishads as the eternal and absolute source and power behind everything else, including the Vedic gods. He is the creator and sustainer. He is bliss and truth and reality; all things are real as they are absorbed in him. He is infinite, beyond space and time and all worldly categories, yet containing all these things within himself. As such he would be totally beyond human knowledge or apprehension were it not for the fact that in addition to being infinite and transcendent, Brahman is also the human self or *atman*.

Humanity. Since Brahman is all things, he is also consciousness. When in self-reflection and meditation we experience our own consciousness, we experience Brahman. Experiencing him is being one with him; we know him, and we are him, since in Upanishad thought knowledge and being are one. As humans we fall short of oneness with Brahman, and this is expressed in evil and suffering. This is *maya*, Brahman veiling or concealing himself. It is expressed in error and illusion. It is focusing on plurality when reality is one. It is turning from the infinite to the finite, from the real to the unreal; it is the pathway to nonbeing.

Living. The Upanishads call upon the individual to follow a life of detachment from the illusionary objects of the world, exercising self-control and renunciation of desires. Since all is one, we should treat other humans with the kindness and compassion we exercise toward ourselves. Nevertheless, the individual's personal salvation through self-knowledge is of greater importance than our concern for our neighbors, and the high point of Upanishad teaching is the final renunciation of all worldly ties by the individual to become a wandering ascetic seeking only Brahman. Those who succeed in this search and become truly enlightened and one with him escape from the cycle of reincarnation that is the fate of most.

TO THINK THROUGH

The change from grassroots polytheism to a fairly sophisticated form of monism was a very big step to take. No one knows what motivated it, though we shall see a similar trend in Zarathustra and in Greek philosophy. What do you think were the factors that caused people to believe in a multiplicity of gods? And why was there a trend toward recognizing just one?

TWO

THE AGE OF ENLIGHTENMENT

THE SIXTH AND FIFTH CENTURIES B.C.

In this chapter we will look at the original philosophies that lie behind Zoroastrianism, Buddhism, Confucianism, and Taoism. We will also explore the ideas of the earliest Greek philosophers.

THE PERIOD BETWEEN THE EARLY SIXTH CENTURY AND THE mid fifth century B.C. was unique in the history of human thought. In a band stretching from Sicily to China, there arose quite independently a group of thinkers whose names are still celebrated today and whose ideas have affected the course of history. Zarathustra, Buddha, Confucius, and the founder of Taoism all belong to this period. So do the Presocratics, who traditionally have been looked on as the first Western philosophers. And, though dates are debated by scholars, it seems likely that the most significant Upanishads also belong to this same period.

ZARATHUSTRA

Compared with what we know of Moses or Abraham, we know virtually nothing about the life of Zarathustra. Guesses about his dates range over a thousand years, starting with the sixteenth century B.C., though the traditional view is that he was teaching, probably in Iran, in the first half of the sixth century B.C. He was a prophetic figure, calling his contemporaries to move from worship of many deities (devas and ahuras, nature gods and other supernatural beings worshiped in the Indo-Iranian tradition and still seen in some forms of Hinduism) to worshiping one supreme God. He is perhaps best known today through the works of Friedrich Nietzsche and Richard Strauss, who both used the phrase "Also sprach Zarathustra" (Thus spake Zarathustra) to great effect, though the philosophical ideas expressed in their works are only very loosely related to Zarathustra's teaching (or, indeed, to each other's). The Greek form of Zarathustra's name is Zoroaster, and the religion of which he is the main prophet is called Zoroastrianism. Though virtually wiped out by the spread of Islam, Zoroastrianism was widely followed in the Middle East up to the seventh century A.D. and still has some 219,000 followers, mostly in western India.

The teaching of Zarathustra is preserved in a collection of *Gathas*, or hymns, to Ahura Mazda. Although it is not easy to distinguish which of the ideas expressed in the Gathas go back to Zarathustra and which are later developments, the following appear to be the main points of his teaching.

Monotheism. In common with much of the ancient world, Zarathustra recognized the existence of a whole range of supernatural beings. But among them and far greater than them all, he insisted, is one supreme God, the Wise Lord, Ahura Mazda, who alone is to be worshiped.

The world. Zarathustra taught that the physical world had a beginning and that Ahura Mazda is its creator. He also probably taught that the world of supernatural beings was created by Ahura Mazda. Creation is essentially good, though some of the lesser deities have chosen evil.

Good and evil. Though at heart monotheistic, Zoroastrianism is sometimes described as dualistic in that it pictures good and evil as two powerful opposing forces locked in conflict with each other. Goodness and light are expressed supremely in Ahura Mazda; evil and darkness are focused in the chief evil spirit, Angra Mainyu. Humans may choose to side with either. The final defeat of evil by Ahura Mazda is certain.

Time and history. It is generally believed that much of the ancient world saw time as cyclical rather than linear. For them time went in an endless series of circles, never getting anywhere different. The moon waxes, then wanes, then waxes and wanes again. Day follows night follows day; seasons follow each other in an endless cycle. Zarathustra, on the other hand, seems to have thought in a much more linear way. He believed in a beginning, a long, drawn-out story of the world and its peoples and the struggle between good and evil, and a final climax, the end of history, when evil is finally and totally destroyed.

Humanity. Zarathustra taught that humans are free; we are able to choose between evil and good, light and darkness, justice and injustice, love and exploitation, and so on. Choosing to worship Ahura Mazda is choosing the good and the right, and will mean eternal joy after the end of the world for those who do so.

Zoroastrianism and Hebrew thought. It is interesting to speculate on the relationship between the teaching of Zarathustra and Hebrew thought. There is no doubt that travel and communication in the Middle East in the second and first millennia B.C. would have enabled ideas to spread either from the Hebrews to Zarathustra or in the other direction. It is impossible to tell exactly what happened, but there can be no doubt that basic Hebrew concepts were established well before the traditional date of Zarathustra and probably even before the earlier dates some have proposed. So it would seem likelier that Zarathustra was influenced by Hebrew thought rather than the other way round, though it is conceivable that the two systems of thought arose quite independently.

TO THINK THROUGH

How do you view the struggle between good and evil?

THE PRESOCRATICS

We can guess that there were other prophets in sixth-century Iran besides Zarathustra, others seeking enlightenment in India besides Buddha, and others seeking the pathway of life in China besides Confucius and Lao Zi. Doubtless there were many who speculated about the nature of the universe and the nature of God and how we as humans should live. Very probably some of their ideas were crazy and others were brilliant. But we have no record of them or their teaching.

In Greece, however, the case was different. Here we do have records of dozens of thinkers and teachers who arose, apparently spontaneously, in different parts of the Greek-speaking world during the sixth and fifth centuries B.C. These records have been preserved largely because a considerable part of the huge literary output of subsequent Greek centuries has come down to us.

We have no complete works of any of the Presocratics; our main source is quotations of their teaching found in later writers. Sometimes we have only an odd enigmatic saying, plucked out of context and open to any number of interpretations. Altogether we have fragments of the work of more than fifty thinkers. Given their divergence and complexity, you will have to be content with a summary of just a few key ideas of the best-known figures. So that you may get a taste of the real thing, here are some of their sayings—without the interpretations offered by the scholars. Have a look at them. Try working out what you think they might mean. Who knows, in some cases your interpretation may be more accurate than the experts'.

All things are full of gods.
—THALES

There is one God, supreme among gods and men, in no way like mortals either in body or mind. —XENOPHANES

God is day night, winter summer, war peace, fullness hunger.
—HERACLITUS

Most divine things escape our knowledge through lack of faith.
—HERACLITUS

No aspect of the whole is lacking; no aspect is superfluous.
—EMPEDOCLES

It is inconceivable that something should come from nothing, and it is incoherent and unheard of that what exists should be totally destroyed.
—EMPEDOCLES

What we describe and think must exist; it needs must be. But nothingness cannot exist.
—PARMENIDES

Whatever existed always existed and always will exist. For if it came into existence, it must have been nothing before it existed. But if there was nothing, nothing could come into existence from nothing. —MELISSUS

All things are one.
—HERACLITUS

It seems to me that all things that exist are other than the same thing and are the same thing. —DIOGENES

Boundless air is the source of everything past, present, and future, including gods and godlike things. —ANAXIMENES

As our soul, being air, holds us together, so spirit and air encompass the whole cosmos.
—ANAXIMENES

All things that become and come into being are earth and water. —XENOPHANES

Air was the first distinct elemental part; the second was fire; then earth. From earth gushed water.　　—EMPEDOCLES

All known things have number. Without it nothing at all could be thought or known.
　　　　　　—PHILOLAUS

You would not step twice into the same river.　—HERACLITUS

All other things share a part of everything; mind alone is infinite and autonomous and is mixed with nothing but is alone by itself.
　　　　　　—ANAXAGORAS

In everything there is a part of everything except mind, and there are some things in which there is mind as well.
　　　　　　—ANAXAGORAS

The explanation of sight is that images, the same shape as the things we see, continually flow from them and fall on to the eye.　　—LEUCIPPUS AND
　　　　　　DEMOCRITUS

Atoms move by hitting and striking each other.
　　　　　—LEUCIPPUS AND
　　　　　　DEMOCRITUS

The earth is in mid-air, not held up by anything, but staying there because of its equal distance from everything.
　　　　　　—ANAXIMANDER

The sun puts brightness into the moon.　　—ANAXAGORAS

So, though almost all the actual writings, such as they were, of the early Greek thinkers have been lost, we have a rich supply of quotations and summaries of their ideas embedded in Greek literature.

The interest of these thinkers, whom we call Presocratics, or Greek thinkers before Socrates, covered a whole range of ideas and concepts. It included philosophy, metaphysics, theology, cosmology, physics, astronomy, mathematics, epistemology, medicine, zoology, biology, anatomy, ethics, and politics. The Presocratics were not philosophers in our contemporary strict sense of the word any more than Moses or Zarathustra were. Nor, with the possible exception of Pythagoras, were they prophets or founders of religious communities, although they all had things to say about God or the gods. Some modern commentators have tended to see them as the first scientists. But though, more than any of their predecessors, they explored areas now covered by science, what they were doing was hardly what we would call scientific. Traditional science has had little time for most of their ideas because their ideas tended to be based on speculation rather than on scientific observation.

Yet they found themselves free to speculate, to develop new theories about the world and the heavenly bodies and the gods and our place in the scheme of things. Perhaps this freedom arose in part from their experience of the diversity of beliefs they encountered around the Eastern Mediterranean. The earliest Presocratics, the Ionians from Miletus, for example, lived on the edge of Asia Minor (Turkey) and would have encountered many ideas from further East, through Mesopotamia and Persia to India. Thales, for example, probably spent some time in Egypt; others traveled west to Italy.

But an additional factor was the structure of the Greek city-states with their incipient democratic principles. The discovery that the world contains a range of concepts and ideas can readily spawn fresh ones, and Greek society of the sixth and fifth centuries, not only encouraged freedom of speech, but provided a ready audience for those with something to say, as is reflected several centuries later when Paul visited Athens.

Many of the Presocratics appear to have been colorful figures. Stories were told of their eccentricities of dress or habits. Some appeared to set out to shock in the way they presented their concepts. Few agreed with any of the others; their teaching makes up a complex and conflicting hodgepodge of ideas. However, some did establish "schools" of those who followed or developed their teaching. Though we have no reason to doubt the sincerity of the majority, as time went by the number grew of those who appear to have been mainly motivated by what they could get out of it rather than by honest pursuit of the truth, and the movement tended to fall into disrepute.

Following are some thumbnail sketches of the best-known Presocratics, giving the place with which they are most associated, their dates, and a few of their ideas. The abbreviation *fl.* (Lat. *floruit*, "he flourished") refers to the date when the person was known to be active; *c.* (Lat. *circa*) means "about."

Thales. Miletus (fl. c. 585 B.C.). Thales is commonly viewed as the first Greek philosopher to try to provide a unified explanation of all things. He is said to have done this in terms of water as the source and basis of everything, but he also taught that all things have soul and are gods. He correctly predicted the solar eclipse of 585 B.C.

Anaximander. Miletus (c. 612–c. 545 B.C.). Everything that exists arises from "the infinite" or "boundless," which is eternal and inexhaustible. He

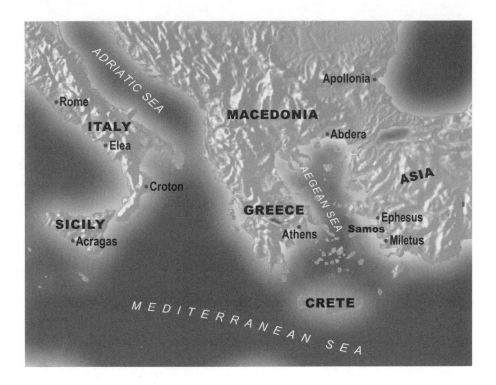

described a process that in some ways prefigured the modern scientific world-view: the disk-shaped earth breaking off from the infinite and existing with-out support, with seasons according to the prevalence of heat or cold, and animal and human life arising through a process.

Anaximenes. Miletus (fl. c. 545 B.C.). The basic stuff of the universe is divine, eternal, life-giving, and in constant motion. Where Thales identified it with water, Anaximenes said it was mist or air, out of which comes fire, which then, by becoming more condensed, produces other objects like water and earth.

Pythagoras. Born in Samos, settled in Croton, Southern Italy (c. 570–c. 494 B.C.). Pythagoras was the founder of a religious, philosophical, and polit-ical community built on high moral principles, which was subsequently famous for its interest in mathematics and music. We know very little about Pythago-ras's teaching except that he taught reincarnation (the soul is immortal and is reborn into animals or humans) and appears to have venerated the powers of number.

Philolaus. Croton (c. 470–c. 390 B.C.). A Pythagorean, Philolaus described the universe as controlling elements (like shapes) and material elements (such as earth and water) held together in mathematical harmony; number is foundational to reality. He also wrote about medicine, psychology, and astronomy, and he probably was the first to state that the earth is a planet.

Xenophanes. Sicily and Southern Italy (c. 570–c. 475 B.C.). Xenophanes vigorously attacked popular and polytheistic theology. He claimed that God is one, omniscient, unchanging, and quite unlike humans in form, and that he accomplishes all things simply by thought. He said that the sun, moon, and rainbows are not gods; they have a naturalistic explanation.

Heraclitus. Ephesus (fl. c. 500 B.C.). The key to the universe is the divine Logos (Gk. for "word") or principle that underlies and directs everything. In some senses this can be equated with Zeus, the supreme God in Greek thought. Everything in the world is subject to change or composed of opposites, but the unchanging Logos is the source of unity. Heraclitus taught that fire is the basic element of the universe, expressing constant change yet remaining the same.

Parmenides. Elea, Southern Italy (born c. 515 B.C.). The real, as opposed to the world around, is eternal, unchanging, and one. Though he taught that the world as we see it is unreal, Parmenides put forward explanations about its phenomena, including teaching that the earth is a sphere and that the moon shines by reflected light.

Anaxagoras. Athens (c. 500–428 B.C.). Behind everything lies Mind (Gk. *nous*), which knows and controls everything and "separates off" from primal matter the objects in the world we perceive, such as air, earth, and things like heat and cold.

Empedocles. Acragas, Sicily (c. 495–c. 435 B.C.). Two forces operate on four basic elements—earth, air, fire, and water. Love joins them in harmony, Strife fragments them. A flamboyant figure and active politician, Empedocles believed in the reincarnation of the soul and the need to live a pure life.

Leucippus (fl. c. 440 B.C.) and **Democritus**. Born in Abdera, Thrace (c. 460-c. 370 B.C.). Leucippus and Democritus were the first "atomists," teaching that everything that exists is made up of eternal innumerable *atoms* (Gk. for "indivisible particles"). These atoms exist in a void that is real, that is, not nothingness. Atoms, in perpetual motion, come together to form different substances, as letters form words. The universe as we know it came together by chance and one day will cease to exist.

Melissus. Samos (fl. 440 B.C.). What exists is one, eternal, infinite, unchanging, indivisible, and bodiless.

Diogenes. Apollonia, on the Black Sea (?fl. 430 B.C.). Everything that exists is one, divine, and intelligent. It is expressed as air, which gives rise to the objects around us through condensation and rarefaction.

The Presocratic philosophers set out to supply an explanation or integrated worldview for the universe and everything in it. Modern commentators, strongly influenced by rationalism and materialism, have tried to claim that they were the first to produce rationalistic and materialistic worldviews in the modern sense, unencumbered by metaphysics (the speculative study of ultimate reality) or theology. This is quite unfair to the evidence. Their systems are in fact highly metaphysical; their concepts of the basic stuff of the universe vary widely. Though they broke with traditional polytheistic ideas, religious concepts—especially those that emphasized the oneness and otherness of God—were well to the fore in their systems.

The primary significance of the Presocratics lies in their conviction that an all-embracing explanation or metanarrative is possible, whether or not this metanarrative includes God. Their secondary significance lies in the multitude of specific concepts they proposed. Some were purely speculative. Others were well supported by evidence. Some appear to us today to be bizarre. Others have become scientific orthodoxy.

But there is a third aspect of their significance. With just a few exceptions, no one Presocratic agreed with any other. And, more significantly, none of their systems was widely adopted by the community at large. Each offered his explanatory worldview, but very few bought into it. In fact, the period of the Presocratics ended in a spirit of disillusionment and cynicism. None of the explanations worked. Instead of giving rise to a new understanding of the world and our place in it, the story ends in cynicism and relativism. For many the conclusion was inevitable: philosophy cannot provide an answer; philosophers are simply producing concepts that will bring them fame or money; we cannot find ultimate truth or principles for living.

TO THINK THROUGH

It is worth asking why the Hebrew worldview lasted so long when the worldviews proposed by the Presocratics were so short lived. Can you think of possible reasons for this?

For Further Study

Curd, P., and R. D. McKirahan. *A Presocratics Reader.* Indianapolis: Hackett, 1996.

Kirk, G. S., J. E. Raven, and M. Schofield. *The Presocratic Philosophers.* Cambridge: Cambridge University Press, 1983.

BUDDHA

Northeastern India (c. 560–c. 480 B.C.). Buddha ("Enlightened One"), or Siddhartha Gautama, was born on the borders of Nepal and India about 560 B.C. He was thus a contemporary of the late Hebrew prophets and of many of the Presocratics. Zarathustra still may have been alive when he was a child. His father was a ruler of some influence and wealth, and Buddha grew up surrounded by royal luxury. Nevertheless, at the age of twenty-nine he left his home, possessions, wife, and young son to seek peace of mind and the answer to human misery. He tried and rejected the teaching of contemporary Hinduism and Yoga meditation, experimented unsuccessfully with the way of asceticism and fasting, and after six years found enlightenment while seated beneath a bo tree. He spent the rest of his life in meditation and teaching and also founded an order of monks. He died about 480 B.C.

The number of Buddhists in the world today is about 359 million, 5.7 percent of the world's population.

Buddhism has developed considerably through the centuries, dividing into a number of sects that have each tended to produce their own scriptures, and it is not always easy to separate later teaching from that of Buddha himself. However, the following appear to be his key philosophical insights.

Suffering. The starting point for our understanding of the world is human suffering. All else must be seen in the light of old age, disease, and death.

God. The existence of suffering makes the existence of a supreme Creator God impossible. It is possible, however, that Buddha retained belief in Hindu-type deities even though they played no part in his system.

The universe. Ultimate questions about the origin and nature of the universe are unanswerable.

The soul. There is no such thing as the self or soul. "I" am not a thing; "I" am a bundle of events. If the events were taken away, the "I" would not remain. Take away the events, and nothing remains. However, perhaps paradoxically, Buddha believed in *karma* (the process of reincarnation to deal with our unfinished business at the close of life) except for those who have been enlightened.

Existence. What is true of the "I" is true of all things. There are events but not enduring entities. There are, Buddha claimed, three marks of existence: Everything is without self, without permanence, and full of suffering.

Enlightenment. However impermanent it may be, the thinking subject is the key to all else. The key to enlightenment is the mind. The essence of the mind is not reasoning, but rather meditating and enlightenment. Though Buddha spoke of "the four noble truths," these are not to be analyzed or debated or even merely accepted as facts. Rather, they are to be allowed to shape and change us, conquering our cravings, curing us of suffering, and leading us to the final release from the cycle of reincarnation in the ultimate calm of nirvana.

Morality and lifestyle. Buddhism is generally seen as a way of life rather than a religion, though the experience of meditation and enlightenment certainly has some mystical overtones. But the main thrust of the Noble Eightfold Path is on ethics and practical living.

THE FOUR NOBLE TRUTHS

1. All life is suffering.
2. Suffering is caused by selfish desire.
3. To be free of suffering we must eradicate selfish desire.
4. Selfish desire is to be eradicated by following the Noble Eightfold Path:

- right understanding
- right thought
- right speech
- right action
- right livelihood
- right effort
- right mindfulness
- right contemplation

The goal of the Eightfold Path is the mystical experience achieved in *Dhyana*, or trance, that enables those who attain it to live free from suffering and escape from reincarnation when they die.

TO THINK THROUGH

To what extent do you think human suffering is a valid base on which to build a worldview?

Compared with Christianity, Buddhism as envisaged by Buddha lacks doctrines and religious activities like prayer or worship. Do you think this is a strength or a weakness?

Compared with the Presocratics, Buddha seems to focus particularly on the negatives of life. Do you think this says something about the differences between Eastern and Western ways of thinking? Could it be a factor in the recent growth of Western interest in Buddhism?

CONFUCIUS

Lu (Shantung), China (551–479 B.C.). Confucius, also referred to as Master K'ung or Master Kong, was contemporary with some of the Presocratics and with Buddha. Raised in poverty, he developed an interest in ethics and politics and spent a brief time as local chief of police before traveling throughout China sharing his ideas with local rulers in the hope they might implement them. When none did, he returned to Lu and spent the rest of his life teaching, establishing a successful school. Not all welcomed his teaching, however; three times rulers who felt threatened by his ideas attempted to kill him. His followers developed his teaching over the years, and six centuries after his death, Confucianism became the official philosophy of the whole of China.

Living in society.

While the Presocratics were primarily interested in the nature of the world, Confucius' first interest was how we should live in society. The world around us did interest him, but, in his thought, as in that of Buddha, the emphasis tended to be less that the external world shapes our understanding of it and more that our concepts and language and behavior shape the world around us. What was of little interest to him was speculation about the details of religion or a future life, since he believed we can never know the truth about either.

Jen and li.

Life and behavior in society need to be governed by two qualities, *jen* (pronounced *ren*) and *li* (pronounced *lee*). *Jen* covers right interpersonal relationships, summed up in Confucius' version of the Golden Rule, never to do to others what you would not want them to do to you. It includes concern for others, selfless love, and a commitment to the well-being of others. Like love in the Hebrew tradition, *jen* is much more than a feeling or attitude; it has to be worked out in practice. The practice of *jen* needs to be cultivated and trained until it becomes second nature. Confucius was concerned to outline in some detail the correct behavior dictated by *jen* in a whole range of relationships and situations, such as between children and parents, and toward superiors or employers.

The key to developing *jen* is *li*. This sets out the codes and principles we need to learn and practice to achieve *jen*. It has been variously translated as ceremonious behavior, rituals, and propriety. It entails the correct observance of society's customs and formal patterns of behavior, adopting the appropriate role, and following the accepted patterns of relating. In particular it entails being balanced and avoiding extremes, and ensuring that our behavior is adapted to its context.

Though the teaching of Confucius was relevant to all, he saw it as particularly pertinent to those who, like himself, sought to be rulers. If these operate according to the principles of *jen* and *li*, thus providing a stable structure and a good example to their subjects, then society will operate harmoniously.

God.

Despite his lack of interest in religion as such, Confucius retained a belief in God, though the heart of his concept is ethical rather than personal. He accepted the Chinese belief in the Mandate of Heaven as the ultimate basis for all human behavior.

TO THINK THROUGH

Some thinkers have focused on the question "What is the nature of the universe?" Others have focused on "How should we live?" Which do you think is the primary question? How could they be related?

Do you think we can draw any conclusions from the fact that the birth of four, or perhaps five, of the world's great religions and the beginnings of Western philosophy all happened at the same time? Are there significant common features in these movements?

LAO ZI

Some doubt has been expressed about the historicity of Lao Zi (Lao Tzu, pronounced *loud*-za), who has traditionally been seen as the founder of Taoism. It may be that the writings attributed to him were, like the Vedas or Upanishads, a collection of works by a number of thinkers. However, if he did exist, he seems to have lived in China in the sixth century B.C., where he is said to have met Confucius. If he didn't exist as an individual, it seems likely that the writings attributed to him still go back to the sixth or fifth century B.C.

The *Lao Zi Book*, or *Daodejing (Tao Te Ching)*, is deliberately mysterious and mystical. The Tao, which literally means "way" or "path," is both something that governs the universe and the way we should follow in our individual lives. But it is far from easy to find. Its nature is beyond our apprehension. It is indescribable. In some senses it is nonbeing, like the emptiness of the valley that holds the mountains in their places. Nevertheless, Lao Zi called upon the individual to seek the Tao through meditation and contemplation, and thus to live in harmony with it.

In contrast to the formal ethic of Confucian thought, Lao Zi urged simplicity of life and spontaneity of action. In this way we are able to become one with the natural world around us and thus with the Tao itself.

Lao Zi also incorporated the concepts of the Yin and the Yang, the two contrasting principles or forces that appear in many aspects of Chinese thought. Traditionally, the Yin was seen, among other things, as female, black, cold, passive, small, evil, soft, and the earth. The Yang was male, white, warm, active, large, good, hard, and heaven. The world and the individual function by keeping these opposing but complementary forces in balance.

THREE

IN LOVE WITH WHAT IS REAL

THE PHILOSOPHY OF PLATO

In this chapter we look in some detail at key aspects of Plato's philosophy. All of these have had a significant role in the development of Western thought.

FIFTH-CENTURY GREECE

Greece in the fifth century B.C. was made up of a number of independent city-states, of which the two greatest were Athens and Sparta. The states tended to squabble among themselves but from time to time formed alliances to face specific crises. Despite a notable victory by Athens over invading Persian forces at Marathon in 490 B.C., Sparta was the dominant state for the first quarter of the century. After that Athens began to dominate and to build a powerful empire. The middle years of the century saw a drawn-out war between Athens and Sparta and its Peloponnesian allies. Though Athens came out on top in this, the first Peloponnesian war, a second war broke out in 431 that lasted twenty-seven years and ended in defeat for Athens.

The period of the Athenian empire was a great time for the city, when magnificent buildings were erected, art flourished, especially sculpture and drama, and the people shared in a democratic form of government and a lifestyle that enabled them to enjoy the many benefits of wealth and the delights of philosophy.

Of the main Presocratics, only Anaxagoras taught for any time in Athens, but from the middle of the fifth century onward there would have been no shortage of teachers of philosophy there. Traveling all over Greece were professional teachers known as Sophists. They offered instruction in philosophy and training in rhetoric. The art of rhetoric was important as a tool to win arguments in the law courts or in the city-state democracies. The best-known Sophist was Protagoras, who had a reputation for theological agnosticism, relativism, and skill at making the weaker argument look like the stronger. Sophists were generally regarded with suspicion, since it was felt that most of them were charlatans, charging high prices for at best a pretty shoddy product and at worst the corrupting of the morals of their students. As a result, philosophy and philosophers tended to have a poor reputation in Athens in the second half of the fifth century. Skepticism and relativism were the order of the day. You pays your money and you takes your choice.

SOCRATES

Athens (469–399 B.C.). Socrates served with distinction in the Peloponnesian War. He was influenced by the philosophies of Parmenides and Pythagoras. He was noted for his lack of good looks, his eccentricities, and his close friendships with aristocratic young men who were strongly influenced by his teaching.

Although perfectly capable of using sophistic tricks in his arguing and branded a Sophist by many of his contemporaries, Socrates probably differed from the Sophists in that he lived an austere life, made no charge for his philosophizing, and saw himself as divinely called and divinely inspired. He wrote no book, but many of his ideas have been preserved in the writings of his younger contemporaries, Plato and Xenophon.

In contrast to the Presocratics, Socrates' interest was not in the nature of the world, but in moral and practical issues like virtue and right living. His method, for which he is famed, was that of dialogue. Typically he would ask someone for a definition of a specific virtue, then proceed to show by further questioning that the definition given was unsatisfactory. Though he had his own views, especially about the nature of virtue, Socrates did not normally teach them directly, aiming perhaps to enable his listeners to find the answers for themselves once the poverty of their proposed definitions was exposed.

After a time of political turmoil in Athens, the seventy-year-old Socrates was brought to trial accused of rejecting the traditional Greek gods, introducing new gods, and corrupting the young men of Athens (at least one of his disciples, Critias, had been one of "the thirty tyrants" who, on the collapse of

Athenian democracy after the defeat of Sparta, had exercised a brief reign of terror in the city). Socrates was found guilty and executed by being made to drink poison.

PLATO

Athens (427–347 B.C.). Born into an aristocratic family, Plato was influenced strongly by Socrates from about age twenty. After a period of travel, he committed himself to teaching philosophy and founded the Academy, a center for philosophical and political training, in Athens in 387, where he stayed until his death. He wrote prolifically, including plays and letters. His philosophy is contained in more than thirty dialogues. It is generally thought that in the earlier dialogues Plato was for the most part expounding the teaching of Socrates, but as time went by he used the dialogues to express his own ideas.

Almost all the works of the Presocratics have been lost. In contrast, many, though by no means all, of Plato's writings have been preserved. The English translation of his works runs to over 750,000 words, the equivalent of eight or so Ph.D. theses. Plato is thus the first philosopher whose works have come down to us in any quantity, a significant indication of his importance, both in his own time and in subsequent centuries.

We might think that having a lot of his writing will make it easier to know just what he taught. Sadly, this is not the case, perhaps for three reasons.

In the first place, Plato was an educator, and as a good educator he tended to operate on the principle that it is better to get students to think things out for themselves rather than spoon-feed them ideas. Many of his works, as a result, spend a lot of time raising issues, challenging current views about them, and pointing out difficulties and problems, but they often stop short of giving any definitive answers.

Second, Plato wrote his philosophy in the form of discussions or dialogues. This makes them interesting to read, but it has a couple of serious shortcomings. Discussions, Plato's included, tend to wander. They raise an issue, talk around it, let it lead on to another issue, pick up that one without really finishing with the first, and so on. Further, different speakers in the discussions express different viewpoints, and it is not always certain which we should take as Plato's. We might assume that Plato uses Socrates as his mouthpiece, but even this is open to question. In many of the dialogues, especially the earlier ones, Socrates plays a dominant part; but it is not certain whether this Socrates is Socrates as Plato remembered him, or Plato expressing his ideas through the mouth of Socrates. In some dialogues, especially the later ones, Socrates doesn't take such

A Taste of Plato

Unlike almost all subsequent philosophical writing, the dialogues of Plato were designed to be fun to read. They are lively, at times even funny, and full of personal glimpses into the character of the participants. If you can, get hold of one of them in a good translation, and read it through. To give you just a taste, here's a short extract from a dialogue called *Laches*, in which Socrates is exploring, with the help of two distinguished Athenian generals, the nature of manliness or courage. Socrates has just reduced Laches to confusion after discussing his concept of courage. I have translated the extract fairly freely to help make it accessible.

Socrates: Come on then, if you can, Nicias. Rescue your friends who're in trouble. You see we've come to a dead end. So *you* tell us what you think courage is, and get us out of this mess, and at the same time sort out your own definition of courage.

Nicias: I've been thinking for some time that you've got your definition of courage wrong. Your problem, Socrates, is that you're not following your own advice.

Socrates: In what way?

Nicias: I've often heard you say that goodness is closely related to wisdom, and badness to ignorance.

Socrates: Right.

Nicias: So courage is a form of wisdom.

Socrates: Get that, Laches?

Laches: Sort of. But I'm not sure what he's driving at.

Socrates: I think I follow him. He seems to be saying that courage is some kind of wisdom or knowledge or skill.

Laches: What sort of wisdom?

Socrates: Why don't you ask him?

Laches: Okay.

Socrates: Come on then, Nicias; tell him what sort of wisdom courage is. I don't suppose it's the ability to play the flute.

Nicias: No way.

Socrates: Or the ability to play the guitar.

Nicias: No.

Socrates: So what is this knowledge?

Laches: Go for it, Socrates. Get him to define it.

Nicias: Okay, here goes. It's the awareness of what's terrifying and exciting in war or wherever.

Laches: That's crazy!

Socrates: What makes you say that, Laches?

Laches: What makes me say it? The fact that wisdom or knowledge or awareness is quite different from courage.

Socrates: That's not what Nicias says.

Laches: No. He's talking rubbish.

Socrates: Let's sort him out instead of having a go at him.

Nicias: Okay. But it seems to me, Socrates, that Laches wants to make out that I'm talking rubbish simply because he was shown to be talking rubbish just now.

Laches: Right first time, Nicias. And I'm going to do it, because you *are* talking rubbish. Try this. As far as concerns illness, isn't it the doctors who know what's to be afraid of? Or are you going to say it's the courageous people who know? Or that doctors are courageous?

Nicias: No way.

Laches: And farmers know what to be afraid of in farming, and other specialists know what to be afraid of in their particular areas. But you still can't say they're showing courage.

Socrates: What's he getting at? He seems to have a point.

Nicias: Maybe he has. But it's not true.

And so the discussion goes on. Nicias doesn't think Laches has destroyed his case, and he continues to defend it, even when Socrates gets him to admit that his definition would mean that animals or children could never show courage. Toward the end of the dialogue, and in the light of the failure to find an acceptable definition of courage, Socrates suggests that our understanding of courage can't be separated from our understanding of other aspects of goodness or virtue and so of virtue itself.

a clear lead, and in some he doesn't appear at all. The result is that scholars frequently disagree over just what Plato is trying to argue in the dialogues.

Third, we can't pin down a systematic body of Plato's teaching for the simple reason that it seems he never arrived at a definitive system himself. He probably shared the awareness of his own ignorance and limitations that he put into the mouth of Socrates. His ideas changed as time went on. In some of the later dialogues, he seems to be criticizing some of the views he has put forward in the earlier ones.

So we have to be content with a certain degree of openmindedness over the details of Plato's teaching. However, it is possible to list the main concepts that appear in his writings that are usually associated with his name and that have had significant impact on the development of subsequent thought.

Reality.

Plato believed in objective, unchanging reality. He was aware that everything in the world around us is open to question; nature, material objects, and human life itself—all are subject to change and impermanence; our concepts of what is right or true or good can constantly be questioned and challenged. Yet Plato was convinced that behind all the change and uncertainty there exists something or some things that are real and unchanging, really true, really good, really beautiful, and so on.

Plato's belief in objective reality was his answer to relativism and skepticism. The attempt to find and establish that reality was foundational to his philosophy. Further, the fact that he thus supplied, or appeared to supply, an objective base for our understanding of the world, was the thing that made his philosophy so successful in his own time and in subsequent centuries.

Reality for Plato is one. He didn't segregate concepts in the way we tend to do. He hadn't been trained to separate them into neat categories: epistemology, science, ethics, aesthetics, theology, and so on. For him it was natural to assume that what is good is true; what is right is beautiful; what really is, is to be loved; and the like. It may be that, unlike the Hebrews, with their strong concept of God successfully tying all these things together, he had no clear basis for this belief, but it is essential to his philosophy.

Goodness.

Faced with moral relativism and the seeming breakdown of ethical principles, "What is goodness?" was both a burning practical question for Plato and the foundational question of his philosophical search. Again, Plato was happy to allow the concept of goodness to be applied in a whole range of ways, without drawing careful distinctions, much loved by some twentieth-century philosophers, between different applications of the concept. Thus Plato could move easily from goodness in a person, that is moral goodness, to the more functional goodness in an object, such as a tool. He was able to do this legitimately because his understanding of goodness was basically purposive, or teleological. He believed that everything has a purpose. A carpentry tool is designed for cutting wood; it is a good tool if it cuts well. A man is designed for living and fulfills that purpose if he lives virtuously.

Though passionately concerned to help his students find the answer to questions of practical morality ("What is right and good for me to do in this or that set of circumstances?"), Plato put his primary emphasis on the discovering of goodness itself. The idea or form of goodness was for him "the greatest thing we can learn about," the thing that gives substance to all other moral concepts. Plato likened goodness to the sun, which not only enables us to see everything else that exists, but also is the source of their "existence, growth, and nourishment."

Plato didn't seem to feel that it was necessary to prove that ultimate goodness exists. It is not the kind of thing we establish by argument. Rather, it is something we seek; if we're philosophers, we spend all our lives pursuing it, experiencing it, and living it.

Beauty. For Plato beauty was closely linked to goodness and so central to his philosophy. We are attracted to what is beautiful. In the first instance, said Plato, this will be to a specific embodiment of physical beauty. Then we move beyond that to the more abstract manifestations of beauty such as harmony or beauty of character. Then behind these again we find the ultimate reality, "the divine Beauty" itself. In the *Symposium* Plato described this as the goal of all our loving, something eternal and unchanging, perfect and absolute, lying behind and apart from all its manifestations in people and things. The very experience of this motivates us to spend our lives propagating beauty and goodness.

God. Plato was not happy with the traditional Greek gods, who couldn't even agree among themselves or work harmoniously together. Rejection of these gods was one of the charges on which Socrates was executed. Plato didn't have a well-developed theology to replace them and still at times used the terminology of Greek polytheism. The world, for him, was made by a demiurge (from the Greek word for a skilled workman), a god who designed and brought everything into being. But this demiurge created the world because he was inspired by his vision of ultimate goodness and beauty and the like, realities that Plato specifically called "divine." In that these are ultimately one, it is possible to say that Plato had a concept of one ultimate supreme God. But it is a very different concept from that of the Hebrews in that it is largely impersonal (though Plato could refer to it as Mind), static, and only really accessible to those who devote their lives to the philosophic quest.

The Forms.

We have seen that Plato had a strong concept of goodness and beauty as ultimate and objective. They are real; they exist independently of us, and they are in many ways the foundation or source of all that exists. Plato called them ideas or forms, and at times he appears to have believed that all the things in the world around us, including, for example, beds and tables, have a corresponding form. However, when he talked about them he tended to major on more abstract concepts like moral values (justice, virtue, goodness) and mathematical concepts (like equality). These clearly fit the theory better than material objects, especially when he insisted that the form of anything itself partakes of the nature of that thing. This works all right when we say that the form of the good is itself good but is a bit harder to envisage if we have to say that the form of a bed is itself bed-shaped, comfortable, or whatever.

Like the form of the good, all forms are the basis for both the existence and the intelligibility of their counterparts in the world around us. They thus provide the pattern or paradigm by which we can recognize their counterparts when we find them in the world. "Recognition" is a significant concept for Plato, since he believed that we all have an innate though suppressed awareness of the forms arising from the fact that our souls existed before our bodily lives began.

Though Plato didn't spend a lot of time discussing his Theory of Forms, it is clear that it was very significant in his thinking. Moreover, it has had a profound effect on the development of Western philosophy. It provided an answer to the question posed by the Presocratics: If all the objects we observe in the world are changing, impermanent, and fragmented, and so ultimately unreal, do we have to conclude that everything that exists, the whole universe, is ultimately unreal? In the East, thinkers tended to answer yes to this question. The Hebrews were confident that God is the ultimate and foundational reality that undergirds everything else and so were able to reply no. Plato also replied no, and the reason he was able to do so was the existence of the forms. Ultimate reality, he said, is eternal and permanent, one and unchanging. Objects in the world partake of reality in that they are copies or expressions of the forms. They are never perfect copies; a just person will never be filled with pure justice; some injustice will always remain. But, however imperfect the manifestations, the perfect forms continue to exist. Though there is no perfect circle anywhere on earth, perfect circularity exists eternally.

Seeing Plato in a Different Light

Plato's Theory of Forms has been criticized, especially by philosophers in the twentieth-century analytic tradition, who saw the key task of philosophy as analyzing the way we use words. They say that Plato has mistakenly assumed that for our concepts to have any real meaning there must be some entities lying behind them. R. M. Hare, for instance, wrote:

It is a mistake to suppose that for words to have meanings is (always at any rate) for there to be entities for which they stand. If we know how to use a word in speaking and thus communicating with one another, it has a meaning; and knowing how to use it is not knowing some solid chunk of eternal verity of which it is the name, but knowing the conventions for its use, and in particular what, according to these conventions, is implied by somebody who uses it in a statement. To know what "circle" means or what a circle is is to know that if we call anything a circle we are implying that it is a plane figure of a certain sort; and in order to know this we do not have to know any celestial entities.

Plato may or may not have accepted Hare's specific point about the meaning of words. But I'm sure he would have replied that Hare had turned things around. He would say:

It isn't the case that I'm concluding the Forms exist because we use words like "justice" and "goodness." Rather, I'm saying that there is such a thing as ultimate reality, which embraces justice and goodness, and it is because there is such a thing that we can experience and talk about goodness and justice in our partial and impermanent world. If you ask me why I'm sure these Forms exist, it is because I find or encounter or experience them, not because I can produce a logical argument proving their existence.

Our experience of the forms is not like our experience of things in the world, through our senses. Rather, we encounter them through the mind or the soul.

Truth. In his concepts of reality and goodness and their outworking through the forms, Plato was able to offer a way of viewing truth that provided a stable base for the development of Western thought through the next two thousand years. Rooted as it was in the forms, truth was objective, eternal, universal, and unchanging. Moreover, it was intelligible to us; we can know it because in our minds or souls we have access to reality. Plato used an interesting range of terms to express our relationship to truth, including aiming at it, pursuing it, discovering it, grasping it, and attaining it. Truth for him was an absolute, an authority to which we are subject. As you would expect, Plato was able to merge truth with reality, goodness, beauty, and so on. What is real must also be true; what is true must be good. Justice and virtue are beautiful and true.

The cave. One of the best-known passages in Plato is his allegory of the cave at the start of Book 7 of the *Republic*. He pictures the experience of ordinary people as parallel to that of prisoners in a cave who see only shadows of objects cast upon a wall before them. The shadows are caused by real objects being passed before a fire, but the prisoners can see neither fire nor the objects. For them the shadows are reality.

Plato then describes a process that is parallel to the philosopher gradually coming to a knowledge of reality and truth, of the forms, and supremely, of the form of the good. A prisoner is freed and, instead of looking just at shadows, he sees the objects that cast the shadows. He would almost certainly find it hard to believe that these objects are more real than the shadows. Then someone makes him look at the fire, an even more painful experience.

But as yet he's still in the cave. Outside is real light, not just firelight. If dragged out into the sunlight, he'd be so dazzled it would take him a long time to be able to see any objects outside the cave. At first he'd go for shadows and reflections, but after a time he'd be able to look directly at real objects and eventually look even at the sun itself, which Plato said pictures "the Form of the Good, seen last and with difficulty, but when it is seen we're forced to the conclusion that it is the cause of what is right and beautiful in all things."

Doubtless with the story of Socrates in mind, Plato adds that, if the person who had made the journey out of the cave returned to tell the other prisoners what he'd discovered, they wouldn't believe him and would end up killing him.

The human person. The worldview that Plato inherited generally looked on the human person as a unity. We are our bodies. That is not to say we are entirely physical or material. The ancient world had none of the Enlightenment's narrow concepts of physics or matter. Our bodies include minds and souls, just as, for many thinkers, the world itself included mind and soul. But, because we are integrated beings, one and not two, it follows that if, when our body dies, our soul lives on, its existence must be something very shadowy, almost unreal.

Plato perhaps would not have been too unhappy with this way of seeing things. But his philosophy was subsequently taken as teaching a radical distinction between the soul and the body. This arose from his stress on the contrast between the forms as eternal and real over against the impermanent and unreal objects around us in the world. Since Plato held that the soul, as opposed to the body, is the part of us that engages with the eternal and the real, it was easy for subsequent thinkers to stress the eternity and reality and goodness of the soul over against the impermanence and lack of goodness of the body. Plato didn't in fact teach that the body is intrinsically evil or that the soul is necessarily good. At times he taught that the soul itself is divided into parts, notably desire, reason (the highest part), and spirit, which fight against each other.

Reason is the highest part of us. Much of the time when Plato is referring to the mind or soul, he is speaking of the rational aspect of us, which has access to the divine Mind and so to ultimate realities. Indeed, it has more than access; it actually shares in eternal being; when I think the truth and the good, I am one with the true and the good. This entails, for Plato, that the mind or soul is immortal; something that merges with reality and eternity in that way can't simply cease to be when the body dies. Immortality for Plato reached back in time as well as forward into eternity. My soul always has existed. Hence Plato agreed with the Pythagoreans and with much of ancient thought in accepting reincarnation, and he used the concept to explain how it is we can recognize the forms and, indeed, come to know anything at all. Our souls in fact already have knowledge that was obscured when they were born into new bodies but that under the influence of education they gradually are able to recollect.

This is not to say, however, that Plato saw the soul as purely rational in the Enlightenment sense. In that it is the part of us that shares in eternal reality, it also shares in the nature of reality, so it is made up of goodness and beauty as well as rationality.

Love. Though Plato didn't coin the term, he was well aware that the Greek word *philosopher* meant not "wise person" but "lover of wisdom." Indeed, his stress was more on "lover" than on "wisdom," since the true philosopher loves not just wisdom but truth, beauty, goodness, justice, virtue, and all that is ultimately real.

This love, for Plato, wasn't some rarefied detached thing. It was full-blooded and passionate, affecting every part of our being. He was able to speak of sexual love, desire for another person's body, and our love of beauty or desire for goodness in the same breath. Philosophers don't just philosophize; they are passionately in love with reality.

Right living. The experience of goodness and beauty and truth in themselves is sufficient warrant for the pursuit of philosophy. But those who find these things will inevitably, said Plato, want to live them out and share them with others. Plato was a teacher, seeking to combat the moral and practical relativism of his day. In several of the dialogues, he acknowledged the difficulty of producing clear-cut definitions of applied moral goodness. Socrates, for example, didn't produce a satisfactory answer to the arguments of Thrasymachus, who adopted a "might is right" approach to morality.

But Plato had a clear reply to the question "How do we know how to live rightly?" in the vision of the forms. Philosophers who have encountered ultimate goodness and have it in their souls will know how to live out that goodness in any given situation. This has the unfortunate corollary that those who are not philosophers (the vast majority of the population) are unable on their own to live a truly good life; they need the philosophers to tell them how to do it.

Virtue is its own reward, but it also brings a range of benefits. On balance it brings happiness. Plato depicted the evil tyrant as ultimately desperately unhappy, in that he is a slave to his passions. On the other side, Socrates, about to be killed for being virtuous, saw himself as truly happy. Additionally, virtue enables us to live in society, with the community and the state functioning harmoniously. And then there's the eschatological element; alongside his doctrine of reincarnation, Plato believed that after this life the virtuous will be rewarded and the evil punished.

Knowledge. Much that passes for knowledge is just opinion. In the earlier dialogues Socrates had no difficulty in tying into knots simple-minded people who made claims to knowledge of truths they had never really worked through. True knowledge comes only after effort, after training, principally in mathematics and philosophical discussion. In time it is possible to build up a whole body of knowledge, a complete system instead of isolated fragments.

Although only philosophers are able to spend the time needed to reach this sort of knowledge, Plato also taught, through his concept of recollection, that everyone has the potential for true knowledge. In a well-known passage in the *Meno*, Socrates managed (through leading questions) to get a slave boy who had no knowledge of math to establish a geometric theorem. The boy, he claimed, already had the mathematical knowledge, but it was latent.

Plato believed we can have knowledge because reality and truth exist in the forms. Thus it is the person who seeks and discovers the forms who is able to attain knowledge. Plato was criticized by analytic philosophers for failing to distinguish differing types of knowledge. Knowing a person, they said, is very different from knowing a proposition. "I know John" (personal knowledge) is quite a different sort of knowing from "I know that it is raining" (propositional knowledge). Plato didn't make this distinction. If it had been pointed out to him, he might have replied, "But knowing John personally necessarily includes knowing propositions about him; the two are inseparable," or "I can only know the meaning of 'It is raining' if I have a personal knowledge of rain." Certainly, as far as the forms are concerned, the personal knowledge of them is essential to possessing true propositional knowledge about them.

Politics.
Plato was concerned to teach right living. This led him in two ways into lengthy discussions of politics. First, right living has to be done in the community, in his context in the city-state. Second, for Plato, the principles he outlined for the running of the state applied equally to the individual. Thus his most famous dialogue, the *Republic*, is both a proposal for a utopian state and an exposition of personal moral philosophy.

In Plato's ideal state, philosophers, who alone know reality and truth and goodness through the forms, will be the rulers. Before they are fit to rule, they must go through a thorough program of training, first in the arts and athletics, but then, more seriously, in math and philosophy. Then they must be tested to ensure they have come to know the forms and not be allowed to exercise any power until they are fifty. Their rule will be absolute and strict, censoring, for example, all the arts to exclude anything that might be detrimental to the state.

It is significant that Plato, disillusioned with Athenian democracy, which had killed Socrates, envisaged a class-structured society. Besides the rulers there would be two classes. Most citizens would be in the lowest class, which consisted of farmers, craftsmen, and traders. Some, including budding rulers, would be in a middle class of soldiers and assistants to the rulers. If this seems discriminatory to us, we could add three things. First, Plato allowed movement between the classes according to merit. Second, the rulers, as opposed to the masses, were compelled to follow a very austere lifestyle lest they should want to rule from wrong motives. Third, Plato clearly stated that women should rule as well as men, thus breaking down one of the strongest discriminatory practices of his day.

The world.

In contrast to most of the Presocratics, Plato didn't show a lot of interest in cosmology or science. When he did explore some of the issues, in the *Timaeus,* he described the universe as the product of intelligent design. It couldn't have just happened. It has been planned and made, and the inspiration and foundation for its structure is in the forms.

There is a parallel between the philosopher and the God who plans and creates the world. Both experience and love the beauty and goodness of the forms. Both want to pass on what they have seen creatively; the philosopher in creating good lives and good society, the God in creating a good world. And both find that, though they have the vision of perfection, what they have created falls short of that perfection. There will be flaws even in the ideal state, and there are flaws in the world as we know it.

The impact of Plato's philosophy on the story of Western thought has been enormous. Even those who disagreed with him have had to take him seriously and seek to answer the points he made. For seven centuries after his death philosophers of the Platonist school were in the forefront of philosophical thinking, teaching and developing his ideas. Then, when Christianity became the leading philosophical force, Platonism still played a major role by influencing the way Christian concepts were expressed and developed.

One of the most significant aspects of Plato's teaching was his dualism. He split off what really is, the world of the eternal and unchanging forms, from the world as ordinary people know it. Though this dualism was not as stark as, say, Parmenides, for whom the eternal and unchanging was unknowable, the split between the real and the shadows, the eternal and the impermanent, the mind or soul and the body, was hugely influential. The problem of tying together a split world was to be a major theme of the history of philosophy.

TO THINK THROUGH

What do you think about Plato's tendency to merge the good and the true and the beautiful? Our society has tended to keep them very clearly apart-- scientific facts and moral values don't mix. Has this been detrimental to our thinking or living? What do you think about Plato's assumption that if we know what is good clearly enough we will do it?

What do you think about Plato's idea that philosophy, knowledge of things as they really are, should be limited to a few, and that these few should rule everyone else?

Plato tried to replace the polytheistic religion of his day with new, more considered, religious concepts, but most authorities think he didn't get as far as monotheism. In what ways do you feel his insights prepared the way for the general acceptance of monotheism in the West? Was his influence in this area a good thing?

For Further Study

Cooper, J. M., ed. *Plato: Complete Works*. Indianapolis: Hackett, 1997.

Hare, R. M. *Plato*. Oxford: Oxford University Press, 1982.

Melling, D. J. *Understanding Plato*. Oxford: Oxford University Press, 1987.

Nash, R. H. *Life's Ultimate Questions*. Grand Rapids: Zondervan, 1999, chap. 3.

FOUR

GETTING DOWN TO THE DETAILS

THE PHILOSOPHY OF ARISTOTLE

In this chapter we will explore some of the main points of Aristotle's philosophy, which most people find less accessible than Plato's. But, again, it has had a great impact on Western thought, so it is worth trying to wrap your mind around his ideas.

Aristotle. Stagira, Macedonia (384–322 B.C.). The son of a doctor, Aristotle was trained in medicine. He went to Athens in 367 and studied under Plato in the Academy until 347. From 347 to 335 he was away from Athens and spent some time tutoring the heir to the Macedonian throne, who was to become Alexander the Great. Back in Athens he set up his own school, named the Lyceum, after the building in which it was housed. The building's colonnaded walk, where Aristotle moved around as he taught, gave the school the name Peripatetic (Gk. for "walk around"). Aristotle died in 322.

Only about one-fifth of his writings survive. Some of them are fragmentary, and most are in the form of lecture notes. They cover a wide range of topics, including physics, biology, astronomy, geology, meteorology, physiology, logic, rhetoric, metaphysics, poetry, psychology, ethics, and politics.

Aristotle and Plato. Aristotle was a pupil of Plato and always revered his teaching, even when he disagreed with it. There has been a tendency since the Renaissance to stress the differences between the two. Plato, it is said, was concerned with mystical ideas, and Aristotle with down-to-earth science and practical living. This is an exaggeration; Plato's concerns were as practical as Aristotle's, and Aristotle can be as metaphysical and mystical as Plato. However, the surviving works of Aristotle do contain much more "science" than Plato's (Aristotle's more philosophically speculative Dialogues have been lost), and the Lyceum in later years was noted as a center of scientific rather than philosophical research.

Perhaps the key difference between the two was one of method. Aristotle always wanted to start with data, especially observations. Speculation had its place, but it must do justice to "the phenomena" (from the Greek, for "things as they appear"), what we observe. In the more scientific field, the phenomena are our observations of the world around us, animals, the human body, and so on, and Aristotle's method here emphasized careful "scientific" observation. In the more speculative areas, the phenomena were people's beliefs and explanations, which were to be analyzed and tested much in the way Socrates did. Once we have formed an explanatory theory, said Aristotle, we should test it by examining further phenomena. One thing we should not do is try to foist a preconceived pattern on the data, as some of the Presocratics had done. In particular, we should not try to explain phenomena in one discipline using the structure of another discipline. Animals do not behave according to the rules of geometry.

Aristotle's philosophy is founded on a belief that we can find explanations for all we observe in the world. These explanations are themselves part of the world, not of some mystical other world, like Plato's forms. The world is not the result of chance; it, and everything in it, is meaningful—indeed, purposeful, or teleological. We understand the world as we come to understand these purposes.

Forms, universals, particulars, and dualism. Aristotle
didn't totally reject Plato's forms. He was willing to use the term as long as it was not taken to refer to some extraterrestrial self-existent entities. For him there were no such entities, no such universals. There were only objects in the world, particular objects. We are perfectly justified in trying to analyze the common form or essence of a group of similar objects, but what we get is no more than an abstraction. By observing a lot of tables, we can arrive at the form or essence of "tabledom." But this is a concept, an abstraction, a universal, not a reality. It's the tables—each specific individual particular table—that are the reality.

The debate over the status of universals and particulars was to occupy philosophers for the next two thousand years. Aristotle's position has the great strength of stressing the oneness of all that is. Instead of dualism, we have just one world, one way of explaining things, one type of existence. Not that this made Aristotle a materialist in the modern sense; his world still included souls, philosophical and metaphysical abstractions, and even God. But his stress is that all is ultimately one, not two.

Three closely linked issues at the heart of Aristotle's teaching are his notion of substance, his contrast between form and matter, and his contrast between actuality and potentiality. A survey of these will lead us into his explanation of change. Then, after a section on explanation itself, we will look briefly at six other areas in which Aristotle had significant things to say.

Substance.

Everything in the world seems to change. Is there anything constant behind the process of change? Heraclitus seemed to say there isn't. Aristotle said there is. And he called it substance.

Substance simply means something that is (Gk. *ousia*). It is the stuff of the world, real existence. A man or a horse or a stone is a substance. Some things are not substances. Socrates may grow pale. Paleness is a nonessential or accidental attribute of Socrates, something that can be added to him or subtracted from him. It is not part of his substance. What is basic, his being as a human, doesn't come and go. It is his substance.

Substances, for Aristotle, can be divided into two groups, primary and secondary substances. Primary substances are individual things, like Socrates or a gray mare or a specific rock. Secondary substances are generalizations, universals, classes of things, such as human beings or horses in general. Anything that is not a primary or secondary substance is a nonsubstance or accident. Sentences like "Socrates is old" or "The horse is white" should not make us think there are substances "oldness" and "whiteness." Such things simply do not exist.

Matter and form.

All substances have two parts. Picture a bronze statue of Pericles. You can describe it in two ways—as a lump of bronze or a statue of Pericles. Bronze is its matter; the statue of Pericles is its form. Without the matter there can be no form; the mere form "statue of Pericles" cannot exist alone. Equally, we may say, matter can't exist alone; it has to exist in some form. If the statue of Pericles is shattered, the bronze matter will now exist in the form of a thousand fragments. Though he rejected the independent existence of Plato's forms, Aristotle retained in his forms much of the sense of vitality and purpose that Plato's forms had. The form adds almost a dynamic element to the matter. When talking about plants and animals, Aristotle saw the form as that which gives them life. In that he tended to look on the whole world as in some sense a living organism, it was easy for him to picture the forms as giving meaning, purpose, vitality, almost life itself even to inanimate objects.

Since it is the form that makes a substance what it distinctively is, the form can be seen as the essence of the substance. The word *essence* has had a long, varied, and difficult journey through the history of philosophy. For Aristotle an "essential" property of something was to be contrasted with an accidental property; humanness is essential to Socrates; paleness is not.

Actuality and potentiality.
An acorn has the potentiality to be an oak tree. The oak tree is the actuality. Equally an acorn is the actuality of an oak tree's potentiality to produce fruit.

Change.
Aristotle used the concepts of matter and form and actuality and potentiality to provide an explanation of change in order to answer two contrasting puzzles raised by the Presocratics. On the one hand, if the world is one, change is impossible. On the other hand, if change really happens, it makes the permanent existence of anything impossible. We can't talk about the river, because every time we step in it, it has changed and so is no longer the same river.

Aristotle's answer was simple. Form, he said, may change; the river may change its shape, and Socrates may grow pale. But the matter, the water or Socrates, remains. Further, he said, change is the actualizing of the potential. The oak tree may not look at all like the acorn, but it has been there all the time potentially in the acorn. And the order of things is fixed. Acorns have the potentiality for oak trees, which in turn have the potentiality for acorns. But neither has the potentiality for producing weeping willows or kiwi fruit. This dependability and stability was essential for Aristotle's scientific investigations, especially his careful analysis of animals and plants into species. It is still, interestingly enough, the basis of scientific investigation today, despite the contemporary belief in evolution that says that one species does in fact change into another. Science simply will not work if the objects under investigation are subject to random meaningless changes.

Explanation.
Among Aristotle's many significant insights is his analysis of explanations, generally called "causes." The word "cause," however, tends to have a mechanical feel about it, and Aristotle was definitely not talking mechanics, so I will call them explanations.

Aristotle analyzed four types of explanation. All of them answer the question "Why?" Some "Why's" will be answered by just one type of explanation, others by two, three, or four. Using the traditional terminology, the types are:

- The *material* explanation, using Aristotle's concept of matter.
- The *formal* explanation, using Aristotle's concept of form. Given the form's almost dynamic nature, the formal explanation can be seen as the principle that directs the object or event.
- The *efficient* explanation, which Aristotle saw in terms of movement—what got the thing going. This explanation is nearest to our scientific concept of cause.
- The *final* or teleological explanation in terms of goal or purpose.

By way of example, we can say that the material explanation of the statue of Pericles is that it is made of bronze. The formal explanation is that it depicts Pericles. The efficient explanation is that So-and-So made it. The final explanation is to remind the Athenians of Pericles.

If that leaves you puzzled, try this: You are on your way out one morning when you meet a friend who is out for a run. In all innocence you ask her why she is running. She replies, "Because I'm an athlete." That is a material explanation. If that doesn't satisfy you, she might say, "Because the muscles of my legs are causing them to propel me forward at speed." That would be an efficient explanation. A final explanation would be "To get fit and keep my place on the team." Formal explanations are harder to think of since we don't share Aristotle's notion of form. A possible one, giving the essence of running, might be, "Because I'm going at ten miles an hour."

Whether or not it is completely accurate in its details, this analysis of explanation can help avoid oversimplifications or outright errors in our search for the meaning of things. It alerts us to the possibility of different types of explanation and of more than one explanation being valid at the same time. You might find it useful when you are confronted with someone who believes that since we have scientific explanations for things, there is no longer any place for God. Aristotle clearly thought Plato's method of providing explanations inadequate, in that he tended to limit himself to just one type and effectively used the forms as the explanation for everything.

The natural world.

In Aristotle's wide-ranging interest in the natural world and the explanation of its phenomena, he was returning to the tradition of the Presocratics, whom he studied and critiqued widely, rather than to Plato. In the works that we have, he explores most of the areas covered by modern science, although not necessarily addressing the issues modern scientists have found interesting. Indeed, despite his emphasis on starting with observations, quite a few of his theories appear bizarre. But we need to remember that he was a pioneer and that the size of the advances he made over his Presocratic predecessors was phenomenal. It would be nearly two millennia before anyone of comparable stature would arise.

Aristotle viewed the earth as an uncreated eternal sphere around which the heavenly bodies move. To the four traditional elements—fire, air, earth, and water—he added ether, of which the heavenly bodies are made.

Among the sciences, biology, interpreted in its widest sense as the science of living things, occupied Aristotle's attention most. It was in this area, to a large extent, that his investigations were most fruitful. His longest surviving work, *History of Animals*, is packed with observations about animals, often in considerable detail. He specifically stated that he would actually prefer to study things that are eternal and thus, in his way of seeing it, divine. But it was easier to engage in study of the rather more accessible things around us. And the animal world gave him plenty of scope to make careful observations (though not to conduct experiments, something that didn't belong to his scientific method), to classify, and to draw conclusions. Among his special studies was one on reproduction and one on how animals move.

The soul. Given his refusal to split reality in two, Aristotle had to reject any concept of the soul that made it radically different from the body and with it any idea of the soul surviving the death of the body. His alternative was to state that the soul was in fact the form of the body, expressed in the various functions of the body, such as breathing, moving, thinking, experiencing pain or pleasure, and so on. Body is matter; soul is form. It is soul that enables the "matter" of the body to have life. But, of course, other living things besides humans have matter and form. Do they also, then, have souls? Aristotle was sure they do, although the type of life, and so the type of soul, differs. The souls of plants are concerned with nutrition and reproduction. Animals have souls that additionally are able to move around and also have perceptions and desires. The distinctive element of human souls is reason.

God. Aristotle spoke about gods or God on three levels. First, he rejected the polytheistic anthropomorphic gods of traditional Greek religion. Second, he spoke often of the divine in the enduring and unchanging aspects of the universe, such as the heavenly bodies. This was no empty epithet, since he concluded from it that the stars and other entities have intelligence; they share in action and life.

On a third level, the process that had begun in the Presocratics and continued in Plato reached its climax in Aristotle's concept of the One, a God who has lost all polytheistic and anthropomorphic elements. He is infinite, eternal, all-powerful, most good, unchanging, indivisible, without parts, without magnitude, and transcendent, a being different from all others. But contrary to some subsequent developments of such a "God of the philosophers," he is not static. Though frequently called the "Unmoved Mover" in accounts of Aristotle's philosophy, he is in fact pictured as very active. He is living and thinking. He is the source and ultimate purpose of all, the prime cause, who gives being and meaning to everything and maintains all existence and life. Again, "prime cause" can seem to suggest he started everything off and then left it all to get on by itself. But this isn't Aristotle's position. His prime mover is always at every moment actively operating as the source and goal of all that happens in the universe. Complete actuality in himself, he is the ultimate goal of the potentiality of all things, the one who gives purpose to the universe itself.

Logic. An area where the innovations of Aristotle have proved invaluable throughout history is that of logic. In his *Prior Analytics* he worked out a scheme of formal logic, classifying and systematizing the forms of argument, just as he had classified the species of animals. Some arguments, he said, are valid, for example:

> All men are mortal.
>
> Socrates is a man.
>
> Therefore Socrates is mortal.

Some are invalid, for example:

> Socrates is a man.
>
> Pericles is a man.
>
> Therefore Socrates is Pericles.

Some issues, like that of statements about the future, pose special problems:

> Either there will or there won't be a sea battle tomorrow.
>
> If there will be, the statement "There will be a battle" is now true, so the battle is inevitable.
>
> If there won't be, the statement "There won't be a battle" is now true, so there cannot be a battle.
>
> Therefore the future is totally determined.

Closely linked to his work in logic was Aristotle's *Rhetoric*, a study of how to use arguments to persuade people.

The categories. We have seen that Aristotle liked classifying things. He attempted to provide a classification scheme for predicates, that is, the things we say about subjects in basic forms of sentences, especially sentences of the form S (the subject) is P (the predicate). In a sense this gives us a way of classifying anything that exists. Normally we would expect categories to be such that any predicate belongs to only one. An example of that would be the two categories Descartes described, mind and matter. What belongs to the mind category doesn't belong to the matter category, and vice versa. Aristotle suggested ten categories and so made it harder to avoid overlap. The first four were the most significant, and substance, the first, was much more important than all the rest.

1. Substance.   Everest is a mountain.
2. Quantity.   Everest is huge.
3. Quality.   Everest is dangerous.
4. Place.   Everest in on the border of Nepal.
5. Relation.   Everest is higher than any other mountain in the world.
6. Time.   Everest has existed since India collided with Asia.
7. Position.   Everest towers above us.
8. State.   Everest is covered in snow.
9. Activity.   Everest draws mountaineers like a magnet.
10. Passivity.   Everest was first climbed in 1953.

Ethics and life in society. Like Plato, Aristotle was very interested in the theme of our life in society. He taught and wrote a great deal in the areas of art, drama, politics, and ethics. His interest in careful research and classifying is seen in his attempt to provide a historically reliable list of winners in Greek athletic contests and in his detailed exposition of 158 constitutions of various Greek states, including Athens.

Perhaps the most famous of all Aristotle's works is his lectures on ethics, known as *Nichomachean Ethics*, after its editor. The book is a wide-ranging discussion and analysis of issues related to our life in society, rather than specific instructions in ethical issues, although Aristotle was careful to say his aim is not that we should just know what goodness is, but that we should live good lives.

Issues he covered include:

- A person's life is not to be seen in isolation. It is essentially life in community. For Aristotle that meant life in the *polis*, the city-state. We are "political" or social animals.

- Like everything in the universe, human life has a purpose or goal—everything aims at the good. Specifically, that good is *eudaimonia*, a term that has traditionally been translated "happiness" or "well-being" but is better understood as right-functioning, living a truly human life, almost self-fulfillment.
- This does not require a life without problems or setbacks; life is to be seen as a whole.
- The essence of a truly human life is not pleasure or success (honor) or even goodness (virtue), but living out the rational principles we find within us (in our souls, the "form" of being human) according to excellence. Aristotle's concept of the soul entails our inherent ability to know and do what is excellent.
- We have freedom to choose or reject the good. Our desires may incline us to choose what we know to be wrong. We must train ourselves, not just to resist our desires, but to eliminate wrong desires, so that our desiring and reasoning both incline us to excellence. This is moral excellence (virtue), a settled state of character achieved, like musical virtuosity, by discipline and regular practice.
- The right choice generally lies between extremes, the mean. We should not eat too much; we should not eat too little.
- We need to develop intellectual excellence or virtues, such as knowledge and good judgment, as well as moral or practical excellence (courage, generosity, and so on). The intellectual virtues are the more fulfilling of the two types, since they are more God-like.

Aristotle's philosophical method and the issues discussed in the *Ethics* were applied and developed further in his political works, of which the best known is his "reply" to Plato's *Republic*, the *Politics*. He discussed the merits of various forms of government; each has its strengths and weaknesses. Aristotle was more inclined toward democracy than Plato, though we need to remember that for him democracy gave no rights to women or slaves.

With Plato, Aristotle set the agenda for a wide range of philosophical discussions over the next two thousand years. We will be picking up many of the issues as we continue our journey through the history of philosophy. Meanwhile, try working out a few things for yourself.

TO THINK THROUGH

Which is the better way--to start with a concept or a principle and interpret what we see in the world accordingly or to start with our observations?

Modern science has taught us that the universe is random, purposeless; Aristotle saw purpose everywhere. Science sees matter as soulless; Aristotle saw souls, or at least forms, everywhere. Who is right?

Try asking a few "Why?" questions and analyze the answers in terms of Aristotle's four types of explanation. (Be warned: Everyone has difficulty analyzing "formal" explanations.)

Aristotle's concept of God has profoundly influenced the Western way of thinking about God. Is this a good thing?

Aristotle would say that anything we'd ever want to say about Everest could be fitted into one of his ten categories. Can you prove him wrong?

Why is the second example under "Logic" invalid? What's your answer to the sea battle puzzle?

For Further Study

Barnes, J. *Aristotle*. Oxford: Oxford University Press, 1982.

Irwin, T. *Classical Thought*. Oxford: Oxford University Press, 1989.

Nash, R. H. *Life's Ultimate Questions*. Grand Rapids: Zondervan, 1999, chap. 4.

FIVE

AFTER ARISTOTLE

SKEPTICISM AND ITS ALTERNATIVES

In this chapter we survey a huge period, more than five hundred years, from the time of Aristotle to the rise of Neoplatonism. Although there were hundreds of philosophers in these centuries, we are only able to look at some of the main ones, surveying cynicism and skepticism, Epicureanism and stoicism, Gnosticism, Philo, and Plotinus.

ARISTOTLE WAS AN OPTIMIST. HE BELIEVED THAT IF WE find what is good we will do it. For the most part those who came after him were a lot less cheerful. They realized the emptiness of the hope that philosophy could change the world. So, instead, the world changed philosophy. The two great systems that developed after Aristotle, Epicureanism and stoicism, accepted the dark side of existence as inevitable. The philosopher's task was not to take it away, but to help the individual live with it. Other thinkers turned to skepticism or cynicism or escaped into a fantasy world of mystery and esoteric religions. Into this world came Christianity, with its own particular brand of realism, but also with a wholly new message of hope.

The loss of philosophical nerve was set against momentous international events: the rise and fall of Alexander the Great's empire, the rise of Rome, its wars and conquests, and the Pax Romana. It was a time of unprecedented freedom for new ideas to flourish. In a city like Egypt's Alexandria, Oriental, African, Greek, Roman, Jewish, and, later, Christian thought mingled and cross-fertilized.

We have seen that the period of the flowering of Presocratic philosophy was followed by a time of disillusionment and relativism, perhaps because there was no way of deciding which of the many systems on offer was the right one. It may seem strange that the period following Plato and Aristotle was also one of disillusionment and skepticism. Surely, we might think, these two great systems, which have had such a profound effect on the history of Western thought, should have been accepted as forming the basis for life and thought. But actually they weren't. Until Christianity became the dominant worldview, no single philosophy was ever accepted in the ancient world by anything more than a relatively small minority. Indeed, there were more adherents of stoicism than there were followers of Plato or Aristotle.

It is easier to be skeptical than to believe. It is easier to destroy than to build. Anyone can deconstruct; construction takes some doing. It takes no time to smash a cup or wreck a car; it takes skill and effort to create a cup or build a car. Knocking down a wall is fun; building a house is hard work. Beliefs are easy to doubt and very hard to establish.

Think of what is necessary to establish a specific belief—for example, that all English people, though they may seem reserved and unfriendly, are in reality, deep down, very friendly. For a start you will have to do a lot of research, checking out all the English people you can find. Some of them will appear unfriendly, so you will need to dig deep to establish that they are actually friendly underneath. All this will take time and effort; after all, there are a lot of English people around, and a lot of them appear unfriendly. But you are a persistent person, so you keep going. It takes you years, and still there are more English people to check out. You grow old, and the job still isn't done. Through all your research you have succeeded in finding at least a bit of friendliness in every English person you have examined, and so you have managed to hold on to your belief. But in a sense, you still have not established it, because there are still others you have not examined. The job goes on forever. Establishing a belief takes some doing.

The person who wants to destroy a belief conclusively seems to have a much easier task. All that is needed is one thoroughly miserable and incredibly unfriendly English person. Of course, finding such a person may take some doing. But it seems a lot easier than checking out every single English person.

And if you want a really easy task, go for skepticism. What does the skeptic have to do? Nothing. No need to do any research. No need to do any thinking. No need to do *anything*. Just be skeptical. Doubt. Refuse to commit yourself. Believe nothing.

Plato and Aristotle's systems of philosophy were brilliant. They offered a way of viewing the world, of understanding and living. But, like all systems ever since, they had their weaknesses, their problem areas, their bits that people found hard to accept. And, by and large, people chose to take the easier option of being skeptical and rejecting their ideas rather than the harder option of working at establishing them.

DIOGENES

Sinope, Black Sea (414–323 B.C.). Diogenes was the originator of a loose philosophical "protest" movement called "Cynicism." A contemporary of Aristotle, he chose to live "like a dog" ("cynic" comes from the Greek for "dog"). He threw off all conventions, lived in a makeshift kennel, and fed himself by begging. He argued for a return to the "natural" life. Against those who saw something "divine" in humankind, he stressed our oneness with animals. He had traveled in the East and maybe picked up some of his ideas from Indian holy men.

The century after his death saw many imitators, and there was a new wave of Cynics in the first century A.D. The movement as a whole used satire and parody to attack the structures of society and the systems of the philosophers and urged in their place the unrestrained freedom of the individual.

TO THINK THROUGH

Nothing divine, just animals, rejecting structures, unrestrained freedom--it all sounds very familiar. But antiphilosophies are parasitic on positive philosophies. Diogenes couldn't live by begging if everyone followed his example. Postmodern relativism would collapse if everyone practiced it. What can you conclude from that? What can we say to those who delight to deconstruct everyone else's beliefs but offer nothing positive in their place?

SKEPTICISM

The original meaning of the word "skeptic" was "enquirer" rather than "doubter," so the spirit of the movement was more one of agnosticism than of total rejection of belief. The generally acknowledged fountainhead of the movement was **Pyrrho,** from Elis in the Peloponnese (c. 365–c. 270 B.C.). As a result, the movement was at first known as Pyrrhonism and only later as skepticism. Since we can never be sure of anything, said Pyrrho, the best way to cope with life is to suspend judgment in all things, including morals and logic.

Pyrrho's disciple **Timon** was born in Phlius and lived later in Athens (c. 315–c. 225 B.C.). He subjected all other philosophies to satirical attack and argued for skepticism on the grounds that we can never prove any of the basic assumptions on which every philosophy (and science) rests. "I can accept that honey tastes sweet," he said, "but I can never know that it *is* sweet." His arguments appear to have been very effective in that they won over the Athens Academy (founded by Plato), which remained in the skeptical tradition for 150 years. As a movement, skepticism continued for some five hundred years. The last main figure was **Sextus Empiricus** (fl. c. A.D. 200).

A standard skeptical argument was based on the fact that we are sometimes deceived by the way things appear; therefore, none of our beliefs can be trusted. A second was based on the range of conflicting theories philosophers and thinkers put forward. Another standard skeptical argument attacked the concept of the justification of our beliefs. For a given belief, we produce a justification, perhaps some evidence, or an accepted principle. But then, says the skeptic, we have to produce justification for the justification, and justification for that justification, and so on—a process we can never finish. Therefore no belief can ever be justified.

TO THINK THROUGH

Can you think of ways of countering the arguments of the Skeptics? How does "Honey tastes sweet" relate to "Honey is sweet"? Does the fact that we sometimes get something wrong have to mean we can never know anything? If two people disagree, must they both be wrong? And how do you stop the "infinite regress" of the "impossibility of justification" argument? You might take as an example: "This is a tree." "How do you justify that statement?" "I can see and touch it, so I know it's there." "How do you know sight and touch are reliable?" "Because they always work well." "How do you know that 'working well' makes a thing true?" And so on.

EPICURUS

Samos (341–271 B.C.). Epicurus taught in Athens, where he developed a philosophy that was highly influential for more than five hundred years. One of its best-known later exponents was the Roman poet **Lucretius** (c. 94–c. 55 B.C.).

Like cynicism and skepticism, Epicureanism was at heart a protest movement. It saw the world and society as corrupt, motivated by selfishness and greed, and dominated by fear, especially of death. As a result, it sought to develop a worldview that would free us from our fears and a lifestyle that would distance us as far as possible from the evils of the world. The goal of Epicureanism was peace or tranquillity, effectively freedom from hassle *(ataraxia)*. One of the keys to this, for Epicurus, was the rejection of the belief that the gods intervened in human affairs and in particular that they would punish us at death. The fact is, said Epicurus, the gods themselves live in perfect *ataraxia* and aren't at all interested in human affairs, so they can be safely ignored. Death, in fact, is extinction. There is no afterlife. Pain is real, but it is not to be feared as it is generally short-lived and is outweighed by pleasure.

Epicureanism was primarily a way of life. Its followers ideally lived in communities; Epicurus founded the first one in a garden. They put great emphasis on the importance of friendship and the pursuit of pleasure, largely through escaping from pain and through the right use of rational thought. Indeed, sorting out our beliefs and our thinking is the secret of dealing with anything that would disturb the serenity and enjoyment of our lives.

But Epicureanism also developed a distinctive worldview on which its lifestyle could be based. Its main points are:

- We can trust our senses and discover truths about the world around us. In reply to the Skeptics, Epicurus conceded that appearances sometimes deceive us, though he pointed out that it is what we infer from these appearances that is the source of error, not the appearances themselves. A straight stick really does appear bent when half in water; error comes in when we infer "This stick is bent." But we have no option but to trust our senses, and provided we are discerning about the way we interpret data, we can do so with confidence.
- The world is not designed; there is no mind or purpose behind it.
- The basis of everything is an infinite number of indivisible eternal (noncreated) atoms in constant motion in an infinite void. From time to time atoms come temporarily together in large groupings to form objects.

- The movement of atoms is determined according to the laws of motion, except for occasional random swerves, which allow for freedom.
- Souls, like everything else, are made of atoms. They therefore cannot be immaterial, as Plato said, nor are they immortal; they die when the body dies. Epicurus also rejected Aristotle's concept of the soul as the form of the body. Given his atomic theory, forms were unnecessary.
- People have experiences of the gods, so they must exist. But they aren't involved in the world; they neither planned nor created it. Since everything is composed of atoms, they are as well. Their atoms are especially fine and are not subject to dissolution.

TO THINK THROUGH

What do you think of "ataraxia" as the primary goal of life?

STOICISM

Stoicism was founded by **Zeno** (c. 334–c. 262 B.C.), who was born in Citium, Cyprus. He taught in the center of Athens in a painted porch (Gk. *stoa*), from which his philosophy got its name. Little of his writing has come down to us. Others, especially **Chrysippus** (c. 280–c. 206), developed his teaching. Even more influential than Epicureanism, the school lasted for well over five hundred years. Well-known Stoics included the Roman writer **Seneca** (c. 5 B.C.– A.D. 65) and the Roman emperor **Marcus Aurelius** (A.D. 121–180).

Stoicism as a general movement had several main points.

God. Despite evil and suffering, the universe is essentially rational and good. It is governed by God, who for Stoics is something nearer to an impersonal force or world soul than a transcendent or personal being. God is expressed as the divine Logos, which pervades everything. The divine Logos is strongly rational, decreeing the best possible overall pattern of events, which is repeated again and again. Each time, the pattern ends in a conflagration in which God's omnipresence is clearly manifested. Then it starts over again. There is nothing we can do about this except accept it and seek to live in accordance with it. Later Stoics dropped the concept of recurring cycles but retained the need to accept the pattern of the world, typified, for example, by the recurring seasons, as inevitable.

Reason. The key to human life is reason, the divine seed or spark in each of us. Through it we can cope with the pain and setbacks of life as it masters our emotions and enables us to realize that everything is ultimately for the best.

Good living. As we accept the world, we also accept ourselves and live in harmony with the divine purposes, with nature, and with others around us. All of these share in the divine Logos and so are to be equally accepted. This enables us to express virtue, which, for Stoics, is essentially rational or cognitive (thinking of things in the right way). The key virtues are good sense, justice, courage, and temperance.

Pain and pleasure. Though life is tough and we need to accept its darker side "stoically," we can still find joy. Stoics spurned seeking pleasure simply for itself and accused the Epicureans of doing just that. Rather, they believed we will find joy in the experiences of life if we approach life rationally, thinking virtuously.

Freedom and responsibility. The fact that the divine Logos governs everything does not mean we are not free or not responsible for our actions. Though we are part of the foreordained process, we have power over the choices we make, especially in choosing to live in tune with the process.

Knowledge and truth. Though we can be deceived by our senses, they are basically dependable, provided we reflect rationally on what we learn from them, moving from observation of specific instances to generic principles. We can therefore develop knowledge and make true statements about the world. Stoic thinkers explored carefully the logic of language and especially of propositions. Truth or falsehood, for them, was conveyed not by single words but by groups of words, axioms, or propositions.

The nature of the world. Everything, including God, is in some sense material. Stoics rejected the Epicurean atomism, saying that what exists is infinitely divisible. At its simplest level, according to stoicism, the universe can be analyzed as a passive principle, matter, and an active principle, God.

At a higher level, given the four elements of earth, air, fire, and water, earth and water can be seen as passive matter, while air and fire correspond to the active principle. Air and fire thus express the rational role of the Logos and can be referred to as spirit or breath (Gk. *pneuma*, Lat. *spiritus*), and they seem to fulfill the life-giving role of Aristotle's forms, giving objects their essential meaning.

Stoicism formed a comprehensive system that had wide appeal. It seems to have been able to adapt itself to changing times and fashions more successfully than Epicureanism. It retained belief in God while still offering a generally materialistic explanation of the universe. It appeared to provide an answer to skepticism, and its stress on reason appealed to the educated and intelligent and at the same time offered more ordinary people a way of viewing the world and coping with its problems.

The adaptability of stoicism can be seen in **Posidonius** (c. 135–c. 51 B.C.), a very impressive thinker, who combined stoicism with Platonic and other concepts. He was born in Apamea in Syria and taught in Rhodes. He traveled widely and studied and wrote on a wide range of topics, including rhetoric, history, geography, astronomy, meteorology, science, philosophy, psychology, and ethics. He sought to add the insights of other philosophical approaches he encountered to his basic stoicism. In his scientific research he was deeply committed to careful empirical observation. He was the first to explain tides in terms of the moon's position.

TO THINK THROUGH

Both Epicureanism and stoicism stressed the role of reason in sorting out our beliefs and our thinking in order to cope with living in a stress-filled world. This ties in with the fashion among some psychotherapists in the last two or three decades of stressing cognitive therapy over against, say, psychoanalysis or behavioral therapy. Sort out your belief structure, they say, and everything else will follow. What do you think?

PLATONISM AND THE ACADEMY

Given the questioning attitude of Socrates, it is perhaps not surprising that the Athens Academy, the bearers of the Platonic tradition, should fall prey to the questionings of skepticism and be dominated by it for 150 years. But in the first century B.C., partly influenced by Posidonius, the Academy and Platonism as a whole emerged into a more positive period known as Middle Platonism, which sought to combine the strengths of Plato, Aristotle, and stoicism. This gave way in the third century A.D. to a further highly significant phase, known as Neoplatonism, in which Plotinus was the most significant figure. Here the insights of Platonism were combined with elements of Gnosticism and Eastern thought.

Gnosticism was a loose religious/philosophical movement that became popular in the first century A.D. and lasted for some three hundred years. Its origins are obscure, but it is likely to have been influenced by Eastern ideas as well as incorporating popularized Platonic and Jewish and Christian concepts together with elements from Greek and Egyptian mystery religions. Its central concept was the radical division between the spiritual and the material. The spiritual is good; the material is evil. The goal of life is to escape from the evil of the world to find union with God. This is achieved through a secret knowledge (Gk. *gnosis*, "knowledge") found through revelation and illumination and perhaps attained through religious practices and meditation. Linked to the *gnosis* was a highly speculative understanding of the influence of celestial spiritual powers, arising perhaps from popular astrological beliefs.

Philo. Alexandria (c. 20 B.C.–c. A.D. 50). A convinced Jew, Philo was trained in Greek philosophy, and he adopted ideas from stoicism, Pythagoreanism (which had developed a number of esoteric mystical elements), and especially Platonism. Many of his writings were in the form of commentaries on the Old Testament, but he also wrote apologetic works defending the Jews. It may be that the primary aim in all his writing was apologetic, seeking to show that Judaism and Hellenistic Greek thought were compatible.

Though strongly theocentric, Philo's worldview had elements of dualism in that he saw a stark contrast between the transcendent God and the world, between the One and the many. This is because he incorporated Greek ideas of the incomprehensibility, immutability, and unknowability of God into his Jewish concept of God. This then created the problem of God's knowability and action in the world. Philo solved this by his concept of the Logos, which he sometimes described as the Mind of God and sometimes described as the firstborn or agent of God, or even a second God. The Logos is the agent of creation, the means through which God is involved in the world. It was the Logos, for instance, that appeared to Moses at the burning bush. The Logos is also the source of human minds, which are made in its image.

Scholars debate the extent to which Philo may have influenced the New Testament writers. There is no evidence, however, that they had read Philo, and it is probably safest to assume that parallels between Philo and New Testament concepts are to be explained by the fact that both drew on current philosophical ideas. Both, for example, used the concept of Logos, which had been in use as a philosophical term for five hundred years, to express key, though different, aspects of their teaching.

Plotinus.

Lycopolis, Egypt (A.D. 204–270). Plotinus studied in Alexandria (Egypt). After traveling in the East and encountering Eastern thought, he moved to Rome, where he taught from about 245. He established the movement later known as Neoplatonism. Though he saw himself as simply applying the basic teaching of Plato, his system was influenced by Aristotle, stoicism, and Eastern thought, as well as by Plato. But perhaps the most significant influence was his own ecstatic mystical experiences of oneness with reality, which were the basis of his belief in the One. Neoplatonism as a movement continued unbroken until the sixth century and resurfaced periodically in subsequent centuries. Plotinus's work was published and developed by his disciple **Porphyry** (c. 234–c. 305).

In answer to skepticism and the materialism of Epicureanism and stoicism, Plotinus taught that reality is ultimately spiritual. Thus we do not have to be concerned by the inconsistencies of our experiences of the material world. True knowledge can be had because reality is constantly presenting itself to our souls and minds.

Levels of reality.

Plotinus taught that there are several levels (Gk. *hypostases*) of reality. The highest level is the most real; as you move to lower levels, you move away from reality until the murky substratum that lies below the fourth level is in effect unreal. Each level flows down into the level below it, giving it at least some degree of being.

1. *The highest level.* This is the One, Plato's form of the good. It is the ultimate source and cause of everything. It is totally transcendent, impersonal, beyond our thinking or knowing. Yet it is not static. It overflows with being. From it flows or emanates all the other levels of being.

2. *From and below the One comes Intelligence or Mind* (Gk. *nous*). This is Plotinus's equivalent of the Stoic God, Plato's divine Mind, and Aristotle's ultimate God. Its activity is thinking. The object of its thought is the Platonic forms. But also, without any activity on its part, by a process of emanation, it is the source of all other intelligences.

3. *From and below Intelligence comes the level of Soul,* a cosmic soul, which also expresses itself by emanation in individual souls. In contrast to the Epicureans and Stoics, the soul is in no way material. Rather, Plotinus returned to Plato's view that the human soul is immortal and can exist without the body. Plotinus didn't, however, accept Plato's concept of reincarnation. At the death of the body, he said, the soul returns back into the cosmic soul. Human souls have higher and lower parts; the higher reaches up to the cosmic Intelligence; the lower links the human soul to the body.

4. *From and below the cosmic Soul comes the level of body and objects in the world.* These emanate from Soul as Soul emanates from Mind and Mind from the One. Plotinus pictured the world of bodies and physical objects as the result of Soul's encounter with a kind of negative substrate, something that doesn't really exist, but gives the soul something in which to express itself. Though this substrate is evil, Plotinus did not stress the radical divide between the evilness of the material world and the goodness of the human soul in the way the Gnostics did. Nevertheless, the gap between soul and body is very great, and the desire of the soul must always be to reach up through the levels to seek the One.

TO THINK THROUGH

In Pascal's words, the God of the Hebrews was the God of Abraham, Isaac, and Jacob, not the God of the philosophers. Nevertheless, the "Greek" concept of God as remote, impassible, unknowable, and so on did have a significant effect on the development of both Hebrew and Christian thought. Why do you think this was so? Do you think it had a good or a bad effect? Similarly, the "Greek" idea of the innate evilness of matter and of the human body infiltrated Christian thinking, contrary to the teaching of the New Testament. Can you think why this happened? Are there traces of this concept still around? If so, what do we do with them?

REFLECTIONS

With Neoplatonism we come to the end of what can be seen as the first great stage in the development of Western thought. It has been a story of adventure, exploration, and speculation. It has sought to find answers to the great questions of the world and its nature, life and its meaning, and ourselves and how we should live. Despite its periodic lapses into relativism and skepticism, it is perhaps possible to isolate three generally common features.

The first is the variety. Even in our brief survey we have touched on a bewildering range of ideas and explanations. And these are only the tip of the iceberg. There were many other thinkers and speculators. Some of their work has survived, but most of them we no longer know anything about—perhaps because their concepts were even odder and more short-lived than the ones that were sufficiently prized to be preserved. One of the reasons for the variety was the lack of an agreed criterion by which to judge any proposed system. Was it, for example, to be compatibility with sense perceptions? Or overall explanatory value? Or its ability to promote a virtuous or hassle-free life?

The second feature is the move from polytheism and traditional religion to some form of monotheism. With the trend to monotheism, there was also a trend to a remote, impersonal, immutable God. The traditional gods had been cast very much in the image of human persons. When they were rejected, the concept of God as personal tended to be rejected as well. Only the Hebrews managed to combine high monotheism with a personal and immanent God.

The third feature is the focus on Intelligence or Mind as somehow basic or ultimate. This may, perhaps, be explained by the fact that philosophy is produced by philosophers, who might be expected to be especially interested in intelligence. It is, perhaps, the one element of personhood that was generally retained in the monotheistic concepts of God. Though he (or it) may no longer love or communicate or be involved in his creation, he still exercises thought.

For Further Study

Irwin, T. *Classical Thought*. Oxford: Oxford University Press, 1989.

Nash, R. H. *Life's Ultimate Questions*. Grand Rapids: Zondervan, 1999, chap. 5.

CHRISTIANITY

PART TWO

SIX

STARTING AT
THE CENTER

THE CHRISTIAN VIEW OF GOD

In this chapter we outline four main aspects of the New Testament concept of God, which forms the basis for all the rest of the Christian worldview.

DESPITE THE FACT THAT NO BOOK HAS HAD A GREATER influence on the development of Western thought, very few histories of philosophy have a section on the New Testament. It is fairly standard for historians to move straight from a survey of Hellenistic philosophy, such as we have just completed, to a discussion of the philosophical issues raised by the spread of Christianity and its encounter with various philosophical movements and concepts. Typically, Augustine, who lived four hundred years after Christ, has been seen as the first serious Christian philosopher worthy of consideration.

This is a mistaken procedure for a number of reasons. In the first place, to understand any worldview, and particularly one founded by a specific teacher, we need at the very least to start with its earliest documents or traditions. This has been the principle we have followed in the first part of this book. Only then can we isolate the original ideas and concepts from later developments and changes.

Second, it is generally agreed that the encounter between Christianity and other philosophies did in fact have a significant effect on the development of

Christianity. This may or may not have been a good thing, but, in order to judge, we need to know what Christianity was like before this happened.

Further, it is undoubtedly true that Augustine has had a profound influence on the development of Christianity and of Western thought in general. But even his influence pales into insignificance compared with the influence of the teaching of the primary Christian documents, the New Testament, containing as they do the teaching of Jesus and of those who were closest to him. Some would dismiss the New Testament as of religious significance rather than philosophical. But despite its primary religious focus, it is in fact full of philosophy. It contains a well-developed worldview with answers, fully formed or embryonic, to many of the questions raised in the previous centuries.

So in this section we are going to outline the philosophical teaching of the New Testament. We could do this in a number of ways. For example, we could examine philosophical issues book by book, starting, say, with Mark or Paul's earliest letters, and working through to those books, like John or Revelation, that are considered to be written last of all. But the approach we will follow is thematic. We will take individual philosophical themes or issues, and, while noting any relevant differences of emphasis between the New Testament writers, seek to build up from the New Testament as a whole a composite understanding of what Christianity in its earliest form had to say on each topic.

The key to the Christian worldview is its theocentricity. All the other philosophies we have surveyed have had some place for God or gods, but their roles have varied widely. In keeping with its Hebrew heritage, the New Testament made God foundational and central to all things. Foundational, in that he is the source and explanation of everything that exists and happens. Central, in that he is personally immanent and actively involved in the world.

Accordingly, in our survey of the New Testament worldview, we will look at the concept of God in some detail. We will then survey seven other themes: truth, anthropology, time and eternity, suffering and death, the world, philosophy, and community.

GOD

In our survey of early Hebrew philosophy, we listed five main elements of its concept of God: God is one; he is Creator; he relates to his creation; he is holy; and he is true. These five points remained central to Jewish thinking down to the time of Christ, despite the varying fortunes of the Jewish people from the sixth century B.C. onward. We will be looking at the last of these five elements in the section on the New Testament concept of truth; the other four we will use as the basis for our survey of the New Testament concept of God.

1. MONOTHEISM

Monotheism in Hebrew thought. In later Hebrew thought monotheism tended to become even more firmly asserted. While in early Hebrew thought there was some willingness to allow that the gods of the nations did exist as supernatural beings, albeit vastly inferior to the one true God, the stress in later thinking tended to exalt YHWH so highly that no other power merited the title "god." Not that this precluded other supernatural beings. Later Judaism in fact developed a belief in a whole host of angelic beings or hypostases, perhaps to compensate for a growing emphasis on God's transcendence. These took the form not just of angels, but of God's Word, God's Glory, God's Wisdom, God's Law, God's Name, and God's Spirit. These were not rival gods; rather they were his servants, working out his purposes in creation and providence.

Monotheism and Satan in Jewish thought. Two seeming exceptions could be seen as challenges to monotheism. The first was Satan, a rebellious angel, who seeks to thwart the purposes of God. But in fact the existence of Satan, for later Judaism, served to emphasize the uniqueness of God rather than to challenge their monotheism. In the first place, he's a creature, made and held in being by God himself. Second, all he does is ultimately under God's control. Third, God, through his wisdom and power, will use even Satan's activities for his own purposes. And, finally, Satan's days are numbered; in the last days he will be destroyed.

Monotheism and the Messiah in later Jewish thought. The second figure in later Judaism, notably in apocalyptic, that might seem potentially to rival God in status was the figure of the Savior King, the Messiah, the one who will defeat and destroy all the enemies of God. But though he is truly a mighty—even heavenly—figure, the Jews again avoided any suggestion that this concept would challenge monotheism. All that the Savior King will do will be done by God's power, and as his representative, with the aim of bringing ultimate glory to God and establishing his kingdom.

Monotheism in the New Testament. New Testament monotheism sat comfortably with Hebrew monotheism, both in its earlier and later forms. Other so-called gods are nothing compared to the one true God. Nor are the other supernatural beings, whether angels (who tend to fulfill a more mundane role in the New Testament than, say, in Philo) or demons. Paul in fact hints that the so-called gods of the nations are in fact demonic powers who hold them under their sway. Though Satan is a powerful figure determined to destroy God's work, the New Testament shared the Judaistic vision of his subservience to the purposes of God and his ultimate destruction. In particular, it demonstrated his defeat in the life and work of Christ.

Monotheism in the New Testament had clear ethical and political overtones. It entailed total obedience and total love. Nothing was to be allowed to set aside the absolute authority of the one God. Simply believing that God is one is insufficient; the belief is to be lived. To live it could be costly. In the first century A.D. Rome declared the divinity of its emperors and demanded that everyone worship them; failure to comply was treason. The result was that many Jews and Christians paid the price of martyrdom for their monotheism.

Monotheism, Christ, and the Holy Spirit. The one area where the teaching of the New Testament came into conflict with the monotheistic vision of Judaism was the status of Christ and, perhaps to a lesser degree, the status of the Holy Spirit. The issue arose most acutely over the relationship of Christ to the one God. The New Testament documents never questioned monotheism, and, indeed, stated it explicitly in a number of places. But they also made it quite clear that Christ not only fulfills the messianic expectations of Judaism, as God's representative bringing in God's kingdom by God's power, but also actually embodies the presence of God in a very specific way. Philo and Middle Platonism tended to preserve the uniqueness of God by distancing him from the world and requiring him to operate through intermediaries. But this tendency was largely resisted in the New Testament. Jesus is the immanent God. Those who see him see "the Father." In him the kingdom or kingly rule of God has come. Despite the need to be circumspect about the way he expressed his claims (to claim to be God was a capital offense in the eyes of Jews; Jesus was executed for just that reason), Jesus made a number of claims to divinity. The most explicit were his application to himself of the divine name I AM. Additionally, divinity was ascribed to him, with greater or lesser explicitness, throughout the New Testament writings.

Yet the distinction between Christ and "the Father" was maintained. The language varied, but it is quite clear that the New Testament writers didn't want to stress the oneness of Christ with God at the cost of his distinctiveness. Just how this was to be understood in terms of substance and nature was a problem the New Testament writers didn't tackle. Their interest was factual and functional rather than metaphysical. Like Aristotle, they were starting with and describing the data—the person, work, and claims of Christ. A metaphysical theory may develop as a result of these observations, but they weren't prepared to allow metaphysics to prejudge the data.

The New Testament experience of Christ as God and yet distinct from God was paralleled by the New Testament writers' experience of the Holy Spirit. They couldn't doubt that this was the Spirit *of God*, nothing less than God (and, indeed, Christ) himself indwelling them in a particularly immanent way, in fulfillment of Old Testament promises. Yet still the Spirit was not to be equated unequivocally with Christ or the Father. Unity and distinction were both to be maintained.

The New Testament writers were describing what they experienced in Christ and in the Holy Spirit. They were sure it was an experience of God. In contrast to concepts of God that emphasized his otherness or his accessibility only to the trained philosopher or earnest mystic, it was an experience of God coming, revealing, being gloriously and personally present to all who would receive him. It was a dynamic experience, an active, living God, not just coming, but doing, speaking, teaching, healing, forgiving, saving, empowering, filling, and so on. And though the New Testament writers may not have worked out the full implications, the threefold form in which they experienced the one God was rich in potential for the understanding of the issue of the One and the many, and of the relationship between God and the world.

2. GOD AS CREATOR

Theocentricity. The New Testament took over the main emphases of the Hebrew concept of creation. It thus proclaimed an understanding of the creative relationship between God and the world that ran counter to most other current views. It presented a world that was radically dependent on God. Whatever it may be composed of, it is not eternal, it is not self-sufficient, it does not possess its own form within itself, it is not self-directing. God is its source, its explanation, and its goal. "From him and through him and to him are all things" (Rom. 11:36; a good example of Aristotle's material, efficient, and final explanations). Here is theocentricity with a vengeance!

Lordship. This kind of creativity entails lordship. Though created beings have been given a degree of freedom, not even the exercise of that freedom can thwart the purposes of the Creator. On the contrary, it enables him to demonstrate the extent of his creativity by using even the free choices of rebellious creatures to bring about his creative purposes, as, for example, in the case of the cross and in the eschatological vision of the book of Revelation.

The creative word. In the Old Testament creation was primarily through God's word. "God said, 'Let X be,' and X was." Besides emphasizing God's sovereignty and absolute power, this stressed God as one who speaks. It stood in contrast to those traditions that pictured God's creative activity as doing (Plato's demiurge), or thinking (later Platonism), or simply emanating. A word is deliberate and personal and powerful. As Confucius had seen, words shape things. (The theocentric biblical writers would not, however, have agreed with Confucius and his more recent counterparts that it is our words that do the shaping. That, they would have said, has already been done by God's word.)

The concept of God creating by his word continued to be central in the New Testament. By his word he creates, and by his word all things are "carried" or held in existence. Even the final defeat of evil and the ushering in of the eschatological kingdom of God is achieved by the pronouncing of God's word, rather than by the performing of an act. In that the agent of creation is Christ, the title "Word of God," applicable for a range of reasons, is especially apposite.

3. GOD'S RELATIONSHIP WITH THE WORLD

Immanence. Linked to the concept of creation is that of God's close relationship with the world he has made. Later Judaism at times felt the strength of the arguments that urged that a transcendent God could not be at the same time immanent. Hence the beginnings of a hierarchy of being, as seen in Philo. The New Testament, however, would have none of it. The incarnation refutes it utterly. Paul vehemently rejected any trace of incipient Gnostic ideas. The concept of the Holy Spirit poured out on and filling everyone without discrimination of age, sex, or status exemplified the central miracle of the New Testament that God can be at one and the same time the gloriously transcendent Holy One and personally present in anyone who will receive him.

In the Old Testament God was a God who comes. In the New Testament he was a God who had come. The kingdom is here; the Spirit is poured out. God is *with us*. For the New Testament writers the infinite transcendent God can be immanent for the very reason that he is infinite. With him nothing is impossible. The power of the Highest One "overshadowed" Mary, so that in her womb she carried the Holy One (Luke 1:35).

Though supremely interested in God's immanence in the individual and in the community of those who know him, the New Testament made it clear that God is immanent generally in all his creation. He is not far from each one of us, claimed Paul in Athens; "in him we live and move and have our being" (Acts 17:28).

Moral dualism. In the New Testament the fact of God's immanence made impossible any form of moral dualism. God has come in a human body. Jesus has made all foods clean. Christ retains his humanity even in heaven. Human resurrection will be of the body. Though the pressure to do so is reflected (and strongly resisted) even in the New Testament, Christianity could never accept that the world in itself is evil, without denying its foundational truths of creation, immanence, and incarnation.

Love. Immanence is motivated by love. The love of God motivated the coming of the Son. In love the Father and the Son come to the individual and make their home there. This concept of a relationship with God rooted in love was the Christian extension of the Old Testament covenant relationship and was radical and unique. Plato gave love a key place in his thinking, but his starting place was human love (Gk. *eros*). Though he could speak of the traditional gods loving in this way, it was an inadequate model for his supreme God, who spent his time in thought, not in involvement in loving relationships. By contrast the New Testament writers modeled their concept of human love on what they saw of God's love, something in essence very different from *eros*. The New Testament word was *agape*, and the essence of *agape* was the opposite of the pleasure or fulfillment of the lover. It was nothing less than a commitment to the total well-being of the loved one, even at infinite cost to the lover. The paradigm of love is the cross. Thus, in the New Testament, the direction of movement was reversed. Plato started with love as we humans feel it, with physical and sexual attraction, which, with the help of philosophy, can be lifted from the level of the love of bodies or of beautiful objects to the love of beauty itself and ultimately of goodness itself. But in the New Testament we learn love from God; we experience it in him, and he then lives it out in us. As a result, his love provides the basis and pattern for all forms of loving.

Accessibility. Confronted with his Athenian audience, Paul started his apologetic by speaking of God as transcendent and Creator. Before he went on to state the fact of God's immanence, he gave as God's purpose in creation that people of every nation should seek him, reach out for him, and find him. This is no esoteric path for the philosophical few. Rather, it is a call to all. Key to our response, said Paul, is the foundational step of repentance. In this he was echoing the basic message of John the Baptist and Jesus and the earliest Christian teachers. "God's kingdom has come," they proclaimed. "Repent, and put your trust in the good news."

Repentance, the response of the individual to God's coming, involves a holistic response from each aspect of the person. The Hebrew word on which the New Testament concept is based means simply to turn round, but in its frequent theological use, it includes turning from evil to God and changing one's behavior, with the consequent experience of God's grace and forgiveness. There is also a rational, cognitive element to repentance. The Greek word most commonly used *(metanoeo)* is cognate with *nous,* the mind. Linked as it is with the acceptance of the Good News, the call to repentance can thus be seen as a call to a change of worldview, the rejection of an old set of beliefs, and the acceptance of new, God-given truth. New Testament thinkers, of course, would have taken it for granted that the adopting of a new set of beliefs entailed a change of lifestyle. To receive the Good News meant both to commit oneself to it, to put one's trust in it, and to start living by it.

The New Testament, then, presented a God who comes and who calls each person into relationship with himself, a relationship that has radical implications in all aspects of life. Here was a concept very different from that of the Epicureans, who could safely ignore God, or from the Platonist tradition, in which experience of God is only for the philosophical few. The New Testament God seeks to be nothing less than preeminent in all things—theocentric indeed!

Communication: God's initiative. Central to the New Testament understanding of the nature of God is that he is a God who communicates. In particular, he takes the initiative in communicating. It is not simply that he responds to us as we seek him. He first seeks us.

This concept of God taking the initiative in communicating ran counter to the dominant Greek tradition. There, God remained relatively remote, to be discovered by the earnest seeker perhaps, but in no way coming or speaking to the ordinary person. The concept was also lacking in the Eastern understanding of God. Even where ancient thought went beyond the idea of the search for God originating in us and suggested that there is something that originates in God and moves toward us, the contrast with the New Testament is still very marked. The Neoplatonists had a concept of mind and soul emanating from the One, but what emanates is impersonal and involuntary. No other philosophy in the ancient world shared the New Testament vision of deliberate, specific, and personal communication.

The roots of the New Testament concept go right back to the start of the Hebrew tradition. Buddha or Plato's philosopher may have attained enlightenment after years of searching; both Abraham and Moses were met, seemingly unexpectedly, by God, who spoke specifically to them, revealing truth about himself and calling them to action. Prophet after prophet had a similar experience; the phrase "The word of the LORD came to . . ." occurs very frequently, with its clear emphasis on divine initiative in communication. The communication was not simply verbal, however. Long before the insights of twentieth-century linguistic philosophy, the Hebrews knew that to view divine communication as simply words was quite inadequate. As we have seen, the divine word was inevitably active, powerful, and performative. What God spoke came to be. His word created, empowered, decreed right and wrong, shaped the course of history, judged, saved, and more.

The content of God's communication.
The message of the New Testament was "good news." As such it had cognitive content. But it was much more than bare propositions or facts. Mark introduced his gospel with a phrase meaning "the good news of Jesus Christ"; Paul started Romans with a similar phrase, "the good news of God." God had spoken not just words, but a person. When Paul preached he "preached Christ," not just truths about Christ (1 Cor. 1:23). The Good News was more than words; it was "the power of God" (v. 24). God's communication is his coming. Christ is the creative, powerful, life-changing word of God.

Communication and the Logos.
Though the word *logos* is common in the New Testament, it is only in a few passages in the Johannine writings, notably in the prologue to the gospel, that it could be taken as being used in a technical sense. Scholars debate just how technically John, especially in his prologue, is using *logos*. Some argue that there is no need to look to Greek concepts; the background to John's use is wholly within the Old Testament worldview. However, though there is no doubt that Jewish thought had a very well-established concept of the word of God that could stand on its own, it seems very unlikely that John used the word unaware of the nuances its use would convey to many of his readers. Thus it is reasonable to assume that in using it he is claiming that in Christ is fulfilled not just what the Old Testament had prefigured, but what Heraclitus or the Stoics or the Platonists were foreshadowing in their use of the term. Christ is the unifying principle (Paul would say the one in whom "all things hold together" [Col. 1:17]), the source of all things ("everything is through him and to him" [Rom. 11:36]), and the

one through whom the transcendent God becomes immanent and acts in the world.

Communication and the "Good News." The concept of God communicating through word and life set a pattern for those who received his communication. The Good News message was to be passed on to others. They couldn't stop speaking what they had seen and heard. Paul and others traveled the world preaching the Good News; Christianity could not but be a missionary religion. But, again, it was not word alone. The proclamation of the Good News was a call to a change of lifestyle. It was the inauguration of a new community. It was a vision with power to change the world.

The justification of God's communication. The New Testament writers didn't deal explicitly with the objections to the concept of divine communication or revelation that have been raised during the subsequent centuries. Challenged to "prove" that the life and teaching of Christ truly were God communicating, they would have replied, "Look at the evidence. Blind people see again and lame people are walking, lepers are healed and deaf people hear, dead people are raised to life and ordinary people are receiving the good news." Jesus was "accredited by God . . . by miracles, wonders and signs" (Acts 2:22), and his resurrection was a demonstration of his power. The evidence for them was overwhelming; they were too near to it and too personally involved in it to doubt it. Later generations were perhaps less privileged; as Jesus said to Thomas, "Because you have seen me, you have believed; blessed are those who have not seen and yet have believed" (John 20:29).

The significance of the New Testament concept of God taking the initiative in communicating with human beings cannot be overstressed. Once again it put the focus of attention on God and his person, actions, and truth rather than on us and our reason or mystical experience. It set a pattern for knowing and for morality and meaning. It made not just religion, but the whole of life, irrevocably theocentric.

4. HOLINESS

The fourth element of the early Hebrew concept of God we listed at the start of this section was holiness. This meant more than divine otherness or the static possession of divine perfection. The holiness of the Hebrew God was personal and active, a key factor in his relationship with his people. It made them holy because he was holy; it sought practical holiness of life in response. This set the

Hebrew concept apart from that of the majority of ancient religions and philosophies, where gods either practiced a morality remarkably similar to human (not so moral) behavior, or were beyond good and evil, or whose form of goodness was remote and philosophical.

Personal and moral holiness.

The New Testament followed the Hebrew concept in seeing the holiness of God in personal and moral terms. Of the two main Greek words for holy, *hieros* and *hagios*, *hieros* lacked any strong ethical feel, something *hagios* was able to carry. *Hagios* is common in the New Testament; *hieros* is rare. Christ as well as God is called holy; so, very frequently, is the Spirit. Indeed, in contrast to the Old Testament, where holiness was experienced in God and received through observation of the cult and obedience to God's commands, in the New Testament the Holy Spirit is the focus of our experience of the holiness of God and the means by which we are made holy and live holy lives.

Dynamic holiness.

Holiness in the New Testament was a particularly dynamic concept, doubtless reflecting the dynamic experience of the Holy Spirit shared by the writers and their readers. Holiness in God cannot be static or inactive. It judges unholiness. It makes the unholy holy. The presence of a holy God produces holiness. Paul referred to early Christian believers as the "holy ones" (*hagioi*). Again, this was a dynamic concept. They were those who were in a living relationship with the holy God. They had been made holy through the work of Christ and the Holy Spirit. They were now living (or should have been living) holy lives because of their continuing relationship with God and the power of the Holy Spirit working in them.

TO THINK THROUGH

What do you think would have been the elements of the Christian concept of God that would have been hardest to accept for those who encountered them for the first time in the first century?

MAKE SURE IT'S THE REAL THING

TRUTH AND PHILOSOPHY IN THE NEW TESTAMENT

> In most of this chapter we will be looking at the well-developed and distinctive concept of truth presented in the New Testament. Then we will glance at the issue of the relationship between "God's truth" and "philosophy," a topic that we will be picking up again on several occasions.

TRUTH

Greek and Hebrew concepts of truth. There has been considerable discussion over the biblical, and in particular the New Testament, concept of truth and its relationship to Greek ideas. Some have argued that the divergence is radical: For the New Testament truth was moral, personal, and practical; for the Greeks it was propositional, impersonal, and theoretical. Others have sought to show that this is too facile a classification; there are elements of Greek thought in which, for example, truth is personal, and elements of New Testament thought in which truth is propositional. This, in turn, has led scholars to reexamine the Hebrew tradition to see if it could be the source of the so-called Greek elements in the New Testament rather than assuming they are the result of the infiltration of Greek ideas. The outcome of these scholarly discussions seems to be:

- It is not possible to establish that either approach fits exclusively into the supposed pattern.

- Neither approach is monochrome. For each of them truth is a rich and wide-ranging concept that can't be pinned down to just one limited aspect.
- However, in general there is a basic difference of emphasis between the Greek and the New Testament understanding of truth. The Greeks tended to see it as static, theoretical, and timeless. The Hebrews tended to see it as dynamic, personal, and practical.
- It is likely that this general emphasis would have permeated all the New Testament uses of the concept of truth. Where, for example, the writers used "true" to describe a proposition, they would, if questioned, have probably asserted that though truth can be predicated of a proposition, this is only possible because a proposition (and so the truth of that proposition) is something that depends on a person.
- It is still an open question whether or not some of the New Testament use of the concept was directly influenced by the Greek approach. As we noted with the Logos concept, it would be safe to assume that Paul and John, at the very least, were aware of current Greek thinking about truth and so may have expressed their ideas, consciously or unconsciously, in ways that took it into account. But even if this is so, it still seems clear that the basic distinctiveness of their concept of truth remained intact.

Theocentricity. The debate over the influence of Greek thought, valuable though it has been, has tended to divert attention from the central aspect of the New Testament concept of truth, and that is its theocentricity. If truth in the New Testament tended to be dynamic and personal and practical, it was because the God who is the source and basis for truth is dynamic, personal, and practical, both in himself and in the experience of his people. Again, if a distinction is to be drawn, we could say that the Greeks started with the question "What is truth as we know it?" while the New Testament asked, "What is truth as it is in God?" or, perhaps more accurately, "How do we apply our experience of a true God to the concept of truth in general?"

For the New Testament writers, the experience of God in Christ was undoubtedly an experience of truth. Jesus' affirmation, "I am the way and the truth and the life" (John 14:6), was a summary both of his entire ministry and of the way he expressed the truth of God. Right from the start, people had been amazed at his teaching. Even those who rejected him conceded that his claims as they stood were absolute. But the paralleling of "way" and "life" with truth expressed clearly the nature of the truth Christ was claiming to be. It wasn't detached or theoretical. It was truth to be followed and lived. Moreover, it was the way to God "the Father"; truth is not something to be sought after for itself. There is only one thing worthy of our searching, and that is God. Similarly, "life" can't be divorced from truth, whether it is the life of God in us through the Holy Spirit or the expression of that life in our daily living and behavior.

Truth was personal because God's revelation in Christ was personal. It was dynamic and practical because the New Testament Christians' experience of God was life-changing and life-empowering. It was true because God was true, and the pattern of truth in God was the model for all other manifestations of truth.

Faith and truth.

Post-Kantian thought has tended to draw a distinction between faith and knowledge. Knowledge, it says, operates in the "scientific" world of facts and so can claim to be dealing with what is true. Faith, which we use in adopting our religious views, makes far less grandiose claims. It is insufficient for establishing truth. At best it can be the basis on which we hold beliefs, which as mere subjective opinions fall very far short of ever being capable of being established as truth.

The New Testament writers used the concept of faith or trust frequently. But, in contrast to the Post-Kantians, they did so without suggesting any element of uncertainty or lack of truth in the objects of faith. They were, for instance, able to use "the faith" as a synonym for "the truth." The Greek word they used (*pistis* and its cognates) never suggested the Post-Kantian element of uncertainty. Instead, it assumed that trust or faith could be exercised in a person or in propositions precisely because they were utterly trustworthy and true. Indeed, a key verbal form of the word is generally translated "I am convinced," and *pistis* itself was used outside as well as inside the New Testament to indicate a conviction as opposed to an unprovable opinion. The concept of exercising faith or belief, therefore, was in no way opposed to the concept of accepting truth. To have faith in God or in the good news of the gospel was to accept God or the Good News as truth.

Truth in the New Testament.

The main features of the New Testament concept of truth can be summarized in twelve points.

1. *Truth is God-centered.* Truth exists because God exists. Truth can be known because God reveals his truth both in creation and the world at large and specifically in Christ and through the Holy Spirit.

New Testament References
to Aspects of Truth

Christ-centered

The Pharisees and the Herodians said, "Teacher, we know you are a man of integrity and that you teach the way of God in accordance with the truth" (Matt. 22:15).

"The Word . . . full of grace and truth" (John 1:14; cf. v. 17).

"I am the way and the truth and the life" (John 14:6).

Holy Spirit-centered

"The Spirit of truth" (John 14:17; 15:26; 16:13; 1 John 4:6).

"The Spirit of truth . . . will guide you into all truth" (John 16:13).

"The Spirit is the truth" (1 John 5:6).

God-centered

"Your word is truth" (John 17:17).

"The truth of God" (Rom. 1:25).

Truth is to be lived, not just believed.

"Whoever lives by the truth comes into the light, so that it may be seen plainly that what he has done has been done through God" (John 3:21).

"If we claim to have fellowship with him yet walk in the darkness, we lie and do not live by the truth" (1 John 1:6).

See also the parable of the two builders (Matt. 7:24–27).

God's revelation, or the gospel, is equated with the truth.

See Romans 1:18, 25; 2:8; Galatians 2:5, 7; 1 Timothy 2:3–4; 3:7.

"God chose you to be saved . . . through belief in the truth" (2 Thess. 2:13).

"If we deliberately keep on sinning after we have received the knowledge of the truth, no sacrifice for sins is left" (Heb. 10:26).

2. *Truth is thus not to be understood in isolation*. Truth is not an independent entity; it is an expression of the nature of God and is thus to be understood in the context of all other aspects of God's nature. It is to be seen as, say, eternal, holy, and personal, in that God is eternal, holy, and personal.

3. The significance of *the personal aspect of truth* is highlighted by the fact that the personal God reveals himself, and thus his truth, to us as persons. In Christ we have a relationship with God characterized by love, life, obedience, and the like; these all operate on a personal level; they require involvement; they do not permit objective detachment. Truth, following this model, also requires personal involvement. As Kierkegaard would have put it, knowing a confession of faith merely by rote, however factually correct it may be, is the opposite of real truth.

4. In a similar way, *truth requires an ethical and practical response*. Because truth in God necessarily puts into practice his holy purposes, truth in us will not be truth unless it is applied and lived out.

5. *Truth predicated of God has a range of interconnected meanings*. It may be that the primary one, going back to the Hebrew concept, is the reliability, faithfulness, and trustworthiness of his nature. It links closely with God's other moral qualities; the book of Revelation, for example, is able to say that God's judgments are true. God and his ways are "just and true" (15:3; 16:7; 19:2) and "holy and true" (3:7; 6:10). We can have confidence that God's communication will be true, whether in verbal statements or in more general revelation or in what we experience of him. That leads on to the truth of God's actions; his "ways" as well as his words are true; all that he does expresses truly the holy God that he is. Finally, there is the nuance we have encountered before. Just as a holy God makes others holy, so a true God makes (or seeks to make) others true. Truth is for spreading, not for remaining inactive.

6. The meaning of *truth as predicated of human persons* is modeled on its meaning when predicated of God. It thus tends to cover the same range, from reliability, to virtue in general, to truthfulness of speech and action, and a sharing in a commitment to spread and establish truth.

7. *Truth when predicated of propositions* has a narrower range of possible meanings, but it is reasonable to assume that at least some of the subtleties of the wider range of meanings would always have been present. New Testament writers would have found it very difficult to conceive of a statement, especially a theological statement, as a "mere" proposition. If a proposition is true, it will inevitably have ethical and practical implications and even some sort of efficaciousness, as seen in concepts like "The truth will make you free" or "The

Good News is the power of God, which results in salvation for everyone who puts their trust in it."

8. In keeping with the predominantly personal and practical thrust of the New Testament concept, *the opposite of true is deceiving or lying*, rather than false in the sense of untrue.

9. Just as truth itself has ethical implications, *the reception of truth has significant ethical overtones*. It is not simply intellectual; the will is involved. We are free to choose to accept or reject the truth. As a result, we are morally responsible for what we do with the truth.

10. In contrast to much post-Kantian thought, *the New Testament writers did not allow for any differences in "logic" in the various areas of truth*. They would not, for example, have claimed that "scientific" truth operates in a different way from "ethical" or "theological" truth. As we have seen, the reason for this was twofold. They didn't recognize any serious divisions between the various types of truth; they all overlapped and interacted; "scientific" truth, for example, had ethical and practical implications. Second, in a very real sense, all truth for them was one in that it was all theological. A "scientific" proposition was as much God's truth as an ethical or theological one. We are back to theocentricity.

11. The issue of *the justification of Christianity's truth claims* was clearly a live issue for the New Testament writers. Luke stressed his careful research, including the testimony of eyewitnesses. Matthew made a lot of the fulfillment of prophecy, an example followed by most of the other writers. Matthew and Luke gave prominence to the question about Jesus' authenticity sent to him by the imprisoned John the Baptist; Jesus' reply touched on three areas: the fulfillment of prophecy, the radical impact for good his ministry was having, and the choice each person had to accept or reject his claims. All the gospel writers recorded and responded to the skeptical rejection of Jesus by the Jewish leaders. John in particular explored the issue from a number of angles. In two extended passages he recorded Jesus as claiming that his ministry was vindicated by the witness or testimony of God himself—the highest justification conceivable. This is not simply a claim that his ministry is self-justifying or self-authenticating. It is a further application of the power of his teaching and the life-giving effectiveness of his ministry. To experience these things was to experience God; and the experience of God is the one thing that needs no authentication.

12. The New Testament writers didn't discuss *the more specifically philosophical issues concerning truth*, such as "What is it that makes a true statement true?" or "How do we account for innocent error?" Had they done so, it is highly likely that their theocentricity and practical concerns would have had

considerable influence in shaping their answers. Paul, for instance, referred to the traditional liar paradox in his letter to Titus who was in Crete. He had warned him of those Cretans who had turned their backs on the truth and so had become "talkers and deceivers" (1:10). The paradox of the statement by a Cretan that Cretans are always liars is an illustration of this (v. 12). Paul dismissed it with "This testimony is true" (v. 13). Language for him was not something to play around with or to manipulate or use for our own ends. Failure to take God-given truth seriously was to settle for universal falsehood, nothing but lies.

PHILOSOPHY

The New Testament writers were very aware that they declared the Good News, with its accompanying worldview, in a marketplace that was crowded with a multitude of alternatives. Religious and philosophical pluralism, frequently of a pick and mix nature, was the order of the day. They thus saw the need to present the Good News in as persuasive a way as possible. The first five books of the New Testament were all written with an apologetic purpose in mind, presenting the Good News in ways that would be relevant and convincing to those who read them. Paul made a point of using appropriate arguments to convince his hearers; in Acts he used the argument from fulfilled prophecy when dealing with those who knew the Old Testament, and he used the argument from the nature of the world when speaking in Lystra or Athens.

Yet another factor went alongside this apologetic aim of persuading people of the truth of the Good News: Christianity is not simply a set of beliefs, a detached objective philosophy. It is a relationship with the living God. Accepting the truth of Christianity is much more than a cerebral act of agreeing to certain beliefs or accepting the conclusion of a rational argument or being persuaded by "proofs." It is far more holistic. It entails the opening up to God of every part of a person's life. The will, the heart, the feelings, the spirit, and the "moral" person are all involved. For a person to respond in these areas, the presence of God and the work of the Holy Spirit are needed.

Christianity has had an ambivalent relationship toward philosophy. For the most part it has accepted it and used it extensively. The majority of Western philosophers of the last two millennia were practicing Christians. But at other times Christianity has had a dismissive attitude toward philosophy, as is commonly held to be the case with Tertullian and Luther. Some have traced this dismissive attitude back to the New Testament, suggesting in particular that Paul urged the rejection of all philosophical activity.

To suggest this is to misunderstand Paul. There is no doubt that, like the rest of the New Testament writers, he was conscious that he was presenting a new teaching, a new philosophy, a worldview that rivaled the other philosophies of his day. In so doing, like any enthusiast, he sought to demonstrate the weaknesses of alternative philosophies, sometimes showing considerable insights into their concepts, as seems to be the case in his letter to the Colossians, where he is attacking some form of Gnosticism. There he warned his readers specifically against "hollow and deceptive philosophy, which depends on human tradition and the basic principles of this world rather than on Christ" (Col. 2:8). But the contrast he is making is not between philosophy as a discipline and the Christian faith as a sort of nonphilosophy. Rather, it is between two sorts of philosophy: one based on human teaching and the principles of this world and this age, and the other that has come to us through the life and teaching of God in Christ and that is based on who he is and what he has done.

TO THINK THROUGH

People around us are quite willing to view Marxism, existentialism, postmodernism, and the like as viable philosophies but are rather less inclined to see Christianity as such. Why do you think this is so?

EIGHT

TO BE LIKE GOD

THE NEW TESTAMENT CONCEPT OF HUMAN BEINGS

> In this chapter we explore how the Christian understanding of God shaped the New Testament concept of human beings and made it radically distinctive in the ancient world.

TWO FACTORS DOMINATED THE NEW TESTAMENT WRITERS' understanding of human beings. The first was theocentricity. To understand who we are, we must see ourselves as God's creatures, planned and made by him and in some mysterious way expressing his "image." Any understanding of human personhood, the soul, or even of men and women as physical beings that started simply with ourselves (as contemporary psychologies and anthropologies almost exclusively do), would have been unacceptable to the New Testament writers. We can only understand ourselves in the context of God.

The second was the incarnation, leading as it did to the death and resurrection of Christ. God became man. Therefore our understanding of who we are can never be the same again. Through Christ's death and resurrection, God has radically changed humankind's relationship to him, and so, in effect, has changed humankind. We cannot understand who we are without taking into account what God has done in Christ.

This theocentricity and Christocentricity make New Testament anthropology unique, affecting, as they did, the concepts of the soul, the mind, the will, and the body, together with issues of morality, relationships, and freedom. No other understanding of humankind in the ancient world came anywhere near it. The Christological element even distances it from the often embryonic views expressed by the Old Testament writers.

In this area in particular, scholars through the centuries have found it difficult to read the New Testament teaching without being influenced by their preunderstanding of the terms and concepts used. The use of the word *soul* (Gk. *psyche*), for example, by the New Testament writers, has been seen as the justification for belief in an entity rather like the Platonic soul, which can exist independently of the body. But this is much too simplistic. *Psyche* was being used in a variety of ways in the world of the first century A.D. and was certainly not bound to its Platonic meaning. Further, as is the case with most of the New Testament teaching, the influence of the Hebrew concept that lay behind the use of *psyche* needs to be taken into consideration. And then there is the overriding influence of Christology. If Christ is real humanity, if who he is is the pattern for who we are and who we ought to be, if his resurrection is the model for our resurrection, then all our concepts about ourselves and, in particular, about our souls, must be subject to what we see in him.

The human Jesus. The title Jesus used of himself most frequently was "The Son of Man." Most scholars agree that this title had a double thrust. It was used in contemporary Jewish thought to describe the coming messianic figure, but it also emphasized Christ's humanity. The discussion on how Christ could be both fully divine and fully human began as early as the first century A.D. While today people probably find it easier to solve the problem by accepting Christ's humanity and rejecting his divinity, in the early centuries there was a marked tendency, arising at least partly from a spirit/body dualism, to accept his divinity and deny his humanity. The New Testament writers fully accepted both his divinity and his humanity. If, then, he was fully human, he can be seen as modeling true humanity. In particular, as the one who gives new life and calls women and men to follow him and be new people living out a new lifestyle in a new community, he is the pattern for specifically Christian human living.

A key feature of Jesus the man was his constant relationship with God and conscious dependence on him. The centrality of God for human living was not just something he talked about; it was something he practiced. The message was clear; outside of a living relationship with and personal dependence on God, human life is seriously deficient.

The resurrection. Jesus' resurrection appearances are a second area in which he provided a significant model for the New Testament writers' understanding of humanity. Jesus lived after bodily death. Quite apart from his teaching, that established that life after death was possible. But the form this life took was of incredible significance. It was not a ghostly semi-existence as pictured in traditional Greek and Middle Eastern thought. Nor was it a bodiless soul, as Plato suggested. Nor was it a soul embodied in some radically different body. No doubt the first-century Christians struggled to cope with the philosophical issues raised by Christ's resurrection body, as Paul did in his first letter to the Corinthians; but it did give them profound insight into the nature of the human person and what it means to survive death.

The image of God. A third strand of New Testament teaching was the concept of image (Gk. *eikon*). In first-century thought an image (of a god or a divine ruler) was looked on as something that expressed the presence and power of that deity. This is at least part of the meaning behind the description in the New Testament of Christ as "the image of God." God is present in Christ; those who see Christ see God himself. But the New Testament writers went a stage further: Christ not only expresses the image of God so that we may see what God is like. He, as the image of God, is the pattern for us. We are to be "shaped" or "changed" or "made new" in his image. The goal of human life is to be as he is.

Createdness and dependence. The fact that we are specifically created beings was hugely significant in the New Testament understanding of humankind. The concept ran counter to Atomistic or Epicurean ideas that we are the products of chance and also counter to those forms of Platonism that saw us as nothing more than inevitable emanations of an impersonal Mind. Even more significant was that the New Testament saw Christ as the agent of creation as well as the agent of the new creation. We are thus made and remade by him. His creative activity is continuous. He holds us in being. He works all things for good. He changes us from glory to glory as we move toward the goal of being like him. Here was a powerful source of meaning and purpose for human life.

Because we are created, we are dependent. We are unable to live without God; it is in him that we have life and being. This is not to say that those who reject God cease to be; God continues to give them life even though they will not acknowledge it comes from him. But apart from God, they will never reach a true understanding of who they are; nor will they be able to live a fully human life.

The essence of the human predicament, according to the New Testament writers, is refusal to acknowledge the lordship of God. The answer to the human predicament is to give God his rightful place, to make the kingly reign of God our first priority. If we do so, everything else will fit into place. The eschatological vision in the book of Revelation describes both the chaos of a world that refuses to accept God's lordship and the certainty that that lordship will finally be established and all that is opposed to it destroyed. But we don't have to wait for the end of the age for the coming of the kingdom. Central to Jesus' message is that it is already possible to welcome God as king and live in a right relationship with him, even when that runs totally counter to the ethos of the world around us.

God has made us rich and complex beings. In common with the Old Testament and the thought of the day, the New Testament writers referred to human beings in terms of body, flesh, blood, mind, heart, "bowels" (KJV), spirit, and soul. These elements are not to be sharply distinguished from one another. On the contrary, the modeling of our personhood on that of God or of Christ entailed a strongly unified concept. As we noted above, the resurrected Christ was not a bodiless soul, but was every bit as much an embodied soul and an ensouled body as before the crucifixion.

The pattern modeled by Jesus of continuous dependence on God applied to all aspects of our being. The New Testament writers could not accept, say, the Platonist concept that God was the ongoing source of mind in us but that our bodies were autonomous and independent of him. Each part of us, or, to put it more accurately, our whole unified being, was dependent on him; God holds us in being, whether physically, psychologically, mentally, emotionally, spiritually, or whatever.

What we are has been made by God and is upheld by him. What God has made is good. Though the New Testament writers were well aware that we can use any part of our body for evil, they didn't believe that any part of us is intrinsically superior or inferior to any other. All that God has made is good. Jesus, and Paul following him, even rescinded the Old Testament regulations about what is "clean" and "unclean." For the person in a right relationship with God, everything is good.

The body.
The New Testament word for body (Gk. *soma*) fulfills two purposes. In general use it refers to our physical body and can even mean "corpse." But in a more theological sense, and especially in Paul, it refers to us as a whole, a psychosomatic unity. In this sense it does not mean our body as opposed to our mind or our soul or the like. It means all of us whom God has created and

holds in being, whether physical, spiritual, mental, or whatever. This is continuing the Old Testament concept and is in stark contrast to most Greek thought, which by the first century A.D. was making a clear differentiation between soul (with or without mind), which is good, and body, which is evil. It is probable that the New Testament writers would have kept something of this inclusive feel about the concept of body even when using "soma" specifically to refer to our physical body.

The New Testament also described human beings as "flesh" (Gk. *sarx*). This, too, can refer to the whole person and certainly does not have any necessary implication that flesh is evil. It is used of Christ, for example, a number of times, as in the prologue to John's Gospel, "the Word became flesh" (1:14). However, it is used at times with a negative connotation, that our flesh is weak or the source of temptation and sin. Paul talked, for example, of "the acts of the *sarx*" as opposed to "the fruit of the Spirit" (Gal. 5:19–23). But the significant point is that the flesh is not sinful or evil in itself. As part of God's creation it is good; it is our sin that defiles it and makes it a source of evil.

Hearts, minds, souls, etc. The New Testament used a range of terms to describe the various aspects of our bodies. We will focus on five of the main ones.

1. *Heart*. Heart (Gk. *kardia*) is a very rich term in the New Testament. Occasionally it is used to refer to the physical organ; but most of the time it is used to indicate the person, the inner self. Its most significant feature is that it is the place where we meet and relate to God. It is with the heart that we believe. It is in the heart that we know God. But *kardia* was also used regularly to indicate the thinking part of humans, the seat of our emotions, and our wills. Here there is no division of the individual; it is the one inner person that thinks or wills or feels or relates to God.

2. *Mind*. The New Testament writers used *nous* and its cognates considerably less than they used *kardia*, but for them its range of meaning is very similar, though with more emphasis on intellectual aspects. In some passages mind and heart are effectively equated. *Nous*, or its cognate *dianoia*, can mean the inner person, the real self, or, more specifically, the understanding, the will, the part of us that believes or exercises faith, our intention, disposition, or wisdom, as well as mind. Though *nous* is applied to God and to Christ by Paul, there is no trace of its specialist Platonist meaning of pure and detached thought. Rather, in keeping with the general practical thrust of the New Testament, the *nous* of God is essentially his purpose and intention to act in grace and salvation.

3. *Inner being.* Parallel to their use of *kardia*, the New Testament writers made use of the term *splanchna*. This was traditionally translated "bowels" but was actually used to refer to any essential organ such as kidneys, liver, lungs, sex organs, and heart. Apart from its literal meaning, it has, like *kardia*, a range of meanings, including mercy, compassion, and love. In particular, it is emotion that stirs us to action, as exemplified by Jesus' compassion on the helpless crowds and the Good Samaritan's willingness to help the wounded Jew.

4. *Soul.* Like *kardia* and *nous*, the New Testament words for soul and spirit had a range of interconnected meanings. The background for the meaning of "soul" (Gk. *psyche*) was a very common Old Testament word (*nephesh/nepes*) that means life or life principle, rather than soul in the Platonic sense. It is the result of the life of God breathed into the lifeless body, giving it life. *Psyche* in the New Testament is thus often best translated "life," as, for example, when Jesus speaks of the Good Shepherd laying down his *psyche* for his sheep, or of our *psyche* being sustained by food. Arising from that basic meaning, *psyche*, like *kardia*, can be used to mean the inner person or the self, the part of us that feels emotions and makes decisions. But what is definitely lacking in the New Testament is any concept of the soul as something to be set over against the body, something superior to it and longing to be free of it, and something that can exist independently of it. Though these concepts would have been well known in New Testament times and were appearing in contemporary Jewish writings including Philo, the New Testament writers clearly rejected them.

5. *Spirit.* Another word the New Testament writers used to describe us is "spirit" (Gk. *pneuma*), a word that is more common and probably more significant than *psyche*. Its meaning goes back to the Hebrew *ruach/ruah*, which basically means "blowing," and so "wind," "breath," and then breathing as the expression of life, and so life itself. Key to the meaning of spirit is that it comes from God. In the creation account God breathed his breath of life into "the dust of the earth" to make a living human being. If God were to withdraw his breath, life would cease.

Pneuma thus carries the special meaning of the part of us that is directly related to and dependent on God. Particularly significant is the use of *pneuma* for God himself. In contrast to *psyche*, *pneuma* is something that specifically expresses his nature. "The Spirit of God" is a common phrase in both the Old and New Testaments; even more common in the New Testament is the term "the Holy Spirit." It is likely that it was the New Testament writers' experience of God as life-giving Spirit (the Holy Spirit came as "blowing" on the Day of Pentecost) that shaped their understanding and use of *pneuma*. Though even those who reject God still have *pneuma* in an impoverished form, it is only as our spirits are united with God's Spirit that they truly are alive. Again, the New Testament concept is a strongly theocentric one. We are not independent spirits (or souls), able to function on our own with our own independent life principle. The life that is in us is God's life; it comes from God and depends on God for its continued existence. No part of us is immortal in the sense that it will continue of itself to live forever. Our souls or spirits will continue to live after our bodies die because God continues to give them his life.

Immortality. Eternal life, then, is a "gift of God" (Rom. 6:23). And, in contrast to the shadowy ghostly existence pictured by many ancient accounts of the afterlife, it is something very real. Indeed, it is the reality of which this life is the shadow. It thus, for the New Testament writers, involved some form of embodiment. Again, here, their thinking would have been profoundly influenced by their experience of the resurrected Christ. He was no ghost; his body was very real and very recognizable, even if its reality was somehow different in that he was able to appear and disappear at will.

Such a concept, of course, both solved and raised philosophical issues. It solved the problem of disembodied thinking, feeling, and so on. But it raised the issue of material bodies existing forever apart from the created universe as we know it. Paul tackled this problem in his first letter to the Corinthians by saying that the resurrection body, though corporeal, is of a different nature from our earthly bodies. He in fact used the adjectives derived from *psyche* and *pneuma* to make his point. The body we have here on earth, he said, is *psychikon*, an earthly living body, the appropriate form of bodily existence for our earthly life. The resurrection body, by contrast, though still a body, will be *pneumatikon*, a body that is alive with the breath of God. Again, such was Paul's confidence in the creative and life-giving power of God that he clearly had no problem accepting that this was possible, though he does concede that the change from our present body to our future one is a "mystery" (1 Cor. 15:51).

For the New Testament, then, immortality is possible, not because of the nature of the soul or the spirit, but by the specific act of God. This act involves not just the sustaining of our soul or spirit, but the sustaining or re-creation of us as an embodied whole, though the form of body will be different from its earthly form. This fits the overall New Testament concept of who we are; we are not a combination of the spiritual and the material that can be divided. Nor are we to be split into various clearly defined areas like the mind, the feelings, the will, and so on. We are one; the terms that apply to one aspect of us, or to us as seen in one particular way, can be applied to the other parts. Nor can it be said that the body is intrinsically evil and the soul or spirit intrinsically good. All are created and held continuously in being by God. Both body, soul, and spirit can be open to God, obedient to him, and indwelt by him; or, conversely, they can reject God, be open to sin, and become evil. In so doing they can be said to be cutting themselves off from the source of life and so, in a sense, are dead.

Salvation. This understanding of human beings as dynamically dependent on God and in relationship with God underlies the concept of salvation, the Good News that is the central message of the New Testament. The message of Jesus and the early preaching to Jewish audiences proclaimed the coming of the kingdom of God (Mark 1:15; Luke 11:20; Matt. 10:7). Speaking to a Greek, or, more probably, cosmopolitan audience in Athens, Paul contrasted their "unknown God" with his God who was near to every person and had made himself known in Jesus Christ (Acts 17:22–31). In either case the message was the same. God was near. A broken relationship could be restored. Sin and evil and rebellion that have marred our relationship with God could be forgiven. God's presence and life in us as individuals and as community could be experienced. We could share in the eternal life of the living God.

Again, this is something that is essentially God-centered. It is not simply the forgiveness of sins or the guarantee of life in heaven when we die. It is the implementing of a life-sharing relationship with God himself that starts now, is lived out in the rest of our time on earth, and, because of the nature of God's life, continues after death. And the effects of it go beyond the individual and even the community. The vision in the New Testament is nothing short of a whole cosmic restoration. A universe that in many ways has got out of gear with its creator will be recreated and renewed so that God may truly "fill the whole universe" (Eph. 4:10).

Ethics, freedom, and community. Ethics for the New Testament writers, in strong contrast to the typical Jewish approach of the day, was not conforming to a code. Nor was it the pursuit of an abstract ideal. Rather, it was the daily practical outworking of the life of God. Those who are in relationship with God and consciously dependent on him, living in Christ, and indwelt by the Holy Spirit, will, almost inevitably, express God and his goodness and ways in their lives. Failure to do so is the result of a breakdown in that relationship and dependence. Of course the New Testament writers did not expect Christians to become perfect overnight. The outworking of our relationship with God is a developing process; at times we get things wrong; old habits die hard. But the expectation is that we will be holy people because God is a holy God. Our morality is nothing short of the expression in us of his holiness.

The New Testament writers had a limited and distinctive concept of human freedom. Their interest was wholly focused on the exercise of our freedom in the making of moral choices, and, in particular, in choosing to respond to God. In a sense we are free to choose to do good or to do evil, to seek God or to reject him. We can therefore be held responsible for our actions and be judged accordingly. But freedom is always limited. Those who choose evil become "slaves" of sin. Conversely, those who choose to open up their lives to God become "slaves" of goodness. Whether we are aware of it or not, ultimate control over our lives doesn't remain with us. Yet it is in this very act of abandoning our own control of our lives and handing them over to God that, according to the New Testament, we in fact begin to taste true freedom. This is because ultimately real freedom is something that only exists in God. Just as he is the source of life and goodness, so he is the source of freedom. Just as rejecting him cuts us off from eternal life and true holiness, so it cuts us off from true freedom. Again, it is very likely that Jesus himself provided the model for this concept; he was seen to be a truly free person, yet he made it clear that he had chosen to surrender his autonomous freedom to the will of God.

Particularly distinctive in the first century A.D., when discrimination of all sorts was common, was the New Testament's radical inclusiveness. Over against Judaism, it declared equality before God of Jew and Gentile. In Christ, it said, the divisions between male and female, slave and free, break down. Social and intellectual barriers are cast aside. Jesus made a special point of including those who had been socially marginalized or rejected, whether on moral, racial, gender, ceremonial, or religious grounds. The poor, women, widows, lepers, prostitutes, non-Jews, and (traitorous) tax collectors were all special objects of his concern and activity. In the structure of the early church, any suggestion that some were of greater importance than others was firmly rejected. Even the leaders, said Jesus, were to see themselves as slaves to those they were seeking to lead.

TO THINK THROUGH

Are there elements of the New Testament concept of human beings and our place in community that we need to reassert today?

NINE

STILL THERE BUT TRANSFORMED

THE NEW TESTAMENT ON SUFFERING AND DEATH

> The radical nature of the early Christian concept of God radically affected all of life. In this chapter we look at its impact on the issues of suffering and death.

BUDDHA SAID THAT THE STARTING POINT OF OUR UNDERstanding of the world was human suffering; everything must be viewed in the light of old age, disease, and death. Many in the ancient world agreed with him. Religions and philosophies sought to confront and solve these issues by atoning the deities, by philosophical detachment, or by Stoic acceptance. By contrast Western philosophy has paid very little attention to these issues; most contemporary books of philosophy completely ignore them despite the fact that existentialism has insisted they are issues that must be faced.

The New Testament writers did not ignore the issues of suffering and death. They accepted their reality and faced the problems they raised. In the Good News they gave their answer to it. Again, it is an answer that is firmly rooted in the nature and actions of God.

Christ and suffering and death. Basic to all is the fact that Christ suffered and died. His suffering was not limited to the cross, though the New Testament pictures the cross as suffering in its most acute form; indeed, on the cross Christ went through the whole totality of suffering, bearing the sin of the world and its penalty in suffering and death, quite apart from his physical pain and personal suffering. But even before the cross, suffering was the hallmark of Christ's life. In him were fulfilled the Old Testament prophecies of a suffering servant, someone who knew sorrow and pain, rejection and injustice.

As with Jesus, so with the early Christians. Those who wrote the New Testament and those to whom they wrote were very conscious that they were following in Christ's steps. Not only did they have to face persecution, torture, and martyrdom, but they lived for the most part in poverty as a despised Jewish sect. Christ was their example and their inspiration. They saw themselves as following in his footsteps, sharing his experience. They could even speak of Christ sharing their experience. As a result, they were able to accept and even welcome suffering, to bear it gladly and even rejoice or boast in it.

For God in Christ had done two things with suffering. He had taken it upon himself, and he had broken its power. Again, New Testament thought is radical at this point. Buddha concluded that the existence of suffering made the existence of any supreme God impossible. More recently Western thought has tended to see the fact of suffering as a powerful argument against the existence of the Christian God. The New Testament writers turned that argument on its head. Instead of suffering settling the issue of whether or not God was real, the reality of what God was and what he had done settled for them the issue of suffering.

A suffering God. For God to suffer would have been as unthinkable for the main Greek tradition as for God to become incarnate. Yet for the New Testament writers the one entailed the other. If, as they were sure, God had truly come in Christ, then God in Christ had suffered. In so doing he had presented us with two startling truths. Suffering was no longer something to be avoided at all costs; if Christ chose not to avoid it, we, in following him, could choose the same. Second, there was no incompatibility between God and suffering. God could suffer. Though the New Testament writers, following the Old Testament, saw the origin of suffering as closely linked with sin, they firmly rejected the concept that our experiences of suffering are always to be associated with sin. Christ was sinless, and he suffered. God does not live in some distant realm in eternal bliss while we struggle with suffering here on earth. He is a God who has chosen to share our pain. The book of Revelation even pictures this sharing as somehow eternal, not just for the time of the incarnation. From the creation of the world Christ was a sacrificed Lamb; and after his ascension he still appears as such.

Suffering broken and transformed. Besides taking suffering upon himself, God had broken its power. Suffering didn't have to be looked on as a curse or a punishment. In a sense it was a privilege given to us by God. In a moving passage Paul spoke of his own experience of suffering a thorn or stake in his flesh. Despite Paul's ardent prayers, God didn't take away the suffering. As a result, Paul was able to see the thorn not as a curse or something to be rejected, but rather as a blessing and something to be glad about and even to boast about. Through it he learned new things about himself and about God's grace. Through it, he was confident, he was a better and stronger person. Suffering doesn't have to destroy us or embitter us. By God's grace it can do just the opposite. Pressures, hardships, poverty, persecution, and even the threat of death don't have to separate us from God. In them all, says Paul, we come out on top.

A further, equally positive strand in Paul's thought was that suffering brings us closer to Christ. We walk the way he walked. We share his experiences. In suffering especially, he walks closely with us. We understand him better. Through sharing in his sufferings we come to know him more. And in the longer term, as we are identified with him in his sufferings now, we will share in his glory in the age to come.

God and death. As with suffering, so with death. The New Testament writers didn't minimize the awfulness of death. It is something that enslaves and destroys, universal and inescapable, fearsome and threatening. In that it is the result of the human rejection of God, it is a constant reminder of our weakness and sinfulness. Death is an enemy. But over against the reality and awfulness of death the New Testament writers set something that enabled them to see it in a wholly different way. That something was the death and resurrection of Jesus.

If for God to suffer was unthinkable to many in the first century A.D., for God to experience death was even more incredible. The New Testament writers knew that the death of Christ on the cross was a huge barrier for many to the acceptance of the Good News. Yet it was something they were sure of, something they kept at the center of all their teaching and preaching. For besides being "scandalous," it was an amazing expression of the nature of God and the extent to which he was prepared to go to restore humankind to a living relationship with himself. Here, they said, we can see the amazing love of God. He loved us that much. He held back nothing. He gave everything, even his life.

Again, as the fact that Jesus has experienced suffering transforms the experience of suffering for the Christian, the fact that Jesus has died enables us to look on death in a completely different way. Since God has gone through it, its edge, its "sting" has been taken away (1 Cor. 15:55–57); Christians can face death knowing Christ has already been that way. We are able to follow in his steps, share his experience, be the same as he was in his death, and know oneness with him even in this final and perhaps darkest experience of life.

The resurrection.

In a way, the resurrection was even more incredible than that God should die. It was Paul's mention of the resurrection that turned off a fair number of listeners to his preaching in Athens. But the New Testament writers were certain of the fact of the resurrection, and they made it the center of their message. Without it there is no Good News; Christianity is vacuous.

The significance of the resurrection for the New Testament writers includes its vindication of the life and claims of Jesus, its demonstration that death's power is broken, its significance as the crowning act of God's purposes of salvation, its expression in the lives of Christian believers, and its role as a pattern and guarantee of their resurrection.

The New Testament accounts state that Jesus told his followers beforehand that he would die and be raised to life again. They clearly found such a claim difficult to believe. But its fulfillment vindicated his claims, not least because dead people do not raise themselves; the resurrection was God's work, and God is not likely to raise an impostor or a liar. It is significant that Luke records in Acts a huge growth in the number of disciples after Jesus' resurrection. Many of those who had not believed before, especially members of Jesus' own family and "a large number of priests" (6:7), now accepted his teaching. It is reasonable to suppose that the resurrection was a significant factor in convincing these people of the truth of Jesus' claims.

One of the pictures the New Testament used to express the significance of the resurrection of Jesus was that of a struggle between him and death, from which he emerged gloriously triumphant. The extent of the struggle should not be exaggerated; this was no dualistic battle between evenly balanced powers. Peter, a few weeks after the resurrection, declared that it was simply not possible for death to hold on to Jesus. God is, after all, the ever-living God, the source of all life, the one before whom all other powers are as nothing. So death has been broken; its seeming power has been destroyed. And, since death is the outcome of human sin, the power of sin has been broken as well. Though the experience of physical death remains, we no longer need to fear it. No longer is it our master. Christ's victory has set us free. And at the end of the age, death will be destroyed finally and forever.

The resurrection is also seen by the New Testament writers as the crowning act of God's purposes of salvation. All through the Old Testament God had shown himself to be a God who cared for and saved his people, both spiritually, in providing means of forgiveness and restoration to a living relationship with him, and physically, rescuing them from Egypt, from their enemies, and so on. In the New Testament these purposes are focused into the person of Jesus, whose name means "Savior," and what he did in his incarnation, his life, his ministry, his teaching, and his miracles. Even before the crucifixion and the resurrection, it was possible to speak of people finding salvation in Jesus. But it was the events of Easter that brought his saving work to a climax, as he gave himself as an atoning sacrifice for the sin of the world and then rose from death. Here was the vindication of all that had gone before. The resurrection was God's demonstration that grace and love and goodness had triumphed. Life had had the final word over death.

The New Testament writers also saw the resurrection of Jesus as the key to what it means to live a Christian life. Christians are not imitators of a dead prophet, nor do they simply adhere to a code of ethics and pattern of behavior. They live in relationship with a Christ who is very much alive. The Christian life is a sharing in Christ's resurrection life. He lives in them, and they live in him. His life is the renewing and equipping power that enables them to face pressures and suffering and all the different experiences of life. Paul frequently used the phrase "in Christ" to describe the Christian life; on occasion he also spoke of "Christ in you." Either way, the fact that he was a risen and living Christ made all the difference.

Finally, the resurrection of Jesus was the pattern and guarantee of the resurrection of believers. The reality of life in Christ and the Christian's living relationship with him were such that death could not destroy them, just as it could not destroy Christ. The life of Christ in believers, which had already broken the power of sin and spiritual death, was powerful enough to deal with physical death. So Christ's resurrection set the trend; as death had been unable to hold him, it would be unable to hold those who were united with him.

TO THINK THROUGH

Why do you think so few philosophers have concerned themselves with the issues of suffering and death?

TEN

BEING IN THE WORLD

MORE KEY NEW TESTAMENT CONCEPTS

> In this chapter we pick up three further topics raised by the New Testament worldview: time and eternity, the world and the political order, and community.

TIME AND ETERNITY

The New Testament writers' understanding of time and eternity was shaped by their understanding of the nature and purposes of God. For most in the world around them time was generally seen as an inescapable power that highlighted human impermanence and the inevitability of death putting an end to life. Two ways of viewing the relationship between God or the gods and time arose out of this way of thinking of time. In the first place, God, gods, and anything that can be called divine, must be free from time, outside of time. Otherwise, they too would be threatened and ultimately destroyed by it. They may, as in Plato, create time, but they themselves cannot be either subject to it or involved in it.

Second, for many, time itself was seen as a god. In the period of the New Testament Greek thought, Gnosticism, Zoroastrianism, the mystery religions, and Philo all used *aion*, one of the main Greek words for time, to describe divinity, either as a specific god, "Aion," or as the title of emanations from the supreme God, "aeons," which rule the patterns of events on earth.

God and time. The New Testament writers stood firmly against the popular concepts of the day. Their experience of God, of Christ, and of the Holy Spirit left them in no doubt that God, whatever his ultimate relationship to time, could not be remote and detached from it. He had involved himself in it and did involve himself in it. Further, he was Lord of it. Paul, in his first letter to Timothy, expressed very clearly his view of the relationship between God and any "aeons": "To the King eternal [of the aeons, or 'ages'], immortal, invisible, the only God, be honor and glory for ever and ever. Amen" (1:17). Far from being something that threatened human life, time was the working out of the gracious purposes of a good and loving God. So, in contrast to those around them, the key Christian attitude with regard to time was positive, one characterized by hope.

There were three key points on the line of time for the New Testament writers: the creation, the coming of Christ, and the end of the age. At each of them God clearly shows his power and lordship. Each happens according to his purpose and according to his perfect timing. The coming of Christ was prophesied and prepared for centuries before the event. Mark's first recorded words of Jesus' ministry were "The time has come" (1:15); the right moment had arrived. Paul similarly spoke about the time being full or completed for Christ's coming. Christ came at precisely the right time according to God's perfect purposes. In the same way, the final establishment of the kingdom of God, the end of the age, will be at a time that is determined by God's wisdom and the working out of his purposes. Like the coming of Christ, its "date" is known only to God. It will be when his purposes, such as the declaration of the Good News to all the world, have been fulfilled.

Those who argued that God could not be involved in time were at least partly motivated by a belief that such involvement would entail change. Since a changing God was, for them, inconceivable, they concluded he could not be involved in time. The New Testament writers were sure that God was unchanging in the sense that he was utterly faithful, his holiness and love never wavered, and so on. But their experience of Christ and the Holy Spirit made it impossible for them to accept a static, detached, uninvolved God. Jesus was promised; he was born; he died; he rose; he ascended. The Holy Spirit was promised; he was poured out. All these were specific events in time. The early Christians were sure they had happened. If the fact that they had happened meant that God had changed in some way, they were prepared to accept that.

The refusal to accept a static God seems to have influenced the writers of the New Testament in their view of God's relationship to time before the creation. A strong body of opinion among New Testament scholars claims that they completely lacked any concept of timelessness and saw time running backward in an unbroken line from the present to the creation and then endlessly on before the creation. Other scholars take a more moderate position and, while rejecting the "Greek" concept of total timelessness, suggest the New Testament writers saw God existing before the creation in time that was of a different sort from that in the created world. Peter's statement that "with the Lord a day is like a thousand years, and a thousand years are like a day" (2 Peter 3:8) might support this view.

A similar issue arises with the concept of time after the end of the age. Here again, even if the New Testament writers would have conceded that time as we know it will cease to exist, it seems unlikely that they thought in terms of a totally timeless eternity. Maybe they would have been happy with John Newton's way of seeing it: "When we've been there ten thousand years, bright shining as the sun, we've no less days to sing God's praise than when we first begun."

The two ages. The New Testament writers spoke of two ages. They did so rather differently from much popular thought in the first century A.D., which contrasted the transience and evilness and time-bound nature of this age with the permanence, perfection, and timelessness of the one to come. For the New Testament writers the two ages could not be totally antithetical since they had experienced the coming of the new age in the coming and work of Christ and the Holy Spirit. The new age had begun. Everywhere Christ went the kingdom of God was inaugurated. Every act of God in the life of the believer was an inbreaking of that kingdom. Christians lived in both ages at once. Thus there could be no incompatibility or radical discontinuity between the two ages. The end of this age will see the judgment and destruction of much that it has contained. But the new age, so far from being something totally different, will be the fulfillment of all that we have already begun to be and to live and experience. In keeping with their concept of the continuance of some sort of time, and parallel to the concept of a resurrection existence in a new sort of body, the New Testament writers pictured the replacement of the universe that ceases to be at the end of the old age with a new universe. New bodies need new time and a new created world in which to live.

Hope. Because of their view of God's gracious involvement in time, the New Testament writers had a distinctive concept of hope. Most of their contemporaries saw no reason to be optimistic about the future, bound as it was with suffering and death. Indeed, in secular usage the most common Greek word for hope (*elpis*), in that it expressed the attitude of anticipating the future, could appropriately be translated "fear." But in the New Testament *elpis* is always used positively. Hope can always be optimistic. Because of who God is and what he has done, Christians can always look forward to a future that is good.

The key expectation was the final fulfillment of the coming of the kingdom, the return of Christ and the destruction of evil and suffering and death. The writers of the New Testament anticipated that this could happen at any time, but the concept of a living hope had many other applications. Every event of life is in the hands of God and will be used for good; we can even view setbacks and suffering in this way and rejoice because God will bring about good even through them. They are the labor pains of the coming of the kingdom. Again, this is a strongly God-centered concept. Our contemporary use of the word *hope* is strongly colored by the fact that we see hope as a subjective attitude. Optimists are hopeful; pessimists are fearful. But the difference for us lies in the subjective attitude or personality of the optimists and pessimists. In the New Testament the thrust of *elpis* is much more objective. Not only is our hope rooted in objective reality, such as God or his promises or actions, Paul is even able to say that Christ Jesus is our hope (1 Tim. 1:1). A paradigm for Christian hope is the resurrection; the darkest gloom of the suffering and evil of Good Friday was transformed by the reality of Easter Day. This is the way God works; hope is a living and powerful reality because it is based on a living and powerful God.

TO THINK THROUGH

The New Testament view of time largely shaped the Western understanding of it. But the theory of relativity is said to have challenged our traditional concept. If this is so, how might we integrate it with the New Testament view?

There is no shortage of philosophers in the late modern period and in the twenty-first century who have replaced hope with despair. Why do you think this is so?

THE WORLD AND THE POLITICAL ORDER

Asked to express their view about the way the physical universe functions, the New Testament writers would have replied "God." For them God in Christ was the creator and upholder of all things. All that happened was according to his design and purpose. This enabled them to have a positive attitude to the physical world of nature. Jesus frequently used the natural order to express and illustrate his teaching. We get the impression that he was at home in the natural order, enjoying the world around him, even to the extent of being accused of being a glutton and drunkard; he specifically repudiated asceticism as practiced by others in his day.

The close relationship between God and his world meant that the New Testament writers didn't need to question the reliability of our perceptions of the world around us. They took it for granted that true knowledge was possible through our observations, in that what we were observing was the work of God, whom we know to be true and trustworthy, revealed to us through his life-giving Spirit. Error or false belief in our understanding of the world was at root a moral issue, a refusal to see and accept God and his truth as revealed in his creation.

The world as we know it, however, will not last forever. At the end of the age, it will cease to be; New Testament imagery of what will happen ranges from a great conflagration to the folding up and putting away of a garment. But, significantly, it will be replaced by a new world, "a new heaven and a new earth" (Rev. 21:1). As we have seen, nowhere does the New Testament imply that the world in itself is evil, something from which we must escape and be set free. The world is good because it is God's world; he created it and holds it in being. Further, it clearly expresses elements of God's nature, his power and divinity. If there is a block to God being known by natural theology, it is in our inability to draw the right conclusions from what we see in the world around us, not in the world itself.

However, there are two factors in the New Testament that strongly influenced the relationship between Christians and the world around them. The first was that they saw the world, however good it was in itself, as subjected to and spoiled by evil. This evil took many forms, both human and superhuman, but in the first century A.D. it was typified by Rome. As an occupying power Rome brought many benefits; for most of its subjects the Roman Empire was a better regime to live under than previous occupying powers. But for the New Testament writers, the essence of anything that claimed to control the world and dominate the whole of human life was necessarily evil. In the case of Rome, this dominance extended to the demanding of worship from its subjects, the ultimate expression of human rebellion and rejection of God. The world may have been good, but the world order was evil. The second factor that influenced the relationship between the early Christians and the world was that they had already had a taste of the world to come in their experience of a personal relationship with Christ, in the power of his life in them to transform such things as suffering, and in the new relationships they enjoyed in the Christian community.

As a result of these two factors, the New Testament Christians had a strong sense of belonging to the world to come as well as to the present world. They could never see this world and this life as of primary importance as others around them did. Consequently, they saw themselves as living in the present world but ultimately belonging to the world to come. Here a key concept was the saying of Jesus, "Give to Caesar what is Caesar's, and to God what is God's" (Matt. 22:21). As far as the current world order had a right to demand it, obedience should be given to it. Taxes should be paid, magistrates and officials treated with respect, and life lived in the community in peace and loving neighborliness. However much it may have contained the seeds of revolution, the New Testament in fact repudiated civil disobedience and encouraged the poor and slaves to follow the example of Jesus who intentionally made himself poor and a slave in the face of the perverted value system of the evil world order.

Despite the phrase in the Lord's Prayer about the coming of God's kingdom on earth, the New Testament writers do not appear to have envisaged the Roman state becoming Christian or to have envisaged any form of world order in this current world other than one dominated by evil. Unlike Plato, they had no blueprint for a Christian state; indeed, like Jesus they had no wish to rule in this age of the world. His time, and so theirs, would be in the coming age. In the place of political power and God's values established in a state system, they saw their calling to change the world in a much subtler way. They were like small seeds planted in the community that grew slowly and bore fruit in kingdom values like love and goodness They were like permeating salt, offering a new flavor and stopping the rot, or yeast, which starts small but eventually makes a huge difference.

TO THINK THROUGH

If the New Testament writers were alive today, how do you think they would view our current world order?

COMMUNITY

At the heart of Christianity, according to the New Testament, is relationship. This relationship is primarily between the individual and God, but such is the nature of God and his concern for all people that relationship with him inevitably involves the individual in relationships with others.

The idea of a community of like-minded believers was a familiar one in the first century, both from the philosophical schools and from the religious communities. In many ways Jesus conformed to the current expectation of someone presenting a new philosophy or religion. He left his home and work and devoted himself to his teaching. He drew a group of disciples around him and shared a common life with them, equipping them to pass his teaching on to others. He clashed with the upholders of traditional views; he was persecuted and, like Socrates, eventually martyred.

Nevertheless, the New Testament doesn't present the community of Christ and his disciples, or even the extended community built up during his ministry, which included women, as a model to be strictly followed. Indeed, the first-century Christians don't seem to have followed any fixed structure in the organization of their communities. In the early days in Jerusalem there appears to have been some communal living, but this was probably difficult to sustain as Christianity spread and included, for example, a large number of slaves. Nevertheless, the sense of community was strong. It transcended family ties and barriers of age, gender, social status, and race. As a community the believers saw themselves as the people of God and the temple of God, the place where God was very specially present and real. They were the body of Christ, expressing not just his lordship, but his presence and manifestation in the world.

The community was to be marked by love, holy living, the presence of God through the Holy Spirit, worship, and service. All, empowered by the Spirit, were to exercise gifts and ministries for the encouragement and strengthening of all. Supremely, the community was called to continue to be what Christ himself had been, the presence of God in the world and the demonstration and proclamation of his nature and truth.

One noteworthy feature was that life in the Christian community was expected to be tough. In keeping with the ministry of Jesus, his followers were to expect rejection, persecution, and even martyrdom. Epicurean *ataraxia* (peace and tranquillity) was not offered as an option.

TO THINK THROUGH

The elements of New Testament teaching we have looked at in the last two sections of this chapter have implications for our contemporary concept of "church." What do you feel might be the main lessons we need to apply in order to make our churches more true to the New Testament concept?

ELEVEN

PERMEATION AND INTERACTION

EARLY CHRISTIANITY AND PHILOSOPHY

We have only limited records of the interaction between Christianity and other worldviews during the first three centuries of the Christian era. In this chapter we will look at some of the leading figures we do know about and see quite a bit of variation in their approach.

THE EXPERIENCE OF GOD COMING IN JESUS CHRIST AND through the Holy Spirit profoundly affected every part of the lives of the early Christians, including their thinking and philosophizing. Every philosophy has to start somewhere. The revelation of God in Christ provided a firm basis for philosophizing and a rich source of ideas that those with a philosophical turn of mind soon started to develop. Additionally, in a relativistic age, it was vital for the early Christians to develop a philosophical defense of their worldview that would stand up to the questionings and attacks of those who followed other philosophies.

The process of the interaction between Christianity and other worldviews started as soon as Christianity began to spread through the Roman world. Much of the interaction would have been through verbal discussion and debate, the kind of thing Paul engaged in wherever he went. In addition, written defenses of Christianity, known as "Apologies" (from the Greek word *apologia*, "answer, defense"), sought to present an argued case for the defense of Christians on trial for their faith, and for the acceptance of Christianity. And polemical writings attacked views contrary to orthodox Christian belief, while numerous attempts were made to explore some of the philosophical issues raised by the Christian revelation, such as the nature of God and of the soul, and the relationships between the members of the Trinity.

Before we look at some of these early Christian philosophical writers, we need to respond to a criticism that has been made over the last two hundred to three hundred years, that these early Christian writers, together with almost all the thinkers from Augustine to the end of the medieval period, weren't doing philosophy at all. Since they accepted the Christian revelation, we are told, they can't have been philosophers, even though they may have discussed philosophical issues. They were theologians. Philosophy effectively ceased for more than a thousand years, until resurrected by the Enlightenment. This attitude, still held by some, has had a serious effect on the way the development of Christian thought from the first century to the end of the medieval period has been treated.

We will meet the arrogant claim "No one before me was a real philosopher" on more than one occasion as we go through the story of philosophy. The answer to it is straightforward. Anyone can choose to invent a new definition of philosophy and make it exclude everyone else. That tends to tell us a lot about the person making the new definition but very little about philosophy. The fact is the term has always had a wide usage, covering a range of worldviews, starting from varied presuppositions, and facing all sorts of issues. To narrow it down and reduce it to just one way of seeing things is not just arrogant; it is ignoring the facts.

The source of the critique that Christian philosophers don't count as real philosophers was Enlightenment rationalism. Locke's statement that "Reason must be our last judge and guide in every thing" could be looked on as the foundational methodological tenet of the Enlightenment. There was to be one authority, that of rational logic. This was to be the test for truth and reality in every sphere. Any other authority was to be rejected.

We in the twenty-first century know that our postmodern age has exposed the inadequacy of such a program. Not only is there no justification for making reason our sole authority; reason as a sole authority in fact does not work. It can't do the task the Enlightenment asked it to do.

Nevertheless, one of the results of the Enlightenment's stress on reason has been the continuing concept that a system of thought that doesn't conform to its rational criteria can't be looked on as a philosophy. So, for example, many twentieth-century philosophers in the Enlightenment tradition rejected existentialism out of hand, simply refusing to accept that existentialists were doing philosophy, since they put other criteria in the place of reason.

But the Enlightenment has no monopoly on the definition of philosophy. For most of its history the word has been used in a much wider way, covering metaphysical and religious concepts just as much as things that can be rationally established. Enlightenment thinkers may have been unhappy with this and wished that things had been otherwise. Viewing the late Middle Ages, they had some justification in their longing to clear away the metaphysical cobwebs religious scholasticism had spun. But clearing cobwebs doesn't have to involve demolishing the house.

Another point is worth bearing in mind. It is true that Christianity is a religion as well as a worldview. But in this it is typical rather than unique. Just about all the philosophies in the ancient world had profound religious implications. Both philosophy and religion sought to answer the basic questions of life. Almost all ancient philosophies gave God or the divine a key place in their systems. A number of them included concepts of "enlightenment" or some sort of direct encounter with the divine. Christianity would not have been seen as something unique, a religion to be set over against the philosophies of the day. Rather, it was a worldview, with religious and philosophical implications, to be set over against the religious philosophies or philosophical religions such as Neoplatonism, stoicism, and Gnosticism.

The first sixteen Christian centuries saw plenty of philosophizing that was truly worthy of the name. The thousand years that followed Augustine were a unique period in which philosophers were able to start from agreed first principles and build constructively on each others' work. Though this may sound less exciting than each philosopher disagreeing with everyone else and trying to start from scratch, it is quite unfair to dismiss it as philosophically invalid.

Nevertheless, we can say that by the end of the medieval period Christian philosophy in the West had lost much of its original vigor. It was obscured by metaphysical cobwebs and as a result was poorly equipped to adapt to the new currents of thought that were circulating. A new start was called for. And it wasn't just the forerunners of the Enlightenment that did the calling. It was in reaction against the apparent sterility of medieval philosophy that Luther and other leaders of the Reformation launched what seemed to be an attack on philosophy in general, appearing to teach that Christianity and philosophy, faith and reason, couldn't mix. This was not in fact what Luther was saying. As we saw with Paul, Luther's attack was on one form of philosophy that happened to be the dominating one of his day, not on the concept of philosophy as such. The conflict, for him, was between scholastic philosophy and the teaching of the New Testament, with its stress on personal faith in Christ. The "reason" he was rejecting was a rationalist approach to God that, in Luther's eyes, offered an alternative way of salvation to the one followed by faith.

Something similar happened in the early Christian centuries. Tertullian in particular vigorously denounced philosophy, giving the impression that faith and reason were to be totally divorced. This was Christianity clashing with and rejecting the philosophy of its day. But even in Tertullian's time another process was well under way. In the interests of effective communication and contextualization, those who sought to commend the Christian message presented it, consciously or unconsciously, in terms of the philosophical concepts of the day.

They in fact had no alternative. Almost every significant word they chose to use to express their ideas had already been used by someone else and came loaded with philosophical connotations. It was impossible to speak of God, resurrection, the soul, Logos, or truth without the words carrying at least something of the meanings the history of philosophy had attached to them. Where such was unhelpful, Christians needed to make clear the distinctive way they were using their terms. At times, however, it was not unhelpful. Familiar terms made difficult concepts easier for their hearers or readers to assimilate. But the recurring problems of any contextualization were bound to arise: To what extent was the contextualizing affecting the basic message? If Christians used Platonist ideas, to what extent was Christianity being influenced by Platonism? If apologists appealed to Plato's concept of one supreme God, was there not a danger that the attendant features of Plato's God, which were incompatible with the God of the New Testament, would infiltrate Christian thinking? These and other issues presented a challenge to the early Christian thinkers, one they met in differing ways and with varying degrees of success.

Most of the apologetic and philosophical writings of these early Christian thinkers have been lost, but some have been preserved. Among the earliest are the works of Justin and Athenagoras. Most of Irenaeus's writings are concerned with biblical and theological issues, but one of his best-known works was a refutation of Gnosticism in which he supported his case with philosophical argument. Tertullian is perhaps the most colorful writer of this group; he is noted for what seem to be violent attacks on philosophy. Clement and Origen were key figures in the Alexandrian school in Egypt who, in contrast to Tertullian, openly encouraged the use of Greek philosophy to develop the Christian faith. These all wrote in Greek except for Tertullian who wrote in Latin.

Justin. Neapolis (Nablus), Palestine (c. A.D. 100–c. 164). As a young man, Justin explored the philosophies of his day, trying to find one that answered his questions and showed him the truth about God. After trying and rejecting stoicism, Aristotelianism, and Pythagoreanism, he settled on Platonism, which he found very satisfying intellectually. Then he met an elderly Christian who entered into philosophical discussion with him about God and the immortality of souls. Convinced by the man's arguments (which took a rather Aristotelian turn), Justin turned to the Scriptures and at about the age of thirty became a Christian.

Having been converted through philosophical arguments and finding all his philosophical questions answered by Christianity, it is not surprising that Justin should both claim that Christianity is the supreme philosophy and that he should use philosophical arguments and concepts in defending it. In particular, he saw many parallels between Plato's teaching and the Christian message; Plato was searching for what God had revealed through the prophets and in Jesus. Indeed, Socrates pointed to Christ, not just in his search for truth, but in the fact that he was rejected and martyred. But Justin didn't find elements of Christian truth just in Plato; he found them in other philosophies as well. Justin emphasized the role of Logos, the reason that philosophers have followed, and which Christianity has shown to be Christ, the Logos of God. Wherever a philosopher truly followed the Logos, said Justin, he was actually following Christ.

Though Justin lived the life of a philosopher and the emphasis of his apologetic writing was strongly philosophical, there was much more to his Christianity than a set of philosophical doctrines. His faith was centered on Christ. He focused especially on the significance of his death and resurrection and on the practical implications of Christian living. Though brought to the point of conversion by philosophical arguments, Justin admitted that the life and witness of those who had been martyred for being Christians had also profoundly affected him. He too remained faithful to Christ to the point of martyrdom.

Athenagoras.

Athens? (fl. second century). During a period of savage persecution of Christians round about A.D. 177, Athenagoras wrote a defense of the concept of the resurrection of the body and a defense of Christianity personally addressed to Emperor Marcus Aurelius. He made an interesting distinction between making a case for a specific truth, that is, showing it is philosophically conceivable, and actually expounding or teaching that truth. He saw his task as the former, though he would have preferred to do the latter. In his work on resurrection, he argued that if God has created human beings in the first place and given them life, it is not inconceivable that he could restore life after death; nor is there any rational reason why God should not want to raise the dead.

The background to Athenagoras's defense to the emperor was that Christians had been accused of atheism, cannibalism, and incest. Athenagoras defended them on all three points but particularly used the first one to argue the case for monotheism. Though not going as far as Justin in his claims about Greek philosophers, he was happy to show where they had produced arguments that supported the concept of God found in the Christian revelation.

Irenaeus. Asia Minor (c. A.D. 130–c. 200). As bishop of Lyons, Irenaeus was particularly concerned to refute Gnosticism, the philosophical hodgepodge that in the second century was infiltrating Christianity. It claimed to offer esoteric knowledge (*gnosis*), and it taught a dualism between God and the world and a system of intermediate beings. Like Justin, Irenaeus sought to show that Gnosticism had inadequacies and that Christianity was the true *gnosis,* providing a better answer to the issues Gnosticism raised. He used philosophical arguments, including a form of the teleological argument, to support the Christian concept of one Creator God.

Tertullian. Carthage (c. A.D. 160–c. 220). Trained as a lawyer and in rhetoric, and influenced by stoicism, Tertullian became a Christian in his thirties and brought his training to bear on his defense and discussion of Christianity. Toward the end of his life, he joined the Montanists, a group that stressed prophecy and practiced strict discipline.

Tertullian was firmly committed to the revealed truth of Christianity and strongly resisted all attempts to combine it with other philosophies. However, he used stoic concepts and philosophical arguments where appropriate, and he covered a wide range of issues in apologetics and philosophical theology. His concept of God as transcendent and beyond change or suffering has echoes of stoicism, as does his use of the Logos concept to describe Christ's (rather subordinate) relationship with the Father. In discussing the relationships of the Father, the Son, and the Holy Spirit, he was the first to use *trinitas, persona,* and *substantia* as technical terms.

Scholars often have said that there is a conflict between Tertullian's own use of philosophical ideas and his vigorous attack on pagan philosophy. In passages that are often quoted to illustrate his philosophical obscurantism, he cried, "What has Athens to do with Jerusalem?" and spoke of believing articles of faith "because they are absurd." These passages, however, are most certainly not saying that to be a Christian we must abandon our reason or deliberately choose what is absurd and make it an article of faith. Tertullian was trained in rhetoric. In these passages he is using devices recommended by Aristotle in his *Rhetoric* to make his point. In the first phrase, he is asserting the primacy of the Christian revelation over all other worldviews; it can stand on its own; it doesn't need to be propped up or watered down by Plato. In the second phrase, he is following Aristotle's suggestion that in some cases things that are believed "are more likely to be true because they are incredible." The resurrection of Jesus is such an "incredible" or "absurd" belief that no sane person would ever adopt it. Yet huge numbers of sane people, including firsthand witnesses, have adopted it. So this actually argues for its truth.

About the same time as Tertullian, **Minucius Felix,** another apologist who wrote in Latin, argued the existence of God on teleological grounds, especially the design of the human body. The ordered nature of the universe is evidence of his oneness and wisdom. Minucius's attitude to pagan philosophers was closer to Justin's than Tertullian's; he wrote with approval of Plato and others discovering divine truth through reason.

Clement. Alexandria (c. A.D. 150–c. 215). Clement was eager to commend Christianity as philosophically respectable and enthusiastic in his view that Greek thinkers had anticipated the gospel of Christ. While he held that philosophical understanding is not needed for those he called "simple believers," a more advanced grasp of the Christian faith and the defense of the gospel necessarily require the help of philosophy. Clement was, however, aware that this runs the risk of compromising the gospel with pagan ideas. Just as God gave the Jews the Old Testament to introduce them to Christ, he said, so he gave philosophy, especially seen in Logos, to the Greeks.

Clement was strongly influenced by Plato and the Platonic tradition but was also eclectic in his use of Greek philosophers. His concept of God had already moved away from the immanent God of the first century and the "simple believers" to a timeless, changeless transcendent being, to be reached only by pure thought and then largely by way of negatives (e.g., without extension, without limit). Creation was through the divine Logos, Christ, who is both transcendent and immanent. Clement used an allegorical method of interpreting the Scriptures of the Old and New Testament, which aided him in his search for higher philosophical truths that lay behind the straightforward accounts and teaching. The use of allegory was not original to Clement; it was widely used by pagan philosophers. It is an approach that is open to abuse by fertile imaginations but that has nevertheless been tried by many philosophers and theologians since, including Hegel and Bultmann.

Origen. Alexandria (c. A.D. 185–c. 254). Orphaned in his teens when his father was martyred, Origen chose to live a strongly ascetic life. He was well trained in Greek philosophy, especially Platonism, and he took the process of merging Christianity with Platonism even further than his teacher Clement. He wrote extensively in the fields of spirituality as well as in apologetics and philosophical theology, building on Clement's allegorical hermeneutic. Origen died as a result of being tortured during the Decian persecution.

He presented a concept of God that was firmly in the Platonic tradition. He saw him as immutable, impassible, timeless, and transcending truth and reason. He argued for God's incorporeality (something Christian thinkers had not necessarily accepted) on the grounds that if he were material he would be corruptible and so imperfect. It is because he is incorporeal that he is utterly transcendent, beyond thought, even beyond being itself. Such a timeless and immutable God could not have created the universe at a specific point in time. The universe therefore is eternal. It, or rather a series of universes, is being eternally created.

Origen's basic concept of the soul is thoroughly Platonic and includes its incorporeal nature and its preexistence, though not its reincarnation. He can be seen as marking the point at which the development of Christian thinking abandoned the New Testament concept of human beings as psychosomatic unities and adopted the Platonic division between soul and body.

Origen wrote widely and discussed issues in many areas. His view of the Trinity and the Logos show signs of Neoplatonic thought with its theory of emanation. He discussed and defended the freedom of the individual in the light of God's sovereignty and addressed issues relating to the existence of evil. Punishment after death, he taught, was purgatorial; everyone will be saved in the end and all things restored.

The spread and impact of Christianity in these early centuries was phenomenal. Despite savage persecution (two of the six thinkers we have surveyed died through persecution) Christianity spread from the obscurest of beginnings in the first century A.D. until it covered the whole of the Roman Empire. By the time of Constantine's Edict of Milan legalizing Christianity in A.D. 313, there were some twenty million Christians, about 10 percent of the total population of the world. Throughout this period of growth, the huge majority of its followers, as in Jesus' time, were very ordinary people. They were the uneducated, the poor, slaves, soldiers, and the like, Clement's "simple believers" who believed because of the impact Christianity had on their lives, not because its claims satisfied philosophical criteria. To study philosophy in those days required a reasonable amount of wealth and quite a bit of leisure time; such luxuries were denied to almost all of the early Christians.

But the attempt to provide philosophical justification for the claims of Christianity was inevitable. There was an urgent need to defend Christians against their persecutors, to answer the unfair charges brought against them. There was a need to present the gospel in forms that commended it to those who had been well educated. There was a need, in an age of religious and philosophical pluralism, when most philosophies included specifically religious elements and most religions dabbled in philosophy, to show that Christianity provided a coherent and plausible worldview, supplying a richer and fuller answer to the issues raised both by philosophy and religion. There was also subtle pressure to seek to show how Christianity in fact included the best insights of other philosophies. And there was a need to wrestle with the philosophical issues raised by the Christian revelation itself.

In this respect Christianity stands in contrast to Buddhism, Zoroastrianism, and Confucianism. Their growth was slower, and perhaps they were seen as less of a threat to their communities. Certainly they weren't persecuted in the way Christianity was. But probably the most significant difference is that there was nothing that these three worldviews had to face that was in any way parallel to the wisdom and vigor of Greek philosophy. Christianity came into a world that was dominated by Greek thought. Thus, for better or worse, Christianity had to interact with Greek thought. It could seek to destroy Greek thought or it could give way before it or seek some sort of compromise with it. What Christianity could not do was ignore Greek thought.

TO THINK THROUGH

Every worldview has to start with some presuppositions. Some have assumed the independent existence of the external world. Others have assumed the nonexistence of an independent external world. Some have assumed the existence of God. Others have assumed that all can be explained without reference to God. Some have made reason ultimate. Others have assumed irrationality is the only way. Can you think of any way of critiquing or choosing between these various approaches?

To what extent do you think the influence Greek thought had on the development of Christianity was a good thing?

The allegorical interpretation of the Bible, as practiced by Clement, Hegel, and Bultmann, among many others, enables philosophers to get behind the "simple" meaning of the text to profound philosophical insights. Do you think this is a valid procedure? What are its strengths and weaknesses?

For Further Study

Grant, R. M. *Greek Apologists of the Second Century.* London: SCM, 1988.

TWELVE

IT ALL FITS TOGETHER

THE AUGUSTINIAN WORLDVIEW

> In this chapter we look at some of the key points of Augustine's teaching, on which much of the medieval world-view was based.

AUGUSTINE'S INFLUENCE WAS IMMENSE. HIS DEFINITIONS of Christian doctrines and his exploration of philosophical ideas and their relationship to Christianity have been seen as foundational down to the present day. Until Aquinas, no Christian philosopher came anywhere near him in significance. During and since the Reformation, both Catholics and Protestants have relied on him as an authoritative resource.

Some would go so far as to say that Augustine's philosophy may yet be proved to be the most significant factor in the development of Western thought after Plato and Aristotle.

AUGUSTINE

Thagaste, Northeast Algeria (354–430). Despite the example of a Christian mother, Augustine rejected Christianity as a young man. He studied rhetoric at Carthage, where, in search of intellectual satisfaction and especially an answer to the problem of evil, he became a follower of Manichaeism, a religion that apparently put no obstacles in the way of his rather dissolute lifestyle. After teaching rhetoric in Carthage and Rome, Augustine moved to Milan. There, through study of Neoplatonism and discussions with Ambrose, the bishop of Milan, he came to an intellectual acceptance of the truth of Christianity. For some time he struggled with the moral and personal implications of becoming a Christian. He described how his struggle ended in a villa just outside of Rome in 386:

> What I needed in order to sort myself out was a paradigm shift, a whole new way of seeing things, accepting God and his truth as a basic premise. But I refused to take this step, basically because I was afraid.
>
> But then God got to work on my heart and my mind. I began to realize that in fact I accepted a vast range of things that I was unable to prove, whether historical, or factual, or cultural. I had to believe these things in order to live. So I moved from refusing to accept the Bible on the grounds that its truth couldn't finally be proved, to allowing that it's valid to accept it as a true message from God, given the strength of its claims.
>
> I kept crying out to God to sort me out. Suddenly I heard the voice of a child repeating in a sing-song way, "Pick it up and read it. Pick it up and read it." Since I couldn't think of any children's game involving these words, I took it that this was God telling me to pick up the Bible and read it, an experience I had heard had happened once to Antony. So I grabbed the Bible, opened it, and read the first passage I found: "Let Jesus Christ fill your life, instead of being dominated by your desires or your sexuality or your feelings."
>
> I didn't need to read another word. As I read that sentence light flooded my heart with peace and security. All the darkness of doubt was scattered.

Augustine returned to Thagaste in 388 and established a small religious community, spending his time studying philosophy, theology, and the Bible. He was ordained in 391 and became bishop of Hippo in 396. For the next thirty years he wrote prolifically in philosophy and theology; from 397 to 400 he wrote his best-known work, the *Confessions*, the first autobiography in Western literature. Very near the beginning comes the statement that is a fitting summary of the whole of Augustine's worldview. Addressing God, he wrote, "You have made us such that you are our focal point, and we are unfulfilled until we find fulfillment in you." In his many other works he defended Christianity against various heresies and alternative worldviews, and he explored a wide range of theological and philosophical issues. He was a conscientious bishop. In contrast to some, he insisted on a simple lifestyle, wearing second-hand clothes and eating only vegetables and herbs.

Augustine's life spans momentous events in the Western world. For the first part of his life, both Christianity and Rome were flourishing. But toward the end of the fourth century, non-Christian religions and philosophies made a comeback, and Rome's power began to crumble. Rome itself was sacked by the Visigoths in 410, and within a few weeks of Augustine's death, the Vandals had overrun the area of North Africa in which he had spent most of his life. The great era of Greece and Rome had ended.

Augustine's great achievement was to state the Christian worldview in a theological and philosophical system that cohered as a unified whole and formed the basis for the thinking and philosophizing of subsequent centuries down to Aquinas and beyond. A man of his time, he did this in the context of current philosophical thought, some of which, such as Manichaeism and skepticism, he rejected, but some of which he used. In particular he was influenced by Plato and Neoplatonism and found no problem in using their insights to help defend and clarify the Christian worldview. Given the wide range of his thought, we will have to be selective in our survey, listing his ideas in three main sections. First we will survey the basic issue of the relationship between philosophy and Christianity. Then we will look at God and the world and finally at individuals and society.

PHILOSOPHY AND ITS RELATION TO CHRISTIANITY

1. What philosophy is. Philosophy is the love of wisdom, a search for truth, goodness, and happiness. Its concern is not just theoretical, but practical—how we should live. The philosopher is concerned with all truth, both truth about the world around us (Augustine used the Latin *scientia* to describe our knowledge here), and about eternal or divine truths (where he used *sapientia*, "wisdom"). Just about all ancient philosophers would have agreed with this definition.

2. Truth. Much of what philosophers (particularly "the Platonists") have discovered is true. Augustine found his study of Neoplatonism showed him many profound truths he later found were part of the Christian gospel. But since philosophies disagree among themselves, they cannot all be true.

3. Whole truth. **There is only one philosophy that is wholly true, and that is the one revealed as truth by God in the Christian revelation.** One of Christianity's greatest achievements is to join together the spheres of *sapientia* and *scientia*, eternal truth and temporal truth. This is achieved throughout Christian teaching but is especially seen in the incarnation, where the divine Logos became a human person.

4. Revealed truth. **This "Christian philosophy" is built on revealed truths that are believed as foundational and authoritative.** It is not the role of reason to create these foundational truths, any more than to create, say, the foundational truth that "I exist." That is not to say, however, that these truths are contrary to or inaccessible to reason. Many of them have in fact been discovered by thinkers quite apart from the Christian revelation.

5. Seeing truth. **To believe (Lat. *credere,* "to accept a truth on authority")** is *cum assensione cogitare,* **"to think with assent."** Some of our knowledge arises from direct experience (what Augustine called "seeing"). For example, you know at this moment that you have a book in front of you. But many things we accept on the authority of others. For example, you have just accepted on my authority that Augustine died in 430. Since accepting authorities can bring a greater risk of getting things wrong, when someone tells us something, we do what we can to check it out before we accept it. We weigh up the reliability of the speaker, say, or check the credibility of the statement. Then, if we're happy, we make a choice (assent) to "think" it, to believe. This applies not just to religious beliefs, but to all sorts of belief. It applies, for example, to beliefs about events in the past. Religious belief, or faith, is accepting truths on the authority of God. It is no different in kind from beliefs we accept on someone else's word or faith we have in the reliability of the writer of a book we are reading.

6. Faith and reason. **Believing and understanding *(intelligere)* or, we might say, faith and reason, go closely together.** Understanding is involved in checking out, say, the acceptability of statements we "believe," so understanding has a role in coming to belief or faith. But belief or faith also provides a base for understanding. Augustine loved to quote his translation of the Septuagint version of Isaiah 7:9, *nisi credideritis non intelligetis,* "unless you believe you will not understand"; we can't wait until we have understood everything (or completed the Enlightenment's agenda of establishing everything by reason) before we adopt beliefs. If someone tells us something, even before our reason can get to work on his or her words, we have to believe, or trust, for example, that we have heard those words correctly. So belief and understanding, faith and reason, work closely together in religion and in the rest of life.

7. The role of reason. Besides having a role in accepting the basic Christian truths, reason also has a significant role in analyzing and examining them, demonstrating their coherence and significance. Augustine had no problem in opening up all Christian truth to the scrutiny of philosophy, though he conceded that some truths, like that of the Trinity, will only be partly understood in this life.

8. The value of reason. Thus we should always be justifying and strengthening our Christian (and other) beliefs through the use of reason. As we do so, they gradually move over from being beliefs to being knowledge, though the process is generally not complete until we experience God directly in heaven.

9. Skepticism. Augustine produced a number of arguments against skepticism. Skeptics argue that it is always possible we may be mistaken, so we should never believe anything. Augustine replied that we have to believe some things in order to live. I have to believe my food is wholesome or I'd never eat. So believing is essential to life. Augustine also countered skepticism with *si fallor, sum;* If I'm in error, there must be a something which is in error. I cannot doubt my own existence. Therefore at least something is irrefutably true. Therefore skepticism is untenable.

10. The highest truth. The highest truths are those we know directly. These include the propositions of math and logic. But they also include our knowledge of eternal things like unity. Here Augustine is applying Plato's concept of forms as universal truths, but in contrast to Plato (and following the Middle Platonists), he identifies these truths as the thoughts of God. God has expressed his beauty, goodness, truth, and so on in the world he has made; he has also patterned our minds on his. We can therefore know these eternal truths. Such knowledge is the highest activity of the human mind.

11. Revelation from God. God is not remote and passive. He is involved in all our knowing. It is fairly easy to see how this applies in our

knowledge of eternal truths or revelation. God expresses his thoughts, and we follow them; God reveals himself in Christ, and we accept that revelation. But Augustine believed additionally that God is active in all our knowing; he illuminates our mind just as the sun illuminates objects in the world. Enlightenment thinkers took it for granted that human beings are totally autonomous, that is, we can live and think and know things without any help from God. As a result, they found this concept of *illuminatio* unacceptable. But for Augustine it followed logically from his concept of God as the creator and immanent and gracious upholder of all that is real and true, including the world around us and ourselves as thinking people.

GOD AND THE WORLD

1. Evidences of the existence of God. Though Augustine did not set out to produce philosophical proofs of the existence of God, he saw many things as evidences of his existence. At root these evidences are all an expression of Augustine's conviction that Christianity is the one philosophy that really works. It is accepting the existence of God that enables us to answer the questions of the philosophers, to make sense of the data of life. God is the only adequate explanation of all we find in the world outside of us or in the human heart or mind.

2. Knowledge of God. Since God expresses himself in the natural world and in the human mind, we can know many truths about him and thus, in a sense, know him. But, in keeping with the Platonist tradition, Augustine at the same time stressed that God is transcendent and beyond all that we can understand or express. He is eternal, that is, outside of time. He is infinite, one, self-existent. He is all-knowing, changeless, possessing all perfections.

3. Creation. In contrast to the Platonists, Augustine taught that God freely chose to create the world, as opposed to the world simply emanating from God, and that he created it out of nothing *(ex nihilo)* rather than from some preexistent matter.

4. God and time. Augustine believed that, since God is outside of time, God created the universe timelessly as part of his eternal purpose. This enabled him to answer the objections "Why didn't he create it sooner or later?" and "Creating must have somehow changed God." The act of creation is both instantaneous and a process; God made the universe complete and yet with potential for development and thus change. Augustine used a seed to illustrate this point. A seed is complete in itself, yet out of it in time comes a plant.

5. The creative mind of God. In keeping with the Platonists, Augustine saw God's creative activity in terms of thought. God is truth. His thoughts are the source of being for the whole created order. When an object in the world truly expresses the mind of God, it is real and good and true. If it moves away from expressing the mind of God, it moves toward unreality and falsehood and evil.

6. The problem of evil. If a perfect God made the world, how do we account for the existence of evil? Augustine's reply is that evil does not exist in the way that, say goodness or beauty or truth exists. While under the influence of Manichaeism, Augustine had believed that evil was in effect another god, to be set over against the God of goodness. Once he became a Christian, he totally rejected this concept. Borrowing from Plotinus, he saw evil as a lack, a deprivation, a falling away from goodness. It is moving away from Being toward non-being. It arises from two sources. The finiteness of the created order entails limits, so even the best things in the world fall short of total perfection. Second, the existence of free will means that created beings may make choices that are less than the best. Nevertheless, in a way we can't understand, God is still working out his perfect purposes, incorporating into them even the things we see as evil, such as natural disasters.

INDIVIDUALS AND SOCIETY

1. The soul. The soul is to be seen as the life-principle. Like Aristotle, Augustine accepted that life-principle is found equally in animals or plants and in humans. Though the human soul is a unity, its activities are on two levels. The higher level, which includes the mind, is rational, and the lower level, which includes sense perception, impulses, and feeling, is irrational.

2. Immortality. Augustine believed that the human person is one; but he nevertheless developed a largely Platonic concept of the human soul as an immaterial, immortal substance. Its immortality arises from the fact that it partakes of divine life both as the source of its own life and as the object of its thought. Though he accepted the concept of the resurrection of the body, Augustine believed that it is possible for the soul to exist apart from the body.

3. Perception. The soul is the part of us that receives and puts together the impressions or sensations of the world around us that we experience through our bodies. The soul thus forms an image of things that are in the world. Since what we come to know through sense experience may sometimes be mistaken, these images may be open to error and thus not as reliable as the eternal truths we know directly. Even so, Augustine argued, running the risk of occasionally getting things wrong is far better than refusing to believe anything our senses tell us.

4. Freedom. Freedom, which includes freedom to decide and freedom to choose, is a very special gift of God, in that it reflects a key part of his own nature. In an early work on the freedom of the will, *De libero arbitrio*, Augustine seems to accept what we would call the liberty of indifference, characterized by the phrase, "I could have done otherwise." Later, however, in the fires of controversy with the Pelagians, who claimed that we have "power to take either side," Augustine took a more morally deterministic position: A good will can only choose good and an evil will can only choose evil.

5. Happiness. Perfect happiness, the goal all philosophies rightly seek, is not just pleasure, though it includes that. Its essence is both rational and practical. It is the fulfillment of our search for truth, both as we discover truths and as we experience God as the final and supreme truth. And it is also the living out of that truth, following the truth, doing what God wills, living rightly, and thus fulfilling our human potential.

6. Virtue. Right living or virtue thus entails moral choice, the exercise of our wills. But it also involves love. In no way do we grudgingly follow God's will. Rather, once we come to know the truth, we love it. Indeed, Augustine would have said that once we come to know the Truth, we love him, since it is Christ or God who is the Truth. Knowing, loving, willing, and doing all flow from one another.

7. The moral law. The basis of human morality is God's moral law, which in turn expresses his own character. This moral law is revealed in detail in the Scriptures, but it is available to everyone, since God has also expressed it in creation as natural law, and its basic principles are enshrined in most human laws. All of God's law can be summed up in the word "love"; if we love God with all our being and our neighbors as ourselves, we will fulfill God's law.

8. Humanity. Throughout history the whole human race can be divided into two, those who love God above themselves and those who love themselves above God. Since love and will are closely linked, this is the same as dividing humanity between those who have aligned their wills with God's will and those who follow their own wills. Augustine called the first group "the City of Jerusalem" and the second "the City of Babylon." All history is the story of the struggle between these two groups. Though the Christian church is an expression of the City of Jerusalem, the two are not to be equated. Nor is the state, however corrupt, simply to be equated with Babylon. Augustine was only too aware that a church leader can act out of selfish motives and not out of love for God, while, say, a magistrate could act out of love for God. Nevertheless, Augustine clearly saw the state in general as opposed to the church. Though the state has a role in curbing evil and keeping peace, its basic orientation is away from God and so from goodness. The church's responsibility is to stand over against the state and seek to permeate society with God's truth and goodness in the hope that the state will come to accept them. Augustine thus clearly separated church and state, a principle the Western church followed for a thousand years, though only at the price of the church developing power structures that enabled it to stand against the state.

9. Sexuality. Augustine believed in marriage and sexual intercourse as a bonding together of husband and wife as well as for procreation. But perhaps partly in reaction to his sexual exploits in his youth, when he became a Christian he committed himself to celibacy. Emphasizing as he did the importance of our wills controlling our behavior, he saw sexual arousal as something that is not subject to our will. In opposition to the Pelagian view that sexual feelings in themselves are morally neutral, Augustine saw them as an expression of our fallenness. This view, which has echoes of the doctrine of the innate evilness of the body (a doctrine Augustine did not accept), was to take a strong hold on the thinking of the Christian church, whose clergy in the fifth century were already beginning to feel that celibacy was in itself spiritually superior to marriage.

TO THINK THROUGH

In all aspects of life, as well as in religion, "I believe in order to understand." Do you agree? How does this work out in science, ethics, politics, and personal relationships?

How would you respond to someone who believes that Christianity is for the "religious" part of life only?

Do you agree that we should "always be justifying and strengthening our Christian (and other) beliefs through the use of reason"? Are there other factors, apart from the use of reason, that might justify and strengthen our beliefs?

What do you think of Augustine's concept of "illuminatio"?

The problem of evil is still a major one for many people today. How could you use Augustine's insights to help them?

How possible is it to merge the best insights of secular philosophy with the Christian worldview? Do you think Augustine succeeded in outlining a truly Christian philosophy?

For Further Study

Augustine. *The Confessions.*

Chadwick, H. *Augustine.* Oxford: Oxford University Press, 1986.

Nash, R. H. *Life's Ultimate Questions.* Grand Rapids: Zondervan, 1999, chap. 6.

THE NOT-SO-DARK AGE:

THE MEDIEVAL SYSTEM

PART THREE

THIRTEEN

WAS IT REALLY AS BAD AS IT SOUNDS?

AN INTRODUCTION TO PHILOSOPHY IN THE MIDDLE AGES

In this chapter we try to dispel a bit of the "darkness" that most people associate with the Middle Ages, and we discover that what they were doing was not as irrelevant and useless as we might have thought.

THE PHRASE "THE MIDDLE AGES" WAS ADOPTED IN THE seventeenth century to describe the period between the end of the Roman Empire and the emergence of the new learning that was expressed in the flowering of the Renaissance and the Enlightenment. But the period has neither a clear beginning nor a clear end. Rome was sacked by Goths in 410, yet the empire continued for another couple of centuries. In many respects the Renaissance was well under way by the fifteenth century, but medieval ways of thinking lingered on into the seventeenth century. For our purposes we will take it as the period from the death of Augustine in 430 to the first stirrings of the Enlightenment, roughly the sixteenth century.

The decline and fall of the Roman Empire signaled the start of a new age in the story of Western Europe. Nomadic tribes swept away much of the fruit of Greek and Roman culture. Centralized government ceased. Education as it had been known was virtually abandoned. Institutions of philosophical learning were deserted. The writings of the wise were lost. The pursuit of philosophy, as it had been known for a thousand years, ceased—that is, except for in

A Little Bit of History

Constantine, Roman emperor from 306 to 337, established Byzantium, later called Constantinople, as the empire's capital in the East from 330. As a result, the empire, though still functioning in many ways as one, was in two halves. In the West in particular it became harder and harder to keep back the hordes of invaders who were constantly attacking its borders. In the fifth century, invaders overran Italy, Spain, and North Africa, and the Western empire was broken up into a number of smaller kingdoms. But though there was no emperor in the West after 476, emperors continued in the East, and even in the West the conquering invaders sought to keep alive the positive elements of the empire, even acknowledging the emperor in the East. Indeed, Justinian, emperor from 527 to 565, made a serious but short-lived attempt to reestablish the political unity of East and West.

Much of the social and commercial structure of the Roman Empire continued into the seventh century despite continuing threats and attacks from invaders, until the rise of Islam and the Arab conquest of the Eastern empire by the middle of the seventh century marked its end.

Meanwhile the development of the churches in the East and the West took different courses. The Western church, perhaps because it had to face a number of heresies, tended to stress the importance of correct doctrine, carefully formulated. This gave particular authority to the church leadership and to the opinions and writings of those who were seen to be orthodox. In the East there was less of a divide between clergy and laity, and the authority of theologians was not so great. There a freedom to indulge in metaphysical speculation was combined with an approach that made worship, rather than correct doctrine, the center of Christianity.

Though study and speculation were kept alive in the East until the seventh century, in the West learning and especially philosophy had by then long been in decline. The cities, formerly a focal point for arts and education, had themselves suffered serious decline. As early as the fourth century, the Western empire had become predominantly a rural society. City culture was focused in the East, in Athens, Alexandria, and Constantinople. Rome itself ceased to be the seat of several of the emperors.

So the light of learning in the West slowly died and remained extinguished until the ninth century, apart from a handful of tiny centers of learning in distant Britain and Ireland, such as the Northumbrian cell of the Venerable Bede (673–735).

one place. In the Christian church, and especially in monastic communities, learning was kept alive. Education continued. Some of the works of the wise were copied and passed on. Scholarship flourished. And from time to time men of penetrating philosophical insight arose.

The Christian worldview.
This learning took a form that had its own special characteristics. The first, as we might expect, was that it was from within the Christian worldview. This didn't prevent it from being truly philosophical, nor did it exclude consideration of concepts that challenged Christians' understanding. But God's revelation in the Scriptures was always accepted as a primary given; that was the basis for all discussion and speculation.

Respect for the past.
The second special characteristic was a respect for the past. For many in the twenty-first century who still believe in the inevitable upward progress of the human race, this may seem strange. But, given their context, we can understand at least something of what the medieval thinkers felt. When civilization has collapsed around you and the future looks bleak, it is very tempting to look back and see the past as a golden age: the Greek city-state with its flowering of art and culture and leisurely discussion of philosophy; Plato in his academy; Aristotle with his incredible systematizing of knowledge; the love of learning; the free investigation of philosophical issues; great thinkers who wrestled with great issues.

Boethius reflected this attitude in the early sixth century. He had access to the works of Plato and Aristotle, and he determined to translate them all into Latin, complete, where possible, with explanations and commentaries, lest they should be lost forever. Of course, the medieval thinkers didn't feel they had to agree with all that the great thinkers of the past had said. That would have been impossible, in any case. And, following Augustine's lead, they were confident that all the issues debated by the thinkers of the past had their fullest answer in the true Christian philosophy. But they did feel they had to take them seriously. Like Augustine, they saw their best insights not as in any way undermining or contradicting Christian philosophy, but rather giving expression to truth in their own distinctive ways, ways that subsequent Christian thinkers can use to supplement and enrich their own thinking.

The appeal to authority.
A third distinctive feature of medieval philosophy, closely linked to the first two, was the appeal to authority. Again, this is a concept that at first sight is alien to us in the twenty-first century. The rejection of authorities was one of the war cries of Enlightenment thought, as it has

been of the postmodern movement. Of course, in neither case has any final rejection of authority actually taken place. The Enlightenment rejected the authority of the church and of the Bible, only to replace them with different authorities, those of reason and the scientists. And the postmodern who uses a website to attack all forms of authority and all structures still has to conform to the structure of language to state his or her message and to the authority of the computer manual or the software package to make the website work. Total anarchy, living without any authoritative structures, is impossible. It was, of course, easier for medieval thinkers to accept authority than it is for us today. In general, they lived in a hierarchical social system; the authority of the state or the king was readily accepted as final. More significantly, Christian thinkers had specifically chosen to accept the authority of God, mediated, almost exclusively by this time, through the Bible and the church. And the tendency to look back with respect to the great figures of the past inevitably meant that their authority had to be taken seriously, though, unlike that of God, not necessarily followed.

For, as we have seen, the accepting of authority for the medievals didn't entail slavish obedience. Nor did it prevent originality. It in fact provided something philosophy has always needed, a starting point for speculation and discussion. One of the greatest reasons why the rejection of all authority by contemporary relativists and postmodernists is philosophically unacceptable is that it completely destroys discussion and so the development of understanding and learning. Discussion or debate of any sort requires at least some agreed (and so authoritative) common ground before it can take place. I can discuss whether or not it was a good thing for the American colonies to declare independence from Britain in 1776 with someone who shares my understanding of history and of goodness, but not with someone for whom history is all subjective and goodness is totally relative.

Compromise and synthesis. The medieval respect for the past and

for the various authorities of the past led to an approach that sought compromise and synthesis. If the Greeks have basically gotten it right, and the Bible and the church have also gotten it right, and Augustine and the other great thinkers of the past have all by and large gotten it right, then fuller truth and deeper understanding is to be found by using the insights of all to build a comprehensive system. To us, perhaps, who know what was to come in the Renaissance and Enlightenment, this may seem to be merely marking time. But to those who were doing it, there was undoubtedly a sense of moving forward. They weren't merely repeating what Plato or Paul or Augustine had said.

Rather, they were quarrying in the rich mines of philosophic thinking to bring out gems they could make into beautiful new works of art.

Despite their interest in the wisdom of the past, most medieval scholars in fact had only limited access to the works of the classical Greek and Roman thinkers. Compared with the large numbers of copies of biblical texts, manuscripts of philosophical writers were few and far between. It was not until the twelfth century that the full works of Aristotle became generally available through the work of Islamic philosophers and that other works were brought from the East into the West. Until then, Western thinkers generally had to make do with limited quotations and summaries and interpretations of what the philosophers had said in place of their original works.

Method.

It is the medievals' respect for the wisdom of the past that gave rise to two distinctive features of their method. The first is the method of raising and discussing issues by means of a commentary on some ancient, or not so ancient, work. Many medieval writings take this form, especially in the earlier period. The second feature, prevalent in the later period, was debates or disputations. An issue or question would be raised and then debated by citing a whole series of comments from a wide range of thinkers.

Contemporary knowledge of medieval philosophy.

In spite of considerable research done in the last few decades, contemporary interest in and knowledge of the philosophy of the Middle Ages is still limited. Most surveys of philosophical history devote just a few pages to it, far less than to the Greek Golden Age or the Enlightenment period, both of which were far shorter than the thousand years or so covered by the Middle Ages. There are a number of reasons for this. The first is that we are still influenced by the attitude of the early Enlightenment thinkers, who could see nothing positive about medieval thought. Their only desire was to clear away the cobwebs of its teaching and get down to the new task of philosophy and build a worldview solidly based, as they saw it, on reason. Second, even if we feel the Enlightenment was unjustified in rejecting medieval thought, we still tend to find the issues debated by the thinkers of the Middle Ages irrelevant and difficult to follow. Their world and their interests seem so different from ours.

A third factor arises from the first two. So far, comparatively little study has been done of the large number of writings of medieval thinkers that we do possess. Many of them as yet remain unread.

Perhaps there is a fourth factor. The philosophy of the period was essentially Christian philosophy. As such, it has tended to have limited interest to non-Christian thinkers. But many Christian thinkers have serious reservations about the period as well. It is seen as a time when Christianity had lost its early vitality and theocentricity and betrayed its essential message. Despite much that was good, especially at the grassroots level, the ecclesiastical history of the period is something of which most Christians feel ashamed. The church became a human institution very different from that envisaged in New Testament times. Bishops and popes struggled for power. Evil was done in the name of the God of love. Both Protestants and Catholics rightly recoil from the mistakes and failures of the period. Protestants, in particular, tend to feel that there was little of value between Augustine and the Reformation. Though Roman Catholics would not agree, the high level of their interest in Thomas Aquinas has tended to mean that other thinkers of the period have not received their fair share of attention.

To a certain extent we will have to follow the trend of spending less time looking at the Middle Ages than at the Greek or Enlightenment periods. But we will at least take it seriously, in contrast to my personal experience of studying philosophy at the undergraduate level at Oxford in the 1960s, when the course leapt from Aristotle to Descartes without any recognition of philosophy done in the period of nearly two thousand years between them. Whatever our reservations about the Middle Ages, no history of philosophy can claim to be complete without covering the period, and we will seek to do that sympathetically, if comparatively briefly.

A DIALOGUE WITH "SAM"

If you are approaching medieval philosophy for the first time, you will probably find there are two major difficulties confronting you. First, the vastness and complexity of the material, made more complicated by its obscure jargon. Second, the seeming irrelevance of so much of it to the present day. So, before we plunge in, we will try to summarize, in as simple a way as possible, what the medievals were doing and why it is significant. We will let you ask the questions, and see if Sam (Some Average Medieval) can manage to answer them. You may also find it helpful at this stage to read chapter 17 on Plato and Aristotle and their role in the Middle Ages.

> You: *Sam, I'm supposed to be studying medieval philosophy, and I'm finding there are masses of the stuff, all seeming to achieve very little. What's it all about?*
>
> Sam: I agree there are masses of it. You're talking about over a thousand years of philosophy. But I can't agree it achieved very little. In fact, it achieved

something fantastic that has never been seen before or since—a world-view that worked beautifully, was universally accepted in the West, and lasted the best part of a thousand years. Beat that if you can.

You: *What do you mean it worked beautifully?*

Sam: Well, it answered all the questions people were asking and built everything together into one big comprehensive system.

You: *What sort of questions?*

Sam: All the same questions people ask in the twenty-first century about what is real and what is true and who we are and how we should live.

You: *I'm not sure people do ask those kinds of questions any more. I think they have given up trying to find the answers. You see, we've just gone through five hundred years of trying to find some answers to replace yours and have now decided there aren't any.*

Sam: All the more reason to go back and look at our answers then.

You: *Well, what are your answers?*

Sam: To what, specifically?

You: *Well, say, how do we escape from relativism?*

Sam: Great! You've put your finger right on the heart of what we were trying to do.

You: *But "relativism" doesn't appear in any of the indexes to medieval works.*

Sam: Right. But that doesn't change the fact that our main aim was to build up a worldview that was comprehensive and that we could know was right, covering all the data and clearly demonstrating that any other approach was useless in comparison.

You: *And did you manage that?*

Sam: Sure. We took the truths of Christianity and the best insights of human reason and found that they fitted together to make a superb overall system.

You: *But that's your great weakness. You combined religion and philosophy, reason and faith. Nowadays people won't let you do that.*

Sam: Then they're idiots. There are far more people who believe in God than there are philosophers. And it's the attempt to produce a world-view that excludes God that has just about destroyed philosophy for your generation.

You: *But what about the Great Pumpkin?*

Sam: The what?

You: *Well, if you base your worldview on faith, anyone can come up with any worldview, like believing in the Great Pumpkin.*

Sam: But we didn't base our worldview on faith. We based it on God, which is something very different.

You: *But you can only believe in God by a leap of faith.*

Sam: Rubbish! Belief in God is perfectly rational. At the very least, it's more irrational to try and build a worldview that excludes God than one that includes him. The Enlightenment fiasco showed that. And in any case, you have to start where people are at. People have always believed in God. He's central to the Greek tradition that came down to us just as much as he is to the Bible's teaching. Listen, the way I see it is that you in the twenty-first century have become stuck in relativism because most of the nineteenth- and twentieth-century philosophers tried to build a worldview on reason alone without any reference to God. And it failed. Now there are two alternatives to that. The first is to build a worldview on God without any reference to reason. I suppose that's what you mean by faith, though its real name is "fideism." That wasn't what we did. We took the other alternative. We built a worldview that was solidly based both on God and on reason.

You: *Okay. But what about all that stuff about substance and essence and things? Why did it all get so complex?*

Sam: Well, I'm not sure that it got any more complex than philosophy ever has been. I'm quite sure I could find you passages in Aristotle or Kant or Heidegger that are as obscure as anything in the medievals. Of course we got into complex details. We had to. It's all part of working out a detailed and comprehensive system. Every time we came across something in the world or in philosophy that raised questions for the system, we had to debate it and work it through. It's all part of trying to understand the world. Failure to explore the issues that arose would have been an abandoning of reason.

You: *You keep talking about a system. What did your system contain?*

Sam: Everything. All knowledge. Not just what you'd call philosophy, but logic, history, law, ethics, religion, psychology, politics, science, and cosmology.

You: *And where did God fit into all these?*

Sam: All over the place. But maybe in two ways in particular. You might say he's the beginning and the end—the source and the goal. He's the origin of everything, its base and foundation, ground of being, if you like.

You: *You mean he's the creator?*

Sam: Yes, but more than that. He's the one who makes things what they are. He makes real things real, true things true, good things good. Actually, that's the only way you can escape from relativism.

You: *And the goal?*

Sam: We saw everything as having a meaning and a purpose. I know your generation has been indoctrinated with the idea that everything is meaningless, based on pure chance and so on. But we had a strong sense of purpose. We didn't invent it, of course. It came from the Greeks as well as from the Bible. But it fit well with reason; it helped make sense of everything. The world exists to express God's glory. Reason's goal is to find truth and goodness in God. We exist to know and love him and enjoy his goodness forever.

You: *But surely your system was riddled with mistakes. You believed in Aristotle's categories and six literal days of creation, and you were tied into a corrupt church that persecuted the Jews. Doesn't that destroy the whole thing?*

Sam: Not at all. Though the overall system was fairly fixed, any of the details were up for grabs. All the issues you've just mentioned, and hundreds more, were raised and debated. As time went on ideas developed and changed quite a bit.

You: *Even the idea of God?*

Sam: Sure. All sorts of ways of viewing God were discussed: who he is, his nature and attributes, the Trinity, how we can know him, how he is the basis for things like goodness, truth, knowledge, and so on.

You: *Then along came Ockham's razor and cut out God, and the whole thing fell to pieces.*

Sam: Not quite. Ockham certainly didn't cut out God. But he was part of a process—the beginning of the end, you might say, where we began to move over from a worldview based on God and reason to one based on reason alone. No one realized it at the time. We thought we were giving just a bit more autonomy to reason. But what we were actually doing was conceding that reason could operate without any input from God at all. And, of course, in effect that was a denial of our central principle that had worked so well for so long, that both are needed to produce a workable worldview.

You: *But why did that happen?*

Sam: In a word, Aristotle.

You: *Aristotle? But he'd been dead for well over a thousand years.*

Sam: True. But something like that didn't worry us medievals. We always had a great respect for the wisdom of the past and especially the great Greek philosophers. And around the twelfth century we discovered Aristotle.

You: *Why, had he gotten lost?*

Sam: Yes. In the days before printing, of course, manuscripts were few and far between. Tons of them were destroyed when the barbarians overran the West. And, as far as the early medievals were concerned, only one or two bits of Aristotle had survived. So they had a rather limited understanding of what Aristotle had said. And then suddenly a load of manuscripts turned up. They had survived out East somewhere and had been preserved by Islamic philosophers. So from the twelfth century on we started reading the real Aristotle.

You: *And he persuaded you to get rid of God?*

Sam: No. Not just like that. But he started a process. Over the next four or five hundred years—

You: *Wow! Did it take that long to read him?*

Sam: Not quite—although we had to translate him into Latin before we could get started. But ideas took time to spread, and medieval philosophers always took their time. They didn't just read Aristotle and take everything he said on board. They'd read a bit and think it through and debate it—you know, typical late medieval stuff: "Aristotle says so-and-so. Plato says so-and-and-so. Augustine says so-and-so." And so on. Putting them all together. Working out compromises. Debating all the issues in fine detail.

You: *The sort of thing Bacon called "spinning cobwebs."*

Sam: Yes, I suppose so. And of course it took time. But eventually Aristotle's way of seeing things tended to come out on top.

You: *But what was so special about Aristotle's way of seeing things?*

Sam: It was much less God-centered than the Augustinian system. Aristotle definitely believed in God and in fact gave him a key part in his system. But he was a pretty remote God. He didn't get involved. The system ran itself. You could explain everything in the natural world without reference to him.

You: *And that way of seeing things caught on, given a few hundred years.*

Sam: Yes. There were other factors as well, all tied in. There was what you'd call the beginnings of the Renaissance—new explorations, new discoveries, a new confidence in human abilities and achievements. "Man come of age," humanism, and all that. And then on the other side, a pretty miserable church scene. Not only was much of the church corrupt; the official representatives of God at the time, popes and bishops and so on, gave the appearance of being stuck in the mud, ready to oppose anything new on principle, whether it was Aristotle or Copernicus. It didn't have to be that way. It was perfectly possible for Christianity to take Aristotle on board and to welcome all the exciting new things that were happening. In fact, Aquinas tried tying Aristotle in with the Augustinian tradition. But the feeling grew that it had to be one or the other—either the God-plus-corrupt-church-plus-stuck-in-the-mud-church-leaders package or the "man-come-of-age"-plus-new-ideas-plus-science-independent-of-God package.

You: *So in a sense the medieval tradition betrayed itself. It started with the vision of combining Christianity and the wisdom of the philosophers into a unified system and ended with a split between religion and science. And human thought has been fragmented ever since. Back to relativism. But we've nearly run out of time, and you've not answered all my questions.*

Sam: Ask me another.

You: *Well, all the stuff about substance and essence and universals. What's the point?*

Sam: I told you we were tackling the same questions you're facing today. And it seems to me that the second biggest question, after "How do you cope with relativism?" is "What is reality?" Is there a real world out there? Or is reality what's in my mind? Or is language reality? That's what we were after when we talked about substance and universals and so on. I know the language seems strange to you, and a lot of the time we were so busy looking at the trees we lost sight of the woods.

You: *And what was your answer?*

Sam: Well, it changed. In the early period we tended to say that reality was something behind and beyond the ordinary things we observe in the world. But later on we were more inclined to say that the things we could see around us were reality, and we didn't have to look any further.

You: *And what about all those other areas you mentioned—logic, history, law, ethics, psychology, politics, science, and cosmology?*

Sam: You name it; I'll spend a year or two telling you about it. We did incredible work in logic and language and meaning. Big stuff. Horribly complex. We sorted out the kinds of issues that no one else thought of until the twentieth century. In ethics we had a go at all the standard questions like "What is goodness?" "What is the relationship between virtue and happiness?" "What happens when moral principles conflict?" The only difference is that we didn't have to struggle with your sort of moral relativism. We believed that there was such a thing as goodness, that it was absolute, that we could discover it and follow it.

You: *And science and cosmology?*

Sam: I've already said a bit about the effect of Aristotle. But the interest in science didn't start when we got hold of his scientific works. We made attempts at all sorts of issues well before then, though we kept very much within a theocentric framework. We were looking at God's handiwork, not at autonomous objects in the world. So we tended to put it all in the context of God as creator, using the biblical account in Genesis and Plato's demiurge.

You: *That brings us to theology. You've not mentioned that.*

Sam: Haven't I? That must be because you've kept talking about other things. Yes, of course, we loved exploring issues in philosophical theology. The problem of evil and the nature of the Trinity alone provided us with plenty to think about for a few centuries. And it was important for us to explore any theological concept in its philosophical context. We didn't just take what the Bible said about, say, the soul, and leave it there. We took what the Bible said and put it alongside what Plato, Aristotle, the Stoics, and others said and let them react with each other. It was philosophical reflection on theological issues, and we loved it. You see, all our theologians were trained in philosophy. Especially in the later medieval period, we wouldn't let anyone loose on theology until they were expert philosophers. So there was no way they could keep theology and philosophy apart—not, at any rate, until the thing began to fall to pieces.

You: *Okay, you've nearly converted me. Maybe what you medievals did wasn't so bad after all.*

TO THINK THROUGH

What do you think about the medievals' respect for the great thinkers of the past and their determination to learn from them? Are the most recent ideas necessarily the best ones? Have you already come across concepts in your study of the history of philosophy that you would like to weave into your current worldview?

Some would say it was a tragedy that the medievals tried to mix theology and philosophy in the first place. Others would say it was a tragedy that the medieval period ended with the two of them drifting apart. What do you think?

I suppose all philosophers have dreamed of just one system (their own system) being universally accepted and followed by everybody. Is this just a dream? Can you envisage, say, postmodernism, or the Christian worldview, being accepted by everyone? Remembering the totalitarianism of Marxism, how could you guarantee philosophical freedom if some such thing did happen?

For Further Study

Martin, C. J. F. *An Introduction to Medieval Philosophy.* Edinburgh: Edinburgh University Press, 1996.

FOURTEEN

NOT EXACTLY TOEING THE LINE

BOETHIUS AND ERIUGENA

In this chapter we start our exploration of medieval thinkers with two whose ideas ran counter to Christian orthodoxy in a number of ways, and we will also glance at one, Pseudo-Dionysius, who was decidedly unorthodox.. All three were widely studied and quoted in the Middle Ages. We don't know Pseudo-Dionysius's dates; perhaps he was roughly contemporary with Boethius in the early sixth century. Eriugena was ninth century.

BOETHIUS

Rome (c. 480–c. 525). Boethius (pronounced bo-*ee*-thee-us) lived in the twilight period of the Roman Empire, when the Goths ruled Italy, but many of the positive features of the empire remained. He was a professing Christian and a well-educated patrician who held high office under the Ostrogoth king Theodoric. However, he seems to have fallen foul of powerful members of Theodoric's court at Ravenna and was imprisoned and executed for treason.

Boethius had high admiration for Greek philosophy and determined to translate into Latin the whole of Plato and Aristotle, adding his own commentary, lest these works should be lost from the West forever. He produced a number of commentaries on Aristotle and other philosophical writings of his own, especially on logic. But he only managed to translate some of Aristotle's work on logic. He also wrote some theological treatises, applying his studies in logic to current controversial issues like the Trinity.

While in prison awaiting execution, Boethius wrote his most famous work, *The Consolation of Philosophy (De Consolatione Philosophiae)*, a personal response to the problem of evil. His writings had a huge influence on the Middle Ages, rivaling the influence of Augustine.

The nature and source of evil.

Boethius agreed with Augustine that evil is a lack or privation rather than something that exists in its own right. It arises from the exercise of free will.

Free will and foreknowledge.

Like others before and since, Boethius tackled the problem of theological determinism arising from the foreknowledge of God. If God knows everything, he knows what I'm going to do tomorrow. So what I'm going to do tomorrow is already fixed today. So how can I make any truly free choices?

Though Boethius tackled this problem in the context of God's foreknowledge, philosophers from Aristotle to contemporary fatalists have realized it is equally problematic even if God is left out of the picture. We could make, for example, two statements: (A) "I will have an egg for breakfast tomorrow." (B) "I will not have an egg for breakfast tomorrow." Given that I make it to breakfast tomorrow, one of these statements must be true. If A is true, I have no choice about what I have for breakfast. I must have an egg. If B is true, there is no way I can choose to have an egg. So I've lost my free choice.

Boethius tackled this problem by looking at the logic of statements like "If God knows I will have an egg, then it is determined that I have an egg." He pointed out that while it is true that if God knows that I will have an egg, I will most certainly have an egg, this does not entail that I have no choice in the matter. It is quite conceivable that God knows that I will freely choose to have an egg. The sense of necessity or inevitability is a grammatical one arising from the way the conditional sentence is formed, not something in the real world. Later medieval thinkers built on Boethius's suggestion; still later thinkers tackled it in terms of the logical flow. The problem tempts us to say that whether or not I have an egg is logically dependent on God's knowledge. But in reality the flow is in the opposite direction. God's knowledge is logically dependent on my free choice. We could illustrate the point by looking backward instead of forward. Yesterday I had an egg. I know that—and God knows it too. But that makes no difference to the fact that I freely chose to have an egg. In fact, it was my freely choosing it that is the basis of the knowledge I have today. And the same applies to God's knowledge. So knowledge, whether mine or God's, whether of the past or the future, is logically dependent on free choices, not vice versa.

But Boethius didn't get as far as that, and he felt the need to tackle the issue further along a different line. Granted, we might say, the problem of inevitability or necessity doesn't seem to arise in the same way when we think about knowledge of past or present events. But there still seems to be something odd about future events. Are they not in a different category? Boethius tended to feel they were. But we can solve that problem, he said, if we realize that God is outside of time. He sees all events, past, present, and future, as we see present events. So, in effect, there is no future to God. Thus the problem is removed.

Christianity and philosophy.
Philosophy is the love of wisdom. Wisdom, for Boethius, is to be equated with God, who is the source of all things and who attracts us to himself by illuminating our minds and drawing us to himself in love.

An interesting feature about *The Consolation of Philosophy* is that there is nothing specifically Christian about it. Although it is full of references to God and his providence, the whole thing could have been written by a Neoplatonist. Indeed, at times it includes Neoplatonist concepts that most Christians chose to reject, such as reincarnation. It seems extraordinary that a Christian facing imminent death and struggling with the problem of evil should make no mention of the Christian hope or God's answer to evil in the cross and resurrection.

It is unlikely that Boethius had rejected Christianity when he wrote the *Consolation*, so we have to assume that he deliberately excluded references to the Christian revelation. But we don't know why. Perhaps the book was addressed to non-Christians, choosing to use their language. Certainly it indicates that Boethius believed that a major issue, one that through the years has been seen as perhaps the biggest philosophical objection to the truth of Christianity, the problem of evil, can be tackled and answered by "pure" philosophy without any appeal to revelation.

Universals.
Boethius spent a lot of energy tackling the problem of general ideas or universals, suggesting more than one possible way of viewing them and providing the starting point for a great deal of further discussion throughout the Middle Ages. The basic issue was whether or not universals really exist. Plato had said they do. Behind every individual example of a man lies the universal, or form, Man. Further, said Plato, it is only the form or the universal that really exists in any ultimate sense. Individual men come and go. While Aristotle's position was a lot less extreme, he still accepted the reality of the forms

in his version and so believed in the existence of universals. The distinction between Aristotle and Plato is that Plato believed that universals would continue to exist even if there are no individual expressions of them. There would still be a universal Man even if all men were destroyed. Aristotle, on the other hand, tied the existence of the universal firmly to the individual expression. When all men are destroyed, the universal Man will cease to exist.

Boethius in general refused to come down on one side or the other, though in his commentaries on Aristotle he tended to take an Aristotelian position, stating that universals cannot exist separate from individual objects, except in our thought. Aristotle had defined a universal as something "apt to be predicated of many." Boethius developed Aristotle's definition, with which he basically agreed, stating that the universal is shared by the many "holistically," that is, not in part; "simultaneously," that is all at one time; and "intimately," that is, sharing in its very nature.

God. In the *Consolation* Boethius argued for the existence of God, without any reference to revelation. He used the Neoplatonic concept of a hierarchy, in which the lesser or the imperfect is dependent on the greater or the more perfect. We know beyond doubt, he says, that the imperfect exists; therefore the perfect must exist, and we innately know that this is God. God is the final peak of all our thinking of good things; he is that of which nothing better can be thought. This is an early version of the ontological argument we will be meeting again later on.

God possesses total happiness or blessedness. So if we seek happiness (as Boethius assumed we all do), we will only ultimately find what we seek by finding him.

In his more theological works, Boethius explored the nature of the Trinity and the two natures of Christ, defending Western orthodoxy. His approach to these issues showed a level of careful scholarship that was a new thing in the West, as he sought to demonstrate that controversial issues could be resolved by careful definition of terms and precise logical arguing.

Like Augustine and the Platonic tradition, Boethius equated being with good and nonbeing with evil. This raised an issue that was to be discussed at great length by subsequent medieval thinkers. If everything that exists is good by virtue of the fact that it exists, or partakes of being, how do we distinguish the goodness of God from the goodness of other things? We may not feel this is a major issue, since we may be quite happy to say that since God creates all things and makes them good, goodness in objects doesn't need to be sharply distinguished from goodness in God. But for Boethius it was important because he believed, with the Neoplatonists, that God had to be wholly other. Thus all that he is in himself, including his goodness, has to be different from the expression of these things in the world. Boethius's answer to the problem was to distinguish between an object's "being" or form, and its substance, the things of which it consists. We, for example, have "being" as human beings, but we consist of various parts, none of which can be said to partake of being or the form of humanness in the way we do as a whole. But God is simple, totally one. So no such distinction between his being and his parts applies to him. Thus God's separateness is maintained.

Boethius enjoyed analyzing and defining things, and he was noted for his definitions, which have served as starting points for debate and critique throughout the Middle Ages and beyond. He defined God's eternity as "the total and perfect possession, at one time, of unending life." Person is "an individual substance [expression] of a rational nature." Happiness, specifically the blessedness of God, is "a condition perfected by the joining together of all that is good."

TO THINK THROUGH

A huge number of philosophers have tackled the issue of free will. Do you think Boethius's approach helps us to find a contemporary answer to the problem?

For Further Study

Chadwick, H. *Boethius: The Consolations of Music, Logic, Theology, and Philosophy*. Oxford: Clarendon Press, 1981.

JOHN SCOTTUS ERIUGENA

Ireland (c. 810–c. 877). (His name is sometimes spelled Scotus Erigena, and it refers to Ireland, which at the time was called Scotia Major or Erin.) Eriugena (pronounced almost like *original*) received a good education in an Irish monastery, one of the few places where knowledge of Greek had survived. Driven from Ireland by the Danes, he was appointed head of the court school of Charles the Bald, king of France. There he translated various Greek works, especially by Pseudo-Dionysius (see below) and Gregory of Nyssa, a fourth-century Eastern theologian strongly influenced by the Neoplatonism of Plotinus. He

Pseudo-Dionysius

Theology and philosophy in the two halves of the Roman Empire had tended to grow apart from the fourth century onward. However, about the early ninth century, some manuscripts from the East incorporating Eastern thinking made their way to the West. Eriugena was asked to translate some of these from Greek into Latin. Among them were the works of someone who claimed to be Dionysius the Areopagite, mentioned in Acts 17 as responding to Paul's preaching at Athens. But their probable date is the end of the fifth century, since they reflect the philosophical concepts of that time. They appear to reflect the pagan Neoplatonism of Athens taught by Proclus in the fifth century A.D.

However, the works were generally accepted in the East as authentic and thus of considerable authority, since they were thought to be written by someone who was taught by Paul. Despite their questionable orthodoxy and divergence from the teaching of Augustine in a number of areas, the West also accepted them as authentic. As a result, they had a significant effect on Eriugena himself, and, through his translation, on subsequent medieval thought.

Key elements of Pseudo-Dionysius's thought include:

- God is the source or principle of all things and the goal of all things.
- The world is the emanation or outpouring of God through his forms or thoughts. When they are created they become distinct from God; but the cycle is completed as they are absorbed back into God and thus deified.
- God can be spoken of in two main ways. (1) Positively (Gk. *kataphasis*; Lat. *via affirmativa*). We can, for instance, say that God is good. However, such is the goodness of God that even if we greatly qualify our terms, for example, that God is superessential Goodness, our description will still fall far short of God's transcendent reality. (2) Negatively (Gk. *apophasis*; Lat. *via negativa*). By using negative terms, we can exclude the imperfections from our concepts of God. God is, for example, infinite. We can't comprehend

what infinity is, but we know it is "not-finitude," "without limit." The first way of speaking about God is inadequate. The second effectively means we can say nothing. So we need to compromise and use concepts like "beyond goodness." The nearer we get to God, the more we are left with only negative concepts.

- God is thus beyond knowing. So our approach to him cannot be through the mind. Reflecting the Eastern tradition, Pseudo-Dionysius gave rise to a mystical approach to God, typified in the phrase "the cloud of unknowing." This ran counter to early Christian and Augustinian concepts of revelation and the illumination of our minds by God's truth.
- Evil is the absence of good and so has no positive existence.

also wrote original works, the most significant of which was *About Nature*, or *On the Division of Nature*. This was a thorough and comprehensive philosophical system, the first to appear in the Middle Ages after Augustine.

Eriugena appears to have been a colorful, independently minded figure, not at all concerned to toe the party line of the day. Though his translation of Pseudo-Dionysius was very widely read, his *About Nature* does not seem to have had a great deal of influence. It was generally seen as unorthodox and was eventually condemned by the pope as heretical in 1225.

Eriugena's System.

Eriugena sets himself the task of embracing in one system "all that is and all that is not." He made four classifications, calling them *species* or aspects. They can be seen as four levels of being, or four ways we think of reality. As a fourfold division, the scheme is not original; Pythagoreanism had something similar to it. The first three aspects also appear in Augustine. Eriugena's fourth aspect highlights the Neoplatonist concept of the cosmic process that originates in God and returns to God; indeed, God is present in all four aspects. The system seems totally dependent on Greek thought and to have lost touch with the distinctively personal vision of God and his relationship with the world described in the New Testament.

1. *What creates and is not created.* This is God. He is transcendent, unknowable as he is in himself. He is essence and wisdom yet beyond essence and wis-

dom. He is creator, yet in a sense he does not create, since all things are manifestations or expressions of his being. Of so great a God we can only speak in negatives.

2. *What creates and is created.* This is the world of Platonic forms, summed up in the Logos. The Logos is the word or thought of God, created or "generated" eternally.

3. *What is created and does not create.* This is all created objects. They arise from or are manifestations of the thoughts of God through the Logos. Since Eriugena viewed the essence of God as totally unknowable to us, he was able to explain the concept of God creating out of nothing as God creating out of himself. He insisted his position was not pantheistic, but many of his contemporaries read him as such, since he denied independent reality to created objects.

4. *What neither creates nor is created.* This is God, viewed in a Neoplatonist way as loving and drawing all things back into himself as the final goal. Ultimately all things will return to God; there cannot be an eternal hell. Evil is nonbeing, a privation of good.

TO THINK THROUGH

What is your answer to those who say that God is so "other" that we can't speak of him at all or only in negatives?

For Further Study

O'Meara, J. J. *Eriugena.* Oxford: Clarendon Press, 1988.

A Bit More History

The medieval period was packed with momentous events and experiences. There were wars, often long and cruel. There was famine and plague; the Black Death in the fourteenth century killed over 50 million people, including one third of the population of England. There were power struggles, secular and religious. There was the establishment of the "Holy Roman Empire" under Charlemagne in the ninth century. There were the Crusades from the eleventh to the thirteenth centuries, culminating in the capture of Constantinople, thus giving the West access to "lost" Greek manuscripts. There were the good things of life; among them were hospitals, schools, and a range of caring institutions, all inaugurated by Christians and arising from something that was unique in the world, a Christlike love for those who were in need.

Two things that had a significant impact on the development of philosophy were the rise of Islam and the founding of universities. Islam arose in the seventh century and rapidly conquered North Africa, the Middle East, and parts of Europe. Like Christianity, it sought to come to terms with secular philosophy and developed its own synthesis from the tenth century onward. This synthesis, together with the preservation of ancient Greek texts, had a considerable impact on the West in the twelfth century.

Up until the middle of the twelfth century, if you had wanted to study philosophy, you would have gone to a monastic school or to a school attached to one of the great cathedrals. Though monasteries were at times something of a law to themselves and certainly developed varying traditions, your education would have been clearly under the aegis of the church. The twelfth century saw the beginnings of a new institution, the university. The first university was Bologna, which dates back to 1113. Paris started in 1150 and rapidly became Europe's center for philosophical study. Oxford was founded in 1167.

All of the universities were specifically Christian institutions, but their structure was such that they began to drive a wedge between theology and philosophy that was something quite new in the medieval period. The two subjects were taught in separate faculties, which meant that each tended to go its own way, with a minimum of interaction with or interference from the other. Philosophy belonged to the faculty of arts, along with logic and dialectic. Theology was in a faculty all on its own; students had to graduate from the faculty of arts to get to it. Those who moved on to theology may have been tempted to feel that they could now leave philosophy and logic behind them. Those teaching philosophy tended to become "professional" philosophers, and some fell to the perennial temptation that always confronts academics, to develop some new and even controversial ideas to attract attention. Because those who taught in the universities were "professional" teachers, they were called "schoolmen," hence the description "scholasticism" for their work.

FIFTEEN

BEFORE THE STORM

MEDIEVAL THOUGHT AT THE COMING OF ARISTOTLE

The impact of the rediscovery of Aristotle's works changed the course of medieval philosophy. In this chapter we look at two philosophers who mark the peak of pre-Aristotelian medieval thought. Anselm and Abelard both used their reason to full advantage. By contrast, Bernard, the third thinker in this chapter, chose the mystic way in preference to that of reason.

ANSELM

Aosta, Italy (1033–1109). Anselm was abbot of a Benedictine monastery at Bec in Normandy and became archbishop of Canterbury in 1093. He wrote widely in theology and philosophy, including works on the incarnation, the Trinity, free will, justice, truth, logic, and the knowledge of God. He saw himself as firmly in the Augustinian tradition, blending elements of Platonism with the Christian revelation into a true Christian philosophy. He had a penetrating mind and, unlike many medieval writers, tended to present his work as his own original thoughts rather than constantly citing authorities and developing highly technical arguments. His key methodology was to present "necessary reasons" for the truths of Christianity, that is, establishing them by rational argument rather than appealing to the authority of revelation.

Reason and belief (credo ut intellegam). This phrase, "I believe in order to understand," had its roots in Augustine. Anselm used it to express his attitude to the relationship between reason and belief, Christian or otherwise. We cannot start with nothing and then get to work on it with our reason. Rather, we start with beliefs and then submit them to the scrutiny of reason and find, to our delight, that reason confirms and strengthens those beliefs. Indeed, Anselm wrote his more philosophical works in the context of his teaching responsibilities at Bec, where he was seeking to strengthen the faith of his students by demonstrating the rationality of their beliefs.

It is important to remember that Anselm wasn't claiming that reason alone could show us the truths of the Christian faith; many philosophers have incorrectly assumed this in their discussion of his so-called "ontological argument." Anselm's reasoning is always from within his Christian worldview. He started his treatise on truth, for instance, with "We believe that God is truth." But he used reasoning to support and justify his worldview even though he knew that reason alone is inadequate. Reason has its limits, as he specifically stated in his discussion of the Trinity. In the paragraph before his statement of the ontological argument, he specifically stated that in presenting it he was not seeking to understand so that he might believe; rather, he believed so that he might understand.

Anselm's "ontological argument."
Anselm put forward a number of arguments in support of his belief that God exists. The most famous is one that appears in four forms at the start of his devotional meditation *Proslogion* (from the Greek, meaning "an address to" [God]). The validity of the argument as a proof that would persuade atheists has been hotly debated ever since. Some, like Descartes and Leibniz in the seventeenth century, and Charles Hartshorne and Norman Malcolm in the twentieth century, have accepted its validity or at least the validity of their adaptations of it. Others, like Aquinas and Kant and most twentieth-century commentators have claimed that they have found logical flaws in it.

In approaching Anselm's ontological argument, it is wise to remember three things. First, Anselm is operating within a basically Platonist worldview. His arguing seems odd to us because we operate with a different worldview. But, given a Platonist way of seeing things, the argument becomes much stronger. Second, Anselm is operating from within a Christian worldview. Indeed, the setting of the argument is a prayer. It is in the same passage of the *Proslogion* that he stresses *credo ut intellegam*. His original title for the essay was "Faith Seeking Understanding." Anselm is not seeking to use the argument to persuade those who do not yet believe in God. Rather, his aim is to confirm the faith of those who already believe. Third, there is a difference between an argument and a total logical demonstration (assuming such a thing is actually possible, which many people doubt). It may be possible to show that Anselm's argument is not a totally watertight proof of the existence of God but still accept that it carries weight as an argument. Almost all, if not all, arguments are in fact in this category. If I argue that it is raining on the ground, that everything is getting wet, that people are holding up umbrellas, and so on, my argument is accepted as valid even though it falls far short of logical proof.

The argument starts with a belief that would have been axiomatic or self-evident to those in the Platonist tradition. It was not original to Anselm; parallel concepts had appeared in Boethius and Augustine and in non-Christian writers such as Seneca and Cicero. Literally translated, this belief says that, if God exists, he is "something than which nothing greater can be thought." We cannot think of anything greater than God. Suppose, for a moment, that this "something than which nothing greater can be thought" does not in fact exist in reality. Even so, we can still think of it; it still exists in thought. Now (and here's the crucial step) "something than which nothing greater can be thought" is going to be greater if it exists in reality rather than just in thought. So although we have assumed for a moment that "something than which nothing greater can be thought" doesn't actually exist in reality, we find in our thought something that is in fact greater than the mere thought of it, that is, the thought of it as really existing. So, by our original definition, "something than which nothing greater can be thought" must exist—that is, God really exists.

It is important to remember that Anselm didn't conceive of God as just one object among many, and he certainly would not have wanted to extend the argument to any other existing thing. God is unique both in his greatness and in his way of existing. This means that his argument can be defended against that of his contemporary, Gaunilo, who claimed that it established that any perfect thing we imagine, like a perfect island, must exist.

Anselm would also probably have used the same point to defend his case against more recent arguments. These have stated that existence is not a predicate or quality that functions like other qualities, so we can't use it, as the argument does, to add something to "something than which nothing greater can be thought." In the case of God, Anselm would reply, existence is quite different from all other types of existence.

The same response could be used to counter Hume's argument that it is invalid to move from the realm of ideas to actual existence. Doubtless this was impossible for Hume, but it certainly wasn't for a Platonist like Anselm. True, if we assume, as Hume did, that there is only one possible way of existing, that is, the way physical things in the world exist, then we will necessarily reject Anselm's argument. Indeed, we will probably reject all concepts of God that bear any relationship to the God of Platonists or Christians.

TO THINK THROUGH

Why does the ontological argument seem so unconvincing to so may people today? Can you think of any way of restating it that would carry more weight?

For Further Study

Southern, R. W. *Saint Anselm: A Portrait in a Landscape.* Cambridge: Cambridge University Press, 1990.

PETER ABELARD

Near Nantes, Brittany (1079–1142). Peter Abelard studied under two men who took opposite sides in the debate over universals. Roscelin was an Anti-Realist, or Nominalist, and William of Champeaux, a Realist. Abelard disputed with both, rejected both positions, and developed an alternative of his own. His life was one of constant controversy, both over philosophical and theological issues, and over his affair with Heloise, one of his students. Though there was much about him that was arrogant (he seems to have quarreled with just about everybody), he was immensely popular as a lecturer. Periodically he was accused of heresy and had to flee from those he had upset or who were alarmed at his views and wished to silence him. He had a brilliant mind and a strong confidence in reason and especially logic. His influence was great. He set a standard of intellectual rigor that was to become a hallmark of scholasticism, with its careful debate and subtle arguing, particularly as it developed at the new universities.

Universals. To us today the issue of universals seems of little interest. This is largely because we neither believe in them, whether in their Platonist or their Aristotelian form, nor see any need for them. In the Middle Ages, however, the situation was very different. The very fact that they were a key issue in the works of Plato and Aristotle made it essential that they be taken seriously. Plato's forms, in particular, had to be reshaped and assimilated into the Augustinian Christian philosophy.

But there was a further reason. The issue of universals appeared to have significant bearing on key Christian doctrines, not least that of the Trinity. In the doctrine of sin, for example, and particularly in the Augustinian concept of original sin, it made a lot of difference if someone said that all that exists is individual sins and denied that there is some further entity "sin," or "original sin," that lies behind them. The same issue arose with the doctrine of the church. Was the church simply the totality of Christians, or was there something extra, something beyond the individuals, a universal, that made the church a universal church?

The discussion over universals was very complex; a lot of different proposals were put forward arguing very subtle points. There is still a great deal of uncertainty over just what many of the writers, including Abelard, were in fact saying. Part of this confusion may arise because those who disagreed with the views of the church hierarchy had to be very circumspect in the way they expressed their position. The church in the later medieval period was very powerful and very willing to use its power to quell dissent. For our purposes it is sufficient to divide the views into two broad camps—realism and anti-realism, or nominalism—while recognizing that there was a range of intermediate positions and that many Anti-Realists tended to present their views as modified realism.

Realism was the dominant view from Augustine until the twelfth century. It arose from Platonism and fit the Augustinian synthesis well. For Realists, universals were realities that existed apart from the particulars in which we see them expressed. There is, for example, a universal Humanity, which would continue to exist if there were no actual human beings. Sin would still be real even if everyone behaved perfectly.

Anti-realism, or nominalism, rejected this view. For Anti-Realists universals are not independently existing entities. Nor are they entities that exist in things in the Aristotelian sense. They simply do not exist at all. When we talk about humanity, we are using a word, a name (Lat. *nomen*), but there is no entity to which the word corresponds. Only individual objects, particulars, exist. Everything that exists is a particular.

Roscelin (1050–1125), who taught Abelard for a time, was the first medieval Anti-Realist of note, but he appears not to have proposed any positive theory in the place of realism.

Abelard saw his position as less extreme than Roscelin's and more in the way of a compromise between the two positions. However, it is nearer to nominalism than to realism.

There are, he said, no universals. There are only particulars, particular substances like Socrates and particular accidents like Socrates' whiteness. However, that is not to deny that we use general or universal terms like humanity and whiteness. But these are merely words, ways of speaking. The existence of a word does not entail the existence of any entity corresponding to it.

But a problem arises. All words have to refer to something. There is no problem seeing what words like Socrates and Socrates' whiteness refer to. But if there are no universals, what are we to say words like humanity or whiteness refer to? Abelard's answer is that they refer to mental images or thoughts in our minds that are formed by abstraction from the particulars. I see many individual humans and extract from them the mental image "humanity." I see many white things and abstract from them the mental image "whiteness." But this mental image is not a "thing"; it is a figment, a no-thing.

Yes and No: Authority and reason. In 1122 Abelard published

a book that was typical of the man, *Sic et Non* (Yes and No). It is a discussion of 150 themes, in each case giving the arguments on one side and then the arguments on the other side, often without coming to any conclusion about the issue. Here we can see the Abelard who disputed with just about every viewpoint he encountered, expressing his love of dialectical discussion. He had great confidence in logic and dialectic as a way of reaching truth. He linked logic with the Logos; to think logically is to think Christianly. Nothing apart from the Bible, he said, is infallible; everything should be tested by reason and logic.

Scholars debate the extent to which Abelard is to be called a rationalist. If rationalism is to be taken in its extreme sense of making reason the only authority, the title certainly does not fit. Abelard thought the role of reason was to strengthen Christian truth, not to create or destroy it. He spoke of reason providing buttresses for the structure that is founded on authority. He could not be an Aristotle, he said, if that meant separation from Christ. Though *Sic et Non* lists conflicting arguments, they are all culled either from the Bible or from the writings of the theologians. Abelard is using reason to debate the relative merits of differing authorities.

Nevertheless, Abelard loved logic and argument, and he implicitly trusted dialectic as a means of reaching truth. In this he could claim to be simply following the Western medieval tradition, which since Augustine had stressed the significance of reason. But, on balance, he does appear to have been more rationalistic than most and to have set the trend for the rationalism of the thirteenth century.

Ethics. In exploring what makes an act right or wrong, Abelard stressed the

role of intention. At root we can choose between intending to do God's will or intending to despise it. If I do a deed with a good intention, then my deed is good even if its outcome is evil. Similarly, if I do a deed that appears good, but with an evil intention, the deed is in fact evil. If I intend to commit a crime but am prevented, I am as guilty as if I had done it. A man who aims his bow at a bird and shoots a man he had not noticed is not morally guilty. Abelard extended his concept of intention to those who do not know the Christian revelation. Though they do not know in detail what the will of God is, they do have a knowledge of God's natural law and are thus able to intend to follow it.

TO THINK THROUGH

Do you agree with Abelard's points about intention? Can it be satisfactorily implemented in, say, a state legal system? How does it fit into much contemporary psychological thinking that sees us as influenced by a complex range of factors, not just one straightforward intention?

From time to time the medieval church tried to ensure orthodoxy by banning any works the church leaders thought were heretical. They are universally criticized for this today. What do you think? Is censorship ever justifiable?

For Further Study

Marenbon, J. *The Philosophy of Peter Abelard*. Cambridge: Cambridge University Press, 1997.

BERNARD OF CLAIRVAUX

Dijon, France (1090–1153). Of noble family, Bernard entered the Cistercian order in 1113 and was abbot of Clairvaux from 1115 until his death. Though he openly deplored the involvement of the pope in worldly matters, he became very influential in ecclesiastical affairs in an age when these seem to have lost sight of most of the principles taught by Christ. Popes fought with antipopes and with emperors. It was the time of the Crusades, and those who dared to disagree with the ecclesiastical authorities were savagely persecuted.

A gifted speaker and writer, Bernard saw himself as the defender of orthodoxy. He encouraged and supported a number of writers in the area of philosophical theology and led the orthodox reaction to Abelard and others who, he felt, had become excessively rationalistic. He has been called "the last of the

Fathers" in that he was the last person to write in the traditional way of speculative theologians, without using dialectic.

Philosophically speaking, Bernard's main significance is that he presents an alternative to the developing rationalism of the twelfth century. Bernard was a mystic. He had personal experiences of mystical and ecstatic union with God. For him the heart of Christianity was not intellectual or theological, but a personal relationship with God. This relationship was primarily one of love. It involved the will rather than the intellect, and it was open to those many ordinary believers who knew nothing of the dizzy heights of intellectual debate.

Bernard saw the goal of life as "to know Jesus, and Jesus crucified." The pathway to this knowledge is through humility, love, and contemplation. The culmination is the experience of union with God in love, which Bernard could call deification. Though he was aware that the experience was incommunicable, he spoke of it in terms of a drop of water falling into a large amount of wine and taking on the taste and color of the wine.

But this union is not the more extreme form of union spoken of by some mystics in which the person somehow becomes God. For Bernard it is our will that merges with God's will; the individual and God remain distinct.

TO THINK THROUGH

Does Christianity have to follow either the mystic way or the way of reason? Can the two modes be combined?

The trend in the twelfth century to value highly the role of reason was to dominate Western thinking for the next eight hundred years. Even today, in the middle of an antireason reaction, many people still make reason the foundation of all their beliefs. Is this is a good thing? What made rationalism so attractive for those eight centuries? Why didn't it arise before? Where do you stand on the issue, compared with, say, Tertullian, Augustine, Anselm, Abelard, and Bernard?

SIXTEEN

STARTING SOMEWHERE ELSE

ISLAMIC AND JEWISH PHILOSOPHY

In this chapter we look at the main thinkers in the Islamic and Jewish traditions up to the twelfth century.

ISLAMIC PHILOSOPHY

Islam arose in the seventh century. With the help of the sword it spread very rapidly, largely at the expense of Christianity. The relationship between the two religions was generally one of firm hostility for the first five centuries of Islam's existence, but from the twelfth century onward, Islamic philosophy began to be read sympathetically by Christian thinkers. A factor here was that Islamic philosophy, like the Augustinian synthesis, had significant roots in Greek philosophy. In particular, it was influenced by Aristotle, whose star was rising in the West in the twelfth and thirteenth centuries.

Muhammad. Mecca (c. 570–632). Originally a merchant, Muhammad was met by the angel Gabriel, who gave him the revelations contained in the Qur'an. The most important of these is that God is one. In Mecca at the time, many gods were worshiped; Allah was just one among many. According to the Qur'an, only Allah is to be worshiped, and although Jewish and Christian prophets are to be acknowledged, Muhammad is his last and greatest prophet.

The Qur'an teaches a simple practical religion with five basic requirements known as the Five Pillars of Islam.

1. Affirming at least once "There is no God but Allah, and Muhammad is his prophet."
2. Prayer.
3. Almsgiving.
4. Observing a month's daytime fast during Ramadan.
5. A pilgrimage to Mecca.

Muhammad set up a religious community in Medina in 622. The new religion grew rapidly and, as a result of the Arab conquests, within a hundred years dominated both the East as far as India and the West along North Africa into Spain. In 661 the movement divided into two groups, the Sunni (the larger, more traditional group) and the Shi'ites.

Islam and philosophy.
Before the Islamic conquests, Arabs had struggled to wrest a living from the desert and so had had little time for philosophizing. But their victories gave them more wealth and thus more leisure and put them in touch with the riches of Greek and Roman thought. By the eighth century they were translating Greek texts into Arabic. The strongest influence on them was Aristotle, though the Aristotelianism they developed was in part tinged with Neoplatonism. The chief areas of interest in specifically philosophical debate were ontology (the philosophy of what is), especially the nature and knowledge of God; creation; free will, prophecy; justice and politics; and immortality. Along with philosophy they explored math, astronomy, astrology, zoology, and chemistry. Though the pursuit of philosophy (in its widest sense, including science and medicine) was encouraged and supported by the state, philosophical speculation that touched on theological issues was generally looked on with suspicion by the teachers of the Qur'an, not least because it was associated with Christianity and paganism.

One of the main tasks the philosophers set for themselves was to find a way that faith and reason could live together, allowing an acceptable coexistence of Greek and Qur'anic thought. Though there were some who argued for the submission of philosophy to theology, their main thrust was toward the separation of the two disciplines. This separatist Islamic tradition stands in contrast to the dominant Western tradition, which, for all its weaknesses, had developed a method of enabling theology and philosophy to work together.

As a result, the discovery of the Islamic tradition, linked as it was with the rediscovery of the works of Aristotle, opened up in the West the possibility of a new understanding of the relationship between philosophy and theology. Instead of working with theology, philosophy could stand over against it, even stand in judgment on it. Philosophy could come of age, dispense with any form of authority, and function entirely independently.

The vision that philosophy could dispense with any form of external authority was one that was to fuel the Enlightenment, and in many ways it was a very fruitful one. It was, however, a mistaken one. Philosophy never can be "pure." It always has to have something to work on. Sherlock Holmes, for all his genius in logical deduction, had to start with certain data. "Data, data, data," he cried. "I can't make bricks without clay." Ibn Rushd claimed that philosophical speculation should not be trammeled by naive or theological understanding of the Qur'an. It should break free from the theologians' way of seeing things, their worldview. But, for him, the breaking free was only in order to submit to Aristotle. One worldview was replaced by another. The authority of the Qur'an was replaced by the authority of Aristotle. We may choose to believe, of course, that Aristotle's worldview is more accurate than the Qur'an's. But this doesn't alter the fact that, whichever we follow, philosophy is not "pure." We will be seeing later that, for all its strengths, Enlightenment philosophy was in just the same position. It managed at last to shake off the authority of the Christian revelation and even the authority of Aristotle. But it did so by replacing them with the authority of the modern scientific worldview. At first this was Newtonian science; then, last century, as science changed its worldview, philosophy followed it and accepted the post-Newtonian worldview.

God and the world. God is one. Islam was prepared to accept that the God of the Jews and the Christians could be identified with Allah, but it firmly rejected any concept of Trinity or the deity of Christ. God is creator of the world by an act of will. In contrast to Neoplatonism, and more in keeping with Aristotle, Islam saw the world as real and good. The Qur'an is the Word of God in an even stronger sense than Christians viewed the Bible. One school of thought saw it as coeternal with God; its meaning is one with the essence of God.

AL-FARABI

Turkestan (870–950). Al-Farabi studied under Christian teachers and spent much of his life teaching in Baghdad. His main source of philosophical thinking was Aristotle; he came to be known as "the second teacher," after Aristotle. But he was also influenced by Plato and Neoplatonism; and believing that all truth is one, he sought to synthesize their concepts. Though stressing the role of logic and reason, he carefully avoided conflict with orthodox Islamic theologians, believing that popular beliefs were a symbolic expression of philosophical truths. Theology, he said, was concerned with God and his attributes, personal and community living, and the life to come. Philosophy is concerned with logic, physics, metaphysics, and ethics. In this he set a trend for the separation of Islamic theology and philosophy in the future.

Al-Farabi argued the existence of God as a first cause or prime mover. His general worldview was Neoplatonic, with its hierarchical structure and concept of emanation. He was a mystic, following Sufism, a strong mystical tradition in Islam that sought union in love with God through *gnosis*.

IBN SINA

Bukhara, Central Asia (980–1037). Ibn Sina was known in the West as Avicenna. He studied Greek philosophy and the Qur'an from his childhood, as well as Arabic literature, math, physics, and law. He was skilled in medicine, and his medical writings were accepted as authoritative until the Renaissance. His influence in philosophy was equally great; he was referred to as "The Supreme Master." He wrote over a hundred books covering a wide range of issues from logic and ontology to politics and prophecy. He traveled extensively, practicing as a doctor, and led an adventurous life, often pursued and at times imprisoned by his enemies. The orthodox theologians were suspicious of him. He developed a close-knit system of philosophy that owed much to Aristotle and something to Al-Farabi, Plato, and Plotinus, but which, in effect, was essentially his own.

Philosophy. Philosophy is to be divided into

- Logic.
- Speculative philosophy, comprising physics, math, and theology. Theology was further divided into that which concerned the philosopher, that is, natural theology and ontology, and that which concerned the theologian, that is, Islamic themes.
- Practical philosophy, made up of ethics, economics and politics.

God and the world. God is absolutely good; absolute goodness must necessarily radiate out from him. God is necessary being (as opposed to contingent being), so all he does must be necessary. The creation therefore must be necessary; it cannot be "might not have been creation." It must also be created from eternity, as opposed to being created at a specific moment, since God is eternal. Nor is there any free choice in creation or any free will in created things; things have to be as they are, since they are the necessary expression of a necessary God. Since God cannot make something unlike himself, he cannot create matter directly. Instead, he creates, or rather emanates, an intelligence, which then creates another intelligence, and so on, to form a hierarchical series of ten intelligences, moving from simplicity to multiplicity and thus eventually creating the world. This scheme has a very Neoplatonic feel to it, but, even so, in keeping with Aristotle's emphasis, Ibn Sina rejected the Neoplatonic low view of matter. It also has a rather pantheistic feel, but Ibn Sina specifically defended himself against pantheism by stressing the basic difference between God and everything else, in that in him alone essence and existence merge.

Reason. Reason was central to Ibn Sina's system. For him God is pure intellect, pure thought; he creates through thinking the intelligences. As the creative thought moves down the levels of being until eventually the human intellect is formed, so the human intellect can rise up the levels of being to God, the ultimate object of knowledge.

Essence and existence. All things have both existence and essence. In God existence and essence are one, but in created things existence and essence can be distinguished. Essence is what makes a thing what it is, its essential characteristics. Existence is the state of existing. A thing can have essence without having existence. I can, for example, describe to you all the characteristics of my dream (but nonexisting) chocolate cake. But a thing cannot have existence without essence. If a chocolate cake exists, it must have chocolate cake-like characteristics. So an object's essence does not entail its existence; to get from an essence to an existing object requires an already existing external object as its cause. To get from chocolate cakeness to an actual cake requires a baker. This establishes the primacy of existence over essence (cakeness will never become cake without an existing baker).

Necessity and the chain of causes. Every existing thing, then, has to have a preexisting (or "prior in rank") thing as its external cause. This lands us in a chain of causes, which cannot be infinite. So there must be an uncaused first cause, a necessary Being. In keeping with his determinism ("nothing has free will"), Ibn Sina saw all the links in the chain as necessary. That is, God necessarily emanates the intelligences; he has no option but to do so. They in turn necessarily emanate the next in the chain and thus in the world and so on until bakers necessarily bake cakes. Therefore, in a sense, everything is necessary. And so there is no such thing as a contingent ("might not have been") object. When we use the concept of contingency, Ibn Sina says, we are referring to the fact that the object is caused; it is not a necessary object in the way God is necessary being. We are not saying it is a "might not have been" object, since it is totally determined by an external cause and, through the chain of cause, ultimately by God.

IBN RUSHD

Cordoba, Spain (1126–1198). Ibn Rushd (pronounced like *pushed*) was known in the West as Averroës (pronounced ah-*ver*-uh-weez or ah-ver-*oh*-eez). Islamic civilization flourished in Spain from the tenth century onward and produced a number of philosophers. Ibn Rushd was the greatest of these; his work influenced Western thought until the seventeenth century, though it had much less impact in the East. He wrote in Arabic; his works were translated into Hebrew and from Hebrew into Latin, and so became available to Western thinkers.

The son of a judge, Ibn Rushd studied medicine, math, science, philosophy, theology, and law. He practiced both law and medicine. He had a very high opinion of Aristotle; most of his works are in the form of commentaries on Aristotle's writings, though often the form of the ideas is Ibn Rushd's rather than Aristotle's. He was particularly concerned to purge the Islamic Aristotelian (Peripatetic) tradition of Neoplatonism. He argued that Islam and Aristotelian philosophy could live happily together, provided we understand their respective and very different roles correctly.

Like Ibn Sina, he produced a wide-ranging system of philosophy, including political philosophy, in which he argued that philosophers and not theologians should lead the state. In some respects his system was more theologically orthodox than Ibn Sina's; for example, it had a less pantheistic concept of God. However, in other places he went against the theologians, for example, in denying personal immortality. After a successful and relatively peaceful life at the Spanish court, Ibn Rushd fell out of favor, not least with the theologians, and he fled from Cordoba and eventually went to Morocco, where he died.

Ibn Rushd marks the end of the flowering of Islamic Peripatetic (Aristotelian) philosophy. Soon after his death, much of Spain was recaptured by

Christian rulers, and Islam in general entered a period during which philosophical speculation was strongly discouraged.

Theology and philosophy.
Ibn Rushd firmly believed that the philosophy of Aristotle was pure and total philosophical truth. One of his aims in his commentaries on Aristotle was to separate "pure" philosophy from the theological accretions (whether Neoplatonic or Islamic) that marred the work of Ibn Sina and Al-Farabi. Philosophy and theology, for him, were to be kept clearly apart. Philosophy was superior to theology and should be given the last word.

However, there are times when the two disciplines speak about the same issues. For example, they both speak about God and the soul. What happens, then, when they contradict each other? Ibn Rushd's answer is that they in fact don't contradict each other. They are both expressing truth but in different ways. In fact, there are three types of people—philosophers, theologians, and ordinary believers—and therefore three types of thinking. The Qur'an (and in this we can see its miraculous nature) speaks differently to each. Ordinary people can grasp its immediate allegorical truth. Theologians can dig into its inner hidden meaning. Philosophers, best of all, can grasp its highest and most real meaning. Individuals of each type should limit themselves to their appropriate level of understanding. It is a mistake to try and combine them or to try and expound philosophical truths to ordinary believers or theologians.

Philosophy, then, according to Ibn Rushd, expresses truth directly; other approaches express it allegorically. Ordinary people rightly believe the picture language of the Qur'an. The philosopher, however, goes behind the pictures to the truth as it really is. This "double-truth" theory has been taken up several times in the history of philosophy, not least in the twentieth century. It can be traced back as far as Plato, who in the *Republic* suggested that in the state where philosophers rule, ordinary people should be told a myth, a "noble lie" that they accept as the truth, while philosophers alone know the real truth that lies behind the myth.

God and the world.
Ibn Rushd retained Ibn Sina's levels of being from God to matter, including the ten intelligences. However, he purged it of the Neoplatonic concept of emanation and substituted a more dynamic concept. Creation is not simply God emanating; it is God in action, his knowledge actively involved in the world. However, Ibn Rushd continued to hold that creation was necessary and eternal, that is, it was not at a specific point of time, and God had no choice but to create.

AL-GHAZALI

Tus, Iran (1058–1111). After teaching law and theology for some years in Baghdad, Al-Ghazali renounced his very influential post and turned to the Islamic mystical tradition of Sufism. He wrote major works in theology and mysticism. His autobiography, *The Deliverance from Error*, tells how he sought truth in orthodox Islamic theology and in philosophy but failed to find it. Neither can give certain knowledge since neither can stand up to the test of reason; it cannot establish the truth of revelation or definitively prove the arguments of the philosophers. Truth can be found only in the mystical ecstatic experience of Sufism, granted by divine grace. Al-Ghazali's influence in the Islamic world was considerable; it has been compared to that of Aquinas in the Christian world.

TO THINK THROUGH

What do you think about developing a "pure" philosophy, independent of any presuppositions or worldview? Is it possible? Is it desirable?

The theory of "double truth" has taken all sorts of forms in the last eight centuries. One of its recent applications is by those who say, for example, that the resurrection is historically false but theologically true. What do you think about it?

For Further Study

Nars, S., and O. Leaman, eds. *History of Islamic Philosophy*. London: Routledge, 1996.

JEWISH PHILOSOPHY

Philo, at the time of Christ, had sought to work out a system that united the insights of traditional Jewish thought and contemporary philosophy. But we know of no Jewish thinker who worked out a comparable system until the tenth century. From then on there was a flowering of Jewish philosophical thinking. A distinctive feature in the eleventh and twelfth centuries was a range of philosophical proofs for the existence of God.

IBN GABIROL

Malaga, Spain (c. 1021–c. 1058). Ibn Gabirol was mainly known in the Western tradition as Avicebron; some scholastics thought he was a Muslim; others thought he was a Christian. His most famous work, written in Arabic but soon translated into Latin, was known as *Fons Vitae*, "The Fountain of Life." It incorporates a number of Neoplatonic ideas, though its contents remain basically true to Jewish insights. It is presented as a dialogue and is an early example of the medieval scholastic form of arguing by piling up demonstration upon demonstration. For Ibn Gabirol this method goes back to the Jewish tradition enshrined in the Talmud, which is presented in dialectical form, that is, incorporating a range of views or comments by former generations of interpreters of the Jewish law, all set down side by side.

God and the world. Ibn Gabirol was concerned to solve the problem of how physical matter could come from something that is nonphysical. Neoplatonism, viewing God as transcendent, linked him to matter through a chain of intermediaries. But these intermediaries took the form of thoughts or intelligences or spirits, gradually increasing in complexity as they moved down the hierarchy. But that still left the problem of the final step from spirit to physical matter. Ibn Gabirol's solution was to use "matter" to describe everything except God. Every object, except God, is composed of matter and form, or rather forms—the matter that makes up Socrates is shaped by the forms corporeality, humanity, whiteness, etc. Some objects, that is physical or material objects, are composed of physical matter plus forms; other objects, that is spiritual objects, are composed of spiritual matter and forms. The concept of objects being made up of matter plus form goes back to Aristotle and was to be known in scholastic writings as hylomorphism (Gk. *hyle*, "matter"; *morphe*, "shape or form"). To describe creation Ibn Gabirol rejected the Neoplatonic concept of emanation and made it an act of God's will, thus avoiding determinism.

JUDAH HALEVI

Toledo, Spain (c. 1075–c. 1141). Judah Halevi, a gifted poet and an ardent Jewish traditionalist and nationalist, reacted against the infiltration of philosophy into Jewish thought. He vigorously advocated the removal of all philosophical ideas and a return to "the God of Abraham, Isaac, and Jacob." The fact that philosophers don't agree among themselves is evidence that human reason is inadequate to show us ultimate truth. Only God can do that, and he has done so in revelation. While the God of the philosophers is distant and uninvolved in the world, the true God has come to us; we meet him not in rationalistic contemplation, but in passionate communion and love. Despite this attack on the kind of philosophy that sought to exalt itself above revelation, Halevi allowed a place for what we would call natural theology; the nations who do not have God's revelation can know his existence and moral law through reason. He traveled to the Holy Land, determined to die in the land of his fathers, and, according to legend, was killed at the gates of Jerusalem.

MOSES MAIMONIDES

Cordova, Spain (1135–1204). Forced to flee from Spain at age thirteen, Moses Maimonides eventually settled in Egypt, where he practiced medicine. He wrote extensively on medicine and Jewish law. He was an enthusiastic philosopher, influenced mostly by Aristotle but also by Neoplatonism. Though he conceded that philosophy unaided could not teach us final truth, he believed it could be used to defend some of the truths of revelation, and he set himself the task of harmonizing revealed truth with philosophy. For those who accepted the Old Testament revelation but found it hard to square with current science and philosophy, he wrote in Arabic his famous *Guide for the Perplexed*. His ideas strongly influenced thirteenth-century Christian thinkers, not least Thomas Aquinas.

Maimonides used three philosophical arguments for the existence of God—the need of a prime mover, a need of a first cause, and the need of a necessary being. However, he said, beyond his existence, philosophy cannot tell us anything positive about God or his attributes. The best it can do is speak in negatives. It cannot tell us how God created the world; Maimonides rejected in favor of the Old Testament account the view of Al-Farabi and Ibn Sina that the universe is eternally created. Their arguments are not conclusive, he said, because they ignore the fact that both time and matter were something very different before creation from what they are now. However, the fact that time did not exist before the creation as we know it now allows us to accept what philosophy is meaning when it speaks of God eternally creating the world; it is possible to say that if creation was outside of time, then it was timeless.

TO THINK THROUGH

What do you think about the concept that people can know about God's existence and moral law through "natural theology"?

Did God freely create? What arguments can you think of on each side of the debate?

SEVENTEEN

OLD RIVALS MEET AGAIN

PLATO AND ARISTOTLE
IN THE MEDIEVAL PERIOD

In this chapter we pause to take stock of the influence of Platonism on medieval thought and to contrast it with Aristotelianism, especially those aspects that were to have a major impact on Western thought from the thirteenth century onward. We end the chapter by looking briefly at the reaction of Bonaventure, a thinker who was reluctant to accept the revolution.

ONE OF THE HALLMARKS OF THE MEDIEVAL PERIOD WAS the appeal to authority. And in matters philosophical everyone acknowledged that the two greatest authorities were Plato and Aristotle.

Ironically, for most of the medieval period very few of the works of either Plato or Aristotle were available in the West. But that made no difference to their status as authorities. There were strong second- and third-hand traditions, or perhaps rather adaptations, of what they had taught. And, in any case, for the most part, medievals were more interested in a living, developing tradition than in meticulous faithfulness to a source. The many centuries of discussion and interpretation and development were not to be ignored; they were all part of their rich heritage.

AUGUSTINIANISM AND THE PLATONIST TRADITION

From Augustine until the thirteenth century, Plato and Platonism were dominant. Augustine set the trend; the Augustinian tradition is basically Platonist.

It wasn't that Aristotle was deliberately ignored or rejected. What was known of Aristotle, mainly his logic, was accepted and set alongside other authorities. But much of the teaching of Aristotle that ran counter to Plato was unavailable, and it was easy for the medievals to assume that, since Plato was the master and Aristotle the pupil, we can gain all we need to know directly from Plato.

There are three key concepts of the Augustinian tradition: philosophy and revealed truth, the priority of ideas, and the hierarchy of being.

Philosophy and revealed truth.

Foundational to the Augustinian tradition was its attitude to the relationship between philosophy and revealed Christian truth, between what we accept through reason and what we accept on authority. Here, as in other issues, there was considerable variation of emphasis within the tradition; the appeal to authority was not a straitjacket, particularly when authorities differed. But at root there was agreement on five principles.

1. Our primary authority is God and the truth he gives us through revelation, which we accept in a spirit of humility.
2. Beliefs precede rational understanding. Reason alone and unaided cannot establish ultimate truth.
3. God is active in all our knowing. He reveals himself and truths about himself to us. He is also active, though we are not conscious of it, when we are using our reason to discover truth. Without his illumination no truth could be known.
4. Reason is God-given and God-illuminated and thus is to be accepted, trusted, and used fully, both in the area of ordinary knowledge and in the area of Christian truth. Since the truths of reason and the truths of revelation are in the last analysis one, there normally will be no clash between what reason and revelation tell us.
5. Where there is a clash, reason, enlightened by God's revelation, should work to resolve it.

The application of these principles gave those in the Augustinian tradition a basis for confidence in reason. They were able to confront and confound both skepticism and relativism without retreating into fideism, that is, the response that says, "I can't rationally defend my position, but I'm still going to hold to it." It also allowed them a considerable amount of freedom in their use of reason. The tradition was able to allow philosophical speculation. It was also able to state the case for Christianity in philosophical terms, that is, without needing to appeal to the authority of revelation.

The priority of ideas.

A second key element of the Augustinian tradition was its conviction that truth and reality lie behind the things we experience in the world around us. The tables and trees and goodness and beauty we see in the world are not ultimate reality. After all, they come and go. Rather, they are expressions of ultimate reality, both of an ultimate concept of what a tree is and of ultimate goodness.

Plato, of course, had located the reality that lies behind what we see in the world in his forms. The Augustinian tradition adapted this and for the most part located it in the mind of God. The forms are God's thoughts or ideas. God thinks the idea of a tree. All trees in the world are expressions or exemplars of his thought. God is goodness and beauty; all goodness and beauty in the world are expressions of his goodness and beauty.

This is not to say that the Augustinians were particularly skeptical about the dependability of their perceptions of things they observed around them in the world, or that they followed the Platonic tradition in viewing the world around them as evil in itself. But it did mean that the movement in their thought was from the idea to the individual object, from the heavenly to the earthly, from the universal to the particular, and not in the opposite direction. We don't start with individual objects and then try to discover universal truths. We start with God and his truth and understand the individual table or expression of beauty in terms of the eternally true ideas in his mind. This priority of the ideas in the mind of God links closely, of course, with the priority of God-revealed truth over what we can discover through reason.

The hierarchy of being.

A third significant aspect of the Augustinian tradition was its way of viewing reality hierarchically. There are levels or degrees or gradations of being. This concept has its roots in Plato. For him trees in the world are less real than the form of the tree. But the main stimulus came from the complex systems of the Neoplatonists, who needed a series of gradations to move from their wholly other God to the very inferior world around us. Christianity, with its doctrine of creation and incarnation, didn't need to follow this system in order to safeguard God's uniqueness, but it fit well with Augustine's account of evil, and it helped to build up a composite and integrated view of the world.

God, the Augustinians believed, is the one true reality. In him are all the perfections, all the ideas, all existences. If we begin to move from God to the world or to objects in the world, such as a beautiful tree or a good man, we are not moving from one reality to another. Rather, we are moving from reality to a lower level of reality, a lesser reality, something less real. In the case of evil, of course, this was a particularly fruitful concept. It saved Augustine having to allow that evil was a thing. Evil is not a thing; it is the absence of the reality goodness. The deeper we go into evil, the further we are moving away from reality toward nonbeing. Total unmitigated evil is nothingness. So, for the Augustinians, everything is on a scale from being to nonbeing.

A noteworthy aspect of these three key elements of the Augustinian tradition is that each is theocentric. Reason is not ultimate; God as truth and giver of truth is. We depend on his illumination even for ordinary knowledge of things in the world. We understand the particulars in the light of his universals; we understand the world in the light of his ideas. Reality in any of its forms is totally dependent on him.

The Augustinians set themselves the task of building up a composite and integrated view of the world, using both revealed truth and philosophy. They started with God. This meant that they gave priority to his truth. But it also meant that they were able to establish their confidence in reason and philosophy on a firm basis. They had what the later Enlightenment lacked. So their rationalism was able to last much longer than Enlightenment rationalism. Nevertheless, in the end Augustinianism by and large gave way to the Aristotelianism of the thirteenth century. This was not so much because it had been proved to be inadequate. Rather, the new way of seeing things opened up new possibilities that were too exciting to be ignored.

AUGUSTINIANISM AND ARISTOTELIAN LOGIC

Aristotle's system was an integrated whole. Nevertheless, for much of the medieval period, the only aspects of his philosophy that were known or used in the West were those that arose from his logic. Here Boethius was a key figure, not just because he was responsible for translating and commenting on Aristotle's logic, but because there were elements of his approach, such as his careful definition of terms, that were specifically Aristotelian. We have already looked at the key concepts in Aristotle's logic, but since the concepts tend to seem obscure to most of us in the twenty-first century, it is worth summarizing them again.

Ultimate reality: substance. The most significant difference between Plato and Aristotle lies in their answer to the question "Where do we locate ultimate or basic reality?" For Plato, the answer was in the forms, that is, not in objects in the world. For Aristotle, though he retained a concept of the forms, basic reality was in objects in the world. Here is a key shift, a change of direction in thinking. Platonists, and thus Augustinians, start with the forms or the ideas in the mind of God and understand the objects in the world in light of them. We could say they approach the world "from above." Aristotelians move in the other direction: They start "from below," with objects in the world. Where they move to after this has been a matter of debate for two thousand years and more.

The reality that is to be found in objects in the world was variously described by the Aristotelian tradition, often using a phrase like "that which is" rather than a noun. However, the traditional term has been "substance," which comes from the Latin word meaning "standing under" (our idiom would say "lying under"). A substance is basic. It really exists. Its accidents may change. That is, we may observe the substance presented in a number of different ways. Socrates, the substance, may appear weary or lively, young or old. Weariness or youth are contingent, short-lived additions to Socrates; they are "accidents"; they don't belong to his basic substance, which remains unchanged.

Aristotle distinguished what he called primary and secondary substances. A primary substance is an individual object such as Socrates. A secondary substance is a generic species such as man. Medievals tended to use "substance" of Aristotle's secondary substances and specified "individual substance" when they meant his primary substance.

Essence, genera, and species.

Another term that arose from Aristotle's definitions was "essence" (translating Aristotle's phrase "the what it is to be"), the thing or things that go to make a substance the specific substance that it is. So the essence of a tree is treeness; and the essence of a man is manness. Two other terms are genus (plural *genera*) and species. In classifying groups, genus refers to the more inclusive group, higher up the scheme of things. Species refers to the subgroup. So when the medievals classify a human being as a rational animal, animal is the genus, and man is the species, while Socrates is the individual substance.

Incorporating Aristotle's logic into Augustinianism.

The concept of substance and the associated aspects of Aristotelian logic came relatively early into the West, largely through the work of Boethius. Perhaps surprisingly, they were able to be adapted and absorbed into the Augustinian scheme without challenging its theocentricity. This was because the Augustinians were able to redefine substance. A twenty-first-century mind would naturally tend to redefine substance by going lower in the Platonist scale of being. We wouldn't want to say Socrates is a basic substance, since we would say he is in fact an accidental collection of various chemical substances. And the chemicals themselves are not basic, because they are made up of atoms. And the atoms are not basic, because they are made up of subnuclear particles. And the subnuclear particles aren't basic, because they are made of energy. So, unless we can think of anywhere else to go, we would want to say that substance is energy. And Aristotle's scheme allows us to do that. After all, we are not very far away from the Greeks who said there were four substances—earth, air, fire, and water.

The Augustinians, however, went in the opposite direction to redefine substance. This, again, was something they could do and still stay within the spirit of Aristotle's logic. If Aristotle himself had conceded that "man," the collective "species" to which the substance Socrates belongs, could itself be called a substance, then it is legitimate to continue to use the concept of substance as we go up, rather than down, the hierarchy of being. So we can then apply it to those ideas in the mind of God that for the Augustinians had taken the place of Plato's forms. If, then, substance is ultimate reality and the ideas in the mind of God are seen as substances, then Augustinianism has preserved the ideas in the mind of God as ultimate reality.

Universals.

At the end of the eleventh century a major difference between Plato and Aristotle came to the fore in the debate over universals. Plato had said that his forms existed independently of their particular expressions. Aristotle had denied this. The term "universals" took the place of forms in the later medieval debate. It covered those concepts that aren't specific objects, or "particulars." Socrates is a particular. The genus and species to which he belongs (animal and man) are not particulars. They are generalizations, universals. The big question was whether or not these universals really exist. The Augustinian tradition, with its Platonism, wanted to say that they do; they are real. Those influenced by Aristotle were inclined to say that they do not exist. The particulars are what exist. Universals are just an abstract concept, a term, a name we give to a generic idea. Those who believed universals were real were called Realists. Those who felt the term was just a name for an abstract concept were called Nominalists (from Lat. *nomen*, "name").

TO THINK THROUGH

The debate goes on. It is still with us in the twenty-first century. But if you had lived in the thirteenth century, where would you have started your understanding of the world--from above or from below?

AREAS OF CONFLICT

The Augustinians had managed to incorporate Aristotelian logic into their system. When his whole worldview, including his physics, metaphysics, and epistemology, became available, they were set the much harder task of incorporating these too. Failure to do so would be to surrender their principle that the truths of reason and the truths of revelation are one. With a lesser philosopher, it would have been open to them to demonstrate by rational argument that his philosophy was false. But Aristotle was already highly revered within Augustinianism and was rapidly becoming even more revered in the Western world at large. In the new universities in particular, especially at Paris, which in the thirteenth century was the most influential center of learning in the West, interest in the ideas of Aristotle dominated everything else. The scene was set for a major clash.

Theocentricity. The key difference between Aristotle's system and the Augustinian was the issue of theocentricity. Everything in the Augustinian system came from God and returned to God. In Aristotle's system most things could function quite happily even if there were no God. It is true, of course, that God didn't play a hugely significant role in Plato himself; it was the Neoplatonists' system that had made him so foundational and indispensable. But that was of small importance. Had "the Platonists" not given God a major role in their system, it is highly unlikely that Augustine would have married their philosophy to Christianity, a revelation that was inescapably God-centered.

Other areas of conflict. It wasn't just that the Augustinians were afraid that the introduction of the Aristotelian system would attack the very basis of Christianity by dispensing with the need for God. In addition, the very existence of a system that was so radically different from theirs yet appeared to work so well and provide such a useful way of viewing the world attacked their foundational concept of the unity of all truth.

More specifically Aristotelianism seemed to conflict with Augustinianism in the following areas:

- In the Islam-influenced form in which it first reached the West, it presented a much more remote and less personal God than the God of Christianity.
- Additionally, in the hands of the Islamic philosophers, it appeared to deny freedom in God and human freedom.
- Also, as interpreted by the Islamic philosophers, it segregated theology and philosophy, and gave the last word to philosophy. It might even teach a theory of double truth: Something could be true in theology and false in philosophy.
- It saw the world as eternal; it has always existed and always will.
- In it the world operates according to natural processes; it doesn't appear to need any input from God.
- The natural processes in the world, including human life, are self-sufficient according to Aristotelianism. They don't point outside of themselves to God. They don't return to God as the ultimate goal of their being.
- Aristotle's theory of knowledge functions without any real concept of forms; it doesn't need the ideas in the mind of God.
- Nor does it need divine illumination. The human mind can know things without any help from God.
- It has a very different concept of the soul, challenging the concept of immortality.

THE REDISCOVERY OF ARISTOTLE

It is not easy for us to imagine the excitement that the availability of Aristotle's work created in the thirteenth century. Until then the West had known only some of his writings on logic. Now a full range of his teaching was available for study, on science, metaphysics, ethics, and psychology, together with the accumulated wisdom of commentaries and interpretations.

At first some attempt was made to control or lessen his impact. In Paris, for instance, some of his works were banned from the educational syllabus in 1210. But the ban was removed five years later, and by 1255 almost all his works had been placed on the curriculum. There were perhaps three factors that caused hesitation in some. The first was natural conservatism in the face of the potential threat to the long alliance between Christianity and Platonism. A surge of enthusiasm for new learning was good, but it posed a substantial threat to what many saw as a secure tradition they did not wish to see overthrown.

Second, at first sight Aristotle seemed to disagree with the teaching of the church on a number of points. Not only was this threatening to the traditionalists, but it also troubled those who had a high respect for the power of the human intellect and the wisdom of the philosophers. With the texts in front of them, there was no way scholars could escape the fact that in places Aristotle appeared to contradict aspects of the Christian revelation. While, with the help of Plotinus and Augustine, Plato and Christianity could be put together into a coherent and satisfying system, Christianity and Aristotle just didn't seem to fit together.

Third, the translations and commentaries that were available in the first half of the thirteenth century had been done mainly by Islamic thinkers and had inevitably been affected by their beliefs. For many, despite the history of Christian/Muslim conflicts, this was not a major problem. The West had viewed Plato largely through Neoplatonist eyes for centuries and thus could cope with viewing Aristotle through Muslim eyes. But others saw dangers in this. A positive outcome of their concern from the middle of the century onward was the retranslating of the original Greek texts into Latin and the writing of new commentaries by Christian scholars, a work in which Aquinas shared.

The thirteenth-century thinkers who chose to remain generally faithful to Augustinianism are not to be seen simply as traditionalist. They were doing what had always been done—citing authorities and using them as a basis for exploring new ideas and new applications of unchanging truth. They were not, for instance, so set in their ways as to refuse to use Aristotelian insights when they suited them. Among them was Bonaventure.

BONAVENTURE

Bagnorea, Tuscany, Italy (1221–1274). Bonaventure was educated at Paris, where he became a member of the Franciscan order. He was later minister general of the order, and he became a cardinal in 1274. He studied and appreciated the newly discovered works of Aristotle but nevertheless sought to maintain a basically Augustinian position.

Aspects of Aristotelianism he rejected include:

- Aristotle's rejection of Plato's forms, which Bonaventure, solidly in the Augustinian tradition, took to be ideas in the mind of God.
- Belief in the eternity of the world, that is, that the world had no beginning. Bonaventure believed he could refute Aristotle here by rational argument.
- The immortality of the soul.

On the positive side, Bonaventure argued:

- The goal of human life is the happiness that comes from union with God. If philosophy becomes an end in itself and leads us away from God, then it is failing in the very thing that should be its main interest.
- Philosophy, using reason, can show us many truths; but for the full truth about God, revelation is essential.
- Creation emanates from God and returns to God. However, Bonaventure removed two of the traditional elements of this Neoplatonic concept. First, this emanation is not necessary; God chooses to create. And, second, there are no intermediate intelligences; creation is direct.
- The illumination of God is needed for human certain knowledge. Our sense experience and even our reason are insufficient on their own; they cannot reach infallibility. Since certainty requires infallibility, only God can give certainty. Bonaventure discussed the issue of illumination at length, acknowledging the distinction between illumination needed for our knowledge of God or the divine ideas and that required for ordinary knowing, and seeking to analyze how God's illumination applied in ordinary knowing. Faced with the options that in all knowing we are actually encountering the divine ideas, or that our minds have the power to know ordinary truth without any need of involvement of the divine ideas, he adopted a compromise. In ordinary knowing two things are happening. Our natural cognitive faculty is work. But at the same time we are thinking divine truth, and so the illumination of God is needed. We are not normally aware of this illumination. The distinction between ordinary knowing and the direct knowing of God is that in the latter case our natural cognitive faculty is not involved.

- Our goal in this life should be to move from contemplating God's works in creation to contemplating God himself. Bonaventure wrote several books that have become classics in the mystical tradition. He expounded "three ways" to God: the purgative way of conscience, expelling sin; the illuminative way of intellect, imitating Christ; and the unitive way of wisdom, uniting us to God.

TO THINK THROUGH

To what extent do your sympathies lie with the Platonist tradition or with Aristotelianism? Were people right to view Aristotle's philosophy as a threat? Some would say that any conflict of ideas has the potential to lead to greater understanding and insight; can you think of illustrations of this?

For Further Study

See the books listed at the end of Part 3, pages 227–28.

EIGHTEEN

ALL THIS, AND HE DIED IN HIS FORTIES

THE PHILOSOPHY OF AQUINAS

> In this chapter we look at Thomas Aquinas, the greatest intellectual giant of the medieval period. We are only able to explore a small part of his huge output and to attempt an assessment of his achievement.

THOMAS AQUINAS

Roccasecca, Southern Italy (c. 1225–1274). From 1239 Aquinas studied liberal arts and philosophy at the new University of Naples. While still in his teens, he decided to enter the Dominican order, committing himself to a life of preaching and teaching. After being detained by his family for a year, he went to Paris and Cologne for further study. By his late twenties he was teaching at the University of Paris, which at the time was the most significant center of learning in the West. For the twenty years between then and his death, he wrote and taught, dividing his time between Paris and centers of learning in Italy. He wrote extensively until 1273, when he had an ecstatic experience during Mass that made him decide to stop writing. All he had written, he said, seemed like straw compared with what was revealed to him in that experience.

Aquinas produced about one hundred works, totaling more than eight million words. Many were commentaries on the Scriptures and on Aristotle. Some were defenses of his ideas on various doctrinal topics. His two greatest works (in both senses of the word) were the *Summa contra Gentiles*, "A Summary (or Compendium) Refuting Unbelievers," and the *Summa Theologica*, "Summary of Theology."

Many of Aquinas's ideas were innovative, and he was involved in various controversies during his lifetime. The value of his works was not immediately recognized by all; in fact, some of his works were even formally condemned. Nevertheless, his reputation steadily grew. He was canonized in 1323, and his influence on Roman Catholic thought was enhanced by a papal encyclical in 1879 making him the "chief and master" medieval authority.

THE TASK

Interpretation. Aquinas was confronted with a double challenge: to interpret Aristotle and to integrate him with the Augustinian synthesis of Platonism and Christianity. The need to interpret Aristotle was particularly pressing in Paris in the middle of the thirteenth century. The new learning was giving rise to all sorts of speculations and radical ideas. To the rest of Europe Paris was seen as a center of dangerous speculation and incipient heresy. A number of thinkers, known as the Latin Averroists, were propagating the teachings of Ibn Rushd. They claimed that these were an authentic exposition of Aristotle and used them to challenge orthodox Christian beliefs. Aquinas was convinced that Ibn Rushd's teaching was a serious misrepresentation of Aristotle and set out to counteract the heresies of the Averroists and the speculations of others by expounding Aristotle's true message.

Integration. But the second challenge that faced Aquinas—to show that it was possible to incorporate the substance of Aristotle's teaching into the Christian worldview—was an even more important one that called for all his brilliance and subtlety. For eight hundred years Christianity had been happily married to philosophy. It had used philosophical method and concepts in seeking to understand and defend Christian truths. For all of that period the form of philosophy with which it had engaged had been Platonism, mediated through Neoplatonism and Augustine. Since very little of the actual work of Plato was available, it had been easy for thinkers to assume there was no real conflict between philosophy and Christian truth and to work at integrating the insights on both sides. Equally, with very limited direct knowledge of Aristotle, it had been just as easy to assume that, being Plato's pupil, he had agreed with his master. Greek philosophy, or, rather, philosophy, was one.

But now the new availability of the works of Aristotle presented a serious challenge. It appeared to demonstrate that philosophy was not one. There were forms of philosophy other than Platonism as the West had known it, and these challenged the assumption that "philosophy" was some kind of extrabiblical divine revelation. In particular, Aristotle offered an alternative methodology, a new way of using philosophy, and so a new way of approaching Christian truth. Where some saw this as evidence that Christianity and philosophy of any hue should not be mixed, and others responded by rejecting Aristotle and holding on to the well-tried Augustinian tradition, Aquinas rose to the challenge and set about finding a way to integrate the ideas of Aristotle with the Christian faith.

On the whole Aquinas succeeded admirably, but at a price. For all the skill of his synthesis, there was no escaping from the fact that the new Aristotelianism was less theocentric than the old Neoplatonism. As a result, he can be seen as marking a new beginning in the development of Western thought, a key step away from a worldview that assumed the priority of the eternal and the nonmaterial, toward one that assumed that foundational reality and truth is to be found in the material world around us.

Firmly in the medieval tradition, and with his deep commitment to integration, Aquinas was happy to make use of the ideas of any philosophers, including Ibn Sina and Maimonides. But for him Aristotle was always supreme. In referring to him, he simply spoke of "the philosopher."

KNOWLEDGE

The primacy of empirical knowledge. In ordinary knowledge there are two factors at work, what Aquinas called *cognitio sensibilis* and *cognitio intellectualis*, knowledge through our senses and knowledge through our intellect. Aquinas took the very significant step of adopting the Aristotelian position that sensory knowledge is primary. That is, there can be nothing in our intellect that is not first experienced through our senses. There are no innate ideas. We depend on sense experience for all knowledge. All intellectual understanding derives from sense experience.

Knowledge and God. However, Aquinas sought to retain the Augustinian (and New Testament) theocentricity by stating very clearly that all knowledge is knowledge of God—that is, everything in the world is created by God and expresses his nature. So when we are examining things in the world, we are viewing God. So even those who don't acknowledge God implicitly know him through his works.

Knowledge and the intellect. Knowledge through our intellect depends on knowledge through our senses. It is our intellect getting to work on what our senses tell us. Sense experience gives us raw data; the intellect processes these data and achieves understanding about them. Sense experience sees raindrops, feels wetness, and so on; our intellect concludes that it is raining.

Aquinas saw the process of knowing in active terms. It is not the case, as some Augustinians might seem to believe, that we are simply passive, doing nothing, while God does all the illuminating. Throughout his system Aquinas emphasized the natural powers that human beings have; we can do all sorts of things, including things in the moral sphere, without any divine involvement. Though Aquinas traced these powers back to God who gave them to us, to Augustinians this was getting perilously close to saying we no longer need God in order to be able to think or make moral decisions.

THEOLOGY AND PHILOSOPHY

The widespread acceptance of the authority of Aristotle's philosophy made the issue of the relationship between philosophy and revealed truth of foundational importance in the thirteenth century. Philosophy was seen to be based on the authority of human reason. Revealed truth, while not irrational, appeared to be based on the authority of God. Can the two live together, or do we have to abandon one in order to follow the other?

Truth is one. Aquinas rejected the extreme Averroist position, which was prepared to segregate philosophy and theology completely and allow that what is true in one discipline could be false in the other. Truth, he felt sure, is ultimately one; truths of faith and of reason cannot be accepted as contradictory. In keeping with the whole Christian tradition, Aquinas was confident that God's revelation in the Bible was true. It must therefore be one with all other truth, however we may come to know it.

Faith and reason. Aquinas was able to state that theology arises from the light of faith, and philosophy (including scientific knowledge) from the light of reason. But it would be unfair to conclude from this that faith is irrational or that the light of reason is unable to tell us theological truth. For Aquinas faith is rational; it involves, like all knowing, the assent of the intellect. And reason can demonstrate the truth of some theological propositions.

Since, following Aristotle, Aquinas believed that sense experience and the application of reason are able to give us knowledge of anything in the natural world, there is for him no need of divine illumination. And he went further. There are even some theological truths we can know through the use of our senses and our reason without the help of revelation. Aquinas saw theological truths, the truths about God that have been made available to us through revelation, as falling into two categories. Some, like the existence and oneness of God, and the existence of the human soul, can be discovered by human reason, quite apart from revelation. Others, like the Trinity, the incarnation, or the last judgment, are beyond human reason, so we need God to reveal them to us. This distinction is not ultimate; it arises from the limitations of our reason; for God all truths are equally apparent. They can be said to be above human reason, but they are not contrary to it. We can only discover them with the help of revelation.

So our senses and our reason give us a great deal of knowledge—all we need to know in the natural world and a fair bit of what we need to know about God. The remaining divine truths we accept through faith. The distinction between faith and ordinary knowledge is not that faith bypasses the intellect. Faith is not irrational. Rather, the distinction is based in the object or proposition about which we have faith. Some objects carry enough weight to convince us of their truth. For instance, I see rain falling, I get wet, and others say it's raining; that's enough for me to know it's raining. But other objects or propositions carry insufficient weight. "This rain is good for the garden" might be an example, since it is arguable that the garden has already had too much rain or that the rain is flattening the flowers. Where an object or proposition has insufficient weight in itself to make us know it, we have to be content with something less than knowledge. At this point an additional factor comes into play, an act of the will. We choose which way to interpret the limited evidence. If even after choosing we are hesitant and doubtful, we would describe what we have as "opinion." But if we are confident and certain, we would use the term *faith*. Faith, then, is the same as ordinary knowledge in that it is rational, "the assent of the intellect," but different in that it involves an act of the will.

SUMMA CONTRA GENTILES

In this apologetic work, Aquinas sought to present a worldview that was built on philosophy and rational arguments alone, without any appeal to revelation. The fact that the result tallies with Christian teaching establishes both the truth of Christianity and the dependability of reason and philosophy.

We can establish, he said, the existence of God as Aristotle did by realizing that anything that is moved has to be moved by something. Therefore, there must be a chain of movers. The chain cannot be infinite; thus there must be an ultimate unmoved mover, which is God. Other similar arguments point us to the existence of God.

Reason (with the help of Aristotle) shows us certain things about God, largely by using negative concepts. He is unmoved, unchanging, incorporeal, indivisible, ineffable. Reason also shows us that God must be good and intelligent. Aquinas explored in some detail the relationship of God as intellect to the world, working through complex arguments about God's knowledge. We can learn from reason that in God is will, delight, joy, and love. His will is free; it wills his own being and the being of all creatures.

Reason tells us God cannot do the logically impossible; he cannot fail, he cannot have bodily feelings like weariness or emotions like anger or sadness. He cannot undo the past, commit sin, or make himself not exist.

As for the human soul, we can learn from philosophy that the soul is the form of the body and is immortal. Animals have souls, but they are not immortal. Philosophy also teaches us how to live. God is the goal of all things; ultimate happiness consists in knowing him. We can't know him fully in this life, so we can't have total happiness here. Details of practical ethics such as marital fidelity can be demonstrated by reason.

The *Summa contra Gentiles* also discusses a range of issues, such as evil and sin, prayer and predestination. Toward its close it becomes more specifically theological and discusses issues that can only be known through revelation, such as the Trinity and the incarnation.

ARGUMENTS FOR THE EXISTENCE OF GOD

Aquinas outlined five theistic arguments, or, as he called them, five "ways" of showing that reason requires the existence of God. Many philosophical books devote more attention to these arguments than to all the rest of his work put together. However, the part they occupy in his writings is relatively small. Though he uses them in the *Summa contra Gentiles* and picks them up in other parts of his writings, his main exposition is in the *Summa Theologica*, which was addressed to those who already accepted the Christian revelation. There the five are grouped in a section at the start of the work. All five together occupy less than one thousand words in a work extending to over three million words.

Aquinas's first four ways are closely related and have a distinctly Aristotelian feel about them. They are all versions of the cosmological argument,

A Sample of Aquinas's Arguing: His Third and Fifth Ways

We see around us that things come into being and cease to be. They have a might-not-have-been sort of existence. It can't be that everything is contingent in this way, since we can envisage contingent things as not having existed at some time, in which case there would have been nothing. But, if that was so, nothing ever would have come to be, since there was nothing to make it come to be. So nothing would exist. This obviously isn't the case. So it can't be that everything is contingent. There must be some being whose existence is necessary.

We can see that inanimate things, like physical objects, operate according to a purpose, in that they always or nearly always work together toward the optimum outcome. This must be deliberate and not a matter of chance. Like an arrow directed by an archer, inanimate things move toward a purposive end only when directed by a knowledgeable and intelligent person. So there is an intelligent being who directs things in the world to a purposive end. This being we call God.

arguing from some aspect of the world as we observe it to a being that is the explanation of that aspect.

None of the arguments was original with Aquinas. Each depends heavily on assumptions that were made by just about everybody in the thirteenth century and so would have appeared stronger to them than they do to us.

We in the twenty-first century have our own versions of the cosmological argument based on our current assumptions, which usually depend on the authority of scientists rather than on the authority of Aristotle. No doubt these would have sounded pretty odd to someone in the thirteenth century. We assume, for instance, on the authority of the scientists, that 15 billion years ago there was a Big Bang. We ask why. No explanation in terms of the natural world, of physics, or of any other branch of science will do, since the laws of physics and time and space and so on came into being only after the Big Bang. So only a supernatural or God-shaped explanation will fit.

The first of Aquinas's ways argues from motion to an unmoved mover. The second starts with the assumption, which we saw in Ibn Sina, that everything needs a cause outside of itself. To avoid an infinite chain of causes, we must posit an uncaused first cause, which we call God. His third way argues for a necessary being from the contingency of everything in the world. The fourth way is perhaps the least convincing to us today. It is in terms of degrees of being and appeals to the medieval Platonic concept of a hierarchy of reality. There are degrees of perfection. Some things are better or truer or more beautiful than others, other things are better than those, and so on. Given two assumptions that Aquinas's contemporaries usually made, that the better is the more real, and that whatever is at the top of the hierarchy is the cause of all the rest, we can posit God as "the real cause of being and goodness and every conceivable perfection."

Though Aquinas himself linked all five ways together, the fifth is generally seen as distinct from the other four in that it is a version of the teleological argument, using concepts of purpose and design to argue for the existence of a designer.

EXISTENCE AND ESSENCE

Aquinas developed the distinction that Aristotle and Ibn Sina had made between existence and essence. (Remember the chocolate cake? See page 180.) Except in God there is no necessary connection between essence and existence. A thing's essence (Lat. *essentia, natura*) is *what* it is, what we are describing when we give a definition. But for Aquinas it is more than just a definition, because a definition can be seen as something that we impose on a thing from outside. Rather, it is something in the thing itself, inseparable from it.

All objects or substances have essence. Most have existence as well, though some, like unicorns, or the perfect chocolate cake, have essence but no existence. If a thing's essence is *what* it is, its existence (Lat. *esse*, "to be") can be called *that* it is. For the Platonists, and so for the Augustinians, the emphasis was on essence, the form of the object. Existence, for them, was something of an optional extra, of no great metaphysical importance. Aquinas, on the other hand—and here he went beyond Aristotle—stressed the primary importance of existence. Existence is "the perfection of all perfections." The world is to be seen as made up of innumerable actual existences, not of forms or essences. The model here is God. Against those Augustinians who said God was pure essence, Aquinas saw God as pure act of existence. "He who is" is essentially pure Being. The glory of all things in the created world is that God has enabled them to share, in however limited a way, in his act of existence.

MATTER AND FORM

Aquinas believed that all physical objects consist of matter and form. Matter is something very basic, the underlying stuff of all physical objects. Form is what makes the matter into a specific object, having its determining characteristics. But Aquinas refused to extend this hylomorphism to angels and spiritual beings, as Ibn Gabirol had done. He also rejected Ibn Gabirol's idea of a plurality of forms. Each object, said Aquinas, has just one basic form that determines its essence. If there are additional aspects of the object that look like an additional form, they can be explained either as aspects of the one form or as "accidental," as opposed to essential, aspects of the object.

POTENTIALITY AND ACTUALITY

Matter, the underlying substance, can be seen in theory as pure potentiality. But since matter cannot exist without a form and it is the form that actualizes the matter's potential, matter never is purely potential; it is always actualized. So everything apart from God possesses both actuality and potentiality. Since potentiality implies some sort of lack or imperfection, there can be no potentiality in God; he is pure actuality.

LANGUAGE ABOUT GOD

While accepting that much language about God has to be in negative terms (e.g., infinite, incorporeal), Aquinas explored the way we can speak affirmatively about God. Apart from negative terms, he said, we can't use ordinary terms univocally, that is, meaning the same when applied to God as they mean in ordinary use. God's love is very different from human love. But God's love isn't totally different from human love; the term isn't entirely equivocal. What is happening, then, when we use such terms of God? Aquinas's answer is that we are using the terms analogically, with a meaning that isn't the same but isn't totally unrelated. This, of course, is happening with words all the time. The goodness we are talking about when we refer to a good story is different from the goodness we praise little Johnny for when he is well behaved. Yet we can see a similarity. We can apply words analogically to God, says Aquinas, because objects in the world about which we use ordinary terms are God's creation; what they are, their "perfections," already exist in him. So there is common ground between objects in the world and God, and we can use this common ground to enable us to speak positively and truly about God.

A Taste of Aquinas

Aquinas was not a scintillating writer. He lacked the urgency and personal involvement of Augustine. He was careful to argue each point through, and his work can appear turgid and tedious. But from time to time he made memorable short comments, and some of them are listed below. In our survey of Aquinas's philosophy, we have only been able to look at a few aspects, so this list helps to illustrate the breadth of his ideas. It is taken from a useful collection of Aquinas's philosophical texts translated by Thomas Gilby.

What is false in nature is false from every point of view.

Love takes up where knowledge leaves off.

A thing can be immediately loved though mediately known

God is before the world in duration, yet *before* does not mean a priority of time, but of eternity, or perhaps, if you like, an endlessness of imaginary time.

Nothing but his goodness moves God to create things.

To hold creatures cheap is to slight divine power.

God does not seek glory for his own sake, but for ours.

Evil denotes the lack of good.

A thing is called evil for lacking a perfection it ought to have; to lack sight is evil in a man but not in a stone.

Pleasure lies in being, not becoming.

Morality depends on intention.

Man has a natural urge toward complete goodness.

Sins are as preposterous in morals as monsters in nature.

Religiosity—religion observed beyond measure.

Peace is not a virtue, but the fruit of virtue.

The divine rights of grace do not abolish the human rights of natural reason.

THE SOUL

The form of the human body, the thing that makes its essence and distinguishes it from everything else, is the soul. While the Augustinians tended to stress the spirituality of the soul, Aquinas stressed its intellectual nature. Human beings are essentially rational. Our basic or substantial form is a rational soul. Since matter and form are inseparable, when we refer to a human being, we are referring to body and rational soul together. It is the soul and body together that experience sensations and so gather knowledge. The soul alone cannot know anything. This may appear to land Aquinas in some difficulty over the immortality of the soul. Indeed, in arguing for the immortality of the soul, Aquinas stated that it is spiritual and thus can survive separation from the body. The Christian doctrine of the resurrection of the body, of course, means that this separation is not forever.

AQUINAS: SUCCESS OR FAILURE?

We have seen that Aquinas had two overall aims. His immediate aim was to incorporate the philosophy of Aristotle into a Christian system. His broader aim was through this system to avert the breakup of the medieval synthesis of theology and philosophy.

Most people would agree that Aquinas achieved his immediate aim admirably. But despite this, he failed to prevent the decline and eventual break up of the Augustinian synthesis. This was partly because his system failed to win universal support. He was unable to persuade many of his contemporaries to accept it. The Augustinians felt he had conceded too much to Aristotle and had thus deserted the true Christian tradition. Some of his teachings were officially condemned by the church in Paris and Oxford three years after his death. The Aristotelians, on the other hand, felt he had compromised too much and had thus taken the edge off of the Aristotelian revolution.

Indeed, though some of his concepts and some parts of his work were influential in the following centuries, it was not until the nineteenth century that his work as a whole received widespread recognition.

But it is arguable that even if Aquinas's system had been more generally accepted right from the start, it still would not have been enough to keep the medieval synthesis together. In incorporating Aristotle, we might feel he had already conceded too much. The door had been opened to autonomous human reason; God was being pushed to one side; a process had started that would eventually push him out altogether.

TO THINK THROUGH

Could Aquinas's aims have been achieved? After all, Platonism conflicts with Christianity at several points, yet the medievals managed to marry the two pretty successfully. What do you think might have happened if Aquinas had succeeded? Would it have hindered or helped the rise of science?

What do you think about Aquinas's arguments for the existence of God? How could they be updated to make them sound relevant today?

Aquinas's insights into existence, essence, potentiality, actuality, and the centrality of Being reappear in twentieth-century existentialism, generally severed from any reference to God. Can you think of ways of presenting what Aquinas is trying to say in terms that would be meaningful to one of your friends for whom life is meaningless?

Talking of existentialists, Kierkegaard is seen by many as totally rejecting Aquinas's compromise that faith is both rational and an act of the will. They see him as declaring that faith has to be irrational, a blind leap. What do you think?

For Further Study

Davies, B. *The Thought of Thomas Aquinas.* Oxford: Clarendon Press, 1992.

Kenny, A. *Aquinas.* Oxford: Oxford University Press, 1980.

Kretzmann, N., and E. Stump. *The Cambridge Companion to Aquinas.* Cambridge: Cambridge University Press, 1993.

NINETEEN

THE BEGINNING OF THE END OF THE MEDIEVAL SYSTEM

In this chapter we reflect on the failure of Aquinas's system to save the medieval synthesis and meet four other thinkers of the late thirteenth century-- Roger Bacon, Henry of Ghent, Siger of Brabant, and Dante.

THE FAILURE OF AQUINAS'S SYSTEM TO WIN COMMON acceptance marks the end of the great vision of the West in the medieval period and the beginning of the end of the whole medieval way of doing philosophy. The vision had been to unite philosophy and theology in one great system of knowledge and living. From Augustine to the thirteenth century, that vision had been largely achieved. For eight hundred years, Western thinkers had basically agreed on the main points of their worldview.

To us today this may seem both odd and a recipe for atrophy or at best dull and unproductive philosophizing. But the medievals didn't see it that way. They saw the alternative, which has prevailed from the fourteenth century to the present day as one in which it was impossible to do any fruitful philosophizing. How on earth can philosophy as a whole make progress, they would ask, if philosophers all start from radically different basic beliefs? How can an atheist and a theist have a fruitful discussion about the nature of God? How can a determinist and a libertarian fruitfully discuss how we should use our freedom? If there is no agreement to start with, then no progress can be made in philosophy.

But in our Augustinian synthesis, our medieval friend might continue, the very fact that we agreed on basics meant we could make progress. Issues could be raised, problems discussed, solutions offered and adopted, and then new issues tackled. The eight hundred years of the Augustinian synthesis were neither static nor dull. True, many of the issues discussed seem obtuse and irrelevant to the twenty-first-century mind, but that is only because those discussing them used terminology and concepts that we are not familiar with today. The fact is, many of the issues they were addressing, such as the nature of reality and knowledge and truth, issues of meaning and language and hermeneutics, and even the existence of God, have remained key problems to this day, even though they are generally presented rather differently.

Was it inevitable that Aquinas's attempt to keep the synthesis going by incorporating Aristotle in it would fail? That is a matter for debate. Those who feel it could have succeeded could point to the fact that Augustinianism had already managed to assimilate views that at first sight might have seemed irreconcilable, not least New Testament Christianity and Neoplatonism. Additionally, there have been many who have felt that Aquinas had in fact produced a workable solution, in that he didn't just absorb Aristotle into the Christian worldview, but used the Christian tradition and Aristotle to form a new and positive approach to understanding the world that could have served as a united basis for theology, philosophy, and science for the future. On the other side some would argue that Aquinas's proposals were too radical to be accepted by those in an eight-hundred-year-old tradition, that there were too many points of conflict between Aristotelianism and Christianity, and in particular, the incorporation of Aristotle's ideas inevitably removed God from his central position in our understanding of the world and so denied the heart of the New Testament message. Additionally, on a more practical note, by the time Aquinas produced his synthesis, the tide was already running strongly in the direction of division and fragmentation.

Again, from our point of view, division and fragmentation are such facts of life that it is very hard for us to imagine anything else. Or is it? Try this. First, in twenty years' time, there will be just one language for the academic world—no more problems of communication, one language with agreed meanings for all the terms used. Second, everyone will agree on basic beliefs and foundational principles. Everyone will start at the same point and play on a level field. Third, all the fragmented disciplines will be reunited. History, zoology, ethics, physics, theology, music, and all the rest will form a united whole instead of each one doing its own thing. In particular, the leading thinkers will be fully aware of all the latest ideas in every area of human knowledge.

Yes, I agree it is an impossible dream. But that was what the medievals had for eight hundred years. And it was at a time when Europe was often in chaos, communication by contemporary standards was appalling, travel was hazardous, and printed books didn't exist. Yet Western thought was united in a common worldview with a common language and embraced all areas of human knowledge. It was indeed a magnificent achievement.

But it came to an end. Ironically, the seeds of its destruction may have been in the universities rather than in Aristotle. For universities, as we have seen, grouped their studies according to topic. So, for instance, at Paris, the most influential university of the thirteenth century, Aristotle was taught not in the theology faculty, but in the faculty of arts. Then, as now, university departments tended to function as independent units, so philosophy was already being separated from theology. Additionally, concentrating academic study in universities, a thing that had never happened before, encouraged both controversy and speculation—speculation, because it is the lecturer with the daring new ideas that draws the crowds (or gets a book published); controversy, because in an academic setting people can be pushed to extremes in the defense of their ideas. Neither controversy nor speculation is bad in itself, but each added its impetus to the gradual fragmentation of knowledge.

Of course there were other factors, not least the new atmosphere of academic excitement and daring. Renaissance humanism was stirring. And there were beginnings of dissent within the Catholic church and a weakening of the top-heavy ecclesiastical power structure. There was a promise of a new age. It took time coming, but there was an inevitability about it, and the first stage of its coming was the breaking down of what had been so painstakingly built up for the previous eight hundred years.

FROM REALISM TO NOMINALISM

At the heart of the shift lay the issue of universals. The shift was a move away from realism to nominalism. Realism believed in the reality of universals, not as independently existing forms, as Plato had suggested, but as ideas in the mind of God. Such a belief provided a basis for all other beliefs and for the whole of human life. It provided absolutes, fixed points, standards. It made knowledge and understanding possible; it provided stability and security. There was such a thing as goodness, so we can know what it is to be good; we have a basis on which to make moral choices; and so on. There was such a thing as truth, so we can discover truth, depend on truth, and build up a system of truth; we don't have to worry that truth will change from day to day. Values and virtues, for the Realist, can all be established and followed; they are unchanging; we can know where we are and live accordingly.

In other words, realism provided an answer to relativism. Just as Plato had produced an answer to the threat of relativism and skepticism of his day, the Augustinian system provided a stable and trustworthy alternative to the fragmentation and relativism that could well have overwhelmed European thought from the fifth century onward.

But, of course, the medieval realism had its weaknesses. It was one thing to say that goodness, truth, beauty, meaning, and so on could be known and depended on because they were rooted in God. It was another to argue that the church or state as it was then constituted was equally a fixed principle in the mind of God. The belief in a hierarchical ecclesiastical and social system didn't come from the New Testament, which in fact taught the opposite. It was one of the results of the infiltration of Neoplatonism into the Augustinian system. But it was firmly embedded in the system and defended in terms of universals. The theory of universals could be (and was) used to undergird excessive conservatism and resistance to change and new ideas.

Though there were exceptions, for instance at Oxford, the fourteenth century saw a general move away from realism toward some form of nominalism. For Nominalists, as a general principle, goodness, truth, meaning, beauty, and the like are not eternally fixed ideas in the mind of God. They are not things at all; they are concepts or linguistic labels we use for convenience when talking about the world.

This is not to say that the Nominalists were consciously opting for relativism. They were not. They wanted to keep fixed principles that would undergird knowledge and human life just as the Realists' principles had done. By and large they were confident that these fixed principles were embedded in the world around them and thus could be extracted and applied by the use of human reason. But there was an incipient relativism in their approach. If concepts or labels are applied by us, then it is up to us to develop new concepts and change labels. And how are we to establish that one concept or label is to be accepted rather than another?

Looking back six hundred years later, surrounded as we are by postmodernism and relativism, we may smile wryly at the cheerful confidence that human reason was sufficient for the task. But the fact is that Western thought did not collapse into relativistic chaos, despite the fragmentation that followed the end of the Augustinian synthesis. On the contrary, it was extremely productive and successful.

The reason is not far to seek. Though the dominant trend from the fourteenth century onward had abandoned realism, it had not abandoned God. The technical understanding of the ideas in the mind of God no longer undergirded the philosophical worldview, but right through until the eighteenth century the human enterprise was seen as one in which we think God's thoughts after him. The world can be known because God has made it and has given us minds that can explore and understand it. Goodness is fixed because God is good. Sixteenth- and seventeenth-century scientists, such as Isaac Newton, saw God as the foundation and guarantor of their systems. Descartes's philosophy similarly was built on the centrality of God.

It wasn't until the nineteenth century that God lost his key position and philosophers and scientists sought to manage without him and the slide into relativism began. Early in the century, so the story goes, the physicist Pierre Laplace, referring to God, said, "I have no need of that hypothesis." Later in the century Nietzsche was declaring that since God is dead, all horizons have been wiped away. There is no up or down left. There are no fixed points, no goodness, meaning, or truth. Without God we are lost in an infinite void.

A TIME OF TURMOIL

Though, for us, Aquinas dominated the thirteenth century, at the time he was one among many who were reacting in a range of ways to the challenge of Aristotle. We will look at three of his contemporaries, Roger Bacon, Henry of Ghent, and Siger of Brabant. Then, after taking a glance at Dante, we will survey briefly another giant of the late medieval period, Duns Scotus, who was renowned for his subtle and often obscure arguments; the English word *dunce* comes from his name. Then we will spend a little longer with William of Ockham, equally great and just as subtle as his master, Scotus, using him as an exemplification of the significant shifts that were happening in the fourteenth century. Following these two we will look in less detail at four contrasting figures who, though still part of the medieval tradition, each in his own way contributed to its collapse. Then we will finish our survey of the Middle Ages with Suarez, who, though in some ways breaking free from the medieval tradition, can justifiably be called the last of the great scholastics.

Even such a brief survey of the final four centuries of the medieval tradition will show that, for all the criticisms of those in the early modern period, medievalism was still alive and kicking and developing new ideas until the end. The ferment and controversies of the thirteenth century continued into the fourteenth, giving rise to creative and original thinking. Though Aquinas failed to win universal assent, there were those, especially in his Dominican order, who defended his position vigorously. Others, including not a few Franciscans, attacked it equally vigorously.

The fourteenth century continued to be a time of turmoil, and not just in the philosophical world. There was continual conflict between church and state and rival factions within Christendom. For much of the century England and France were at war. Europe was ravaged by the Black Death. A third of the population of England died within one year. The plague is probably the reason why there was a decline in philosophical activity in the second half of the century and into the fifteenth century, particularly in Britain.

Roger Bacon. Ilchester?, England (c. 1215–c. 1292). A Franciscan who taught at Oxford and Paris, Bacon was one of the first to lecture on Aristotle's newly discovered works at Paris. But subsequently he reacted against Aristotelianism and denounced it, preferring to retain a basically Augustinian framework, including a belief in divine illumination. Everything, he said, comes from God; as we explore the secrets of nature, we are lifted up in worship and wonder to God. He developed his own comprehensive system covering all fields of knowledge, stressing among other things the need for controlled experimentation in science. He was especially noted for his contributions to chemistry (alchemy) and visual perception.

Henry of Ghent. Ghent, Belgium (c. 1217–1293). Henry, like Bacon and Siger, taught at Paris. He sought to retain a basically Augustinian worldview but to incorporate into it elements of Ibn Sina and Aristotle. However, he saw some aspects of Aristotelianism, such as its denial of the creative act of God, as unacceptable and supported the condemnation of Aristotelian doctrines at Paris in 1277. Henry interpreted universals relationally rather than ontologically; they are a relationship between God and the individual rather than independent existences. He stressed the priority of essence over existence. In metaphysics we are able to study the intelligible essences and so can attain unchanging truth. In physics, on the other hand, we are looking only at individual existences. If we stay merely on the level of individuals, we will not be able to reach universal truth. He retained the need for God's illumination in our knowing but accepted Aristotle's insight into the key role played by sense experience. His work was very influential in the fourteenth century; both Duns Scotus and William of Ockham were influenced by it and responded to it.

Siger of Brabant. Brabant, France (c. 1240–c. 1284). Siger taught at Paris from the 1260s. He was an enthusiastic supporter of Aristotle but was also influenced by Ibn Sina and Ibn Rushd. His views were seen as extreme and dangerous; Aquinas was among those who attacked him and succeeded in ousting him from Paris two years before his death. He appeared to teach on the authority of Aristotle that the world was eternally created and that we do not have individual immortal souls. Instead, there is only one rational soul or intellect. All humans participate in this soul during our lives, but after death it is this unitary soul that survives, not the individual. Siger may have modified these views later in life. He was accused, probably unjustly, of holding to the theory of double truth attributed to Ibn Rushd.

Dante Alighieri. Florence (1265–1321). Though famed as a poet, Dante was a profound thinker and political philosopher who was influenced both by Aquinas and by the Arab Islamic philosophers. He referred to Aristotle as "the master of those who know," and in the *Divine Comedy* he placed Ibn Sina and Ibn Rushd in Limbo (the best he could do for non-Christians) and Siger in heaven, eulogized there by Aquinas. In his political philosophy, he decisively separated church and state.

TO THINK THROUGH

We accept fragmentation as a fact of life, but was it inevitable that with the founding of universities the various academic disciplines all went their separate ways? What could we do today to encourage greater dialogue and crossover between the disciplines?

For Further Study

See the books listed at the end of Part 3, pages 227–28.

TWENTY

THE MIDDLE AGES' FINAL FLING

SCOTUS TO SUAREZ

Though the modern approach gradually replaced the medieval, it never showed it to be untenable, and thinkers went on using and developing medieval methods and ideas up to the seventeenth century and beyond. In this chapter we will look at two very significant late medieval figures, Duns Scotus and his pupil William of Ockham. Then we will look more briefly at John Wyclif, Nicholas of Cusa, Desiderius Erasmus, and Niccolo Machiavelli before ending our survey of the Middle Ages with Francisco Suarez.

JOHN DUNS SCOTUS

Maxton, Scotland (c. 1266–1308). A Franciscan, Duns Scotus studied and taught mainly at Paris and Oxford. He earned the nickname "the subtle doctor" because of his careful and meticulously detailed arguing. He, more than any other medieval, is responsible for the image of complex and tedious "scholasticism" that early modernism rejected. He balanced his high regard for logic and careful argument with an insistence that the role of reason was limited: Emotions and the will also play a vital role. Seeing himself primarily as a theologian, he also stressed the need for divine illumination. Scotus was committed to retaining the Augustinian tradition, though he accepted that some of the insights of Aristotle could be integrated into that system. However, he felt that Aquinas had gone too far in that direction and sought to moderate his ideas, though he rarely attacked Aquinas directly. His teachings were well received and followed by his fellow Franciscans.

God. Scotus rejected the view that we can speak of God only in negative terms or by analogy, stating that we can speak of him univocally; human love is patterned on divine love. He expounded and discussed rational arguments for the existence of God in great detail. But he also stressed that we must approach God through the will and especially through love, not just through the intellect. In the same way God is not to be viewed in the Aristotelian way simply as pure intellect; will and love are also central in him.

Human persons. Just as God is much more than pure intellect, we are made up of reason plus will plus passions and desires. The key virtue is love, not reason. Scotus believed strongly in free will; his theology verged on Pelagianism.

Theology and philosophy. Though Scotus made copious use of his reason in debating theological issues, he stressed that the source of theological knowledge was God's revelation rather than our natural reason. He thus tended to widen the gap between theology, in which revelation is prior to reasoning, and philosophy, in which natural reason operates without revelation.

Metaphysics. Scotus distinguished a thing's "whatness" (quiddity) or common essence from its "thisness" (haecceity)—a term Scotus coined from the Latin for "this" (*haec*) to indicate a unique individual essence. A quiddity is something that can be shared by several individuals or particulars. A haecceity is unique and limited to one particular or individual. Being Socrates is a haecceity; being a man is a quiddity. Making this distinction enabled him to reject the view of Aristotle, reflected in Aquinas, that the key to a particular's uniqueness is in its matter. In answer to the question "Do a thing's quiddity and haecceity really exist (like Plato's forms) or are they just concepts or names (as the Nominalists would say)?" Scotus took a (subtle) middle position, making them less than real but more than just concepts.

WILLIAM OF OCKHAM

Ockham, England (c. 1285–1347). A Franciscan, educated at Oxford, Ockham soon fell foul of the pope because of his teaching on corruption in the church and the relative authority of church and state. He fled England and spent most of the rest of his life on the Continent, especially in Bavaria. He continued to be very involved in the ecclesiastical and political controversies of his day, generally arguing against the power-seeking policies of the church hierarchy.

Ockham saw Aristotle as his philosophical master. His approach has traditionally been viewed as rather more radical than that of his fellow Franciscan and teacher Duns Scotus. It was a key factor in the developing disintegration of the medieval way of doing philosophy and theology. It encouraged a new attitude of criticism and skepticism toward the past, an attitude that came to be known as the "modern way" (Lat. *via moderna*). In many ways it set the agenda for the next two centuries. His writings were all polemical, or responses to specific issues; he did not publish a comprehensive system. Recent scholarship has tended to stress that his ideas were not as radical as some have thought; rather, he was part of an ongoing development of Franciscan theology's reaction to Aristotle. However, he is a very significant figure, not just because of the way he has been traditionally viewed, but because he exemplifies the shifts that were occurring in the fourteenth century that mark the transition from the medieval period to the modern period. Ockham isn't the cause of these shifts; they were already happening and would have happened without him. Rather, he is a specific expression of them.

Universals: The shift from realism to nominalism.

Ockham took the decisive step of denying any reality to universals. Not only do they not exist either in the Platonic sense or as ideas in the mind of God; it is not even true to say they somehow exist in the particular individuals. Only individuals exist. Universal terms like humanness or whiteness are only our abstractions, our way of identifying and naming common elements. Ockham thus was committed to a form of nominalism. Traditionally he was looked on as a thoroughgoing Nominalist, but most contemporary scholars feel he took a less extreme Nominalist position known as "conceptualism," since he believed the element that is abstracted is a concept in the mind rather than just a name or label.

Ockham's razor: The shift from complexity to the search for simplicity.

Most contemporary scholars tend to stress that the principle known as "Ockham's razor" was not in fact introduced by Ockham. Certainly the most frequently quoted form of the principle, "Entities are not to be multiplied any more than necessary," doesn't appear as such in Ockham's extant works. But there are passages where he says something very similar, and it is safe to say that even though others, including Aristotle, had urged following the same basic principle, it is undoubtedly one that Ockham believed in and followed wherever he could. Also called the principle of parsimony, it assumes that the simplest theory or explanation is the most likely to be correct.

Ockham exemplifies the use of the razor in the way he cut Aristotle's categories from ten to two, retaining just substance and quality. Given the extreme complexity of many medieval theories and explanations, it is not surprising that the razor was a very useful tool in the hands of the early modern thinkers.

The shift from the primacy of metaphysics to the primacy of epistemology.

Ockham can be seen as marking a significant shift in interest from metaphysics to epistemology, a shift that exemplifies one of the key differences between the Middle Ages and the modern period. Though the two areas intertwined, the medievals tended to be primarily interested in metaphysical issues, such as what exists, the status of universals and matter and essences. Ockham's "nominalism" greatly reduced the number of existences to be investigated, appearing to solve at a stroke the biggest medieval metaphysical problem, that of the status of universals. But "solving" the metaphysical issue in this way didn't get rid of the basic problem. Indeed, Ockham admitted as much.

To put it simply, universals as metaphysically existing entities were posited to enable us to make sense of what we are doing when we think and talk about the common element shared by, say, a good person, a good book, and a good day. After Ockham we have to say that there is no detachable common element; all we have is three completely distinct and unique individual items with nothing in common. And yet we still think and talk about goodness. So we have a continuing problem explaining how we can do this. But after Ockham, and especially in the modern period, the problem has become an epistemological one rather than a metaphysical one—seeking to understand what are we doing when we extrapolate and conceptualize a common (nonexisting) element, "goodness," from these three.

Ockham believed that there are two sources of knowledge, revelation from God and our direct experience of individual objects. Both are to be used; both are dependable; but the two, he believed, are to be kept apart. We are not, for example, to base our knowledge of objects in the world on the truths of revelation. Ockham was fully aware that this raised the question of how we know that the perceptions we have of objects in the world and the concepts we form as a result are correct. Objects themselves change; perceptions we have of them change; one person's concepts will be different from another's.

How can we know anything for sure? Ockham's answer was straightforward: We simply trust our observations and our mental processes. Our cognitive faculties are reliable. This, of course, was more of a pragmatic assumption than an answer to the question. It was, however, an assumption that science has been happy to make throughout the modern period. Philosophers, by contrast, have realized that the question of the justification of what we know does not go away simply because our knowledge works, and the struggle to find an acceptable answer has continued throughout the modern period down to the present day.

The shift from an integrated worldview to the separation of theology and philosophy.

Again, in this Ockham is part of a general process rather than a radical instigator. But there is no doubt that he was happy with the process and that he helped further it. Our understanding of the natural world, he felt, can be and should be built on nothing more than our observations and experiences interpreted by our natural reason. No undergirding by God's revelation is necessary. Revealed truths, of course, have their place; but that is the realm of theology, not philosophy. Ockham applied this principle consistently in several areas, including ethics and the issue of the separation of church and state.

The shift from objectivity to subjectivity.

Ockham also exemplifies the beginnings of another significant shift, which ties in with the widening gap between theology and philosophy and the consequent gradual loss of theocentricity. It is the shift to a "me-centered" way of seeing the world, from objectivity to subjectivity. A belief in actually existing universals, particularly in the Augustinian version of ideas in the mind of God, provided an objective basis for our thoughts and ideas. Goodness is something independent of us; we can discover it and seek to practice it, but we don't control it. But when goodness becomes a concept in our own minds (or perhaps rather a concept only in my mind, since the objective existence of any other mind is only a concept in my mind), then it has moved from being something primarily objective to something primarily subjective. The Renaissance and the Enlightenment, of course, were confident that the objectivity of our thoughts and ideas could somehow be guaranteed by the world around us. But we now know that this was a misplaced confidence.

The shift toward empiricism.

Traditionally Ockham has been seen as laying the foundation for an empirical approach to our understanding of the world, that is, accepting only what we can observe and experience through our five senses as the basis for our understanding and knowledge of the world. This is true to an extent, though we could note two points. The shift was, of course, already well under way, since it was inherent in the reestablishing of the Aristotelian approach to the world. And, second, Ockham was still a long way away from anything like a "pure" empirical approach, if such a thing is possible. He still retained, for example, Aristotle's concept of matter and form and assumed a number of basic universal principles, such as the uniformity of nature and the impossibility of being coming from nonbeing.

TO THINK THROUGH

Ockham's razor has been a favorite tool of thinkers in the empiricist tradition. But the twentieth century seems to have shown that the simplest explanation is not necessarily the right one, for instance, in Freudian theory or subnuclear physics. What do you think?

What do you think about the six "shifts"? Were they inevitable? Are they cases of either one thing or the other, or could the best insights of both sides have been held together?

For Further Study

Adams, M. M. *William Ockham*. 2 vols. Notre Dame: University of Notre Dame Press, 1987.

LATER MEDIEVAL THINKERS

Ockham, then, can be seen as exemplifying the shifts that were taking place from the thirteenth century onward, taking Western thought from the Middle Ages to the modern period. But there were to be another three centuries before the arrival of the philosophers who are generally looked on as the heralds of the new era. During that time the process of change continued steadily but slowly. The powerful momentum of the medieval synthesis still continued to shape the thinking of society at large and of some thinkers. Meanwhile, the new freedom of thought, together with concern at the corruption of the church, gave rise to a range of more radical ideas.

The five thinkers I have selected to represent the final centuries of medievalism demonstrate between them many of the contrasting features of the period: radical innovation and a desire to return to the past; deep spirituality and a freedom from all moral restraints; revolution and moderation; specialization and an attempt to produce a comprehensive system.

JOHN WYCLIF

North Yorkshire, England (c. 1330–1384). Wyclif taught philosophy and later theology at Oxford, and he wrote widely in both fields. He was Master of Balliol College and was also a popular teacher. He attacked corruption in the church and challenged a number of official doctrines, such as transubstantiation. With a vision of making biblical truth (as opposed to church teaching) available to all, he started translating the Bible into English. His work was condemned by the ecclesiastical authorities, and all available copies of his writings were destroyed. His followers, known as the Lollards, produced the first English version of the Bible, which was condemned by the church in 1408 and suppressed. The Lollards themselves were persecuted, and several were killed. John Hus, the chief exponent of Wyclif's ideas on the Continent, was burnt in Prague in 1415. Wyclif has been called "the morning star of the Reformation."

Metaphysics.
Oxford was dominated by realism from the middle of the fourteenth century and through much of the fifteenth century. Wyclif started with two basic principles: Nothing simultaneously exists and doesn't exist; and being exists. Everything participates in being, so being exists in particular objects and can be known through them. But being in itself is transcendent. Wyclif adopted a comprehensive approach toward universals, accepting that they are both concepts and forms common to sets of individuals. But in addition, and foundationally, he accepted the Realist position that they exist in the mind of God independently of particulars. Wyclif believed in predestination and explored at length the issue of free will.

Ethics and politics.
Wyclif's commitment to universals and his high view of Scripture enabled him to develop a system of ethics that was independent of the teaching of the church. Key to his thinking was the concept that God is the source of virtue and authority, so power, whether ecclesiastical or political, should only be exercised by someone who is in a relationship with God through grace and thus can exercise true justice and virtue in a spirit of love. He believed, in Augustinian fashion, that the true church was made up of those who have a relationship with God and that the ecclesiastical hierarchy showed little evidence of such a relationship. As a result, he taught that a

truly Christian secular ruler had more right to rule in matters both secular and religious than the authorities of the church. He also emphasized that our natural rights—such as a ruler's right to rule or an individual's right to own property—are not absolute in themselves; they are subject to the principles of virtue and justice we find in God.

NICHOLAS OF CUSA

Kues, Germany (1401–1464). Nicholas was active in church politics; he did much to establish the Vienna Concordat between the Eastern and Western churches in 1448. Basically an eclectic, his thought was specially influenced by the Neoplatonist tradition. He was one of the first to deny geocentricity and the finiteness of the universe: "The universe has no center and no edge." He is best known for two related concepts, the limitation of our knowledge and the coming together, or "coincidence," of opposites in God.

Nicholas's best-known work, *On Educated Ignorance*, examines the limitations of our intellect. In it he pours scorn on those who claim to know truths about God. Only those who are aware of their ignorance, he says, are wise. The gap between the infinite God and our limited minds is too great for us to cross. God is ineffable. The most we can grasp about him is what he is not. Nor can we know ultimate truth in other matters. We cannot know reality; all we have are finite images of reality constructed by our minds from the finite images of reality found in objects in the world. These images are most clearly seen in math, a subject in which Nicholas was particularly interested. So all our knowledge is partial and uncertain. The best we can do is opt for a sort of Platonic skepticism.

Linked to his views on the limitations of our knowledge is Nicholas's doctrine of the "coincidence of opposites in God." God is such that opposites meet in him. Things that in our finite world would be contradictory are united in his infinity. His transcendence is able to embrace even opposites. For example, God is both maximum and minimum; he is the greatest of all, and he occupies no space at all.

DESIDERIUS ERASMUS

Rotterdam (c. 1466–1536). From a poor background, Erasmus attended the University of Paris, where he was influenced by some of the leading thinkers of Renaissance humanism. Like them he developed a lifelong interest in the classical Greek and Latin writers. He was himself an elegant writer and for much of his life lived as a traveling scholar, urging a blend of classical and Christian virtues, such as gentleness and tolerance. He was one of the first to make good use of the new medium of printing. He edited the works of a number of the church fathers and prepared an edition of the Greek text of the New Testament.

Erasmus shared many of the concerns of the Reformers and voiced a number of criticisms of abuses in the church. His ideal would have been a return to the practices and spirituality of the early church, replacing scholasticism with *philosophia Christi*, the philosophy of Christ, and replacing ecclesiastical complexities with the simplicity and piety of the early Christians. For a time he worked with Luther but eventually broke with him. In a situation in which most people were taking up polarized positions, neither side was willing to listen to Erasmus's urging of tolerance and moderation.

Though firmly committed to the certainty of Christian truth, known to us through revelation, in other matters Erasmus was epistemologically skeptical. He urged the consideration of arguments on both sides of an issue but then recommended the suspending of judgment.

NICCOLO MACHIAVELLI

Florence (1469–1527). Machiavelli was a historian, a diplomat, and a playwright. But he is chiefly known as a political philosopher. His best-known work is *The Prince*, in which his recommendations for a ruler have cut free from any Christian or conventional morality. Applying such morality, he says, may bring disaster, so the ruler is free to do anything that will achieve his ends, including using deception and violence. The task of the ruler is to succeed in running the state, so anything that will promote that success is justifiable. There is no greater authority, no further moral absolute or control, such as God or an ultimate moral principle, to which the ruler should be subject. Virtue in *The Prince* has become wholly naturalistic and pragmatic. The division between philosophy and theology is being applied with a vengeance. Inconsistently with what he says in *The Prince*, Machiavelli also wrote a much more moderate defense of republican government based on his studies of the ancient Roman republic.

FRANCISCO SUAREZ

Granada, Spain (1548–1617). After a period of relative decline, the sixteenth century saw a vigorous renewal of interest among Roman Catholics in theological and philosophical studies, not least in response to the ferment of the Reformation period. This was partly expressed in the founding of new centers of learning, especially by the Dominicans and the Jesuits. Suarez was a Jesuit, trained in law, philosophy, and theology. He studied and wrote extensively and had considerable influence. He was studied not just by Jesuits and those in the Thomist (Thomas Aquinas) tradition, but by Protestants and philosophers including Descartes, Leibniz, and Wolff. He was a creative thinker, standing generally in the tradition of Aquinas and Aristotle. Many would consider him second only to Aquinas among the scholastics. His method in metaphysics was more modern than medieval, considering one issue at a time and breaking free from the medieval habit of following the agenda laid down by Aristotle in his *Metaphysics.*

Metaphysics. Suarez defined metaphysics as the science of "being insofar as it is real being"; its object of study he expressed as "the objective concept of being." Thus he was part of the furthering of the move away from seeing metaphysics as a study of existing entities to a study of concepts. Only individuals actually exist, he said. We are able to experience them directly and form concepts of them without the intervention of any process of reflection. More general concepts arise through a process of analogy. While accepting reason or intelligibility as a key aspect of being, Suarez also stressed the aspect of will. God, who is being itself, freely and omnipotently wills the existence of all created things, which are thus totally and continuously dependent on him for their being and actions.

Philosophy of law. Suarez's writing on law was influential on the development of modern concepts of law and on the doctrine of the just war. Though he taught that all law is ultimately rooted in God, he accepted that reason alone was sufficient to discover and enact law, though he criticized Aquinas's definition of law as "an ordinance of reason for the good of all, made by the one who has the oversight of the community, and promulgated." Suarez felt this was too rationalistic; the elements of obligation and the will need to be stressed as well. He accepted four varieties of law that had been laid down by Aquinas:

1. God's eternal law: the free decree of the will of God, the basis of all other law.
2. Divine law: God's revealed law, such as the law of Moses.
3. Natural law: law according to nature. This is ultimately rooted in God but is evident to reason even for those who do not have revelation.
4. Human law: specific enactments and applications of natural law.

Suarez stressed the significance of natural law. For him it was both an expression of the will of God and wholly accessible to reason. The mood of the times was such that, given its accessibility to reason, the fact that natural law is rooted in God could readily be forgotten.

Middle knowledge.

Suarez is noted for his contribution to the debate on human free will in relation to the foreknowledge of God. Along with his contemporary and fellow Spanish Jesuit **Luis de Molina** (1535–1600), he developed the theory of middle knowledge. Aquinas had said that God has two sorts of knowledge, knowledge of what actually is and knowledge of what potentially could be. Suarez suggested there was a third kind of divine knowledge, which he called "in between" or "middle" knowledge. This is knowledge of what would have been if certain conditions had been fulfilled which in fact have not been fulfilled. For example, God knows how you would have solved the problems of the Middle East if you had been elected president of the United States in 2000.

TO THINK THROUGH

So far, so good! Now that you have made it through the Middle Ages, were they what you expected? What things have you found there that are worth incorporating into your own worldview or philosophical method?

Philosophical fashions come and go. Do you think there are any aspects of the medieval worldview that will ever gain wide acceptance again?

The medieval Christian thinkers tried to walk a tightrope between incorporating secular philosophy into their worldview and letting secular philosophy control their worldview. How well do you think they succeeded? Should Christianity (or any religion) try to incorporate secular philosophy into its worldview?

For Further Study

For a general introduction to the background and ideas of the Middle Ages:

Martin, C. J. F. *An Introduction to Medieval Philosophy*. Edinburgh: Edinburgh University Press, 1996.

For more detailed study of individual philosophers:

Armstrong, A. H., ed. *The Cambridge History of Later Greek and Early Medieval Philosophy.* Cambridge: Cambridge University Press, 1967.

Copleston, F. *Mediaeval Philosophy.* Vol. 2 of *A History of Philosophy.* 1959; reprint, New York: Doubleday, 1993.

Kretzmann, N., A. Kenny, and J. Pinborg, eds. *The Cambridge History of Later Medieval Philosophy.* Cambridge: Cambridge University Press, 1982.

Marenbon, J., ed. *Medieval Philosophy.* London: Routledge, 1998.

THE SEARCH FOR A SYSTEM

PART FOUR

TWENTY-ONE

SETTING THE AGENDA

In this chapter we begin to explore the modern mind-set, setting it in the context of the Renaissance, the Reformation, and the rise of modern science, and listing some of its differences from the medieval mind-set. Then we look at two contrasting approaches that set the agenda for modern thinkers: skepticism and the "scientific" method.

THE TRANSITION FROM MEDIEVAL TO MODERN

It is impossible to fix a date for the end of the medieval period and the beginning of the modern period. Various suggestions have been made, ranging from 1500 to the publication of the work of Descartes well over a century later. The fact is that, like the end of the modern period and the rise of postmodernism, the process of change was a slow one; elements of the modern mind-set were appearing as early as the thirteenth century; the influence of late medieval thought lingered on well into the seventeenth century.

The shift from medieval to modern was a change of attitude. It was linked closely with three major features of the fifteenth and sixteenth centuries, the Renaissance, the Reformation, and the new developments in science.

The Renaissance. The Renaissance was self-consciously a period of new beginnings. There was a sense that Europe had emerged from a dark period, which had reached an awful climax in the Hundred Years' War and the catastrophic Black Death, and entered a new era characterized by new learning, new travel, new trade, and new investigations and discoveries. A spirit of adventure and exploration prevailed. Freedom replaced the structures of feudalism and the oppressive power of a corrupt church, which were beginning to crumble. There was a new interest in ideas and learning outside of the medieval tradition; texts of classical Greek and Roman writers were now widely available and were avidly studied. Art blossomed.

Linked in with it all was a new focus, called man. In a sense this focus was the start of individualism, the move from the significance of the community to the independence and importance of the individual. But it was also an awareness of the abilities and incredible potential of humanity. The rediscovery of Aristotle had opened up a new awareness of the world, and the severance between theology and philosophy had encouraged a new attitude toward it. For the medieval mind, it was God's world, and though we can use our observations and reasoning to explore it, we are both dependent on God for ultimate truth about it and responsible to him for what we do with it. But now philosophy and science had been detached from theology, and it was open to Renaissance thinkers to investigate the world without having to keep referring back to God. Through the power of their unfettered reason, it was theirs to explore and discover. And discovery is power and control. Unashamedly Descartes proclaimed the goal of humanity, to become "lords and possessors of nature."

This thinking did not entail a wholesale rejection of God. On the contrary, God was still of crucial importance in the early modern worldview. Until Hume all Western philosophers were practicing Christians, and the vast majority of scientists saw themselves as exploring God's handiwork. God was still central to the systems of Descartes, Spinoza, and Berkeley. Renaissance and early modern humanism was Christian humanism, not atheistic humanism. But the change of focus was significant. The direction of travel for the next five hundred years was being set, and it was away from theocentricity.

The Reformation.
The Reformation was a protest against the corrupt nature and practices of the Roman Catholic Church. Central to its concern was the individual's relationship with God. The Catholics taught that the only way into this relationship was through the church, by means of its sole authority to dispense the sacraments. Martin Luther and the Reformers taught that this relationship was a gift of God's grace received by faith. No church and no priest were needed. All those who had faith, all believers, had direct access to God through the work of Christ and the presence of the Holy Spirit.

But Protestantism's stress on the individual and its concept of the priesthood of all believers didn't entail the rejection of all external authority. For the Reformers the Bible was to be their authority. Of course the Catholics also claimed the Bible as their authority; but their understanding and interpretation of the teaching of the Bible was shaped by centuries of tradition. Taking their cue from one of the catch phrases of the Renaissance, *ad fontes*, "back to the originals," the Reformers sought to return to the original meaning of the biblical texts and to the understanding and practices of the early church.

Science. Science in the Renaissance period was very different from what it is today. It was still seen as a branch of philosophy and was only just beginning to develop a truly empirical approach. Much of Renaissance science was permeated with attitudes and beliefs that to us seem very unscientific. Chemistry, for example, or *alchemy* as it was called, was a strange mixture of superstition, sorcery, spiritualism, the investigation of the nature of substances, the development of medicines, and the like. **Giordano Bruno** (1548–1600), who supported Copernicus's heliocentrism and was burned by the Catholics in 1600, has generally been looked on as a martyr for the cause of modern science in the battle against obscurantism. But his support of Copernicus was not on scientific grounds; it arose from his belief that the earth was alive and so must move. His worldview was based on ancient Egyptian occult texts, and a large part of his interest lay in the field of magic.

Renaissance science had a mixed relationship with Aristotle. On the one hand, it was Aristotelianism that had laid the foundation for the development of a new way of viewing the world. But, on the other, the Aristotelian worldview was seen as the straitjacket from which the new discoveries were liberating humanity. Again and again, it was Aristotle's specific teaching, now nearly two thousand years old, that was being disproved and rejected. Typically, **Galileo** (1564–1642) disproved a number of the tenets of Aristotelian science through mathematical calculation and observation and experiment. For example, he rejected Aristotle's claim of the perfection of the heavenly bodies on the grounds of sunspots and the existence of mountains on the moon, and he showed, contrary to Aristotle, that different sized rocks accelerate at the same speed by dropping them off the Leaning Tower of Pisa.

Renaissance science also had mixed relations with Christianity. In general Christian leaders were wholly committed to its development. Almost all those involved in it were practicing Christians. Some were monks or clerics. But problems arose in two areas—where science involved occult or magical practices or beliefs, and where its conclusions contradicted what were seen as foundational Christian beliefs.

Medievals and Moderns

If we bear in mind the fact that the transition from the Middle Ages to the modern period was a process rather than a revolution, and the fact that generalizations in philosophy need to be treated with caution, we could summarize points of contrast between the two periods as follows:

- Medievals saw themselves as part of a long, rich tradition. Moderns saw themselves as breaking exciting new ground.
- Medieval thinkers were almost all clergy or monks; in the later medieval period they were educators in monasteries or universities. Most modern thinkers were laypeople following secular professions.
- Medievals wrote in Latin. Moderns increasingly moved over to writing in the vernacular. Medieval Latin was heavy, obscure, and inaccessible to all but trained academics. Those who used it were scholars writing for scholars. The language of the people was accessible to all; those who used it for their writings had a message for all.
- In the medieval period the authority of the church was a force to be reckoned with. In the modern period the church's monolithic authority was broken, and in many cases it could safely be ignored.
- In the medieval period the agenda was set by Plato or Aristotle. In the modern period thinkers were free to set their own agenda.
- In the medieval period reason used the truths of revelation as data. In the modern period they were subject to its critique.
- The medievals operated within a secure framework of agreed truths with a strong confidence in the dependability of their reason and knowledge. For the moderns skepticism was a constant threat and the justification of knowledge a continuing problem.
- Medieval thought included a teleological element. That is, it saw things in terms of purpose or Aristotelian final explanation. Moderns sought to understand the world without reference to teleology.

- The medievals viewed humanity corporately. The moderns stressed the individual.
- The medievals accepted authority. The moderns challenged all authorities except that of reason.
- The medievals accepted data from a number of sources, notably the philosophy of the past, the Christian revelation, and their experience in the world. The moderns limited their data to their experience.
- The medieval approach was thus basically objective. The modern approach was basically subjective.
- The medievals saw God as ultimate. The moderns made human reason ultimate.
- The medievals believed all truth is one and thus that all areas of knowledge and living can and should be integrated. The modern period saw increasing fragmentation. Science, for example, claimed the right to operate without the interference of religion or ethics.

THE PERSISTANT FALLACY

At this stage, it may be worth picking up again the fallacy we touched on in chapter 1 of the naive assumption made by people throughout the modern period that the latest is the best and is destined to supersede all that has gone before it. This no longer applies in the realm of automobiles, and it has never applied in the realm of philosophy. Philosophical ideas have come and gone almost as fast as new models of cars. Many of them have pointed out faults in their predecessors and have claimed to be rectifying them. But very few can claim they have actually demonstrated that any of the views they sought to replace were untenable. Christianity replaced paganism, but it didn't do so by showing pagan concepts were untenable. There are plenty of people around today, for instance, in the New Age movement, who believe paganism is still a viable worldview. The scientific worldview claimed that it had superseded Christianity, but in fact it was only offering an alternative. Postmodernism has rejected the scientific worldview and made extravagant claims about the end of all metanarratives. But metanarratives still thrive, and most people still live according to the scientific worldview.

The fallacy itself arises from a specific philosophical idea of inevitable historical progress, expressed specifically by Hegel but assumed by plenty of others. Linked with this view is the concept of irreversible trends. In the middle of the twentieth century, sociologists identified a process of secularization in the West and were quick to claim that it was irreversible. We were divesting ourselves, they said, of religious trappings left over from our primitive past. Now "man come of age" can manage without God and can finally excise all elements of religion. A couple of decades later the story had changed radically. Sociologists were rejecting secularization as a myth. Religion and a desire for the transcendent were not on the decline after all, even if the forms they took were changing. Given the many times the bold pronouncements of one generation of thinkers have been rejected by their successors, we may justifiably be skeptical of the confident claims of those who are currently pronouncing the death of God, truth, morality, meaning, philosophy, and so on. With even greater confidence we can predict that a new generation will declare them wrong.

MICHEL DE MONTAIGNE

Bordeaux, France (1533–1592). Many books will tell you that the modern period started with Descartes. We, however, are going to start with another Frenchman, Michel de Montaigne, who was born over a century before Descartes produced his first philosophical work, but who effectively set him his agenda. Then we will look at Francis Bacon, an Englishman who saw himself as setting the agenda for a new age.

The collapse of the medieval synthesis, together with the conflict of ideas around the time of the Reformation, inevitably created an atmosphere in which skepticism could flourish. An additional factor was the rediscovery of ancient skeptical writings. Montaigne was particularly influenced by reading the newly available work of Sextus Empiricus, a spokesman for Greek skepticism who wrote about A.D. 200. Perhaps surprisingly to us, skepticism in the sixteenth and seventeenth centuries was directed more at the claims of philosophy than at those of religion. Skeptics, for the most part, continued to accept the truths of Christianity, largely, perhaps, because they viewed them as received by faith rather than by reason.

Montaigne reacted strongly to the sixteenth century's growing confidence in reason. In a series of essays, or "attempts" to express himself (the first in the genre), he advocated tolerance and the suspension of judgment, arguing that no claim in any field could be supported by sufficient rational evidence to establish its truth. He advocated moral and cultural relativism, using the "admirable" lifestyle of South American Indians as an object lesson. Neither philosophers nor scientists can give us certain truth. Philosophers cannot agree among themselves or persuade each other by their arguments. Scientists change their views from one generation to the next. Both our experience of the world and our processes of reasoning are notoriously fallible. Even if they are only occasionally mistaken, we can never trust them, since we have no way of distinguishing between true and false information they give.

Montaigne set the trend for a skeptical element particularly in French thought. Pierre Bayle (1647–1706), for example, argued that reason only leads to paradox and that, apart from the Christian revelation, we can never know ultimate truth. Montaigne also directly influenced Montesquieu (1689–1755), who said that "goodness," "beauty," "perfection," and the like are terms "relative" to those who use them. All these helped set the agenda for Descartes and others who sought to escape from the destructive implications of skepticism.

FRANCIS BACON

London (1561–1626). Bacon was a lawyer, politician, and philosopher. He entered politics at the age of twenty-three and rose to become lord chancellor of England. But he fell from power as a result of a charge of corruption. He is said to have died as a result of catching a chill after experimenting on the effects of refrigerating a hen.

The new age. Bacon was an iconoclast and a visionary. He consciously rejected the concepts and methods of all who had gone before, and he called for a new start and a new method in the development of knowledge and understanding, especially in science. In particular, he called for the casting down of what he called the four intellectual idols, or ways of thinking that lead us away from the truth.

- Idols of the tribe: popular assumptions, such as that nature is teleological.
- Idols of the cave: personal biases, indoctrinated by education or personal background.
- Idols of the marketplace: linguistic confusions, arising, for instance, from using words that describe things that don't exist in reality.

- Idols of the theater: philosophical or scientific presuppositions. For Bacon these were especially Aristotelian presuppositions, but they also included most of the basic assumptions of sixteenth-century science.

Bacon expressed unbounded enthusiasm for the new age of adventure and discovery typified by the exploits of Magellan and Columbus and the discoveries of science. But the structures of study and learning, he said, and especially the universities, were still operating according to ancient and outmoded ideas and methods. All these must be cleared away; there must be a new beginning, a "Great Instauration." He worked out in some detail how this might be done by separating religious ideas from scientific investigation and reclassifying the areas of scientific research. Though he tried hard to find a sponsor to put his plans into practice, they were never implemented. But his vision inspired many later thinkers and educators.

Knowledge and power. Knowledge, Bacon said, gives us power over nature and enables us to promote the good of humankind, particularly in practical and technological ways. But it needs to be true knowledge. He used insects to illustrate three different approaches to learning. Spiders, he said, spin lovely webs that have nothing to do with reality. These are the speculative philosophers. Ants make untidy heaps. These are scientists who collect information but don't structure it. Bees produce a structured system. This was what Bacon set out to do.

Induction. We should start, Bacon said, with observation and experience. Since our observations and experiences are limited and we wish to develop general principles and universal truths, we will have to use induction rather than deduction. In deduction we keep within the strict limits of our data; we cannot conclude anything that is not originally given. In induction we move beyond our data to something new. We observe, for example, a swan and see that it is white. We see another swan, and that one is white as well, and so on until we have observed one hundred swans, all of which are white. Deduction can tell us there are a hundred white swans, a hundred white birds, or a hundred white creatures. Induction concludes that all swans are white. The assumption of the reliability of induction is, of course, foundational to science, but it is also very open to the attacks of skeptics, since we can never establish the nonexistence of black swans.

Straightforward induction, then, or induction by simple enumeration, is inadequate. So, said Bacon, we need to develop it into a more satisfactory tool.

To do this he suggested a more rigorous program of observation and experimentation, which, he claimed, would give us certain knowledge. Scientists, he said, must work slowly and thoroughly, keeping careful records. They must not just examine the instances that support their theories; they must make a study of anything that appears to contradict them or only partially supports them. After patient and careful observation, a preliminary hypothesis may be formed, which is then tested by carefully planned experiments. Once one hypothesis has been established, others should be added until a comprehensive system of laws has been established.

This inductive principle, Bacon said, can be applied to other areas of human knowledge, such as his own area of law. Here too we extract principles by careful study of individual situations, test them, and then are able to apply them back again to other specific cases.

There are few today who would accept that Bacon's improved inductive method is able to give us certain or ultimate truth any more than its rather naive predecessor could. However, his influence on succeeding generations of scientists was profound. After all, for the most part, modern science was amazingly successful and fruitful. For most people, that alone justified their faith in it. But if Bacon appears to have provided a philosophical justification, so much the better. As late as the nineteenth century, leaders of American thought waxed eloquent in their praise of Bacon, whose inductive method had been so hugely successful in the development of modern understanding and technology.

TO THINK THROUGH

Do you believe the earth is spherical or that water is composed of hydrogen and oxygen? If so, on what basis? On authority? Through experience? By faith? By logic? Is Bacon right in saying we can only know these truths by using induction? If induction is so imperfect a tool, how is it people are so sure of these truths?

TWENTY-TWO

TWO RESPONSES TO SKEPTICISM

DESCARTES AND PASCAL

In this chapter we look at two very different attempts to counter skepticism. Both turned inward. One used reason alone; the other used reason and "the heart."

Although there are a number of ways to respond to skepticism, one thing we can't do is refute it. Isolated items put forward by a skeptic can be refuted; we can get a flat-earther to travel with us in a more or less straight line round the world. But a full-fledged skeptic won't be put off by bits of refutation. He or she may say, "Okay. You claim we've flown round a spherical world in a straight line, and you've brought me back to where we started. But it's still possible that what you've actually done is fly in a huge circle over the flat earth." Records of the flight path won't convince her or him; they could be fakes or could be mistaken. If a person really wants to go for skepticism in a big way, there is nothing we can do to refute it.

But in fact most people aren't that skeptical. Or they accept that being that skeptical makes life impossible. But they still feel the need to work out at least some answers. And down through the ages plenty of answers have been put forward.

We are going to look in this chapter at two seventeenth-century Frenchmen's responses to skepticism. The two men are very different. One has been looked on as the epitome of rationalism; the other has been strongly criticized for his fideism. And yet they have points in common. Both had graphic "mystical" experiences. And both made God the key to their approach.

RENÉ DESCARTES

La Haye, France (1596–1650). After education in a Jesuit college, Descartes (pronounced day-*cart*) took a degree in law. He left France and fought briefly in the wars of religion. In 1619, during a period of deep meditation, he conceived in a moment of inspiration what he felt was a whole new way of understanding the world. He then had a series of dreams that gave him a strong sense of vocation for the rest of his life. For some years he gave himself to further reflection and meditation, taking the opportunity to travel in Europe. After 1628 he only occasionally visited France, spending most of his time in Protestant Holland. He lived the life of a gentleman of leisure, supported by his own fortune that he had realized by selling his French estates.

Descartes had a brilliant mind and studied and wrote on a wide range of topics. Mathematics particularly fascinated him and gave him a desire to find in other areas the kind of proof and certainty we find in math. He carried on a lengthy correspondence on philosophical matters with Princess Elizabeth, the daughter of Frederick V of Bohemia. She clearly had a very capable philosophical mind and made constructive criticisms of his ideas at a number of points.

Descartes's first (unpublished) work was on musical harmony. He made significant discoveries in math, including the Cartesian coordinates (*Cartesian* is the adjective formed from Descartes). He also published groundbreaking work in optics and meteorology. He wrote a comprehensive account of the origin and nature of the universe, in which he adopted heliocentricity. But when he heard that the Roman Catholics had condemned Galileo's work, he decided not to publish it.

Descartes's first philosophical work was written in French and published in 1637. It was designed as a preface to a collection of three of his works on geometry, optics, and meteorology and was called *Discourse on the Method of Rightly Directing One's Reason and of Seeking Truth in the Sciences*. It is elegantly written in the form of an autobiography and describes Descartes's approach to science and philosophy and how he came to adopt it. In 1641, in response to criticisms of the *Discourse*, he wrote (in Latin) six *Meditations on First Philosophy Wherein Are Demonstrated the Existence of God and the Distinction of Soul from Body*. With the *Meditations* he also published his responses to objections to his ideas by various other thinkers. The *Discourse* and *Meditations* were both fairly short works. Descartes subsequently published lengthy works called *The Principles of Philosophy* and *The Passions of the Soul*, but neither of them provoked the level of interest shown in his earlier philosophical works.

The foundation for science.

Like Bacon, Descartes stressed the practical value of philosophy in the widest sense of the word. Mere metaphysical theorizing produces nothing in itself, he said, but it lays a foundation for the key science of physics, which in turn gives rise to the more practical sciences like medicine and ethics. Our ultimate goal, he says, is to make ourselves "lords and possessors of nature."

It is because Descartes recognized the importance of laying a firm foundation for our scientific knowledge that he occupies a key position in the development of modern thought. Before we use reason to establish anything else, we must be able to justify its dependability. Soon Locke will be declaring, "Reason must be our last judge and guide in every thing." If this is so, how can we be sure reason is telling us the truth? In fact, Descartes didn't spend a great deal of time on this issue. Once he felt he had sorted it out, he was able to go on and spend much more time elsewhere. But a satisfactory answer to this question was foundational to all else. For this reason most philosophical attention has been focused on Descartes's epistemology outlined in the *Discourse* and *Meditations*. One generation of philosophers after another has tested its validity and tried to find alternative answers where Descartes failed.

Skepticism and doubt.

The basic epistemological agenda for Descartes was set by Montaigne and the skeptics. They had demonstrated quite clearly, and to Descartes's satisfaction, that the sure and certain knowledge Descartes so admired in the field of mathematics was unobtainable in our knowledge of the world around us. We are often deceived; our senses tell us things that are false; for example, a straight stick looks bent if it is half in water. Bacon's reply to the skeptic was to be more thorough in checking what our senses tell us. But Descartes realized that no amount of thoroughness was sufficient to defeat the skeptics. How can I know, for instance, that I am not asleep and dreaming that I am making those truly thorough observations, or that some evil genius is not maliciously deceiving me?

But if skepticism is not to be defeated by more careful observations and experiments, how are we to provide a firm base for our knowledge? Descartes's answer was to turn away from the external, objective world to what is inner and subjective.

Just about everything can be doubted. Authorities sometimes give us false information, so we can never trust any authority to give us certain knowledge. Our observations and sensations sometimes deceive us; a wise man, says Descartes, will never put full confidence in things that have once cheated him. Some experiences are very immediate—that I'm sitting reading, for example. Can I not be sure of that? No, says Descartes; I could be asleep and dreaming, or deceived by God or an evil spirit. Nothing, he concludes, is beyond legitimate and well-considered doubt. So nothing can be known for sure.

Descartes is sometimes said to have invented the method of doubt. This is not so. The method of doubt had already been practiced for over two thousand years. Skepticism, though held at bay by Platonism and the medieval synthesis, had never gone away. The removal of God as the foundation for philosophical and scientific truth inevitably allowed all the old relativism and skepticism to come flooding back. In expressing his doubts, Descartes was only echoing the arguments of Montaigne and the others of his time who realized that once God ceases to be the basis, all our knowledge begins to crumble.

The answer to doubt.
What is original in Descartes is not his doubt, but his answer to doubt. He gathered together a number of arguments from Augustine and the medieval tradition and built them into a sustained argument that takes us from total doubt to complete certainty, each step seeming to be logically established, just like a proof in a geometry theorem. Descartes was convinced that any person with a logical mind would have to allow the conclusiveness of his arguments and so accept his conclusions. He was seeking to argue deductively, as in math, a way of establishing his conclusions much more powerfully than Bacon's inductive method.

Sadly, every step in Descartes's argument has subsequently been shown to be inadequate. Brilliant though it is, it in fact fails to do what he set out to do. But it is a great example of philosophical arguing. Following is my summary of Descartes's argument. You may want to work slowly through it and see how convincing you find it before looking at my summary of some of the standard objections.

1. I can be deceived about, and so doubt the existence of, everything—the world, minds, even my body.
2. But I cannot doubt that "I exist." There must be something that is thinking, doubting, being deceived. *Cogito, ergo sum.* I am consciously aware; I think; so I exist. This is what Descartes calls his "first principle" of philosophy, the foundation of all else.

3. The "I" that exists is a conscious being that thinks, reasons, wills, has experiences, imagines.

4. Since I can doubt the existence of my body but not of my "I," the "I," which we will call my *mind* or *soul* (Descartes used the terms interchangeably), must be able to exist without my body.

5. The thing about *cogito, ergo sum* that enables us to be sure of its truth is the fact that it is "clear and distinct." Therefore, whatever we perceive very clearly and distinctly must be true.

6. Since knowledge through our senses or observations of the external world are unreliable, true knowledge can come only through the mind.

7. I have in my mind an idea of God as an infinite, independent, supremely intelligent, all-powerful Creator. This idea can only have come from God. Therefore God exists.

8. God is perfect in every way. Perfection in God must include existence; existence must be part of his essence. If he lacks existence, he is less than perfect. Therefore God exists.

9. Since God must possess every perfection I can think of, it is impossible that he should be deceitful.

10. Since God has planted reason in me, my reason is to be trusted when I use it rightly.

11. So everything I conceive very clearly and very distinctly may be taken as true since it is guaranteed by God.

12. Therefore I can have sure and certain knowledge.

Mind and matter: Cartesian dualism.

Descartes made a clear distinction between mind (or soul or self) and body, in effect splitting the world in two. The medieval period had resisted this division, finding a basic unity in God and, for the most part, emphasizing the unity of mind and body, not their separateness. For Descartes the "I" is a conscious, thinking thing; its essence consists in thinking. The essence of body, whether my body or objects in the world, is spatial extension. That is, they have length, breadth, and depth; they occupy space; they can be measured. Other attributes, like color and shape, come and go. So there are two very different types of things or "substances": thinking things, which occupy no space, and spatially extended things, which exercise no thought.

Princess Elizabeth pointed out that an immaterial human soul such as Descartes described would be unable to "propel" the body. If the two types of thing, soul and body, are so utterly different, how can they interact? Descartes replied that though they cannot normally interact, there is a part of the brain, the pineal gland, where they do so. He conceded, however, that it was very hard to conceive of how this could happen. He used gravity as an illustration but had to admit that even that was a "lame" simile.

Matter, motion, and God.

Every nonmental thing in the world is matter whose basic attribute is spatial extension. However, Descartes also stated that it is matter in motion, thanks to the creative activity of God. Indeed, for Descartes, God is needed to hold the world in being at every moment. Simply to have created it in the first place is insufficient; creative power must be continuously at work. Matter in motion, divided as it is into tiny particles, forms shapes and objects strictly according to mathematical principles. These form deterministic laws that mean that everything functions mechanistically.

Freedom.

One of the most powerful "clear and distinct" ideas we have, said Descartes, is that our wills are free. Indeed, they are no less free (though much more limited in potential) than God's will and thus are an evidence that we are made in the image of God. Having stated this, however, Descartes greatly limited human freedom by saying that the will has no choice but to follow clear and distinct ideas. Since these ideas come from the world around us, which operates in a mechanistic way, it would seem that our "free" choices are in fact determined.

The split world.

Quite apart from providing fuel for endless philosophical discussions, Cartesian mind/body dualism has profoundly influenced the development of Western thought. Linked with the accelerating separation between theology and philosophy, between religion and ordinary life, it validated a radical splitting of the world, one Descartes himself as a Christian would have rejected but which follows from his position. From now on there are two types of things in the world, each totally different from the other. Mind is the sphere of thought, emotions, free will, beliefs, values, and moral decisions. But none of these things applies to matter. Rather, matter is the sphere of fixed rules, of facts, of machines (Descartes referred to animals as machines). So values and morality only apply to us, not to the world.

This dualism gave the go-ahead to the modern concept of scientific exploration in which matter is investigated by mind. While matter operates blindly according to fixed rules, mind is free to think through and work out how matter functions. Since the personal aspects of the mind don't apply to matter, scientific investigation can (and must) leave aside personal feeling, issues of morality, value judgments, and the like, and operate in a detached dispassionate way. And, since mind is clearly superior to matter, the scientific enterprise is basically one of asserting mastery. Though for a few generations yet, scientists were still open to being humbled by what they observed, and worshiping God for his handiwork, the goal of becoming "lords and possessors of nature" had dangerous overtones of conquest and exploitation.

PROBLEMS AND OBJECTIONS
TO DESCARTES'S ARGUMENTS

Just about every philosopher since Descartes has had to take notice of his arguments. Here are some of the objections that have been raised.

- *Cogito, ergo sum* does not establish the existence of the "I." It only establishes the existence of thinking.
- Descartes assumes that the "I" who was thinking yesterday is the same as the "I" who is thinking today. He fails to prove our ongoing personal identity.
- How can a free will exercise significant freedom in a mechanistic universe?
- Descartes argues in a circle. He wishes to reach the conclusion "Whatever I clearly and distinctly conceive is true." To get there, he says, in effect, that he has a clear and distinct concept of a God who would not let him be deceived; and he accepts it because it is clear and distinct. (Descartes would respond to this that his concept of God, like the *cogito*, is in a special logically undeniable category of its own.)
- Descartes also argues in a circle in another way, since he depends on reason to establish that reason is trustworthy.
- Existence is not a perfection. Mathematicians conceive of a perfect circle, but no such circle has ever existed.
- Has the "evil genius" been defeated? Surely he or she would be clever enough to counterfeit clear and distinct ideas or even make a falsehood look like an intuitively obvious truth.
- It does not follow that if I have an idea of God in my mind, it must have been put there by God. Descartes here is unconsciously following medieval thought, which assumed that an effect (that is, my concept of God) cannot have a cause or source that is smaller or lesser than itself.

- Descartes's system produces an impossible dualism. If mind and matter are totally distinct, they can never interact.
- If Descartes's argument for the existence of God is less than rationally watertight, his whole system fails.
- The quality of being clear and distinct is difficult to apply. Did not everyone clearly and distinctly conceive of the earth as flat for many centuries?
- Descartes's inspiration for knowledge and his model for clear and distinct ideas are taken from math. But the principles of math apply only to math. They do not apply in the real world. For example, a mathematician's right angle is precisely 90 degrees. What we call right angles in ordinary life are never precisely 90 degrees.
- Descartes appears to provide a totally rational argument for the dependability of our knowledge. But, at best, it is based not on reason, but on intuitively known truths—the *cogito* and our innate knowledge of God. Reason cannot establish these foundational intuitions. Descartes's argument is therefore no more rational than, say, the medieval system that started with a belief that cannot be finally established by reason, namely, the fact of God's revelation.
- Descartes's main interest was understanding and mastering the external world. To do so he starts with the internal world, the mind. But if the gulf between mind and matter is so great, how can he then justifiably move back from the internal to the external, from the subjective to the objective?

TO THINK THROUGH

Was he right? Was he wrong? What aspects of Descartes's philosophy do you think are worth taking seriously?

People tend to say that Descartes's philosophy was the first modern "scientific" system. Yet in fact everything in it depends on God. Can you think of any way in which Descartes could have developed his system without giving God a key place?

How do you see the relationship between your mind and your body?

For Further Study

Descartes is one of the few philosophers who is fun to read. Try reading the *Discourse* and the *Meditations;* plenty of good translations are available.

Cottingham, J. *Descartes.* 1986; reprint, New York: Oxford University Press, 1998.

BLAISE PASCAL

Clermont-Ferrand, France (1623–1662). Though Descartes's philosophy was to exercise a dominating influence on subsequent thought, he was by no means the only person to be working out a philosophical system in mid-seventeenth-century France. Pascal, a man of equally brilliant intellect, was doing the same, with very different results. Sadly, he died in his thirties before he could complete his work. It is left to us to speculate whether, had he lived to publish his system, it would have been as trendsetting as Descartes's.

Educated by his father, who was an accomplished scientist, Pascal had published a treatise on conic sections and invented a calculating machine while still in his teens. In 1646 he became associated with the Jansenists, a French religious group that adopted a number of the insights of Protestantism. It sought to return to the simplicity of New Testament Christianity and rejected much of the teaching of the Catholic church after Augustine. However, the effects of this association seem to have worn off somewhat, until one November night in 1654, as he was meditating on the sufferings of Christ, he had a profound experience of God that affected him so strongly he wrote a "memorial" of it and kept it sewn into his clothing for the rest of his life.

Pascal was a brilliant mathematician and physicist. Among his several inventions was the *omnibus* (Lat. meaning "for all"), a carriage with a number of seats, which people could pay to use. Pascal gave the income from the bus to the poor and needy of Paris. He intended to write a defense of Christianity but died leaving only fragmentary notes and short passages. These were published after his death as his *Pensées* (Thoughts).

Skepticism, reason, and the heart. For a time Pascal had been influenced by the skepticism of Montaigne. He described the method followed in geometry as the best the human mind could do to achieve certainty. There we deduce a series of truths from basic principles and axioms. But, even in geometry, these basic axioms, though accepted by everyone, are ultimately unprovable. We accept them not on the basis of reason, said Pascal, but with

Pascal's Memorial

The year of grace 1654
Monday 23 November, feast of St Clement, pope and martyr
    and of others in the martyrology; eve of St Chrysogonus,
    martyr, and others.
From about half past ten in the evening until about half past
    midnight
Fire.
"God of Abraham, God of Isaac, God of Jacob"
not of the philosophers and wise men.
Certitude. Certitude. Feeling. Joy. Peace.
God of Jesus Christ
"My God and your God"
"Your God will be my God."
Forgetful of the world and of everything, except God.
He is to be found only through ways taught in the Gospel.
Greatness of the human soul.
"Righteous Father, though the world does not know you,
    I know you."
Joy, joy, joy, tears of joy.
I have separated myself from him.
"They have forsaken me, the spring of living water."
"My God, will you forsake me?"
May I not be separated from him for all eternity.
"This is eternal life, that they may know you, the only
    true God, and Jesus Christ, whom you have sent."
Jesus Christ.
Jesus Christ.
I have separated myself from him; I have fled from him,
    denied him, crucified him.
May I never be separated from him.
He is kept only through the ways taught in the Gospel.
Renunciation total and sweet,
Total submission to Jesus Christ and to my director.
Eternally in joy for one day of trial upon earth.
"I will not neglect your word." Amen.

"the heart." Knowledge in practical sciences or in ordinary life is rarely able to use the deductive method of geometry, and it too is based on principles or axioms we cannot justify by reason. Thus in two ways it falls short of rational certainty. Pascal was well acquainted with the arguments of Descartes and was convinced that they were inadequate because they depended on reason alone. Not only is reason inadequate to establish knowledge, said Pascal; it can even be used to destroy it.

But skepticism too is inadequate. No one, said Pascal, can live as a total skeptic. Skeptics have to believe some things in order to live, and since they don't believe them on grounds of reason, they have to accept them on other grounds.

So we can have grounds other than rational grounds for holding our basic beliefs. We do not have to limit knowledge to what can be rationally proved. Supremely, we have "the heart." For Pascal the heart is where we know truth immediately; we encounter it personally. He listed "heart, instincts, and principles" together. We know truth, he said, not just through a reasoning process, but in the heart. It is in the heart that we know first principles, like those of geometry, space, time, and movement. Reason can neither establish nor destroy these first principles, and yet we know them for certain. Further, these first principles are foundational to the operation of reason: "Reason relies on and has to base all its arguments on the knowledge gained by the heart and the instinct." We shouldn't expect reason to establish our first principles any more than we should require the heart to give us emotional conviction of the truth of rational arguments. "The heart has its reasons which the reason does not know."

Reason, God, and the Christian worldview. Just as reason cannot prove truths of science or ordinary life, it cannot prove the existence of God in any ultimate way. If it could do so, said Pascal, it would be a logical absurdity to deny his existence. That is not to say that belief in God is irrational. Pascal accepted that the "metaphysical proofs" may convince a few people for a time, and he planned to demonstrate in his *Defense of Christianity* how reasonable its basic doctrines were. Once we have experienced in our hearts the first principles of Christianity, we don't need rational arguments. But rational arguments have a place for those for whom that has not yet happened. Pascal was sure that as they responded positively to the arguments, God would work in their hearts. Even his famous "wager" argument was an attempt to show that it is more rational to accept Christianity than to reject it.

Pascal listed a number of "proofs" or arguments that show it is more reasonable to accept Christianity than to reject it. He included:

- The gentle way Christianity became established against the odds
- The good effect it has on an individual's life
- Jesus Christ
- The Bible
- Miracles
- Fulfillment of prophecy
- The comprehensiveness and adequacy of Christian teaching
- The way it has survived through history
- Its morality

Overall, says Pascal, the Christian worldview is the one that best fits and explains the world and the human condition as we know it. It is the only philosophy that really takes seriously the brokenness and need of the individual and provides an answer to it.

Given, then, that the case for Christianity is a powerful one but not such as to force someone to accept it on logical grounds, what do we do? Pascal, in one of his mathematical writings, had investigated probability theory and had devised a way of making decisions by assessing not just the balance of probability but also the value of the alternative outcomes. He applied this to the decision of those who are wavering between accepting or rejecting Christianity. He pictured them as well aware that Christianity may be true, but influenced by their "worldly" feelings to reject it. Other things being equal, he says, they should opt to accept Christianity, because if the Christian God exists, they have everything to gain, while if he doesn't exist, they won't lose anything. On the other hand, if they reject Christianity and it is in fact true, they have gained nothing and lost an infinite amount. This "wager" has been depicted by its critics as a totally unjustified leap of faith. Pascal didn't see it as such; for him it was the most rational thing to do. But his approach was also influenced by his own experience and his firm belief in the grace of God. When we do turn to God, he believed, God turns to us and shows himself to us. When he does so, we will know him in our heart and so have fullness of knowledge through reason and the heart.

There are two foundational truths of Christianity, said Pascal, both of which are revealed to us in Jesus Christ. There is a God whom we may know. And without God humanity is corrupted and unworthy. Jesus Christ is thus the "only object" of Christianity. Through him, and not through philosophical arguments, we find God, whom Pascal described as a God of love and comfort, who fills the souls and hearts of those who are his, who causes them to feel deeply within themselves their own need and his great mercy, and who unites himself with them in the secret places of their hearts, filling them with humility and joy, confidence and love, and joining them forever to himself.

Pascal, then, didn't reject the use of reason. But, in contrast to Descartes, he conceded its inadequacy. And, in answer to skepticism, he argued for a more holistic concept of knowledge. His stress on the need for basic principles, which are prior to reasoning, and on the role of the heart, prefigure a lot of more recent thought, not least that of the existentialists.

TO THINK THROUGH

Pascal's religious experience clearly influenced his philosophy. Sartre and Russell's atheism clearly influenced their philosophy. What would you say to someone who argued that religious beliefs should not be allowed to influence philosophy?

To what extent can Pascal's arguments be used to counter contemporary skepticism and relativism?

For Further Study

Krailsheimer, A. *Pascal.* Oxford: Oxford University Press, 1980.

TWENTY-THREE

DO WE STILL NEED GOD?

> In this chapter we review philosophy from the late sixteenth century into the eighteenth, tracing the way the modern worldview gradually pushed God out of his role in the universe.

I<small>F REASON IS OUR AUTHORITY, DOES IT HAVE TO OVER-</small>rule all other authorities? Does God have to become subject to it? Do we have to choose between the authority of reason and the authority of God? Is it possible to have two authorities? Is it a matter of being unable to serve two masters? Or can we give to Caesar what is due to Caesar and to God what is due to God? Or should we merge the two? Could we say that God is the author of reason, and so what reason says, God says? Or, perhaps, whatever God says will necessarily be reasonable?

These issues weren't new in the modern period. They had all been faced before, especially in the early centuries of the Christian era. But they came with new force in the first part of the modern period, and not surprisingly, they were answered in a number of different ways. The philosophers we are looking at in this chapter all wanted to retain a role for God in their systems, though they differed in the way that role fit with the role of reason. But they all shared a common feature—they assumed reason could establish its own first principles. The medieval period had, for the most part, consciously accepted that reason must start with presuppositions, which, though not contrary to reason, aren't able themselves finally to be established by reason. Nearly every philosopher today would agree that the twentieth century saw the abandoning of any attempts to show that reason could establish its own first principles. So today we all have to concede that we have to start with faith. For the average person in the twentieth century, that was faith in the basic assumptions of the scientific worldview. For the medieval, it was faith in a God who has created the world and communicated with it. Then, given the basic presuppositions, reason could get to work. Faith could seek understanding.

But this need to start with foundational presuppositions was something the modern age rejected or chose to ignore. And it was because of this that philosophers were confronted with the issue of the role of reason in relation to God and revelation and the other areas, like ethics, which traditionally had been closely linked with religion.

The issue of the relationship between reason and revelation was a central one especially in the seventeenth century. Different thinkers tackled it in different ways. The Cambridge Platonists viewed reason as the voice of God, which speaks more clearly than revelation. The deists, for the most part, decided that revelation failed the test of reason. Others, like Hobbes and Newton, though they continued to believe in God, were committed to following where reason led even if it led to places where there seemed no room for him. In the realm of ethics, it was inevitable that thinkers should seek to analyze concepts of goodness and obligation with the help of reason alone and move away from explanations that had their base in God. Meanwhile, those committed to defending the orthodox faith, like Butler, were happy to do so on the ground marked out by their opponents. If miracles or Christian moral principles are to be accepted, it is because they can be shown to be reasonable.

DEISM

If reason is our authority, then revelation is to be subjected to it. Those in the seventeenth and eighteenth centuries for whom revelation failed the test of reason, but who wished to retain at least some elements of Christianity, were generally called "deists" by their more orthodox opponents. This use of the term needs to be distinguished from its later specific meaning of someone who believes in a God who created the world but plays no part in it.

Deists argued that a benevolent God would make sure that all people have access to truths of religion and morality regardless of whether or not they know of the Christian revelation. This access, they claimed, is through human reason. They differed among themselves over how many and what truths reason could show us. They also differed over their attitude to revelation. Some were prepared to accept that reason confirmed some of the truths of revelation. But most tended to feel that reason was able to demonstrate that revelation, requiring as it did the miraculous intervention of God, was itself unreasonable.

They all agreed, however, that at least some of the claims of revealed religion (including Judaism and Islam, as well as Christianity) were false, that is, they were unacceptable to reason. They also agreed that purported revelations should be allowed no special status. The Bible, for instance, should be subjected to historical, moral, and rational criticism like any other book. While Locke claimed that reason supported belief in miracles and fulfilled prophecy, deism found these contrary to reason and sought to explain them away.

Deists saw themselves as clearing away unacceptable elements of superstition, supernaturalism, and institutionalism in order to establish a new pure form of Christianity, or natural religion, that would be acceptable to thinking people. Their ranks included Herbert of Cherbury (England), John Toland (Ireland), Voltaire (France), Reimarus (Germany), and Thomas Paine (America).

Edward Herbert.
Shropshire, England (1583–1648). For a time Edward Herbert was English ambassador in Paris, where he mixed with thinkers such as Thomas Hobbes. Dubbed "the father of English deism," Herbert sought to counter skepticism by showing the rationality of five basic religious truths, or "common notions," which everyone knows innately:

- There is one supreme deity.
- This deity should be worshiped.
- Virtue is the chief part of worship.
- We need to repent of wrongdoing.
- We are rewarded or punished in this life and the next for what we do.

Revelation may develop and add concrete images to these truths, but it can't contradict or establish them. Rather, it is to be judged by them.

John Toland.
Londonderry, Ireland (1670–1722). John Toland was successively a Catholic, a latitudinarian, a deist, and finally a pantheist; he coined the word "pantheist" in 1705. His best-known work, written in his deist phase, was *Christianity not Mysterious: Or, a treatise Shewing That there is nothing in the Gospel Contrary to Reason, Nor above it; And that no Christian Doctrine can be properly call'd a Mystery* (1696). In it he argued for freedom of religious

beliefs and developed further Locke's contention that religion should not be contrary to reason. "Mysteries," he said, being contrary to reason, should be excluded from the doctrines of Christianity.

TO THINK THROUGH

Can you desupernaturalize Christianity without destroying it?

CAMBRIDGE PLATONISM

A movement that shared the rationalistic approach of the deists was Cambridge Platonism. It was centered on Cambridge for the half century up to 1688, but it had considerable influence through much of the eighteenth century. The philosophy of the Cambridge Platonists was mostly Neoplatonic. They were generally opposed to any form of empiricism that exalted experience over reason. They were particularly opposed to all forms of materialism with their mechanistic view of the world that left no room for God or the spiritual element. They also reacted against the dogmatism of Calvinistic Puritanism, which was dominant in Cambridge at the time, preferring a more broad-minded, tolerant form of Christianity known as latitudinarianism. Reason, for them, must play a central role in religion as well as in ethics and philosophy. According to **Benjamin Whichcote** (1609–1683), in many ways the leader of the movement, reason is "the Candle of the Lord." "To go against Reason is to go against God. . . . Reason is the Divine Governor of Man's Life; it is the very Voice of God." So reason and true religion can never conflict. Forms of Christianity that appealed to revelation over against reason are to be rejected. The Cambridge Platonists staunchly defended the concepts of innate moral realism and human freedom.

THOMAS HOBBES

Malmesbury, England (1588–1679). Thomas Hobbes was a mathematician, classical scholar, physicist, philosopher, and political theorist. At times his political views made England unsafe for him, and he spent a considerable part of his long life on the Continent, especially in Paris, where he was highly respected. He was for a time tutor to the future King Charles II. He published works in legal and political theory as well as philosophy. His best-known work is *Leviathan* (1651), a study in political philosophy written during the time of upheaval leading up to the Civil War.

Matter, mechanism, motion, and minds.
Hobbes believed in God and spent quite a lot of his time defending himself against the charge that his philosophy had no place for God. Nevertheless, he held a strongly materialistic and mechanistic view of the world that left little for God to do and seemed to exclude significant human freedom. He attacked Descartes for his "immaterialism"; "I exist," he said, should be taken to mean that a conscious material being exists, not that an immaterial soul exists. Everything in the universe can be explained as matter in motion. All effects have motion as their cause. Our thoughts and other forms of mental activity are motions in our heads; external events cause these motions in immediate perception, and they continue to vibrate in our heads, like waves after a storm, and thus cause further thoughts and memories. All motions are governed by the laws of mechanics, so there is no freedom in the full libertarian sense of the word.

Politics.
In political theory Hobbes was basically a royalist, who argued for strong sovereign rule to enable the state to function. Without it, he said, there would be anarchy and war. In our natural state, that is, before the formation of societies and states, we all selfishly seek our own fulfillment and happiness, and as a result, life is "solitary, poor, nasty, brutish, and short." So the alternative is to form a "social compact" in which the people agree to follow their ruler or rulers, who would then exercise absolute authority for the good of the people on the basis of natural law.

In the rest of this chapter, we will look briefly at three moral philosophers who exemplify the trend to seek explanations that did not involve God. Then, after a glance at Butler, who sought to defend Christianity, we will turn to Newton, who, for many, is the key figure in the development of the "scientific" worldview that made God redundant in Western thought.

THREE MORAL PHILOSOPHERS

Third Earl of Shaftesbury.
Wimborne St. Giles, Dorset, England (1671–1713). Shaftesbury, who had John Locke as his tutor for a time, served in both the House of Commons and the House of Lords. He sought to separate morality from religion. Rather than accepting Locke's idea, shared by most people of the time, that morality is rooted in God, Shaftesbury sought for a more naturalistic source for morality and said that we each have a "moral

sense," something unique to humans. In contrast to Hobbes, who highlighted the selfish egoism of the individual, Shaftesbury stated that the moral sense is basically altruistic; it inclines us to what is good not just for ourselves but for the community. This moral sense is parallel to an aesthetic sense by which we know and respond to what is beautiful. Though Shaftesbury was later seen as principally emphasizing feeling as the basis of morality, reflective reason had a role to play in his theory. His approach led the way for a widespread trend in the eighteenth century to seek a basis for morality in the natural world rather than in the nature or commands of God.

Francis Hutcheson. Drumalig, Ireland (1694–1746).

After a time as a Presbyterian minister in Dublin, Francis Hutcheson was appointed professor of moral philosophy in Glasgow, where he was the first major figure in a fruitful period of Scottish intellectual life known as the Scottish enlightenment. He developed Shaftesbury's moral sense theory, particularly emphasizing feeling as opposed to reason as the basis of our moral decisions, though, again, he had a place for reason, especially in its role of justifying moral acts. He claimed that we have other senses in addition to the standard five, sight, hearing, touch, taste, and smell. In particular he proposed a sense of beauty and the moral sense as distinctive ways of experiencing the world. Like Shaftesbury, he saw human nature as essentially benevolent rather than egoistic. Virtuous behavior brings us an experience of pleasure through our moral sense; wrong behavior brings us pain. Consequently, we do not have to be told what is virtuous; we know it through our feelings. Virtue, for Hutcheson, was to be summed up as benevolence, a concern for "the greatest happiness for the greatest number," a phrase he originated.

Adam Smith. Kirkcaldy, Scotland (1723–1790).

Adam Smith was educated at Glasgow and Oxford. He was appointed professor of logic at Glasgow in 1751 and professor of moral philosophy in 1752. Later he resigned his position to devote himself to study. His first book, *The Theory of Moral Sentiments* (1759), was very well received and attracted the praise of Hume and Kant. His second book, *An Enquiry into the Nature and Causes of the Wealth of Nations* (1776), was equally successful and earned Smith the reputation of being the founder of modern political economy. He intended to complete his philosophical system by publishing a third book, but he was unable to complete it to his satisfaction and destroyed the manuscript.

In seeking to analyze the basis of morality, Smith rejected three possible answers: the religious answer, that morality is rooted in God, the "moral sense" theory as presented by thinkers like Hutcheson (who was for a time Smith's teacher), and any rationalistic form of answer that claimed that moral judgments are in fact rational inferences. In their place he developed a theory of "sympathy" borrowed from Hume, combining it with a concept of the "impartial spectator," which he in part inherited from Hutcheson. It is as we are imaginatively able to appreciate the situation of another and find pleasure in seeing virtue at work there that we are expressing virtue. And, just as we play the part of impartial spectator of others' situations and actions, so we are aware that they are spectators of our conduct, and equally we are able to assume the role of spectators of our own conduct. In each of us is a theoretical "man within the breast" who passes moral judgment on our actions, praising or blaming as appropriate. Neither the judgments of others nor of our own "man within the breast" are infallible, but they point us to an ideal, and as we strive for it, we develop our moral virtue.

Smith recognized that making pleasure and approval of specific conduct a criterion ran the risk of moral relativism, since different cultures found pleasure in different patterns of conduct. But he believed certain patterns of behavior won approval in all cultures, and it was the task of the moral philosopher to identify these. Moreover, even if we have difficulty identifying specific positive virtues, certain negative virtues—those that keep us from injuring others—are much more readily agreed, and these form the basis of social and legal justice.

JOSEPH BUTLER

Wantage, England (1692–1752). Joseph Butler was an Anglican clergyman, later bishop of Durham. His *Analogy of Religion* was a defense of Christianity in the context of deism. In it he argued that the claims of revealed religion are probable in a way that is analogous to the probability (accepted by the deists) of the truths of natural religion. His moral theory rejected crude egoism but argued that one form of self-love, "cool" or long-term self-love as opposed to immediate selfishness, will ultimately turn out to be for the good of others. He adopted elements of the moral sense approach while criticizing it for excessive dependence on feeling. His *Fifteen Sermons* present a carefully argued analysis of human nature and stress the role of conscience, the highest element of our nature, above self-love and benevolence. Conscience is supreme because it has its origin in God, though Butler did concede that it can be affected by education or culture.

ISAAC NEWTON

Woolsthorpe, Lincolnshire, England (1642–1727). Educated at Grantham and Cambridge, Isaac Newton was a professor of mathematics and fellow of the Royal Society while still in his twenties. His scientific research actually occupied a relatively small part of his life. He is said to have spent considerably more time studying theology and alchemy than he did math and physics, and toward the end of his life much of his time was taken up by politics. He made brilliant discoveries in the fields of math and the behavior and nature of light, but his greatest contribution to science was his theory of universal gravitation, which established a new way of understanding the working of the whole universe. His major work, first published in 1687, was *Philosophiae Naturalis Principia Mathematica*, "The Mathematical Principles of Natural Philosophy." His influence in his own time was considerable, although some rejected his theories. But as they were increasingly confirmed, not least by the return of Halley's comet in 1758, they took on the status of universally accepted dogmas until the twentieth century.

Newton saw his discoveries as supporting belief in God. Though not entirely orthodox in some of his beliefs, he accepted the Bible as God's revelation and explored a number of theological issues at considerable length.

Newton's method started with empirical observation and applied mathematical principles then went on to establish through induction "laws" that apply throughout the universe. From these laws, by a process of deduction, specific applications and predictions can be made. His theory is thoroughly mechanistic. Every body continues at rest or in motion unless influenced by an external force, which will cause a change of motion in proportion to its action. Every action results in an equal and opposite reaction. Between any two bodies there is a gravitational pull proportional to their respective mass and distance apart. Time and space and motion are absolute and boundless. However, Newton believed that God was still essential to and involved in the universe. He was its creator; the more Newton unlocked the wonders of the order and design of creation, the more he worshiped the divine orderer and designer. God is also the upholder of the system, making sure it runs smoothly and sorting out the irregularities that Newton was unable to explain.

But for all of Newton's personal belief in God, such a clockwork universe appeared increasingly to subsequent generations to make God redundant. God as an explanation was no longer needed. Everything in the universe could manage without him. From praise of God for his wonderful handiwork, subsequent generations turned increasingly to praise of humanity for its wonderful understanding of how our world functions.

Despite the Newtonian worldview's incredible usefulness in the development of science over the next two centuries, it had a very distinct downside. Such a mechanistic view of the universe turned out to have no place for those things that make human life most meaningful. Purpose, value, moral principles, human freedom, and the like don't belong in Newton's world. We are just cogs in the great machine. For some this was acceptable. For others it destroyed the essence of what it means to be human. Though Newton's theories dominated science for two hundred years and more, many philosophers found it unacceptably narrow and inadequate. The world may operate according to the fixed laws of physics, but we don't. We are something more than machines.

TO THINK THROUGH

What went wrong? Newton believed in God and retained values and morals. No conflict existed between his science and the rest of life. Did his system have to turn us into machines? How could that have been avoided?

TWENTY-FOUR

IT'S ALL THE SAME TO ME

SPINOZA'S PHILOSOPHICAL SYSTEM

In this chapter we look at the rationalistic and pantheistic system of Benedict de Spinoza.

IN THE NEXT THREE CHAPTERS WE WILL LOOK AT THE philosophical systems of three of the best-known thinkers in the Western tradition—Spinoza, Locke, and Leibniz. All three were contemporaries of Newton, and all were committed to the primacy of human reason. None of them were professional philosophers. The three philosophies they produced were very different from each other and had different receptions. Spinoza's was virtually ignored. Locke's had widespread influence; toward the end of his life he was feted as perhaps Europe's best-known thinker. Leibniz's did have some influence, but it took second place in his lifetime to his mathematical work and to the debate over whether he or Newton was the first to discover calculus.

BENEDICT DE SPINOZA

Amsterdam (1632–1677). Benedict de Spinoza's parents were Portuguese Jews who settled in Amsterdam to escape persecution. They gave him a traditional Jewish education, though he also studied secular subjects including philosophy. By 1656 he had broken with Judaism and was excommunicated. He devoted his life to philosophy, supporting himself by lens grinding and private teaching of philosophy. In 1673 he turned down an invitation to become a professor at Heidelberg on the grounds that he wished to retain his philosophical freedom. The two main philosophical influences on his thinking were Descartes and Hobbes; his first published work was an exposition of Descartes, based on his own tutoring. However, much of his philosophy was very distinctly his own. In the preface to his work on Descartes, he stated some of his points of disagreement. He rejected the concept that the human mind and the body were independent entities; he rejected free will; and he didn't believe that anything was beyond the reach of human understanding.

Spinoza published one other work during his lifetime, the *Tractatus Theologico-Politicus* (Theological/Political Treatise). In it he challenged the authenticity of the Old Testament as a revelation from God and argued for democracy and freedom of speech and religion. Because of the contentious nature of some of his ideas, Spinoza published the *Tractatus* anonymously. As a result of its hostile reception, he published nothing else during his lifetime. After Spinoza's death in 1677, friends published some of his writings, including his major work, *Ethic, Demonstrated in Geometric Order.*

Spinoza's philosophy won no followers, and no one took him particularly seriously until toward the end of the eighteenth century. However, his ideas have inspired a number of thinkers since then, and his monistic system, though equally rationalistic, provides an interesting counterbalance to Descartes's dualism. While dualism dominated for three hundred years, the second half of the twentieth century saw a reaction back to a unitary concept of all that is, very much in the spirit of Spinoza.

Substance. Like Descartes, Spinoza sought to build a systematic understanding of the world on the basis of reason. Whatever reason tells us is true and is to be accepted as infallible. But where Descartes started with the *cogito*, Spinoza started with substance. Descartes had defined substance as "that which requires nothing but itself in order to exist." But he appeared to accept at least three sorts of substance. God was the one ultimate substance. But mind and matter were also substances. This, as we have seen, raised problems about the relationship between the different substances. Spinoza was unhappy with the way Descartes applied his notion of substance, though not with his basic definition, so he set out to provide an alternative.

To do so Spinoza had to establish, by the use of reason alone, the existence of substance. He argued this in a version of the ontological argument based on the Cartesian definition of substance as having its own cause or source within itself. This means, said Spinoza, that for any substance, essence must involve existence. Since we define God as a substance, the notion of a nonexisting God is self-contradictory. So substance, that is, God, exists.

Monism.

However, says Spinoza, there cannot be more than one substance. For him this followed rationally from the definition of substance in terms of independence from anything else. So, since God exists, and he is the only substance, everything that exists exists in God as a mode or a modification of God. Scholars have debated whether this means that Spinoza was a pantheist. Certainly his system has clear pantheistic elements; his God, for instance, lacks the personal qualities of the biblical God, and Spinoza frequently used the expression "God, or Nature," in effect identifying the two. Indeed, he was able to use God, Nature, Substance, Being, and Reality all to mean the same. It is worth noting, however, that his concept of Nature is rather more intellectual than that of later pantheists; it is the rational order of things rather than the material universe.

A further rational conclusion Spinoza drew from the oneness of God and the world was the oneness between each individual and any other individual, and between the individual and God. God is not distant or unknowable. Nor should the divisions and conflicts that arise from our emotions be allowed to destroy the basic unity all people share.

God and the world.

Judaism and Christianity, with their clear concept of God as creator, saw the relationship between God and the world in causal terms and thus allowed some degree of separateness between the two. We might parallel it with the relationship between a parent and a child. Spinoza's concept is more like the relationship between a mother and a fetus she is carrying in the early stages of pregnancy; we are able to describe the existence of the fetus totally in terms of the mother: "She is pregnant." The world and human beings, for Spinoza, are not seen as objects God has made, but rather as attributes or descriptions of God. Spinoza is able, in referring to the world as possessing extension, to say "God is extended," something the Judeo-Christian tradition would find very hard to accept.

God and us.

God, the one substance, says Spinoza, consists of "an infinity of attributes." In us, however, just two attributes, thought and extension, are expressed. This enables Spinoza to escape from Cartesian mind/body dualism. There is no dualism; mind and body are one. Both mind and body are modes or expressions of the divine attributes thought and extension. Mind doesn't need to interact with body, or vice versa; rather, mental and bodily processes occur together.

The mind.

In keeping with his rationalism, Spinoza minimized the significance of sensations or empirical experience. For him there were three levels at which the human mind can operate. Most people function at the lowest level, accepting a mass of largely unrelated images or concepts arising from their experiences. A higher level of mental activity is attained by those who use their reason to form general and universal concepts about the world, building a rational and comprehensive system of scientific understanding. The highest level, attained only after much effort, is the divine understanding of the "infinite idea of God or nature." Spinoza called this "intuitive knowledge" or knowledge *sub specie aeternitatis*, seeing things from the standpoint of eternity.

Freedom and ethics.

Spinoza's system is highly deterministic. Everything, he said, exists and happens in a way that is determined by God. Even God's actions are determined by his own nature. However, Spinoza did attempt to salvage a limited concept of freedom for both God and humans. God is free, he said, in that his actions are determined by his own nature and not by something outside of him that controls him. And though we are totally determined, we can feel free by accepting and conforming to things as they are.

Again, in true rationalist fashion, this acceptance comes through the exercise of our reason. Much of the *Ethic* is devoted to a discussion of our emotions, how we understand them and how we cope with them. Through our thinking we are to eradicate negative or "passive" emotions and accept the determined order of things. Why feel fear of death or hatred of someone when death and the person's actions are inevitable? As we increase in our understanding of and acceptance of the way the world and we as individuals operate, we are, says Spinoza, in effect showing love for God. Spinoza has been called "a God-intoxicated man." But in true rationalist fashion, Spinoza saw our oneness with God and our love for him basically in intellectual terms. His concept is very different from the Christian concept of a relationship of love in which God loves us and expresses that love toward us. For Spinoza the only way God can love is if we, as part of God, express this intellectual acceptance of the way things are. As we develop this "intellectual love," we participate more fully in the eternal rational order and so obtain some sort of immortality.

Spinoza called his major work *Ethic*, indicating the practical aim of his system. Since his God is impersonal, ethical behavior is not a matter of obeying God's commands or responding to God's love. Rather, it is the application of our understanding of the nature of the world, that is, God, and, in particular, the right handling of our emotions. Emotions are confused ideas about the way things should be. Once we accept that things are as they are and that there is no question of them being anything else, we can become intellectually one with the rational order of things and so obtain "bliss." Although Spinoza defined good in terms of what is personally advantageous to us, his concept of the unity of all individuals and their unity with nature enabled him to assume that what is good for the individual is good for the whole. Though he didn't work out a detailed code of ethical behavior, the virtues he extolled are essentially altruistic: acceptance and love for others, toleration, honesty, and the like.

TO THINK THROUGH

Plenty of people today are attracted to a basically pantheistic concept of the universe. Why do you think this is so? In what ways can we learn from the pantheistic worldview?

For Further Study

Donagan, A. *Spinoza*. Chicago: University of Chicago Press, 1989.

TWENTY-FIVE

LET'S BE REASONABLE

LOCKE'S PHILOSOPHICAL SYSTEM

> In this chapter we have a conversation with Locke, whose philosophical system, despite contradictions and unjustified assumptions, had a huge influence on contemporary and subsequent thought.

JOHN LOCKE

Wrington, Somerset, England (1632–1704). Locke was born the same year as Spinoza, but he outlived him by twenty-seven years. A comparison of the two illustrates the similarities and differences between the Continental and British traditions of philosophy.

- In contrast to the scholastic tradition, neither was a teacher of philosophy or involved in theological education.
- Both were influenced by Descartes.
- Both valued the role of reason very highly.
- Both sought to produce a philosophical system that applied to the whole of life.
- While Spinoza sought to build his system on reason alone, Locke built his by applying reason to the data of experience.
- Spinoza's system is thus essentially a rationalist one. Locke's is an empiricist system in that it starts with the data of experience, though Locke would insist it is totally rational.

◆ Spinoza, like Descartes, operated in the sphere of pure thought, drawing conclusions for the logical principles of his thinking, without reference to things around us in the world. Locke claimed that this was impossible. There is nothing in the mind that has not gotten there through our senses. Pure thought, unaffected by experience, does not exist. Nothing in our mind is "innate"; everything comes there from the world around us.

Born into a Puritan family, Locke was educated at Westminster School and Christ Church, Oxford, where he studied philosophy and medicine. The philosophy he studied at Oxford was still strongly influenced by scholasticism. But Locke developed a keen interest in the ideas of Descartes and was to number among his personal friends leading scientists of the day, including Isaac Newton and Robert Boyle. In 1683 he had to leave England for the Netherlands because of his political views. It was there he wrote his best-known philosophical work, the *Essay Concerning Human Understanding*, which he published in 1689 on his return to England. His writings include political theory (which was to influence the development of both the British and American constitutions) and theological issues. He was a great letter writer.

A DIALOGUE WITH LOCKE

Let's have a chat with Locke to see if we can get him to describe some of the main points of his philosophy.

You: *We have just been looking at Descartes and Spinoza, who are generally known as rationalists. Where do you stand on the significance of reason?*

Locke: I stand with them. Reason is God's gift; without it all is darkness. It must be our last judge and guide in everything. But I believe that the human understanding has its limits. And I can't agree with Descartes and Spinoza over their rejection of the significance of our observations of the external world.

You: *Perhaps that's because you're British and they're Continentals. Descartes started with his "cogito," Spinoza with the nature of substance. Where do you start?*

Locke: I can state my foundational principle positively or negatively. Positively, all knowledge comes from experience. Negatively, there are no such things as innate ideas.

You: *You mean we can only know things directly?*

Locke: No. There are two ways knowledge can come from experience. Directly, as when I see a tree. Or on reflection, as when I draw conclusions on the basis of a number of observations or experiences.

You: *What do you mean by innate ideas, and why do you reject them?*

Locke: Some people believe we all are born with certain basic principles and concepts. This belief has a long history and goes right back to Plato himself. It was held by Descartes and is held by most people in my century, but I reject it. There is no evidence for it. Babies or children don't spontaneously come out with the principles of logic or the basic truths of mathematics. It is much more reasonable to accept that they learn these things through experience. Our minds—and by the way, I accept Descartes's distinction between mind and body—start off as a *tabula rasa*, a "blank tablet." They contain nothing until experience starts writing on them.

You: *Your principle that all knowledge comes through experience is a profoundly influential one. It has been the basic presupposition of the empiricist school of philosophy and has been very fruitful as a principle of modern science, and it is still widely (and often unthinkingly) held in my century. But if all knowledge comes from experience, what precisely is it that we know?*

Locke: Ideas. We don't know things directly; we know our ideas of them, which arise from the sensations we experience. From these ideas we form other ideas as the result of reflection.

You: *Hmm. So it's a three-stage process. Things exist. They cause the sensations that we experience. And we think ideas that arise from these sensations. It sounds a bit complicated. I have a suspicion that it gives rise to the very difficult problem that skeptics love to raise over how we can be sure that our ideas accurately reflect the objects that lie behind them. But tell me more about our sensations. You say we experience them rather than the real things. What are the sensations sensations of?*

Locke: Qualities. As I said, we don't experience the thing itself, what I call the object's "substance." Rather, we experience its properties or qualities. Someone reading a book is experiencing the qualities of the book, such as its shape, mass, and color. He doesn't experience the book itself, its substance. Instead, he infers the existence of the book from its qualities.

You: *You have some distinctions to make over qualities?*

Locke: Yes. I distinguish primary qualities, which are in the object, like its mass, motion, or number, and secondary qualities, which are in us, like its color, taste, and sound. I do this because I'm aware of the relativity of such things as color, exemplified, say, in color blindness.

You: *If you'd known twentieth-century theories of the relativity of mass, you may have had to conclude that the number of primary qualities is in fact very limited or even nonexistent. But if we only experience qualities, how can we know that there really is a substance behind them? Can we not say with Buddha that nothing real exists behind the perceived qualities?*

Locke: No. I have to assume that qualities can't exist without a substance. There must be something underlying them even though we're unable to say what it is.

You: *But surely this provides a pretty shaky foundation for our knowledge of things in the world around us. Can we ever have certain knowledge on the basis of our empirical observations?*

Locke: I'm afraid not. The best we can have is probability. If we have adequately observed or experienced something or received something on good testimony, then we can accept that it probably is true. Our minds have the ability to assess the strength of the probability of any given proposition. Mind you, there are two nonempirical types of knowledge where we can have certainty. These are the propositions of mathematics and ethics, where, of course, we're only dealing with abstract ideas, not with the real world.

You: *But surely science and society will collapse if we can't have knowledge about things in the real world.*

Locke: Not necessarily. Where we can't have knowledge, we can operate with beliefs.

You: *What do you mean by "beliefs," and how do they help?*

Locke: Beliefs are the opinions that we all hold about every conceivable subject. For the most part, we accept them without verifying them, and as a result many of them turn out to be false. But with some effort we can regulate and govern the formation of the beliefs that we hold. We can seek to establish them more firmly. We can collect and examine the evidence for and against them; we can decide how probable it is that they are true and the extent to which we should trust them. We can then continue to make rational and regular experiments and so get nearer and nearer to the truth. But we can never arrive at total certainty.

You: *You said something interesting about ethics just now. Do you really believe we can have total certainty in ethics? That's something most people of my generation find very hard to accept.*

Locke: Yes, I do. For two reasons. First of all, our reason tells us clearly that there are basic moral principles that apply universally. And, second, God, who is the source of these moral principles, has revealed them to us in the Bible. I've shown in some detail in my treatise *The Reasonableness of Christianity* how closely the biblical principles and the principles reason shows us agree.

You: *So you believe that Christianity is reasonable?*

Locke: Yes, I do. And I believe that in the seventeenth-century atmosphere of skepticism and the questioning of everything, it is essential that we seek to defend Christianity by showing that it is perfectly rational to believe in it. Some of the truths of Christianity, like the moral laws and the existence of God, can be established by reason apart from revelation. Indeed, in my *Essay* I've shown that the existence of God is something we can know with mathematical type certainty—more certainly than we can know the existence of external objects in the world. But I accept that some truths of Christianity are above reason. That's why we need revelation and faith. But none of them must be contrary to reason. Any claim to being a revealed truth must be tested by reason. As I said before, reason must be our last judge and guide in everything. I personally believe that the essence of Christianity can be summed up in just a few propositions. You don't have to accept all the Thirty-nine Articles. That's why I believe we should let even Dissenters practice their Christianity the way they want to.

You: *That brings us to your social and political theory. Can you sum that up in a sentence or two?*

Locke: Not really. It has taken me several treatises to express it. But I suppose the key point is that I've no time for the divine right of kings. Reason teaches us that we're all equal and that every one of us has a right to life, liberty, and the owning of private property. The foundation of government is a contract with the people to protect these rights. We give up some of our freedom in order to enjoy the benefits of this social contract. Generally the people should trust their government, but if a government fails to protect their natural rights, it should be removed and another set up in its place. As for toleration, though I belong to the Church of England, I can't accept that all should be compelled to belong to the state church. Churches should be voluntary associations, independent of the state.

TO THINK THROUGH

Where do you stand on the empiricist principle that everything in our minds has gotten there through our empirical experiences?

The postmodernists have totally rejected Locke's principle that reason must be our last judge and guide in everything. But have they thrown the baby out with the bath water?

Locke conceded that empirical experience can never give us certain knowledge. Does that matter? Was he right?

For Further Study

Jolley, N. *Locke.* Oxford: Oxford University Press, 1999.

TWENTY-SIX

GETTING REALLY FANCIFUL

LEIBNIZ'S PHILOSOPHICAL SYSTEM

> In this chapter we explore one of the oddest of philosophical systems. But don't let that put you off. As you look at Leibniz's philosophy, watch out for the things you can accept and use in your own thinking, rather than just the things with which you disagree.

GOTTFRIED LEIBNIZ

Leipzig (1646–1716). Gottfried Leibniz was the son of a professor of philosophy at Leipzig. He trained in math and in law, and he earned his living at the court of the electors of Hanover until 1714, when the elector George left Germany to become George I of England. Leibniz spent four years in Paris from 1672, where he interacted with the latest philosophical and scientific ideas of the day. He wrote prolifically but published very little in his lifetime. He did, however, publicize his views in journal articles and through correspondence. He was a brilliant mathematician, and his interests included history, law, linguistics, etymology, symbolic logic, theology, geology, medicine, and physics. Essentially an optimist, he had visions of a united Europe, a universal logical language, and the unity of Christian denominations.

Leibniz was a Protestant Christian who made God foundational for his understanding of the world. He was eager to defend the Christian concept of God against those who attacked it, as he did in the only book-length work he published in his lifetime, the *Theodicy* (1710). In that his philosophy is strongly rationalistic, the rational God he depicts there seems to lack many of the qualities of the God of Abraham, Isaac, and Jacob, yet, unlike Spinoza's God, Leibniz's God and the God of the Bible are not incompatible.

Three factors complicate understanding of Leibniz's philosophy. First, his style and his terminology tend to be heavy and hard to follow. Second, he never worked his ideas into a coherent system, and he doesn't seem to have paid much attention to making the different aspects of his work consistent with each other. Third, many scholars believe that he in fact had two philosophies, a "popular" one that he made public, and the other, his true philosophy, that he recorded in some of his unpublished works. Nevertheless, it is possible to summarize what are generally accepted as his most significant insights in seven points.

1. All that is, is rational and is to be understood through our reason.
2. Everything that is and everything that happens is according to a principle of sufficient reason.
3. The basic stuff of the universe is an infinite number of independent individual "simple substances."
4. God is the self-sufficient transcendent creator and rational basis of all that is.
5. The universe as it is, is "the best possible world."
6. Everything in the world is determined, yet human choices are free.
7. The existence of evil in the world does not count against the existence or goodness of God.

Some of these concepts need unpacking.

2. The principle of sufficient reason.
Leibniz distinguished two kinds of truths. "Truths of reason" are based on the law of contradiction. To deny them would be to make a self-contradictory statement. A standard example is "A bachelor is unmarried." Kant was to call this kind of truth "analytic." But most truths are not like this. "John is a bachelor" can be denied without producing a self-contradictory statement. We can use various terms to describe this second sort of statement, such as contingent (because it is contingent upon, or depends upon, whether John has gotten married), synthetic (Kant's term), or empirical, because it is something in the world around us that we observe through our senses, not something wholly within the mind. Leibniz called it a "truth of fact," using "fact" in the empirical sense.

What makes a "truth of fact" true? Leibniz's answer is "sufficient reason." Nothing happens without sufficient reason. Sufficient reason for our concluding John is not a bachelor would be the existence of his wife, his wedding photos, his marriage certificate, and so on. Leibniz conceded that we are never able to amass all the sufficient reasons to establish a truth of fact, so we may get things wrong. God, however, knows all the sufficient reasons, so he always gets things right. Leibniz drew a very significant conclusion from this. If God knows all the sufficient reasons for everything, then he knows everything. He doesn't need to experience John getting married. He knows even before creation all the reasons leading up to John meeting Mary, why they fall in love, and so on. Or, to put it another way, because there are sufficient reasons for every event, every event is totally predetermined.

Leibniz accepted that this conclusion was one that people found hard to accept, so he tended to keep it to himself. But it did seem to follow logically from his way of understanding the principle of sufficient reason.

3. Substance and monads.

Descartes and Spinoza had tried to understand the nature of substance. If we get behind the appearances of physical things, down to a deeper reality, the real basic stuff of the universe, what do we find? Leibniz asked the same question and came up with a very different answer. In place of Spinoza's one basic substance, or Descartes's mind and matter, he said that basic to the universe was an infinite number of individual substances, which he called "monads."

These monads are not physical. Trained as we are in the current scientific worldview, we in the twenty-first century find no problem in thinking of an infinite number of subnuclear particles as the basic stuff of the universe. But because we have been thoroughly indoctrinated in materialism, these particles are still for us basically physical, even if we think of them in terms of energy. But Leibniz's monads are not physical; they are not subnuclear particles or even atoms, which was as far as they had gotten in his day. (Leibniz did in fact accept a mechanistic concept of the physical world, which for him consisted of tiny particles in motion.) But in speaking of monads, he is seeking to answer the question "What lies behind the physical world, which is only the world of appearances, where things come and go?" It's a bit like Descartes's body and mind. The body is the physical reality; but behind, and very different from, the body is the mind or soul. So Leibniz's monads lie behind all the physical things in the universe, and they are very different from them.

Since they are so different, it is hard for us to conceive what they are like. But Leibniz tells us monads are

- Immaterial; that is, nonphysical.
- Immortal. Physical things may be broken down. A monad, being a simple substance, must continue to be as it is forever, unless annihilated by an act of God, parallel to his act of creation.
- Alive. The form of life they possess is not physical life; it is more like spiritual or soul life.
- Many. There is an infinite number of them.
- Independent. Each monad is totally self-contained. It complies with Descartes's definition of substance, "that which requires nothing but itself in order to exist."
- Isolated. Monads don't communicate with each other. They are "windowless"; they can't see the monad next door.
- Perceiving. Though monads don't perceive each other, they are all programmed to know everything that is going on in all the other monads. Think of it this way: Your local team is playing a football game. You're ill in bed, so you can't go; in Leibniz's terms you can't perceive the match. But suppose God, who knows in advance every detail of the game, at the moment of creation put the whole thing on a computer so that you can lie in bed and by virtual reality experience the match just as though you're there. You'd even be cheering at the identical moment the crowd in the stadium is cheering. That is how it is with the monads. God at creation put into every monad the potential to perceive every action of every other monad forever. If monad X jumps at time T, all other monads will perceive the jump exactly at time T, not directly, but because God, knowing X would jump at T, programmed them at creation to have an internal and private perception of that jump at time T. Leibniz called this "preestablished harmony."
- Varied. Leibniz pictured a hierarchy of monads arranged according to their level of perception or awareness. At the bottom are very basic monads with very little perception. They may potentially be able to perceive everything, but they don't because they are three-quarters asleep. Higher up are the monads that can be seen as constituting the life force in animals. Higher still are the monads that form human souls or spirits, one monad per soul. These exercise a high level of perception; they are rational and have will as well as perception. And highest of all is the supreme monad, God.

Q and A on Preestablished Harmony

If you are still puzzling over preestablished harmony, here are a few questions and answers that may help.

Q: *Why such a long way around? Surely it is much easier if monad Y can perceive monad X jumping directly rather than having to find it out via God's programming at creation.*

A: True, it would be a lot easier. But this is Leibniz's answer to the problem of the link between mind and body. Why is it when my mind or rational soul decides to kick, my leg moves? Science has shown that physical effects need physical causes. Descartes fudged the issue by saying something happens in the pineal gland in the brain. Leibniz was more consistent, and he accepted that my immaterial mind can't move my leg. Yet we know beyond any doubt that my mind's decision to kick is followed by my leg moving. How can this be? His law of preestablished harmony was his answer. The monad that is my mind and the collection of monads that make up my leg both have an internal and private program implanted in them at creation that means that at the very moment my mind decides, my leg moves.

Q: *But surely that's asking too much. An infinity of monads and an infinite number of events—how could God synchronize all that?*

A: For us it would be a problem, because we're finite. But it's no problem for an infinite God. He's had all the time and resources of infinity to set up the system.

Q: *But listen. Every time I decide to kick, my leg moves. Surely that proves that it's my deciding that makes my leg move. It has to be cause and effect, not preestablished harmony.*

A: It doesn't have to be. Think of a skilled clock maker, says Leibniz, who makes two clocks such that they strike every hour, week in week out, absolutely simultaneously. Clock B's striking always accompanies clock A's striking. But A doesn't cause B to strike. Rather, it's all done by preestablished harmony.

5. The best possible world. God, as creator, is the one who set up the whole system of "sufficient reasons" that causes everything to be as it is. In theory he had an infinite number of systems to choose from. All systems, or possible worlds, would have their good points and their not-so-good points. For example, world A where John marries Mary makes Mary very happy (since John's a nice guy) but makes Gladys and Maud, who have both taken a shine to John, pretty miserable. But world B, where John marries Gladys, would make Gladys happy and Mary and Maud miserable. What God did, says Leibniz, in his infinite wisdom and goodness, was to select out of all the infinite possibilities "the best possible world," that is, the one that has the greatest number of good things and the minimum number of bad things.

6. Determinism and free will. Everything in Leibniz's universe is totally determined by the principle of sufficient reason. How, then, can he explain the experience we have of making free choices? Did John freely choose to marry Mary, or did he not? Leibniz's answer is that since at creation God had an infinite number of possibilities before him, there must have been an infinite number of ways he might have designed John. For instance, he could have created John such that he freely chose Mary or Gladys or Maud. But, in the end, and for the best possible reasons, he chose to create a freely-Mary-choosing John. So John's choice is both totally determined and totally free.

7. Evil and theodicy. In his *Theodicy* Leibniz argued that the existence of evil in the world does not count against the existence of God. Not all evils can be directly attributed to God, he said. Some arise through the physical makeup of the world. Some are caused by the wrong use of human freedom. Some are essential so that a greater good may come. But we need to look at the whole picture, not just the individual evils. The whole picture, the world as we have it, including the fall and redemption through Christ, is the "best possible world" that God has chosen out of the infinite number of possibilities.

TO THINK THROUGH

"What a weird system. How could anyone even begin to believe that?" you may ask.

I agree it's weird. But anyone living in Leibniz's time would have thought it much less weird than what we all now believe about the behavior of subnuclear particles, none of which anyone has ever seen. And, interestingly enough, some subnuclear physicists have developed ideas that have uncanny parallels to Leibniz's preestablished harmony to explain the behavior of some subnuclear particles. Why do we accept the subnuclear physicists' way of seeing things and reject Leibniz's? Remember, subnuclear physics may well be out of date in a generation or two. And where does Ockham's razor fit in?

If you don't like preestablished harmony, try "occasionalism." Since mind and matter can't interact, every time I decide to kick, God is aware of the decision and steps in and moves my leg. Just as weird? Or just as possible? Or is it another example of the lengths to which people will go to maintain Cartesian dualism?

How would you get out of Leibniz's determinism?

Descartes, Spinoza, and Leibniz all claimed to produce a purely rationalist system, using logic and the content of the mind alone, unpolluted with unreliable empirical experiences. What does the fact they each ended up with such contrasting systems tell you about the pure rationalist approach?

For Further Study

Mates, B. *The Philosophy of Leibniz*. Oxford: Oxford University Press, 1989.

TWENTY-SEVEN

THE IDEAL SYSTEM

BERKELEY AND EDWARDS

In this chapter we look at the "idealistic" philosophies of George Berkeley and Jonathan Edwards. In an age when the almost universal trend was to make the world as the scientists viewed it the basis of all our knowledge and living, they both made something of a last-ditch stand to make the God of traditional New Testament Christianity the key to everything.

To LIVE IN THE WORLD WE NEED TO UNDERSTAND WHO we are and what the world is. We need answers to the big questions about truth, reality, meaning, goodness, and the like. Where do we find the answers to such questions?

The answer of the medieval period had been God. He is the source of us and of all things; he is wise and good; and he has revealed his truth and himself to us. This answer didn't preclude the use of reason; the medievals gave reason a very significant part to play in their worldview. But God was the primary authority.

The answer of the philosophers of the early modern period was our reason. Reason must be our only authority. This answer didn't preclude the inclusion of God; almost all the early moderns gave God a key place in their worldview. But reason was the primary authority.

The early moderns used reason as their primary authority in two slightly different ways. Some, notably Descartes, Spinoza, and Leibniz, chose the way of pure reason. That is, they chose to start with reason alone, not with anything in the world, and to build up a worldview purely through rational arguing, again without any reference to the way things actually are in the world around us. But, as we have seen, the sad fact was that the three who were most brilliant and successful at doing this ended up with three different systems that were irreconcilable with each other at several points. This is profoundly disappointing. If reason is our authority, we need it to be a reliable authority. Yet it led three of the most brilliant minds of their age off in three mutually contradictory directions. We might feel that this demonstrates once and for all that reason is not a sufficient authority.

Maybe the problem these three shared was that they chose the way of pure reason. The alternative way, which Locke followed, was to make reason our authority but to link it with our observations of the world around us. Locke, like Aquinas before him, believed that if we didn't have any experiences of the world around us, we wouldn't have anything to reason about. There is nothing in our intellect that hasn't first been in our senses. We have no innate rational ideas, principles, or truths. So we have to take the two, reason and our experience of the external world, together. Those who followed the way of pure reason might reply that this approach in fact removes reason from the position of authority and makes our empirical observations our authority instead. Locke and the empiricists might reply that this is not so, since they are prepared to let reason have the last word over which empirical experiences we should accept as reliable and which we should reject.

The question we might ask is, was the empiricist way of combining reason and experience any more successful in establishing an agreed and reliable worldview than the way of pure reason? To that question, the eighteenth century had to answer no.

Before we turn to that answer, as expressed by Hume, we will look at two fascinating philosophers who independently of each other produced systems based on remarkably similar presuppositions. Both George Berkeley and Jonathan Edwards were Christian ministers, and both built their systems firmly on God. In so doing they solved the problems inherent in earlier systems over the relationship between mind and matter, but only at the price of going against what was becoming the foundational scientific principle, that the things around us that we can examine through our five senses are the basic realities of the world. Perhaps because of this, or perhaps because of the prominent role given to God, neither philosopher had much of a following. It was their younger contemporary, David Hume, with his demonstration that the project to explain all things through human reason without any reference to God was in fact self-destructive, who was to receive the attention and set the agenda for the next generation of philosophers.

GEORGE BERKELEY

Kilkenny, Ireland (1685–1753). Berkeley graduated from Trinity College, Dublin, at age nineteen. He became fellow of Trinity and published his three best-known philosophical works by the time he was in his mid twenties. They were *An Essay Towards a New Theory of Vision* (1709), *A Treatise Concerning the Principles of Human Knowledge* (1710), and *Three Dialogues Between Hylas and Philonous* (1713). He lived an active and philanthropic life. He traveled on the Continent and to America, and he attempted to establish a missionary college in Bermuda. He became Anglican bishop of Cloyne in 1734 and remained there until his retirement in 1752. Among his other claims to fame is that he published a book promoting the medicinal virtues of tar-water, a substance similar to turpentine.

Berkeley has traditionally been seen as the second of a trio of British empiricists (with Locke and Hume) to match the trio of Continental rationalists, Descartes, Spinoza, and Leibniz. The fact is that Berkeley and Hume, though they were both empiricists in the sense that they started, like Locke, with the priority of sense experience, each did more to challenge the validity of the empirical approach than to establish it.

At first sight there is a radical difference between Descartes's and Locke's theory of perception. Descartes had said that all the objects of knowledge are ideas in our minds. Locke, by contrast, had said that the external world is the source of our knowledge. But, if pressed, Locke had to concede that our knowledge of the external world is severely limited. We don't know external things as they are in themselves; all we know is our experiences or sensations of some of their qualities. So, though Locke started with experience as opposed to pure reason, his position in fact is not very far from Descartes's. The objects of our knowledge are in us, not in the external world. In Berkeley, this admission is pushed to its logical conclusion.

You are reading a book. You see certain shapes and colors. You feel the texture of the paper. You hear the rustle of the pages as you turn them over. Almost certainly, unless you are in a very skeptical frame of mind, you are quite sure that you are having genuine experiences of black printing on white paper, of rustling noises, and so on. And probably you are equally sure that underlying your experiences are a number of things that genuinely exist in their own right, such as paper, printing, and a book. They would continue to exist even if you put the book away and forgot all about it.

But since you are into philosophy, you are aware that it is very hard to move logically from your experiences of the book to the book's genuine existence. All we ever experience is our experiences; we never experience the book as it is in itself. There are at least two reasons why this is so. First, it is impossible to produce enough evidence to convince a skeptic that there has to be a book that gives rise to our experiences. We might, after all, be asleep and dreaming. Second, given the Cartesian-Newtonian worldview, it is very hard to see how a material thing, the book, can produce nonmaterial ideas in our minds.

Descartes proposed God as the answer to the first problem and the pineal gland as the answer to the second. Berkeley's answer was to dispense with the existence of material substance. We cannot move, he said, from our experience of a book to some underlying material thing we might call the book in itself. We have to start and stop with our experiences. So, since we can't infer the existence of a nonexperienceable material substance or substratum on the basis of our experiences, let's simply dispense with it.

To put it another way, if holding a dualistic belief in two substances, mind and matter, causes problems over the relationship between the two, the simplest way out of the problem is to reject one of the two. Since matter is inaccessible to us, while mind is something we are experiencing all the time, it is matter that has to go.

So Berkeley set out to build a philosophical system that contained only mind, or, to be more accurate, that allowed for matter not as something that existed in its own right, but as something that was dependent on and subordinate to mind. This is a form of "idealism," the philosophical doctrine that reality is mental (or formed by "ideas") rather than material.

Berkeley listed a number of criteria for a satisfactory philosophical system. They included compatibility with the truths of science and religion, ability to solve philosophical issues without raising new ones, and compatibility with common sense. You may like to apply these criteria to the main points of his system, which can be summarized in seven points.

1. Locke was right to say that the key to all knowledge is experience. But he was inconsistent in allowing that matter in itself, some substratum we cannot experience, exists.
2. If we use words with strict accuracy, we can never say that we experience a material object like a table. We can only say that we experience a cluster of table sensations or a collection of tabley ideas.
3. Consequently, existence needs to be defined in terms of experience. Though Berkeley wrote in English, he used the Latin phrase *esse est percipi*, "to exist is to be perceived or experienced." For us (or God) who have minds, to exist is to perceive *(esse est percipere)*.

4. We might object that Berkeley's system doesn't work because ideas are so different from material objects. Tables, for instance, are hard and occupy space, while our idea of a table is neither hard nor space-occupying. Berkeley's reply would be that the hardness of the table is itself an idea, one of the cluster of ideas we link with tables. Hardness isn't a thing any more than table-substance is a thing.

5. But if matter doesn't exist in itself, how do we safeguard continuity? Berkeley's answer is God. Though we may only think of things intermittently, God's mind, which is omnipresent and eternal, is continually focusing on everything in the universe and so can be said to be holding them in being. There are echoes of both Leibniz and the Neoplatonists here, though in contrast to them Berkeley has arrived at his idealist conclusions from an empiricist starting point.

6. Berkeley has here an opportunity to present an argument for the existence of God:

   - Only ideas exist.
   - Ideas can only exist in a mind.
   - No finite mind is capable of holding every idea permanently.
   - Yet we are aware that there is a dependable continuity of ideas.
   - Therefore there must be a mind that keeps thinking them.
   - This mind must be infinite and eternal.
   - Therefore God must exist.

7. A further objection to Berkeley's idealism might arise from the fact that two independent observers experience and are able to describe the same properties of the table, its brownness, hardness, and so on, and their descriptions tally. Does this not prove that it is the table that is the basic reality that shapes their experiences, not the other way round? Berkeley's answer is that it is God who ensures that each person has the same experience; God's mind thinks the properties of the table and causes all observers to think them too. This solves the problem of matter influencing mind, since what in fact is happening is God's mind influencing human minds.

A contemporary engraving of George Berkeley in later life pictures his achievements as a bishop, a defender of Christianity, and as an authority on tar-water. But it doesn't mention his philosophy. His influence, especially compared with Locke and Hume, was limited, largely because of his idealism. The trend of the age, with the emerging successes of science, was to stress the reality of matter over that of mind, rather than the other way round, and to seek explanations that did not involve God. Nevertheless, Berkeley is today recognized as a very able philosopher who made a brilliant attempt at producing a system that would defeat skepticism and answer the philosophical problems of the day. The failure of his system to win general acceptance led almost inexorably to the work of David Hume, who was forced to concede that in a system that had no room for God, the problems of philosophy could not be solved and skepticism could not be avoided.

TO THINK THROUGH

Well, how did he do? How does Berkeley's philosophy fare in the light of his stated criteria of compatibility with science and religion, compatibility with "common sense," and the ability to solve philosophical issues without raising new ones?

What do you think about the role of God in Berkeley's system? Is he foundational and central? Or is he pulled in to get Berkeley out of a hole?

For Further Study

Berman, D. *George Berkeley: Idealism and the Man*. Oxford: Clarendon Press, 1994.

JONATHAN EDWARDS

East Windsor, Connecticut (1703–1758). Edwards entered Yale as a thirteen-year-old and by 1724 had been appointed senior tutor after pastoring a church in New York City for two years. From 1727 to 1751 he exercised a very significant ministry at Northampton, Massachusetts, both as a church leader and as a key figure in the religious revival of the Great Awakening. In 1756 he was appointed president of Princeton, America's leading Presbyterian college. While at Yale he had a profound experience of God, which he looked upon as his conversion, and which was followed by a number of similar experiences throughout his lifetime. He wrote of "sweetly conversing with Christ," being "wrapt and swallowed up in God," "a sweet burning in the heart, an ardour of my soul." Though disassociating himself from the extremes of the revivalists, Edwards argued strongly that Christianity is much more than intellectual belief. True religion, he insisted, lies much in the emotions; these emotions may well express themselves in bodily manifestations, such as were widespread during the revival. He was a prolific writer. His works range from sermons through theological discourses and autobiography to scientific essays and "pure" philosophy.

The Puritan background.

At the start of the eighteenth century, New England thought was dominated by Puritanism and the learning that had been brought from Britain and Europe during the previous century. Though most of the early colonists had little opportunity to indulge in academic pursuits, the clergy were generally well educated, and their interests ranged over many topics besides theology. In particular, they welcomed and furthered the new scientific developments; almost all the early scientific investigations in New England were done by clergy. The Puritan worldview was strongly theocentric, and this theocentricity encouraged rather than precluded a keen interest in the world around them. The world, they believed, is God's creation; we can see his handiwork everywhere we look. Because God is faithful and consistent in all that he does, and because he has made us in his image, we are able to appreciate and explore his handiwork. We can depend on what our senses tell us of the world because the creator has patterned our minds on his mind. True, our creaturehood and fallenness cause us sometimes to make mistakes, but God's revelation in the Scriptures and his grace at work in the regenerate mind are sufficient safeguards against error.

Empiricism and idealism.

The work of European thinkers took some time to reach many of the colonists. It was only in 1714, two years before Edwards arrived there, that Yale received its copies of works by Newton and Locke and their contemporaries. Edwards and his fellow students read them with enthusiasm; the work of Locke, in particular, profoundly influenced him. The theocentricity of Edwards's Calvinism, however, meant that though he accepted the Newtonian mechanistic universe and Lockean empiricism, he remained firmly committed to the primacy of the spiritual over the material. God alone exists in himself; there is no "proper substance" but him. Everything else derives its being from him; things are only real in a derivative sense; they depend for their being on the mind of God as he expresses his eternal purposes.

Objects in the world are like the reflections in a mirror; they have no reality in themselves but are totally dependent on their source. Similarly, all events are caused by God and only derivatively by other agents. All that happens in the world, and, in particular, all the wonders of the Newtonian system, are out-workings of the divine mind and purposes.

Though it is almost certain that Edwards was unaware of the teaching of Berkeley, like him he turned the tables on those who used the new science to develop a form of mechanistic materialism that threatened to exclude God. Being, he argued, must be infinite and eternal. It cannot be spatially located, and it cannot be material. It must be omnipresent and omniscient. It is to be equated with both space and God. All that is "exists in God's mind" and is revealed by God to other minds that he has created. The world, he concluded, "is an ideal one."

Epistemology. Edwards's epistemology took Locke's teaching about the primacy of our perceptions and linked it with the Puritan concept of the faithfulness of God and his image in human beings, thus avoiding skepticism. Through the grace of God, the regenerate person is not only able to discover truth intellectually, but has a "new sense of the heart." Knowledge is more than rational; it is personal and "experimental." Edwards's idealism meant that our knowledge is dependent on the constant activity of God. The ideas in our minds of objects in the external world arise not as the result of some mysterious exchange between the objects and our minds, but as the result of the continuous activity of the mind of God upholding both our minds and the world we perceive.

Ethics. In ethics Edwards followed a moral sense approach based on benevolence and closely linked with beauty, though again he remained thoroughly theocentric and criticized Hutcheson for his secular approach. Benevolence is love of being in general and so is ultimately love of God. Though everyone has a natural sense of beauty, harmony, and so of benevolence, we are still tainted with self-love except for those in whom the grace of God has worked to eradicate it.

Free will. Both Calvinism and Newtonianism led Edwards to deny significant human freedom. God's predestination ties in with a wholly determined clockwork universe. We do not choose randomly; our choice is always dictated by "the strongest motive," which is itself caused by factors outside of our control. Our sense of freedom arises from the compatibility of our choices with what is in fact determined rather than from truly open possibilities.

Edwards thus merged his Calvinism with Newtonianism. His own experiences of God as a living personal reality, encountered not just through the intellect but very powerfully in each part of his being, meant that he did this in a distinctive way. Some forms of Calvinism stressed the transcendence of God at the expense of his immanence. Newtonian physics led many, especially in England, into deism. By contrast Edwards's theocentric worldview linked to his personal experiences enabled him to merge his theology, philosophy, and personal religion into an integrated whole.

Though Edwards was generally acknowledged as America's most significant philosopher before the civil war, his philosophical influence was small. This may be partly the result of a general lack of interest in philosophical speculation, particularly if it did not seem to accord with the practical mood of the times. But there was an additional factor. The dominant philosophy in America in the later part of the eighteenth century and into the early nineteenth was Scottish realism, which, while still giving a high place to the insights of Locke, had also taken into account the apparently devastating attacks on it by David Hume.

TO THINK THROUGH

To try and persuade ordinary people that matter does not exist was hard enough in Berkeley and Edwards's day; it is even harder today. Can you think of a way of moderating their idealism that would allow for the real existence of matter but would keep their basic insight that all matter is totally dependent on God?

For Further Study

Lee, S. H. *The Philosophical Theology of Jonathan Edwards.* Princeton, N.J.: Princeton University Press, 2000.

TWENTY-EIGHT

IT DOESN'T WORK

THE ANTI-SYSTEM OF HUME

> In this chapter we face the challenge Hume presented to the whole modern worldview. Philosophically, he said, the modern worldview is unjustifiable. Most ignored his challenge and simply got on with living or applying the scientific worldview. But Hume was right. Though it took two hundred years to work through, his skepticism effectively demolished the modern worldview.

DAVID HUME

Edinburgh (1711–1776). Hume studied at Edinburgh University from 1723 to 1726, leaving when he was fifteen. His studies included classical authors, especially Cicero, and a general introduction to philosophical topics, as well as science and history. He started a course in law but abandoned it to devote himself to philosophy. He lived for a time in France and in London and then returned to Edinburgh. He took a number of jobs to support himself. Toward the end of his life he was secretary to the British embassy in Paris and an under-secretary of state in London. His first book, setting out what he felt was a new approach to philosophy and knowledge, was *Treatise of Human Nature*, published in 1739–1740. Its reception was disappointing; Hume described it as falling "deadborn from the press." He recast his basic ideas and published them in 1748 as *An Enquiry Concerning Human Understanding*. This work was more successful, and as he published further philosophical works, Hume's reputation began to grow, though ironically it was his six-volume *History of England* that was seen by most of his contemporaries as his most significant work. Born into a strict Presbyterian family, Hume abandoned any Christian beliefs and declared himself a pagan.

At the start of the *Treatise*, Hume expressed dissatisfaction with all previous philosophy on the grounds that it gave an inadequate place to experience. He set himself to remedy this by applying more rigorously the "experimental" or empirical approach advocated by Bacon and used by Newton. The *Treatise* was to present a new science of human nature that would be the basis for our understanding of all other subjects. It would do so, promised Hume, drawing no conclusions but those authorized by experience.

CAUSALITY AND SKEPTICISM

Of all his achievements, the one Hume emphasized most was his demolition of the accepted understanding of the relationship between a "cause" and its "effect." Both science and ordinary life took it as axiomatic that the relationship is one of causality, some necessary link between one event and another. But when we come to examine just what "causality" is, Hume said, we can't find any such thing. A flame, we might say, causes heat, or one billiard ball strikes another and causes it to move. But we can observe no "causal link" between a flame and heat or between one billiard ball and another. All we can observe is that an experience or idea of a flame is followed by an experience or idea of heat. Now, if we observe an event A followed by another event B on just an isolated occasion, such as our favorite song being played on the radio and Uncle John's car turning into the drive, we don't link the two events in any causal fashion. But if A keeps being followed by B, we do begin to assume a link. If, for instance, every time the phone rings the dog barks, after a time, because our minds are so constituted, according to Hume, we assume the ringing of the phone causes the dog to bark. But, in fact, he said, when we look for the link, we don't find anything in the external world, in the phone or in the dog. The link is just in our minds; we form a habit of connecting the barking with the phone ringing. But we can't find any more "causality" in the phone than in the playing of our favorite song. Logically, we are no more justified in saying that the phone causes the dog to bark than in saying that our favorite song causes Uncle John to arrive.

Hume is saying two things about causality. He is saying that, however many times event or object B may follow event or object A, we have no rational grounds for believing in such a thing as causality in A that makes B happen. All we can do is observe a lot of cases of succession, that B regularly follows A. Even if thunder is preceded by lightning a million times and we observe no counterexample of thunder occurring without lightning, we still have no grounds to speak in terms of causality or to predict that the next time there is a flash of lightning it will be followed by thunder.

The second thing Hume is saying about causality is that what we take to be a function of things in the world around us is really a function of our own minds. We observe A and B regularly "conjoined," and we project the concept of causality onto them. Causality is thus a subjective concept we impose on the world. It is interesting to note that Hume assumes that it is the continual "conjoining" of B with A that causes or "determines" us to have this idea of causality. But to be consistent he should have conceded that conjoining of events cannot cause ideas in our minds any more than, according to him, fire can cause heat.

Hume realized the radical implications of his argument. If A cannot be rationally shown to cause B, then I have no rational grounds for believing that B will follow A tomorrow. Further, since, as Hume fully accepted, all I can ever know are the ideas in my mind, if there is no necessary link between one idea and another, then both coherent living and rational thought are impossible. At present a red traffic light "causes" me to brake; tomorrow it may "cause" me to accelerate. Today the evidence of my observations and experience may lead me to conclude there is a tree in the garden, or that other minds exist, or that there is an external world; tomorrow the same observations and experience may cause me to conclude that none of these things exist.

The outcome, said Hume, is philosophical skepticism. It wasn't that Hume didn't in fact trust his senses or the logic of his thought. Nor did he deny in real life that fire causes heat or lightning causes thunder. But what he had shown was that if we consistently apply his atheistic empiricist principles, there can be no philosophical or rational justification for these things. We believe in the foundational principle of causation because we have certain ideas that, according to Hume, arise from our feelings, our instinct, and our habits, not because we can understand it or justify it rationally. But to admit that a foundational principle is based on feeling or instinct or habit, rather than on reason, is in effect to show that the Enlightenment trust in reason is misplaced. As Bertrand Russell famously put it, Hume

> represents the bankruptcy of eighteenth-century reasonableness. He starts out, like Locke, with the intention of being sensible and empirical, taking nothing on trust, but seeking whatever instruction is to be obtained from experience and observation. But having a better intellect than Locke's, a greater acuteness in analysis, and a smaller capacity for accepting comfortable inconsistencies, he arrives at the

disastrous conclusion that from experience and observation nothing is to be learnt. There is no such thing as a rational belief: 'If we believe that fire warms, or water refreshes, 'tis only because it costs us too much pains to think otherwise.' We cannot help believing, but no belief can be grounded in reason. Nor can one line of action be more rational than another, since all alike are based upon irrational convictions. This last conclusion, however, Hume seems not to have drawn. Even in his most sceptical chapter, in which he sums up the conclusions of Book 1 [of the *Treatise*], he says, 'Generally speaking, the errors in religion are dangerous; those in philosophy only ridiculous.' He has no right to say this. 'Dangerous' is a causal word, and a sceptic as to causation cannot know that anything is 'dangerous.'

"HUME'S FORK"

Hume distinguished between "relations of ideas" and "matters of fact." In the area of ideas it is possible to move deductively from one idea to another. That is, the truth of the first idea is sufficient to establish the truth of the second. This happens in math, where we start with foundational first principles and then make valid deductions from them. However, in the world of science and ordinary life, we cannot proceed in this way. We make a series of observations, such as "This swan is white," "This swan is white," "This swan is white," and so on, and conclude, "All swans are white." But that conclusion is not a valid deduction. It is an inference, but it is no more than a guess. There is no way we can conclusively establish it through reason. In matters of fact, we can never have certainty.

SUBSTANCE, OBJECTS IN THE EXTERNAL WORLD, AND THE SELF

Hume's skepticism was not limited to the principle of causality. In a parallel way, he demonstrated that neither our senses nor reason could establish the existence of external objects, that is, any of the things in the world around us. It is rather by use of our "imagination," he said, arising from a series of ideas we have that show constancy and coherence, that we assume their existence. Berkeley had shown that we can't justify belief in some underlying substratum or substance that gives rise to our experiences of external objects; Hume extended this argument further to show that empirical observation or reason cannot justify belief in the existence of the self or mind or soul. When I look inside me, he said, I only ever observe perceptions of heat or cold, pain or pleasure; I never catch myself without a perception. All I find is a bundle of perceptions, constantly changing, each rapidly succeeding the other, with no evidence of anything permanent underlying them.

Again, Hume was not saying that external objects do not exist, or, indeed, that we have no grounds for believing in them. He accepted that we have to believe in them, and he did in fact do so. But he was saying that we have no empirical or rational justification for this belief. His presentation of his skeptical argument about the self, however, is rather more dogmatic. He does seem to be claiming that he has empirically and rationally established that there is no such thing, and he has been widely interpreted as "proving" the nonexistence of the self. However, in the nature of the case, it is as impossible for Hume to prove the self's nonexistence as it is to prove its existence; the best he can do is to show the inadequacy of our observations and reason to "prove" anything either way. And, in fact, Hume later retracted his early dogmatism against the existence of the self.

HUME AND RELIGION

Hume's personal rejection of Christianity made him less willing to give ground over his skepticism about God and miracles. Consistency might have demanded that he dealt with these things in the same way as he dealt with causality and the existence of underlying substance and objects in the external world: We cannot produce rational or empirical arguments that establish these things, but we still can be justified in believing in them. Granted, Hume does state in conclusion to his skeptical arguments that "our most holy religion is founded on *faith*, not on reason." But he seems unwilling to accept that this sort of faith is viable in the way that "imagination" or "feelings" are viable as a basis for other beliefs.

Natural religion. Hume's *Dialogues Concerning Natural Religion*, published three years after his death, have sometimes been taken as disproving the existence of God. They do not in fact do this, nor was this Hume's aim. Rather, he was trying to do much the same as he did in his earlier investigations—to explore whether "natural religion," that is, the use of unaided reason, can provide us with truth about God. His answer was that it cannot. This answer, of course, needs to be set alongside Hume's belief that unaided reason cannot provide us with truth about the world or the self or about the basis of scientific investigation. It also needs to be set in its context. Locke had said that reason must be our judge and guide in everything. Many of the deists had concluded from this that only what could be rationally proved could be real. So for them Hume's claim to show that the existence of God cannot be rationally proved was disastrous. For those who claimed grounds for belief in God that were based on something other than rational argument, his skepticism was less damaging.

Proofs for the existence of God.
In the *Dialogues* Hume examined the teleological and cosmological arguments for the existence of God in considerable detail and showed that neither of them are such that they rationally compel us to believe in a designer or necessary being as the basis of the universe. It is perfectly possible, he said, just to accept that there is no reason for the existence of the universe; it simply exists. And the so-called evidences of design are largely open to challenge; there are evidences of lack of design as well as of design; and even the latter can be explained without reference to a designer by positing some sort of developing process.

Miracles.
Hume did not believe in the miraculous, and it has often been claimed that he proved miracles cannot happen. He didn't in fact do this, though some of his claims make it sound as though he thought he had done so. What he in fact did was to seek to show that a rational person would have to conclude, on examining the evidence for a purported miracle, that it is insufficient to provide rational justification for accepting its viability. Such an argument, of course, would not carry any weight with someone who actually experiences a miracle, though Hume, usually keen to stress the significance of personal experience, chose to pass over this point. But it does affect us, he said, when we have to decide on the truth or otherwise of a claim by someone else that he or she has experienced a miracle. Since in our general experience nature is uniform (that is miracles do not happen), any time we are confronted with an alleged miracle, it will be more reasonable for us to assume the person making the claim is lying or deluded than that a miracle has occurred. After all, lies and delusions are much more common than miracles. Further, said Hume, it is generally credulous, biased, or "ignorant and barbarous" people who believe in the miraculous. A "wise man" will not.

Religion.
In Hume's attack on religion in general and Christianity in particular, he claimed that religion originally arose from fear and ignorance, and that the practice of religion, so far from helping to counter fear and ignorance, actually fosters them. Early forms of religion, he said, were polytheistic and much to be preferred to monotheism, which gives rise to zeal, intolerance, and debasing "monkish virtues."

Ethics and values.

In keeping with his general approach, Hume stated categorically that moral values are not based on reason. Rather, morality is a matter of feeling, located in our moral sense. We are moved to action by our "passions," especially our desires, and by "sympathy," the ability to share in others' feelings. Hume rejected any concept of an objective moral law, which is binding on everyone, in favor of ethical relativism.

Free will.

Not surprisingly, Hume also denied significant freedom of the will, allowing only that we may feel we are acting freely when our predetermined act is one we wish to perform. He argued for this view on the grounds that the mind, like the universe, is totally mechanistic. A set of circumstances A always leads us to make the decision B, or to be more accurate, we observe that A is always conjoined with B. Confronted with a choice between a piece of chocolate and a sticky toffee, I always choose the chocolate. If we reply that it is perfectly possible for me to choose a toffee one day simply to demonstrate my significant freedom, Hume can answer that my desire to assert my significant freedom is itself a determining factor, so though I seem to be freely breaking a regular pattern, I am only expressing some broader pattern in which I have no choice, presumably to assert my significant freedom whenever it is challenged.

Some people believe Hume was the greatest English-speaking philosopher, at least before the twentieth century. Others point out that there was very little in his work that was original; practically all his skeptical arguments had been put forward by others, and he was merely reproducing them in his own very persuasive way. A possible test of any philosophy is to ask what positive contribution it makes to our understanding of the world and our living in it. If a philosopher simply demolishes the views of others, something some twentieth-century philosophers in particular loved doing, but puts nothing in their place, we may be justified in feeling that she or he has only done half a job—and that the least important half. After all, it is always easier to destroy than to build. What, then, did Hume offer in place of all that he took away?

At face value Hume offered very little. Not only did he produce no system or set of beliefs that we could follow; he claimed to have shown that no such system was rationally possible. How then are we to live? By "habit" and "custom," by "carelessness and inattention." By forgetting philosophy and going away and having a meal or a game and just getting on with life. Hume himself built up a reputation for being a sort of Epicurean *bon vivant*.

Perhaps this is all Hume offers. But perhaps there was something else, something more positive. Those who feel that Hume's contribution was not all negative suggest that his underlying aim was to urge tolerance in all our beliefs. If none of them can be conclusively rationally established, then we have no right to be dogmatic and to reject the beliefs of those with whom we disagree. Apart from his strong intolerance of Christianity, Hume was known in his lifetime as an advocate and example of toleration, so there may be some truth in this view. Nevertheless, the impression remains that Hume's main contribution to philosophy was a negative one, to show that reason and empirical observation are inadequate as a basis for a worldview.

TO THINK THROUGH

Hume showed that we have no rational grounds for accepting the presuppositions and beliefs that underlie both ordinary life and the whole scientific enterprise. But everyone, including Hume, went on living, and science continued to be enormously successful. What conclusions can we draw from this? Do beliefs have to have rational grounds? What other sort of grounds might they have?

What reply could be made to Hume's attack on religion?

For Further Study

Norton, D. F. *The Cambridge Companion to Hume.* Cambridge: Cambridge University Press, 1993.

LIVING WITHIN OUR LIMITS

PART FIVE

TWENTY-NINE

WHERE DO WE GO FROM HERE?

RESPONSES TO HUME

In this chapter we begin to look at reactions to Hume. Thomas Reid's response was enormously influential; many felt he had successfully answered Hume's skepticism. But it was at least in part a capitulation, accepting that we can't rationally justify our beliefs. Jean-Jacques Rousseau represents a different reaction, one that predominated in the long run. He accepted the severe limits of reason and looked elsewhere for a basis for living.

BERTRAND RUSSELL RIGHTLY SAW HUME'S PHILOSOPHY as the turning point of the attempt to establish a worldview on the foundation of reason. No philosopher who followed Hume could ignore his skeptical conclusions. Yet life had to go on. And science continued to make impressive progress, whether philosophy could justify its presuppositions or not. Apart from ignoring him, the eighteenth century responded to Hume in a number of different ways, of which we will look at three. The first was the way of "common sense," as advocated by Thomas Reid. This was widely accepted as a satisfactory answer to Hume that provided an adequate, though not entirely rational, justification for our faith in ordinary experience and science. The second type of response to Hume was a rejection of rationalism in favor of a stress on feeling. An example of this is seen in Jean-Jacques Rousseau. A third response was Immanuel Kant's, which sought to rescue rationalism but only at the cost of making major concessions to skepticism.

THE EIGHTEENTH-CENTURY ENLIGHTENMENT

Before we turn to these three, we will sketch in a little more of the background against which they were operating. Though the term *Enlightenment* can be used to cover all the period when modern thinkers were seeking to stress the primacy of reason, it is generally agreed that the eighteenth century marked the high point of the Enlightenment and that the three countries where its influence was most felt were the homelands of Reid, Rousseau, and Kant, that is, Scotland, France, and Germany. In looking at Hutcheson, Smith, and Hume, we have already seen something of the Scottish Enlightenment, which had close links with the parallel movement in France.

The French Enlightenment. The term "the French Enlightenment" is generally used to describe the eighteenth-century period of intellectual excitement and adventure that led up to the French revolution. The spirit of seventeenth-century rationalism was popularized and spread through France and beyond into Europe in the first half of the century by a group of writers, scientists, conversationalists, and "men of affairs," known as *les philosophes*. Best-known figures among them are Pierre Bayle (1647–1706), **Baron de la Brede et de Montesquieu** (1689–1755), **Voltaire** (the pen name of François Marie Arouet, 1694–1778), and **Etienne Bonnot de Condillac** (1714–1780). They were eloquent in praise of the achievements of science, enthusiastically confident in the powers of reason, and strongly opposed to traditions and superstitions, especially those of religion. The human race, they said, is essentially good. Science, education, and reason are setting us free and opening up a future of unlimited progress and opportunity. Between 1751 and 1772 an eighteen-volume encyclopedia "of the Sciences, Arts and Trades" was published under the editorship of **Denis Diderot** (1713–1786) and **Jean le Rond d'Alembert** (1717–1783). Known as the *Grande Encyclopédie*, it contained 17,818 articles surveying all the achievements of reason and science, and advocating secularism, rationalism, and social and political reform. Both the *philosophes* and the *Encyclopédie* used Locke as a major source of their philosophical and social ideas.

It is perhaps ironic that at the very time this wave of confidence in rationalism was emanating from France to Europe and beyond, Hume was in France writing his *Treatise of Human Nature* and demonstrating the inability of human reason to do any of the things the French Enlightenment claimed for it. Even the dissemination of Hume's views did nothing to counter the terrific confidence in reason, a fact that might suggest that the confidence in reason was itself somewhat irrational. For though the *philosophes* and Encyclopedists ardently advocated the liberation of the human race from the metaphysical and religious chains that had so long bound it, their alternative worldview, with its faith in reason, progress, science, education, and the innate goodness of the human race, was itself a metaphysical system that rested on very unsure foundations. Nevertheless, it was the worldview that prevailed and set the trend for the secular rationalism that has continued to dominate popular Western thought through the last two centuries.

The German Enlightenment.

Two key figures in the German Enlightenment (known as the *Aufklärung*) in the eighteenth century, before Immanuel Kant came to dominate the movement, were **Christian Wolff** (1679–1754) and **Gotthold Lessing** (1729–1781). Wolff used elements of Descartes, Locke, and Leibniz to develop a thoroughly rationalistic system that incorporated belief in God into a mechanistic view of the world and claimed that the truths of both reason and science could be known *a priori*, that is, without reference to empirical observation. He wrote profusely, both in Latin and German, using a pedantic heavy style that set the trend for subsequent German philosophical writing.

Lessing, on the other hand, was deeply involved in literature and the arts. He studied Protestant theology for a time but gave it up and developed an anti-dogmatic rationalistic approach to religion that eventually came very near to Spinozan pantheism. He rejected revealed religion and attacked orthodox Christians (while urging religious toleration), proposing a form of religion that saw humankind progressing through history in a process of evolution toward personal and spiritual maturity and perfection. His ideas were very influential in the German Enlightenment.

A further significant figure in the German Enlightenment was **Moses Mendelssohn** (1729–1786). He was a German Jew whose thought was influenced by Leibniz and Wolff and who was a close friend of Lessing. He began his studies with the Bible and the Talmud but developed wide interests in philosophy, psychology, and aesthetics, as well as theology. He was a capable linguist, and his writing style was clear and elegant. He argued for religious toleration; all religions, he said, agree in their basic moral and metaphysical beliefs. Reason is able to demonstrate the truth of the foundational beliefs of every religion, particularly the existence and providence of God and the immortality of the soul. He defended Judaism on the grounds that it was a way of life rather than a body of doctrines.

THOMAS REID

Strachan, Kincardinshire, Scotland (1710–1796). After serving for fifteen years as a parish minister, Reid was appointed professor at King's College, Aberdeen, where he taught math, physics, and philosophy. In 1764 he was appointed professor of moral philosophy at Glasgow. After his retirement in 1780, he was instrumental in the founding of the Glasgow infirmary. His first published work, on philosophy and science, and in part a response to Hume, was *An Enquiry into the Human Mind on the Principles of Common Sense* (1764). On being asked to read the manuscript before publication, Hume is said to have remarked that "parsons" should mind their own business and leave philosophical controversies to philosophers. However, he did agree to read the manuscript and was willing to commend it. Indeed, he took the "parson's" philosophy sufficiently seriously to seek to defend his view against it in the *Inquiry*. Reid's two other major works were *Essays on the Intellectual Powers of Man* (1785) and *Essays on the Active Powers of Man* (1788). The first explored the nature of perception, memory, "conception," abstraction, and judgment. The second dealt with the will, the principles of action, freedom, and morality. Both were widely used as textbooks.

Scottish Common Sense philosophy. Reid was the founder of what is known as the Scottish school of Common Sense philosophy, or Scottish realism. Other members of the school included **James Beattie** (1735–1802), **Dugald Stewart** (1753–1828), and, to an extent, **William Hamilton** (1791–1856). The influence of Reid and the school were substantial, not just in Scotland, but on the Continent, and particularly in France and America. For some fifty years Reid's was seen as the definitive response to Hume's skepticism. Even when Kant's response to Hume began to oust it, it continued to be an accepted alternative to Kantianism right into the second half of the nineteenth century, particularly in America.

The rejection of the theory of ideas. Reid said that the key feature of his philosophy was his rejection of the theory of ideas, the doctrine "that all the objects of my knowledge are ideas in my own mind." For a time he had believed this theory "so firmly as to embrace the whole of Berkeley's system in consequence of it." But his reading of Hume's *Treatise* made him aware that the concept, which he claimed was as old as Socrates, and which had been developed by Descartes and Locke and followed by Hume as well as Berkeley, led only to a dead end. Hume had pushed the theory to absurd conclusions.

No evidence can be adduced, said Reid, that the theory of ideas is true. But there are good reasons to conclude that it is false, quite apart from the fact that it leads to skepticism. It contradicts experience, it is contrary to common sense, it leads to absurdities, and it creates more problems than it solves. So, said Reid, it needs to be rejected. Instead of holding that the only things we can know are our subjective "impressions and ideas," we are to accept that we really directly perceive external objects.

Reid argued his case by a careful analysis of the way we use words and of the experience of perception and the attainment of knowledge. Those who accept the theory of ideas, he said, have failed to appreciate the difference between language that describes our inner thoughts and feelings and language that describes our experience of the external world. They have assumed that the sentence "I think a thought" functions in the same way as the sentence "I see a tree." But it doesn't. The second sentence has an actually existing object, a tree. But the first, despite its parallel grammatical form, does not have an actually existing object. Though seeing a tree means more than just seeing, thinking a thought means no more than just thinking.

Common sense. In support of his case, Reid appealed to the common experience of all people and to "common sense." His analysis makes it clear that this "common sense" is something much more complex than naive acceptance of immediate experience. The mind is active in perception and knowing; Reid carefully analyzed the complex roles and relationships of sensations, instincts, conceptions, estimations, beliefs, and judgments, all of which are involved in perception.

Self-evident truths. How then do we answer the doubts of the skeptics and prove the dependability of our perceptions and knowledge? How can I prove rationally that it really is a tree that I'm seeing? Reid's answer is that we don't need to produce rational proof to establish it. We all know it is so without it being proved, even without it being taught. It is a self-evident truth. Reid used "self-evident truth" in a number of ways, for instance, of the axioms of math. But in this context he seems to be saying that the existence of objects in the external world and the dependability of our experience of them is simply something we cannot doubt. The general dependability of our perceptions, the existence of the external world, the continuity of our personal existence, and the existence of other minds are foundational "first principles." We cannot but accept them; even the skeptics have to assume them in order to live. They cannot be more clearly established than they already are in the very constitution of our natures. Though no argument is needed to establish them, the fact that to deny them lands us in absurdity demonstrates their truth.

It is interesting to note that though Reid was a clergyman and often referred to God as our creator, he didn't use God as the basis for his trust in the dependability of our experiences in the way that, say Descartes or Berkeley had done. Rather, he saw himself as describing how things actually are. He left open the questions of why they are as they are and how we can be sure they will stay that way.

TO THINK THROUGH

Are there self-evident truths? If there are, how do we answer those who say they aren't self-evident to them?

What do you think about Reid's arguments against the theory of ideas?

For Further Study

Lehrer, K. *Thomas Reid*. London: Routledge, 1989.

JEAN-JACQUES ROUSSEAU

Geneva (1712–1778). Jean-Jacques Rousseau was one of the most interesting thinkers of the eighteenth century, expressing many of the ideas of the French Enlightenment but also reacting against it. He was a gifted writer, a musician, and a botanist; he had a deep Christian faith, a deep love of nature, and a deep distrust of the way the human race had developed. He spent much of his adult life in France, especially Paris. Starting as a Calvinistic Protestant, he became a Roman Catholic and then changed back to Protestantism. In keeping with his romanticism, religion for him was a matter of the heart rather than the head.

For a time Rousseau was a friend of Diderot, and he contributed to the *Encyclopédie*. But many of his basic convictions were at odds with those of the *philosophes*, some of whom attacked him mercilessly. Toward the end of his life, he found his views rejected by just about everyone, revolutionaries and traditionalists alike. Suffering perhaps from a form of paranoia, Rousseau moved from place to place seeking refuge but frequently alienating those (including Hume) who sought to befriend him.

The romantic reaction.

Rousseau marks the beginnings of a reaction against the excessive faith in reason and stress on the mechanistic worldview of the eighteenth century. For him nature and sentiment were the key to virtue and happiness, not science or the artificial structures of eighteenth-century culture, based as they were on power, position, and money. He had a highly romantic philosophy of nature, believing that before the coming of civilization, humans were happy, independent, content, and naturally good. This concept of the "noble savage" was to become one of the central tenets of subsequent romanticism.

Human nature.

Rousseau's book *Émile*, a treatise on education, starts with the observation that everything God makes is good, while everything man touches degenerates. It goes on to recommend that children be allowed to develop unaffected by the ideas of society. Growing children are to live in the country communing with nature and developing naturally according to their own needs and natural goodness, without being corrupted by books, theoretical concepts, and rational thought. In this way their character and relationships will be based on wholesome natural feeling and direct experience of the world of nature rather than on the training of their intellect.

The world and society.

The source of our innate goodness is God. Since nature is his handiwork, living in accord with nature enables us to express that goodness as we develop a spiritual bond with the world around us and so with the community in which we live. Rousseau's social and political views were expressed in his *Social Contract* (1762), a work opportunistically exploited by the French revolutionaries, with its radical ideas and ready catch phrases, including "Man is born free, and everywhere he is in chains." There he proposed the concept of the "general will." Individuals come together in free association and form a social contract, choosing to submit to the agreed corporate expression of human goodness in the general will. Not only is this submission a free act of the individuals involved; through it they find true freedom and self-fulfillment through living as part of the corporate being, or state. Rousseau did not advocate any specific form of government; a state could be ruled by an individual or an elected government, provided they rule according to the general will. If they fail to do so, their power should be removed.

In the fifty years after Rousseau's death, the romantic reaction to the mechanism and rationalism of the eighteenth-century Enlightenment permeated

Europe and America. Apart from rejecting the dominance of reason and empirical experience, its hallmarks were feeling, emotion, spontaneity, intuition, free self-expression, and the centrality of nature.

TO THINK THROUGH

Did romanticism get it right? Or was it an over-reaction?

THIRTY

ACCEPTING THE LIMITS OF REASON

KANT

In this chapter we look at some of the ideas of Immanuel Kant, whom many people would call the greatest philosopher of the modern period. We see how he responded to the challenge of Hume by redefining "reason" and making many areas of human life inaccessible to what most of his predecessors had meant by reason.

LIFE AND WORK

Königsberg, East Prussia (1724–1804). Kant spent his whole life at Königsberg. After being educated there, he spent eight years as a private tutor and then taught at Königsberg University from 1755, becoming professor of logic and metaphysics there in 1770. Interestingly, being a university teacher of philosophy sets Kant apart from most of the main figures of the Enlightenment, who had tended to be philosophical "amateurs" rather than "professional" university teachers.

Kant's inaugural dissertation in 1770 marked a significant change in his outlook. Until then he had published a number of works that had been well received. They showed the influence of Leibniz and his German successors, and of Locke, Hume, and Rousseau, but lacked the radicalism of Kant's later, or "Critical," period. From 1770 to 1781 Kant was working on his new approach and published nothing. Then, after his fifty-seventh birthday, came a rush of publications that have given him a place among the world's leading philosophers: *Critique of Pure Reason* (1781; much revised edition, 1787),

Prolegomena to Any Future Metaphysics (1783), *Groundwork of the Metaphysics of Morals* (1785), *Metaphysical Elements of Natural Science* (1786), *Critique of Practical Reason* (1788), *Critique of Judgment* (1790), *Religion within the Limits of Reason Alone* (1793), and *Metaphysics of Morals* (1797).

Kant summed up the four tasks he set himself as answering the questions "What can I know?" "What should I do?" "What may I hope?" and "What is man?" He answered the first question in his first *Critique (Pure Reason)*. His second *Critique (Practical Reason)* and other writing on morals answered the second. The third was answered by his work on religion. Kant did not live to answer the fourth question fully, though it was partly answered by the publication in 1798 of his lecture notes on anthropology.

Kant's philosophy is often referred to as transcendental idealism. Idealism, in this sense, is a philosophy that centers on our ideas, whether experiences or judgments, rather than on the external world. "Transcendental" means beyond ("transcending") sense experience. Kant defined his transcendental idealism as the belief that all we experience is representations or appearances, not things as they are in themselves.

Most people find Kant very hard to understand. Part of the reason for this is that he deals with complex and deep issues. An additional factor is that he seems to have a number of strange ideas that we find difficult to take on board. Of course, these two factors apply to most philosophers and are not in themselves sufficient to explain why we find Kant so difficult. Some have suggested that it is because, unlike most, he was a professional philosopher, completely immersed in his esoteric philosophical world into which ordinary mortals can only occasionally peep. But, mercifully, being a professional philosopher doesn't have to entail an obscure and difficult style. Much of the problem, sadly, has to be put down to Kant's unwillingness or inability to express himself clearly. His heavy, complex style, his use of ponderous technical terminology, and his often tortuous use of the German language all serve to make even the simpler things he is saying hard to grasp. So, before listing Kant's main ideas, let's get an understanding of some of his technical terms.

Analytic propositions. This is Kant's name for the "truths of reason" we encountered in Leibniz. An analytic proposition is one whose truth is established simply by an "analysis" of the terms involved. The predicate is completely contained in the subject. One doesn't need to check anything in the surrounding empirical world. To deny an analytic proposition produces a contradiction or absurdity. "A bachelor is unmarried" and "Quadrupeds have four legs" are analytic. Because they don't tell us anything about the real world, analytic

propositions are of very limited usefulness. Someone who spends all his or her time saying things like "Bachelors are unmarried" or "Quadrupeds have four legs" will hardly be the life of the party or be offered a job as a university professor. In effect, analytic propositions are merely tautologous. All propositions that are not analytic are "synthetic."

Synthetic propositions.
Kant's term for Leibniz's "truths of fact" is "synthetic propositions." The huge majority of beliefs we hold and statements we make are synthetic, that is, "synthesized" or put together from sources other than just the words used, supremely from our observations and experience. "Today is Monday," "There has been a plane crash," and "Mike is crazy about Linda" are all synthetic propositions. We can't tell whether they are true or false simply by looking at the words used. The fact that just about all the propositions that really matter are synthetic is a great disappointment to a rationalist philosopher like Kant. Inevitably, philosophers who have high confidence in human reason are happiest dealing with clear-cut propositions whose truth or falsehood can be definitively established. They are a lot less happy having to cope with things like empirical synthetic propositions whose truth or falsehood can never be definitively established. Descartes and the early rationalists had hoped to be able to establish that there are very many propositions whose truth can be clearly established. But Hume had shown this was a vain hope. So the world of certain truth has suddenly become very small, limited in effect to tautologous, and so virtually useless, propositions.

A priori and a posteriori.
An *a priori* truth is one we know "prior" to experience. It is the opposite of *a posteriori*, which we know "post," or after, experience. *A posteriori* thus means the same as empirical—based on our experience through our senses. Rationalist philosophers believe that a lot of significant truth is *a priori*. Indeed, those convinced by an approach like Descartes's could claim that their whole system was *a priori*. A very extreme empiricist would presumably deny the existence of any *a priori* knowledge; everything is "post" experience. In fact, most empiricists didn't go that far. They were prepared to accept that there were *a priori* truths even though we come to know them through experience. We experience two oranges set alongside two oranges and discover four oranges. We do the same with two apples plus two apples. From these experiences we extract a truth "2 + 2 = 4," which we see to be independent of apples, oranges, or even experience. It is an *a priori* truth. So, in this case, the "priority" of *a priori* truths is a logical priority rather than a temporal priority. *A priori* propositions can be seen to be necessary; *a*

posteriori propositions are contingent on our experience of things in the world around us.

The problem.

Kant wholly accepted the Newtonian scientific worldview. He was confident that what the scientists of his day were discovering and saying was dependable and correct. After all, no one could dispute that science worked.

But the success of science created a major problem. To put it crudely (which Kant did not!), it made everything else redundant. If everything operates according to fixed laws in a determined, mechanistic clockwork way, there is no room left for anything nonmechanistic, like freedom, morality, the self, or God. Nor is there any room for reason; if I can only think what scientific laws make me think, then I am nothing more than a machine; I am not a thinking, reasoning person. Further, even causality, one of the foundational principles of the Newtonian worldview, had been shown by Hume to be untenable as it was normally understood. But such conclusions are impossible. I know that I think, that I choose freely, and that nonmechanistic things like goodness and beauty and God and causality are highly significant aspects of human life.

THE ANSWER

So Kant set himself the task of finding a way to hold on to the mechanistic Newtonian worldview in its totality, but at the same time to find a place for the nonmechanistic realities of life. He did it by taking three radical steps: inventing a new way of defining propositions, dividing everything that is into two irreconcilable parts, and proposing a "Copernican revolution."

A new class of propositions: synthetic a priori.

Kant rejected the belief that all propositions or judgments must be either analytic, and so effectively tautologous, or synthetic, and so unable to be rationally established. He said there is a third class of propositions that are neither. They are not analytic, and so they are synthetic. But they are not *a posteriori* or empirical. They are *a priori*; they can be established by reason alone, and so can be held with confidence. We can be sure of them and can build our worldview on them.

Into this class of synthetic *a priori* propositions Kant put a wide range of key propositions. Very usefully they include the propositions of math and geometry and the inductive generalizations of science. Causality, for example, cannot be known analytically, so we have to concede that causal statements are synthetic. But we do not have to concede that they are therefore uncertain. On the contrary, they are *a priori*; we can see their evident truth simply by the use of our reason. This, of course, is a bold claim, and Kant regarded his main task in his first *Critique* to justify it. He did this by taking his second and third radical steps.

The splitting of the universe: the divided mind and the divided world.
In his first *Critique*, Kant dealt with the realm of "pure reason." By "pure reason" he meant what most people would simply describe as "reason"; it is the faculty that we use to find rationally established truth about the world around us. To distinguish it from what he called "practical reason," we can think of it as "scientific" reason, the form of reasoning scientific thinkers have traditionally followed. His second *Critique* moved on to practical reason. This is something very different from pure reason. It is not rational in the usually accepted sense. When we are using our practical reason, we don't have to argue and produce evidence as we do in the ordinary world or the world of the scientist. The rules of the game are quite different. This splitting of "reason" or the mind was a hugely significant step. It was accompanied by an equally significant splitting of the universe and all that is in it.

Reid had analyzed Hume's theory of ideas as the source of his skepticism and had concluded that the way to escape Hume's skeptical conclusions was to reject the theory of ideas. Kant was scathing about this way out of the problem. He agreed with Hume and the empiricists that the objects of our knowledge and experience are ideas, not things in the world. So he bravely faced the implications of this and accepted that in the sphere of "pure reason," that is, of things that we can establish with rational certainty, we can't know anything beyond our ideas. He drew a firm line between things as they actually are and our ideas or perceptions of them. Things as they actually are, things-in-themselves, he called *noumena* and said that they are beyond the reach of the kind of reason we use in science and in ordinary life. We can't have any "scientific" knowledge of what lies behind our perception of a table, or our experience or other people, or our concept of an external world or of God. We can't even speculate rationally about these things or follow Hume in simply assuming them. We are totally limited to "appearances," *phenomena*, our experiences and perceptions.

So we have a divided universe, and corresponding to it, divided "reason." Ordinary reason works in the ordinary world. But when we try to reach out for the realities behind the ordinary phenomenal world, we have a wholly different way of operating. For Kant this splitting of reality was a triumph; it enabled him to keep both the world of Newtonian science, where we use pure reason, and the non-mechanistic realities of freedom and morality and God, where we use practical reason. But we may feel it solved one philosophical problem only by introducing another: Granted we can now keep both worlds, how are we to relate the two?

The "Copernican revolution." Copernicus changed our way of viewing the universe. In physical terms, most people before him thought that planet earth was the center and that everything else revolves around us. Copernicus announced that we are not the center; our position is a rather humbler one. Kant claimed that he too was introducing a revolution comparable to Copernicus's. As far as concerns its radical nature, he was justified in his claim. If he was right, everyone else before him had been seriously in error and needed to revolutionize their thinking. But as for putting us in a humbler position in our universe, Kant in fact did the opposite. In order to safeguard the Enlightenment project of making human reason the last judge and guide in everything, he introduced a way of viewing the role of human reason that made the human mind the center of the universe.

Most people have assumed, he said, that the objects in the world order our perception of them. That is, if I see a tree, it is the tree that somehow forms a series of concepts in my mind, of shape, color, distance, duration in time, and so on. But the fact of the matter is the other way around. The tree may supply something, but because it is the thing-in-itself, we can't have any knowledge of it. So what is significant is not what the tree supplies but what our mind supplies. And it is significant for Kant, not just because it shapes our knowledge, but because it does it necessarily; our minds have to operate in this way. So, by analyzing the fixed way our minds work, we can establish some actual and incontrovertible, that is, synthetic *a priori*, truth about the world, even if the truth about things in themselves is lost to us.

So, said Kant, when we examine the way we perceive objects in the world, we find that we have to think of them in terms of space and time. Space and time, then, are not things-in-themselves or things in the world; they are things in our minds. For us at any rate, they have no objective reality; they are purely subjective. In the same way, causality is in our minds, not in things in the external world. Here Kant went a step beyond Hume. Hume had decided that we can't locate causality in objects or in their relationship, but he hadn't offered any explanation for it other than habit and custom. Kant located it squarely in our minds. He stated in fact that there are twelve subjective "categories" our mind uses to view the objects of perception.

1. Concerning quantity: unity, plurality, totality
2. Concerning quality: reality, negation, limitation
3. Concerning relation: substance, cause, community
4. Concerning modality: possibility, existence, necessity

Kant referred to the twelve categories as forms of understanding, and space and time as forms of sensibility.

Kant's Antinomies

Kant claimed that his philosophy was able to solve many of the puzzles that philosophers had struggled with through the centuries. One of the ways it did this was by providing us with a tool for solving "antinomies." An antinomy is a pair of contradictory statements, each of which can be supported by apparently valid arguments. The contradictory statements he called "thesis" and "antithesis." He gave four common antinomies:

1. Thesis: The world had a beginning in time and is limited in space.
   Antithesis: The world has no beginning and no limits.

2. Thesis: Space is infinitely divisible.
   Antithesis: Space cannot be infinitely divisible.

3. Thesis: Humans have real freedom.
   Antithesis: Everything is determined by natural laws.

4. Thesis: There must be a necessary being.
   Antithesis: There cannot be a necessary being.

The solution to these paradoxes, says Kant, is to recognize that they involve us in making statements about things, the beginning of the world, space, freedom, and God, that are not part of our actual experience. We have crossed the line from speaking of the phenomenal world of appearances, the only world we are really able to speak about, to trying to speak about things-in-themselves, the noumenal, the sphere where we should be silent. No wonder we have trouble.

I have called Kant's categories or forms "subjective," in that they are in the "subject's" mind rather than in the objective world. Kant, however, would not have accepted the twenty-first-century concept that makes subjectivity arbitrary and as a result provides the basis for relativism. He is not saying that we are free to pick any category or form and impose it on the world around us. We can't, for example, arbitrarily take the category "red" and choose to see everything through red spectacles and so claim that everything is red. All we can do is look into our minds and see what categories are already there. When we do so, we in fact find two things that we might think are pretty objective. One is that everyone's mind works the same, so we can all agree to a common understanding of the world. The other is that there is a limited range of forms of sensibility and understanding, which, Kant thought, we can definitively list.

For Kant it was very important that these things were fixed, *a priori* as opposed to subjectively relative. Their being fixed enabled them to provide a firm basis for science, something Hume had removed. Of course, this firm basis is now in the mind of the observing and experiencing subject and not in the world as it is in itself. But at least something had been salvaged, and Kant clearly thought that that something was pretty considerable. But there was more to come. Kant was determined not to stop with epistemology; he had defined the boundaries of our knowledge and the limits of our reason in order to provide a foundation for his next task, to establish a basis for morality and true human living.

The world behind the world.

Kant's second *Critique* moved on from the world of science, of pure reason, to the world behind the world of science, where we leave pure reason behind and move on to practical reason. In this new world we find all the things that don't fit the scientist's world: free will, goodness, beauty, morals, the soul, and God. Kant was absolutely sure that these are genuine and significant realities; he certainly didn't want to follow the line taken a century and a half later by the logical positivists that anything that wasn't "scientific" was necessarily nonexistent or meaningless. But once he had set them beyond the reach of normal reason, he was confronted with the difficult task of justifying any rational discussion of them at all. In that these things belong to the noumenal sphere rather than the phenomenal, in a sense we can only be silent about them. But that was something Kant didn't want to be. He was eager to provide a justification for them and so supply a firm basis for practicing morality, making free choices, worshiping God, and so on, just as he believed he had provided a firm basis for the practice of science and ordinary thinking. In the same way, just as he had, he believed, established the existence of synthetic *a priori* truths as a foundation for knowledge in the phenomenal world, so he wanted to establish synthetic *a priori* truths that operated specifically in the world of morals.

Kant emphasized the importance of two concepts that were basic to his idea of goodness, the concepts of the good will and duty. The good will seeks goodness not as a means to some other end, but simply because it is good. Kant is scathing about those whose actions appear good but are done from some ulterior motive; that, for him, is not goodness at all. This approach causes him to have a very demanding concept of duty. To enjoy doing our duty, to find fulfillment, for instance, in practicing kindness to others, is for Kant of little moral worth; we are actually fostering our own happiness or self-fulfillment. So for the practice of duty to be morally laudable, we must do our duty against the odds, with gritted teeth, deriving no pleasure or any benefit from it. This approach stands in stark contrast to that of, say, Aristotle, who said that the truly virtuous person should enjoy the practice of virtue.

Morality, for Kant, is not rooted in the nature of God. In keeping with his principles, he stated that pure or, as we might say, "scientific" reason cannot establish the existence of God. Accordingly, he sought to demonstrate the fallibility of the ontological, cosmological, and teleological arguments as rationally watertight proofs of God's existence. He did, however, see a basic continuity running through the various "nonscientific" aspects of human experience. Just as we find the forms and categories by looking into our own minds, we find equally clearly moral categories that we find to be synthetic *a priori*. In particular we find a major moral principle. Kant called this the "categorical imperative." He formulated it in various ways, stating, for example, that we should act only in accordance with principles that we would be happy to see as universally binding laws. Moral awareness, an acceptance of the categorical imperative, and a sense of moral law are things we all share and cannot reasonably ignore.

But the existence of a moral awareness has very significant implications. One of them is that we have free will in order to be able to make meaningful responses to the promptings of this awareness. And if we have free will, then there must be more to us than the bodily machine described by the scientists. There is thus something beyond the physical world, something that is not subject to its laws. This in itself opens up the possibility of the existence of spiritual or supernatural reality. Additionally, Kant developed other lines of thought that could be taken as arguments for the existence of God. The moral law, for instance, must have come from somewhere, from a mind, a moral law giver; God is an obvious candidate. The moral law demands that justice should be done; but justice is not always done in this life: the evil prosper and the good suffer. So the moral law requires that in the end someone—God—puts all the records straight in a life to come.

Of course, by his own rules, Kant can't offer these "arguments" as rational "proofs." In a sense he is being inconsistent with his principles, even talking about them. In this area, he says, it is not a question of using our "scientific" reason or ordinary knowledge. Indeed, here we lay aside reason and knowledge to make room for faith. Some have criticized Kant at this point for seeming to make morality foundational and God as a kind of afterthought, rather dependent on morality for his significance. Kant would have been able to counter this criticism by saying that to argue from morality to God no more lessens the significance of God than the traditional ontological, cosmological, or teleological arguments do; all that we are doing is starting with an aspect of our own experience and following it back to God. Indeed, in the area of practical reason, Kant can justifiably claim that he has an integrated and interdependent system, tying in together all the significant nonmechanistic elements of life. Where he is perhaps more open to criticism is over his failure to link the world of the scientist with the world of practical reason. Many of his predecessors had, of course, been able to do this by acknowledging that God has a significant part to play in the creating and sustaining of the physical world, quite apart from his role as the basis and guarantor of freedom, immortality, the moral law, and the like. Kant, in his desire to give "scientific" reason total autonomy, chose not to give God any role in the physical universe and so made it inevitable that his philosophy should split both the human mind and the world.

KANT AND CHRISTIANITY

Of the four questions Kant set himself to answer, we have explored "What can I know?" and "What should I do?" Kant did not live to complete his answer to the final question, "What is man?" But he did explore "What may I hope?" This question gave him the opportunity to recast Christianity into a form that was acceptable to a pure rationalist. He did this in *Religion within the Limits of Reason Alone* (1793), in which he sought to establish what he saw as the key truths of Christianity without having recourse to revelation.

Kant's background was Lutheran pietism. Though he retained some of pietism's beliefs, such as the innate root of evil in our souls, he clearly rejected its narrowness and what he called its fanaticism, together with its stress on a personal experience of God. We cannot *feel* the immediate influence of God, he said, since the idea of God lies only in reason.

At times Kant appeared to reject the concept of special revelation totally. But at other times he allowed it a place. In the second edition of *Religion within the Limits of Reason Alone*, he described two concentric circles. The inner circle is the Christian religion as it is accessible to the unaided reason. This circle contains all the essential truths of Christianity. The outer circle, overlapping the inner circle but holding some additional truths, contains the truths of revelation. There is enough in the inner circle to enable those who use their reason alone without the benefit of revelation to be true Christians. Nevertheless, Kant himself on occasion drew from the outer circle, as in the case of his belief in original sin and the Lutheran concept of the bondage of the will. Kant had to discuss this issue because his moral philosophy entailed a belief that "ought" implies "can." That is, if there is a moral obligation, such as we find in the moral law or categorical imperative, it must be possible for us to obey that moral obligation. "Ought" without the ability to comply would be absurd. Kant's solution to this problem also seems to lie in the outer circle; he accepted our need of the grace of God to enable us to do what the moral law requires. "Ought" thus implies "can" with help from God.

Kant chose not to involve himself in Christian observances and practices. This may stem partly from his pietist background, which tended to distrust organized religion. But it is more likely that it expressed his disdain for popular beliefs and practices. As a rationalist he felt he was able to get behind the superficial concepts of traditional Christianity and grasp the rational realities that they represent. This concept that the philosopher can grasp theological reality while ordinary people have to be content with shadows is one we have already met. It goes back to Plato and was to dominate German philosophy and theology throughout the nineteenth century and well into the twentieth.

TO THINK THROUGH

Are we machines? Or are the really meaningful aspects of life nonmechanistic?

Descartes had split mind and matter. Kant divided in two both the human mind and the universe. Can we live with such divisions?

Your mind may appear to you to be the center of your universe. But does that mean it is the center of "the" universe? Is it inevitable that if God ceases to be the center of the universe the only thing we have left to put there is our own minds?

Do you think Kant's arguments in the area of practical reason could be used today to help someone accept the viability of a belief in the existence of God?

For Further Study

Guyer, P., ed. *The Cambridge Companion to Kant*. Cambridge: Cambridge University Press, 1992.

THIRTY-ONE

BUT WE STILL WANT TO WORK OUT A SYSTEM

GERMAN IDEALISM AFTER KANT

> In this chapter we look at three German thinkers who largely accepted the main points of Kant's philosophy and continued to develop idealism. We will spend more time looking at the philosophy of Hegel than at the philosophies of Fichte and Schelling, since, though no one followed it in all its details, Hegel's system has had a powerful effect on both philosophy and history, not least through its influence on Marx.

LESS THAN A QUARTER OF A CENTURY AFTER THE DEATH of Kant, in 1827, the American Charles Hodge arrived in Germany to acquaint himself with the latest theological and philosophical situation in Europe. Friedrich Tholuck, professor of theology at Halle, told him, "Kant's system is universally abandoned. Fichte, who followed him, is also forgotten. Schelling has shared the same fate. The reigning philosopher of the day is Hegel."

The reign of Kant was brief, like the reign of most of his successors. No one accepted and continued to teach his system as a whole. But the impact of his ideas lasted far longer. Aspects of his idealism were adopted and developed by thinkers throughout the nineteenth century. The three Germans Tholuck mentioned each were profoundly influenced by him and, in their way, furthered his impact. Through Hegel, Kant's influence reached to such contrasting thinkers as Karl Marx and the late-nineteenth-century idealists. Romantic and Existentialist thinkers alike owed much to him. But the impact of Kant's ideas was not limited to those who were sympathetic toward him. Those whose philosophical viewpoint was very different from his still had to take notice of him and of the impact of his ideas.

Kant had hoped that his system would provide the means of structuring all our thinking into one unified worldview. Ever since the rejection of the medieval synthesis, philosophy and science had been fragmented and struggling, failing to find a unifying feature that would fulfill the role that God had played in the thousand years after Augustine. It seemed that this unifying feature had to be either the world around us or ourselves. Given the huge confidence in reason, this in effect meant our reason itself or the world as understood by our reason.

Descartes and Leibniz had confidently claimed that they had built systems that used reason alone and provided an answer to all philosophical and practical questions. But it was clear they had failed to do so. To Kant it was also clear that no one could do this. Reason, for all our confidence in it, was insufficient to establish a total and satisfying system or worldview. So, in his system, he had aimed for something less. He had sought to analyze how reason functions and thus to show both where and how it can be used and where it cannot be used. The capabilities of the human mind are limited to the structuring and understanding of our ideas. It can never reach beyond our ideas to the world around us, to things-in-themselves. Yet we all are convinced that things-in-themselves exist, that they are more real than our ideas, and that in fact we can't live without allowing them to be a highly significant part of our world.

Given the limits, and so the inadequacy, of the human mind, as shown by Kant, we have a number of possible ways forward:

- We can accept the role of the reason or the mind in the area where it is successful, that of the phenomenal world, which includes the world of the scientist, and seek to use some other means of grasping reality for things-in-themselves, the noumenal world. In a sense this is what Kant did, limiting the role of reason in order to make room for "faith." It was an option gladly seized upon by many in the nineteenth century, particularly romantic thinkers and theologians. While the scientist or ordinary person explores the world around us by means of reason, we, the poets, speculative thinkers, and theologians, have a further, higher means of knowing reality. Where ordinary reason stops, the soul, the spirit, intuition, a "higher reason," or faith takes over and enables us to know with certainty what reason can never tell us. This is the way of the split universe and the split human subject.

- We can conclude that by showing the inability of mind or reason to grasp ultimate reality, Kant has in fact shown the inadequacy of idealism. Mind is not ultimate reality; ultimate reality lies beyond mind's limited abilities. So ultimate reality must be greater than mind, and if we are to have an integrated universe, mind must be subject to and part of and hopefully explicable by ultimate reality. There are two possible contenders for the role of ultimate reality, God and matter. For those trained in the idealist tradition who wanted to take the radical step of rejecting the priority of mind, matter was the most attractive option.

- Alternatively, we can salvage idealism by assuming that ultimate reality is mind rather than matter. Kant had said that all we can know is the content of our own human minds; what lies beyond, whether it is mind or matter, can't be known by us. But let us suppose that it is mind. After all, such an idea has a long pedigree, especially in Neoplatonism. If ultimate reality is mind, then we have a bridge between the world of phenomena and the world of noumena, between the world of the scientist and the world of things-in-themselves. Both are the province of mind. The problem of the split universe is solved. Accordingly, those idealists who immediately followed Kant sought to develop systems based on a belief that everything that is, is the product of mind. To do this they had to go beyond human minds, with all their limitations, and posit an ultimate or absolute Mind, which not only causes all things to exist, but is the basis for the ideas that human minds are able to think. This is the way followed by Fichte, Schelling, and Hegel.

JOHANN GOTTLIEB FICHTE

Rammenau, Saxony, Germany (1762–1814). The son of a ribbon maker, Johann Gottlieb Fichte studied at Jena and Leipzig, starting with theology and then majoring in philosophy. He was professor of philosophy at Jena from 1794 to 1799, and he wrote his most influential works while he was there. In 1810 he took up a professorship at Berlin but died of typhus four years later. He started out as a determinist, but his study of Kant convinced him of both the reality of freedom and the validity of Kant's basic approach. Other influences on his thought were Spinoza and Lessing.

Idealism, freedom, and dogmatism.

Fichte's first book, *Attempt at a Critique of All Revelations* (1792), was published anonymously and was thought by many to be by Kant himself. It rejected the dogmas of orthodox Christianity and proposed morality as the main interest of religion. An aversion to "dogmatism," together with an insistence on freedom, marked all Fichte's thinking. As a result of Kant's discoveries, Fichte stated that we have to choose between starting with the free subject, the observing and experiencing "I," or the objective thing-in-itself. To choose the first is the way of idealism; to choose the second is the way of materialism or dogmatism. Fichte chose the way of idealism, since this alone offers freedom and opens the way to an acceptable philosophical system. He accepted, however, that those who were less mature and so less capable of exercising their intellectual freedom would incline toward "dogmatism."

Transcendental egoism.

Fichte outlined his system in his book *Grundlage der gesamten Wissenschaftslehre* (Foundation of an Entire Theory of Knowledge, 1794). At its heart is a theory of mind that combines elements of Kant with the conclusions of rationalistic deistic religion. Fichte posited the existence of Mind that lies behind or transcends human minds, a transcendental ego, an Absolute Mind. He called the theory "transcendental egoism." The word he used for the Absolute Mind was *Geist*, which is the word from which we get the English "ghost." It has a broader feel to it than what we today would think of as mind. Many today would effectively equate mind and brain, but for Fichte, and for Schelling and Hegel after him, mind was something very different from brain. A better translation of *Geist* would be "spirit." The idealists were saying that reality is spiritual, though they were careful to insist that the essence of spirituality is rationality; its activity is thought. Fichte didn't picture this ultimate mind as an entity in an objective sense. Rather, it was an activity. Conceiving it as an entity would take us back into the world of objects and of dogmatism. Seeing it as an activity retains the element of freedom. Part of the transcendental ego's activity is to posit its own existence and, by working in the minds of human observers, to posit the existence of Nature, the world around us.

Moral philosophy.

Fichte's stress on freedom shaped his moral philosophy, which has a distinctively existentialist feel about it. Each of us is striving toward self-expression, self-realization. The higher part of us, which is rational and spiritual, resists our lower nature and moves us stage by stage nearer to being truly human and truly free. As in the individual, so in humanity and in the world at large, the absolute spirit is moving on to maturity and perfection.

FRIEDRICH VON SCHELLING

Leonberg, Germany (1775–1854). Son of a Lutheran pastor, Schelling studied at the theological seminary at Tübingen, where he met and became friends with Hegel. He studied math and science at Leipzig and was appointed professor of philosophy at Jena in 1798, the year before Fichte left. He held teaching posts at other universities, ending up as professor at Berlin. His works include *Ideas Concerning a Philosophy of Nature* (1797), *On the World-Soul* (1798), *System of Transcendental Idealism* (1800), *Presentation of My System of Philosophy* (1801), and *Philosophical Investigations into the Nature of Human Freedom* (1809). Schelling was a deep and often original thinker. In his attitude to nature and the priority he gave to aesthetics and (later) religion over the intellect, he was a romantic rather than a rationalist. Though to an extent eclipsed by Hegel, his ideas prefigure those of Schopenhauer and of the existentialists and perhaps even of the postmodernists.

Mind and the world. Like Fichte, with whom he collaborated for a time, Schelling firmly rejected mechanistic materialism and proclaimed the priority of mind. But he went beyond Fichte in developing his "philosophy of nature." The natural world, or Nature, is to be seen as mind in the process of becoming conscious. Like Fichte, Schelling saw this mind primarily as active. It is dynamic and alive, and as a result, everything, even "inert" inorganic matter, is alive. Everything is pervaded by the force or life-force of mind. Force is directed either inward or outward. It is attraction or repulsion. When it is matter, it is attraction; when it is spirit, or the subjective ego, it is repulsion, thrusting outward.

Art. A further departure from Fichte was Schelling's stress on art. God is an artist. The world is a work of art. The dramatic self-revelation of the Absolute through history is a work of art. A work of art is a manifestation of the Absolute. As a result, the aesthetic sphere is more ultimate than the moral or the religious sphere, though religion has value because it is especially able to express the aesthetic.

Monism. Throughout his life Schelling's philosophy changed and developed. For a time his position was near to pantheism as presented by Spinoza and the monistic Giordano Bruno (1548–1600). In order to solve the problem of the relationship between the subjective ideal world of spirit and the objective "real" world of Nature, Schelling proposed that in the Absolute the distinctions between subjective and objective, ideal and real, mind and matter ceased to exist. The Absolute is the vanishing of all distinctions. Hegel criticized this, parodying it as "At night all cows are black."

Religion. Later Schelling moved away from pantheism, accepting more of a distinction between the Absolute and the natural world. At this stage he began to feel that philosophy is insufficient to explain the world and, as a result, religion replaced art as of primary significance in his thought. He saw himself as developing a "positive" philosophy, as opposed to the "negative" philosophy of Hegel and of his own earlier phase, which he now rejected. In this he accepted that there is such a thing as Being, which is beyond our rational thinking, but which reveals itself (generally irrationally) in religion and not least in the biblical revelation. In exploring this Schelling saw the origin of the world as a cosmic fall, as God alienating himself from himself, the finite becoming something that "stands out" (the literal meaning of the word "exist") from the infinite. Involved in this is a sense of the tragic, of the deep hurts and dreads of the human condition, which religion is able to heal.

GEORG WILHELM FRIEDRICH HEGEL

Stuttgart, Germany (1770–1831). Georg Wilhelm Friedrich Hegel studied theology at Tübingen University but didn't impress his teachers, who noted his ineptitude at philosophy and unsuitability for Christian ministry. Earning his keep as a private tutor, Hegel wrote a treatise on economics and began work on a life of Christ purged of all supernatural elements. He got to know Schelling and his work and began to teach philosophy at Jena, where he was appointed a professor in 1805. Subsequently he was made professor of philosophy at Heidelberg (1816) and Berlin (1818). By the time of his death in a cholera epidemic, he had become the dominant figure in German philosophy.

Among Hegel's best-known works are *The Phenomenology of Mind* (1807), *The Science of Logic* (1812), and *Outlines of the Philosophy of Right* (1820). Many of his lecture notes and his students' notes from his lectures were also published. His very early works were written in an attractive, clear style. But when he became a professional philosopher, he followed (and surpassed) Kant in adopting a heavy, obscure style that for most people makes his work unintelligible.

But even though Hegel's system is famous for its obscurity, its impact has been enormous. This was partly because it had very practical applications in concrete historical situations and covered areas like economics, society, politics, revolution, and war. It also had particular application to Prussia and the development of Germany. In the longer term, its greatest impact was through its influence on Karl Marx, but it was also significant in that much of subsequent philosophy was a reaction to Hegel's ideas. Hegel's philosophy also significantly affected the development of German theological thinking and thus of liberal theology generally.

Hegel's philosophical writings are so obscurely written that some philosophers have decided he is not actually saying anything at all. But most agree there are some key concepts that underlie all the obscurity and that can be presented comparatively simply, even if Hegel himself would not have recognized them stripped of all his verbosity.

Idealism.

Idealism. Hegel was an idealist. He saw himself as a more consistent idealist than Kant. Kant had said that for us our minds shape reality, and so, in effect, reality for us is mental. But Kant had conceded that reality in itself may well not be mental; the problem is that we can't know anything about it, so we can't know whether it is mental or not. Hegel dismissed Kant's unknowable thing-in-itself as unacceptable. We do know things as they are, he said, and the reason we can know them is because everything is mind. We, the perceiving subjects, are minds. The objects of our perception, the things in the world around us are mental, not material. There is no underlying material substance behind them. Everything is mind.

Mind, spirit, and God.

Mind, spirit, and God. Like Fichte, Hegel used the word *Geist* for mind, with its connotation of "spirit." For him reality is spiritual. Everything is spiritual. We are perceiving spirits. All that we perceive is spiritual, and all that exists is spiritual. In that Hegel saw everything that exists as one, and so one ultimate or absolute Spirit, some have seen him as a pantheist. Others say his position was nearer to panentheism, in that he believed that Spirit is manifested in everything but not to be identified with everything.

Hegel's Absolute Spirit doesn't create, in the traditional Christian sense. Rather, it expresses itself as everything in the world. Everything is Mind thinking, the Absolute actualizing itself, the rational expressing itself as the real. Hence Hegel's most quoted line, "The Real is the Rational and the Rational is the Real." The more rational my thought, the more it partakes of reality, or perhaps, rather, the more reality expresses itself in me. But into this self-expression of God/Mind/Spirit, Hegel introduced a special quality that was to have a far-reaching influence—the quality of being in process.

Process, history, and dialectic.

Process, history, and dialectic. Jewish and Christian thought had established the concept of all history being an expression of the purposes of God and so moving forward in a teleological process. The replacing of God with the Newtonian scientific system tended to destroy this concept. What happens, just happens. A clock isn't going anywhere. Hegel restored the concept of a process, but rather than rooting it in God in the way Christianity had done, he rooted it in the world as the expression of Mind/Spirit and in particular in the history of Western Europe, culminating in Hegel's own philosophy and the political situation of the Germany of his day.

History, said Hegel, is the dynamic process of the gradual development and self-actualization of Absolute Mind through human minds. Key to Hegel's understanding of this process was his application of Kant's concept of thesis and antithesis. He applied this both in the realms of logic and of human affairs. Up to the time of Hegel, people had generally assumed that the way out of the conflict between two contradictory ideas or situations was to reject one of them. Either the thesis or the antithesis had to go. So, in the conflict between "All swans are white" and "Some swans are black," one of the statements must be rejected as false if the other is true. In the conflict between the interests of the community and the interests of the individual, one or the other has to give way. Hegel famously rejected this response and said that instead of the conflict between thesis and antithesis leading to the rejection of one or the other, it leads to what he called "synthesis." That synthesis in its turn can be viewed as a new thesis, to which, sooner or later, will come another antithesis. Out of the new conflict will come a new synthesis and so on. The emergence of a synthesis is not to be seen so much as a compromise between the thesis and the antithesis as a whole new concept that grows out of their conflict.

Two of the key conflicts that Hegel saw as exemplifying this process were the conflict between reason and desire and the conflict between morality and self-interest. In each of these conflicts, it is not so much a case of one element having to give way to the other, reason giving way to desire or morality giving way to self-interest. Rather, the outcome is the developing of a new way of integrating our desires with the dictates of reason or of merging self-interest with the principles of morality.

Hegel's process, known as the dialectic (thesis and antithesis in "dialogue" with each other), is always upward and forward. Each conflict gives rise to new truths and situations that are one step nearer to being in tune with the Absolute Mind. Such was Hegel's confidence in himself and his philosophy that he was able to say that it was in his work that the great goal of all the process was being realized.

The implications of the concept of the dialectical process were radical. It moved Western thought one stage nearer to relativism. Even logic, for so long the bastion of absolutes and fixed points, was subject to change and development.

Truth is no longer fixed; moral principles develop and change. The theory of dialectic also made conflict and innovation both inevitable and desirable, a concept Marx was to exploit very effectively. It also entrenched the belief that all that has gone before, whether in history or in the realm of ideas, is inferior to what we have now. This is a belief that has dominated Western thought for far too long, with detrimental results. In theology it contradicted the call of the Protestant Reformers to get back to the teaching of Jesus and the early Christians, and it encouraged theologians to claim that their new way of seeing things was at last the true one; all that had gone before was primitive and superstitious and unenlightened.

Alienation. Hegel originated the concept of alienation, which was then taken up and applied extensively by Marx and later by the existentialists and social theorists. Hegel used two terms, one meaning estrangement (*Entfremdung*) and the other externalization (*Entausserung*). He illustrated alienation by the "unhappy consciousness" of those who, in Hegel's way of seeing things, have lost the support and security afforded by being at one with the community around them and with themselves, and turn inward and direct their focus toward an other-worldly kingdom of God. The cure for such alienation, said Hegel, is to realize that we as individuals are in fact the expression of Absolute Mind; as such we are one with reality, not alienated from it.

Hegel also saw alienation as more than just a part of the overall process; in a sense the process itself expresses alienation. The fact that the goal of the process is the full self-actualization of the Absolute Mind entails that while the process is going on, the Absolute Mind is somehow alienated from itself. This is in part at least due to the fact that it has involved itself in nature and society.

Freedom. One of the key aspects of the process is that it is working toward freedom. Hegel believed that the synthesis that arises out of each conflict would be both a fuller expression of Absolute Mind and a stage nearer to freedom. The final culmination of the process will see Mind totally free of any limiting forces. Since we all participate in Mind, Hegel believed that each individual's freedom would develop as the process goes forward.

It is salutary to reflect that despite Hegel's confidence in the inevitability of the development of individual rationality and freedom, it is probably true to say that his system, more than anything else, was the philosophical justification for the two most savage expressions of totalitarianism and the suppression of individual freedom seen in the twentieth century. In accordance with

Hegel's vision, Hitler saw the German state as the culmination of history; all who opposed it had to be ruthlessly oppressed and eliminated. And Marxism, adopting the philosophy of Hegel almost wholesale, has been responsible for the oppression and murder of innocent citizens on a scale that makes even Hitler pale into insignificance.

Nature and society. Nature, the natural world around us, is seen by Hegel not as existing in its own right, but as the expression of the Absolute Mind or Spirit. In contrast to many pantheists, who see the world as the necessary emanation of God or Mind, Hegel stressed that the Absolute expresses itself freely. It is a dynamic expression, not an inert inevitable emanation. Again, nature is essentially in process; if we wish to understand it, we are not to view it as it is now but rather in the context of what it has been and what it is becoming. It is not the particular object or event that matters, but all the objects in relationship with each other and in the context of all events past and future. What is expressed in nature is always less than the idea that is expressing it, just as a work of art is always less than the idea in the mind of the artist. Like the Neoplatonists, Hegel thought of this process as two-way—the minds of individuals reflect back the thought of the Absolute Mind and thus further the ongoing dynamic process.

Besides expressing itself in nature, Absolute Spirit expresses itself in social institutions, notably the family, society, and the state, and in art, religion, and philosophy. The family, society, and the state are thus to be seen and accepted as an expression of Absolute Mind. For all the value we are to put on the individual, individuals cannot be seen as complete in themselves. Individuals are part of the larger unit. Since only the whole, the Absolute, fully partakes of reality, it is only as we share in more and more of the whole through social institutions that we get near to experiencing full reality. Since Absolute Mind is rational, rationality is to be a hallmark of social institutions. They are to be regulated in such a way that all individuals are free and able to express their own rationality.

Art in all its forms is similarly an expression of Absolute Mind, particularly in its spiritual aspect. But even at its best it can only express it partially. Religion gives us a fuller expression, clothing the ideas of the Absolute in images, pictures, and stories that ordinary people can grasp. The best expression of all is in philosophy, where truth can be grasped without the mediation of pictures or stories. In the philosopher the human mind reaches the high point of rationality; indeed, in the philosopher, the Absolute Mind finally comes to its full self-actualization.

TO THINK THROUGH

From Plato to Berkeley to Hegel, the belief that mind is more real than matter has kept recurring. Yet many people would say that evolutionary theory has finally shown that it is untenable. What do you think?

Maybe you noticed the way the interest has shifted from "reason" to "mind" to "infinite mind" to "spirit" to a cosmic process. In the last decades of the twentieth century, when people's confidence in the rationalism of the scientific worldview was shaken, there was a parallel shift to an interest in spiritualities and cosmic processes. Does this tell us something significant about human nature?

What do you think about Hegel's dialectic, both in its logical and in its historical applications? Has he got it right? Does it demolish traditional logic? Even though its historical application has lent itself to a great deal of abuse, is there some truth there?

For Further Study

Beiser, F. C., ed. *The Cambridge Companion to Hegel*. Cambridge: Cambridge University Press, 1993.

Pinkard, T. *German Philosophy 1760–1860: The Legacy of Idealism*. Cambridge: Cambridge University Press, 2002.

THIRTY-TWO

GETTING RID OF GOD

THREE RADICAL POST-HEGELIANS

> Our main interest in this chapter
> is the philosophy of Karl Marx.
> But we will get to it via two
> other key figures on the Hegelian
> left, Ludwig Feuerbach and D. F.
> Strauss, who in different ways
> prepared the ground for Marxism.

PHILOSOPHERS IN THE GERMAN TRADITION WHO FOL-
lowed Hegel fell into two main groups. One group, the Old or Right Hegelians,
accepted Hegel's philosophy as it was, complete with its claim that it was definitive and that the current political situation in Prussia was the climax of the
great historical process. Given these two things, there was little fresh to be
done. A rather watered-down version of Christianity, Hegelian philosophy, and
the political and social status quo could all live reasonably happily together.

Others, known as the Left or Young Hegelians, were more radical. They saw
elements in Hegel's philosophy that were not yet fulfilled. They saw the current
political and religious situations as falling far short of an adequate culmination of
all history. There was yet much to be changed and much to be achieved. As a
result, the Hegelian Left tended to be revolutionaries; they explained Hegel's failure to advocate revolution by the fact that his salary was paid by the state.

As one might expect, the impact of the Hegelian Right on philosophy and
history was slight. The influence of the Hegelian Left was very considerable.
Among them were Ludwig Feuerbach, D. F. Strauss, and Karl Marx.

LUDWIG FEUERBACH

Landshut, Germany (1804–1872). Son of a celebrated legal philosopher, Ludwig Feuerbach studied theology for two years at Heidelberg and then studied philosophy under Hegel at Berlin. Converted to Hegelianism, his first published work attacked the concepts of the transcendence of God and personal immortality. Later he turned his attack on Hegel himself, particularly for his idealism and for retaining elements of religion in his system, but also for his failure to work through the revolutionary implications of his philosophy. For a time Feuerbach collaborated with Marx and like him moved from idealism to atheism and materialism; he originated the concept "We are what we eat." Matter, he decided, cannot be dependent on mind, so mind must have arisen out of matter.

Getting rid of God. The heart of Feuerbach's attack on Christianity, expressed in *The Essence of Christianity* (1841), was his theory that all our ideas of God are our own creation, the fulfillment of our wishes, the projection of our humanity. Theology is nothing more than anthropology; God is "man" writ large.

The developing of this theory marks a particularly significant stage in the implementing of the modern period's hidden agenda of removing any traces of God from human thinking. Feuerbach was doing two things. Like others before him, he was attacking the idea of God and seeking to show its problems and inconsistencies. Even though Hegel had already greatly watered down the traditional concept of God and made it little more than a mental undergirding of everything that is, Feuerbach went further and sought to purge Hegelianism of even that concept of God.

Second, Feuerbach's argument that God is a projection of our human attributes goes a significant step further. In seeking to explain how the concept of God had arisen in the first place, he was taking away the ground from under the feet of those who, consciously or unconsciously, assumed that the universal awareness of a concept of God supported belief in his existence. Many, like Descartes, had believed that the fact we have an idea of God is a good reason for believing he exists. Traditional Christianity had claimed that our idea of God has its origin in God himself. Feuerbach's argument sought to undermine these positions and thus to remove God from human thought altogether.

Though Feuerbach was never able to prove his theory, his influence, especially through Marxism, has been considerable, not least in the areas of psychology and the social sciences.

DAVID FRIEDRICH STRAUSS

Ludwigsburg, South Germany (1808–1874). Though D. F. Strauss taught for a time at the theological seminary in Tübingen, he saw himself as the opponent of traditional Christianity and particularly of its doctrine of a transcendent and personal God who is supernaturally involved in the world. This meant supremely that Jesus could not be God incarnate and that the historical Jesus could not have done the things the Bible records. Starting from these presuppositions, he launched a vigorous attack on the New Testament, particularly in his *The Life of Jesus Critically Examined* (1835). Strauss's impact on German theology was perhaps greater than his scholarship warranted; most of those who followed him made the mistake of accepting his antisupernaturalistic presuppositions, which he had never established, and approaching the Scriptures as a purely human book. Starting out with a philosophy of nature, he was strongly influenced by Hegel; but then, like Marx, he moved on to a more materialistic and atheistic position.

KARL MARX

Trier, Germany (1818–1883). The son of a Jewish lawyer who became a Lutheran Christian, Karl Marx studied law at Bonn and then Berlin, but influenced by members of the Hegelian Left, including Feuerbach, changed to philosophy. He completed his doctorate in philosophy in 1841 but had to leave Berlin when the political situation made things dangerous for the Hegelian Left. He spent time in Cologne, Paris, and Brussels, mostly engaged in radical political journalism. After the unsuccessful European revolutions of 1848, Marx settled in London, where he lived until his death. Though he was supported financially by Friedrich Engels, who had been a fellow student with him at Berlin and was now a successful industrialist, he and his family suffered severe poverty during their early years in London, and Marx's health was damaged. With Engels he wrote *The Communist Manifesto* (1848). The first volume of his greatest work, *Das Kapital* (Capital) was published in 1867. Two further volumes, unfinished at his death, were completed and published by Engels. Marx also wrote numerous newspaper articles. For a time he was the European correspondent of the *New York Tribune*. Some of his more serious philosophical writings remained unpublished until the 1930s and later.

Dialectical materialism. Trained in Hegelianism, Marx took over many of Hegel's doctrines, especially those of alienation and of the dialectical process that proceeds by way of conflict to a final culmination or synthesis. But, in his own words, he stood Hegel on his head in one crucial aspect. Instead of the whole process being the expression of Mind, everything for Marx was matter. From idealism Marx swung to materialism.

His matter, however, under the influence of Hegelianism, was in no way inert in the way that it was in the systems of other materialists of his day. Marx's system was dialectical materialism; he retained the dynamic concept of an ongoing process that Hegel had given him, including the upward development of the process of thesis and antithesis. But instead of the conflict being between ideas or concepts, for Marx the conflict was thoroughly material. Its causes were material: economics, working conditions, the forces of material production. The conflict itself was material: a very real clash between the oppressed and the oppressor. For the idealists it was ideas that caused the events that made history. For Marx it was the concrete situations and events of history that formed ideas. Windmills created feudalism, spinning wheels created the industrial age.

Human beings. Four further key beliefs followed from Marx's materialism. The first was his understanding of the nature of human beings. Where Hegel had seen us primarily as minds and others had seen us primarily as souls, Marx saw us primarily as workers. By our labor we produce; through our creativity and productivity we express our true humanity and thus our dignity. Tragically, in the urbanization and industrialization of the nineteenth century, many workers were being exploited; instead of expressing their true nature through their labor, they had become slaves of the capitalist system.

Changing the world. The second key belief that followed from Marx's materialism was his conviction that the way forward was by stirring people to action, not by disseminating ideas. The world, and so the suffering and needs of the people, were shaped not by ideas but by economic and social conditions. So it is the economic and social conditions that need to be addressed. He derided other philosophers who had merely offered interpretations of the world. Our concern, he said, must be to change it.

Truth. A third result of Marx's materialism was his attitude to truth. He agreed with Hegel in rejecting truth as fixed and static. But in making "truth" subservient to material factors, he opened the door not just to relativism but to any form of propaganda, manipulation, and indoctrination. It is significant that, apart from attacking aspects of Hegel's idealism, Marx did not see the need to argue the case for the truth of his materialism. He simply assumed that it was true. Or, perhaps we should say, he simply assumed it.

Religion.

A fourth result of Marx's materialism was his attitude to religion. There could not, of course, be any spiritual reality lying behind people's religious beliefs. God cannot exist. But it was undeniable for Marx that religion was a powerful social force. It was therefore to be understood in social, that is, material, terms. Religious beliefs and aspirations were the result of social needs and pressures. Unable to cope with alienation and the evils of their condition, the oppressed turn to religion for comfort and hope. It is in this sense that Marx saw religion as the "opium of the people," providing heart in a heartless world. The oppressors, meanwhile, find that it is in their interest to foster religious hopes and aspirations, since they discourage the workers from revolution. As a result, the oppressors, consciously or unconsciously, use religion as a tool to keep the oppressed down. But its system of beliefs, by giving a degree of meaning, dignity, and hope, actually furthers alienation because it prevents people from seeing alienation's true source in the oppressive structures of society; and in the long run it prevents the essential radical change that was society's only real hope. Thus it is to be ruthlessly removed, its false props knocked away.

Marx saw the critique of religion as fundamental. In a sense he was aware that the system of beliefs he was offering was a rival religion, an alternative worldview that had repercussions on every part of life. So he had to break the hold of religion, and especially Christianity, on the people's minds and lives. He developed his critique in three areas. Sociologically, the religious consciousness is the product of social factors, such as the need for the ruling class to keep the workers under submission. In the area of history, Marx sought to show that Christian beliefs about God's acts in history were simply false. In this he was able to draw on the work of his contemporary skeptical German theologians. As an alternative historical fact, Marx argued that Christianity arose as a development of the Phoenician cult of Moloch, which included the sacrifice of the firstborn. In the area of psychology, he drew on Feuerbach and argued that God and the spiritual realm are projections arising from our unmet needs.

Society and alienation.

Marx's stress on the key significance of economic and social conditions meant that for him society at large was of greater importance than the specific individual. In this he went against the trend encouraged by Locke and others of stressing the rights of the individual as in some sense absolute. For Marx it was essential that individualism and, where necessary, the individual be sacrificed for the good of the whole and for the furtherance of the process of history. The exercise of individual freedom was to be severely curtailed at any rate until the final establishment of the perfect society that Marx saw as the goal of history. Nevertheless, Marx's theory had a message of hope for the individual worker in that it embodied a deep concern for equality. All workers should be rewarded, not according to the value of their labor to their employer, nor even according to their ability or skill, but rather according to their needs. Hence his famous saying, "From each according to his abilities to each according to his needs."

Like Hegel, Marx saw alienation as a fundamental human condition. Not surprisingly, however, his main stress was on the economic and social aspects of alienation. The basic physical needs of the people of his day were being denied them by the social and economic structures. Capitalism, by using workers as a commodity, took away the meaning from their labor and so from their life. As a result, they lived in alienation and despair. But where Hegel had prescribed the individual's realization of true integration with the Absolute Mind or Spirit as the cure for alienation, Marx saw the answer in much more practical and material terms. The material structures that cause the alienation must be removed.

Marx's application of the Hegelian dialectical process was wholly in material terms. The story of history is a story of conflict between classes, between exploited and exploiters, slaves and free, serfs and lords, poor and rich, workers and capitalists. One class forms Hegel's thesis; their oppressors are his antithesis. Out of the class struggle eventually will come a synthesis, which will take the form of a new social structure, arising perhaps from the collapse of both the contending classes or from a revolution in which the oppressed throw off their oppressors. Either way, a new conflict situation will arise. Even if those who were formerly exploited succeed in throwing off their chains, society will not be liberated, because that group will in turn become the exploiters of some other group. So the process continues throughout history until the day comes, confidently expected by Marx, when there will be no one left to exploit; the lowest class, the proletariat, will have taken control.

In keeping with his materialism, Marx saw every aspect of the class struggle in material terms. It was not a battle of ideas or principles, nor was it furthered just through words; it was a war in which guns would be fired and people killed. Violence would be inevitable; Marx hoped for a worldwide, or at least Europe-wide bloody revolution. In an industrial society, this would take the form at first of workers standing up against their exploiters through strikes. These would escalate into a general strike and civil war, leading to the overthrow of the government and the liberation of the workers and the establishment of the "dictatorship of the proletariat." But even after the revolution there cannot be true freedom until all traces of exploitation have been removed and all dissent ruthlessly quashed.

Like Hegel, Marx felt that the long process of history was coming to its final climax in his day. The coming clash between thesis and antithesis would result in the final synthesis and the ultimate cleansing and perfecting of society. With the removal of economic and social injustice and exploitation, all other forms of evil would disappear. Even the controlling role of the state would fade away; all would live in peace and harmony, fully satisfied. Private property would cease to exist; all would be shared.

TO THINK THROUGH

Leszek Kolakowski, who taught philosophy under the communists at the University of Warsaw until dismissed for unorthodoxy, called Marx's system an irrational and antiscientific faith. In what ways do you think he was right?

For Further Study

Wood, A. *Karl Marx*. London: Routledge, 1981.

THIRTY-THREE

THE AGE OF REASON

> Confidence in reason ran high in the late eighteenth and early nineteenth centuries. In this chapter we look at some of the ways this was expressed in America and France.

REASON AND REVOLUTION

Reason brought revolution. It cleared away the dusty cobwebs of tradition, authority, metaphysics, and theology. It threw off the shackles of the mind and in some cases threw off other shackles as well. Despite Hume and Kant, confidence in reason, and in science as the outworking of reason, ran high in the last decades of the eighteenth century and well into the nineteenth.

The phrase "The Age of Reason" was the title of a popular book by Thomas Paine, an enthusiastic rationalist and supporter of revolution, both in America and in France. Though hardly a serious philosopher, he typifies the spirit of the age, and in this chapter we will look briefly at him and at two of the key American thinkers in the revolutionary period. Then we will return to France and in particular to the radical scientific positivism of Auguste Comte.

Thomas Paine. Thetford, England (1739–1809). Thomas Paine emigrated to America in 1774 and settled in Philadelphia, where he became a writer and political agitator, expressing and spreading the fervor of late-eighteenth-century rationalistic revolutionary thought. He argued vigorously for the American Revolution; in support of the French revolutionaries, he moved to France and became a French citizen. According to his own account, he escaped the guillotine by divine providence. He returned to America to find that his popularity had waned, and he died in comparative obscurity. His best-known works are *The Rights of Man* (1791–1792), in which he argued that the individual's rationality and knowledge of natural law should be accepted as sovereign, and *The Age of Reason* (1794), in which he outlined a rationalistic deistic religion as the proposed basis of society.

Thomas Jefferson. Shadwell, Virginia (1743–1826). Trained as a lawyer, Thomas Jefferson soon became involved in politics, first in his home state of Virginia and then in the country at large, rising to become the third president of the United States. An empiricist, materialist, and deist, he drew much of his thinking from Locke. He followed a natural rights and social contract theory and argued for religious freedom, universal education, and equality of opportunity as the basis of a democratic society and a "natural aristocracy" of "virtue and talents." He was the author of the Declaration of Independence. Besides being a statesman, he was an educator, scientist, writer, and architect.

Benjamin Franklin. Boston (1706–1790). Born into an orthodox Puritan family, Franklin was early exposed to the literature of the European Enlightenment, especially Locke, through his brother who returned from England in 1717. As a result, he rejected Puritanism for deism. In 1724 he went to London, where he published his first philosophical work. He returned to Philadelphia in 1726. After flirting with polytheism, he returned to a position incorporating deism and Unitarianism, which included a concept of God's special intervention in human affairs. He was a successful businessman and a polymath, pursuing interests in various areas of science, especially electricity. As a statesman and diplomat, Franklin played a leading part in the battle for American independence. As a social reformer and popular moralist, he saw the maximization of happiness, defined as the satisfaction of needs of all God's creatures, as the basis of virtue.

THE APPLICATION OF SCIENCE: SAINT-SIMON AND COMTE

After the upheavals of the revolution and the Napoleonic era, nineteenth-century French intellectual life soon reasserted itself as a significant national institution. Some urged a return to traditional concepts and values, including divine revelation and the monarchy. Others, such as **Victor Cousin** (1792–1867), offered a moderate position based on Scottish Common Sense philosophy. Rather more radical were the social and positivistic philosophies of Saint-Simon and Comte.

Comte de Saint-Simon.

Paris (1760–1825). Of an aristocratic family, Claude Henri de Rouvroy, Count Saint-Simon served in the French army until the Revolution. After losing his fortune through unwise speculation, he supported himself by writing, developing his interests in science, history, and social issues. Many of his ideas were taken up by Marx.

Saint-Simon took as the foundation of his social theory the concept of brotherly love, which is, he said, the essence of Christianity. In keeping with his strong commitment to science, he saw the application of science through industrialization as the key to the development of society. Feudalism, he said, collapsed because of the economically based conflict between the emerging social classes; a successful society will be one that eliminates conflict by being organized scientifically according to economic interest. His scientific analysis of society recognized three categories, each of which should be encouraged to make its distinctive contribution. The doers are the workers, managers, and administrators. The thinkers are the scientists. The feelers are artists, poets, and religious and ethical teachers. As these fulfill their role and work harmoniously together, poverty, the major cause of evil, will be eradicated. To avoid conflict the less able should defer to the more able. As this happens interference by the state will become unnecessary, and central government will wither away.

Auguste Comte.

Montpellier, France (1798–1857). Two months before his death, Auguste Comte crowned himself "the founder of the universal religion, the high priest of humanity." The pope, he said, was but a minister. He, Auguste Comte, was the very personification of the Great Being.

As a student at the École Polytechnique in Paris, Comte gained a deep respect for the scientific worldview as a result of his studies in science and technology. He was, however, expelled for causing trouble before he was able to graduate. His commitment to science meant that throughout his life he sought to understand the operation of all areas of life in terms of the action of laws such as the scientists were said to be discovering. He spent seven years as secretary to Saint-Simon, but the two men quarreled and separated in 1824. From 1826 he gave private lectures on his philosophy and published two lengthy works, *Positive Philosophy Course* (1830–1842) and *Positive Political System* (1851–

1854). From the early 1840s he focused increasingly on developing his Religion of Humanity. He died estranged from most of his former supporters and friends.

The three stages.
Comte described the development of science, expressed in astronomy, physics, chemistry, and biology, as divided into three stages. He called this development a "law," which he then sought to project onto other areas of human knowledge and life. The concept of the three stages was not original to Comte, though their rigid application as a "great fundamental law" that applies with "invariable necessity" to all areas of knowledge was his own development.

The first stage was the theological stage. Here primitive people sought for supernatural explanations for phenomena. This stage lasted from the dawn of time to the end of the Middle Ages. Then came the metaphysical stage, in which abstractions like force or nature or energy were posited as explanations. This was the approach of the modern age. But this, like the theological stage, was to be superseded by the third stage, Comte's scientific stage, to be called "positive" because it replaces groundless speculation with positive scientific fact.

Comte produced three arguments for his law. The first was that even today we can still see traces of the first two stages. Second, all individuals develop through these three stages. Children are theological, young people are metaphysical, and adults are scientific. So it is reasonable to assume that the human race as a whole has passed through them. Third, there had to be early stages based on theological or metaphysical beliefs, since the scientific beliefs we now have are based on observations, and humans were incapable of building a system based on observations before they had some conceptual framework, however false, into which they could fit their observations.

Empiricism.
Science is based on empirical observation. Comte was very insistent that what cannot be observed cannot be a part of science. Some of his contemporaries postulated unobservable substances like ether or fluid to explain phenomena, rather in the same way as physicists today posit subnuclear particles. But Comte would have none of it.

Natural laws.
The key to positive philosophy, said Comte, is that it regards all phenomena without exception as subject to invariable natural laws. It is the scientific observer's task to "detect" these laws and to state them as economically as possible. Any area of study where observations cannot lead to the formulation of such laws cannot be a science and therefore cannot be an area of human study and knowledge; Comte put psychology in this category.

The six sciences. Comte stated that there are six sciences. All areas of knowledge and thought belong to one of the six. They are, in his order, math, astronomy, physics, chemistry, physiology/biology, and "social physics," for which he invented the name *sociology*. This order of classification is according to the order in which they have achieved status as positive sciences. It is thus also the order of increasing lack of positive precision. Thus math is a highly positive and precise science; sociology is as yet the least positive and least precise. Study, he said, should begin with the first and go through each in turn, ending with sociology. He later added ethics as a seventh science.

Though others before Comte had attempted to apply the presuppositions of the Newtonian worldview to all areas of life, he was the first to develop a system that rigorously applied scientific procedures to social, moral, and political development. He believed that it was possible and desirable to develop sociological understanding to the point where the sociologist has identified all the laws that govern human behavior, social interaction, government, and so on, and is thus able to predict future behavior as confidently as an astronomer can predict an eclipse.

Comte was an enthusiastic classifier, and he subdivided sociology into statics and dynamics. Statics dealt with social organization as it is presented in the whole range of social systems. Dynamics dealt with the development of social phenomena and structures, particularly through the three stages. Comte's concept that this development is in accordance with fixed laws was taken up by Marx.

TO THINK THROUGH

What do you think of Comte's concept of law? Are there fixed patterns of development like his three stages? Do different areas of human life all function according to the same laws?

What do you feel about Comte's declaration that an area of interest that doesn't fit the "scientific pattern" cannot be an area of human study?

For Further Study

Kramnick, I. *The Portable Enlightenment Reader.* New York: Penguin, 1995.

THIRTY-FOUR

IF REASON WON'T WORK, LET'S TRY SOMETHING ELSÉ

THE ANTI-RATIONAL REACTION IN GERMANY

> After the rationalistic approaches of the last two chapters, we turn in this chapter to those who reacted against rationalism and stressed the significance of other aspects of human personhood. We look at the German romantics and then at Arthur Schopenhauer and Friedrich Schleiermacher.

THE REIGN OF REASON WAS LONG. THOUGH ITS FAILINGS and inconsistencies were clear by the eighteenth century, its incredible effectiveness meant that most people continued to treat it as their last judge and guide in everything. But a reaction was setting in, not just among romantics and philosophers, but among those concerned with philosophical theology.

In this section we will look briefly at German romanticism and then turn to Schopenhauer, who replaced reason with will as the key element of what it is to be human. We will then go on to look at five differing reactions to the dominance of rationalism from those starting from a more or less Christian position. The first was from a German and thus belongs in this chapter. The other four will need a chapter to themselves.

GERMAN ROMANTICISM

Romanticism was not a school of philosophy; it was a movement that affected all areas of life. As such it is hard to define, and it is not always easy to decide which thinkers are to be classed as romantics and which are not. **Madame de Staël** (1766–1817), a French romantic writer who stressed the integration of thought and feeling, claimed that all German culture, as opposed to French, was romantic. As a movement in Germany, romanticism spanned the last years of the eighteenth century and the early decades of the nineteenth. The collapse of the reason-inspired French Revolution into a reign of terror gave it special impetus.

The key to philosophical romanticism is its rejection of the absolute authority of reason. In this sense, Schelling was a romantic, in that he gave art and religion primacy over intellect. So was Schleiermacher, with his call to accept Christianity as a matter of feeling rather than of intellect. Similarly, Samuel Taylor Coleridge, quite apart from the romanticism of his poetry, was a philosophical romantic in that he debarred understanding from having anything to do with morality or religion.

Philosophers who were influential in the romantic movement included **Friedrich Jacobi** and **Johann Herder**. The pietist philosopher Friedrich Jacobi (1743–1819) attacked Spinoza, Wolff, and Kant for their excessive rationalism and urged the centrality of feeling and faith. Johann Herder (1744–1803) urged a holistic approach, both to the person, which is much more than a mind, and to the world, which is much more than a machine. The poet and philosopher **Novalis** (Friedrich von Hardenberg, 1772–1801) called for faith, love, imagination, poetry, and religion to be set alongside reason as authoritative. **Friedrich von Schlegel** (1772–1829) was a central figure in the movement, stressing the centrality of aesthetics but also developing his own system that included ethics and politics, and ending up virtually in mysticism.

In a broader sense, the German idealists after Kant tended toward a romantic position insofar as they acknowledged that things-in-themselves were beyond the reach of reason. **Johann Schiller** (1759–1805), a key literary and philosophical figure in the movement, shared much of Fichte and Schelling's idealism. He stressed the role of aesthetics in our relationship with both the phenomenal and the noumenal.

The romantic movement was not confined to Germany; each European country had those who expressed their protest against the excessive significance given to reason by stressing that there is much more to human life than the rational and there is much more to the world around us than the mechanistic. In America it was the merging of romanticism with idealism that gave rise to transcendentalism.

ARTHUR SCHOPENHAUER

Danzig (1788–1860). Born into a wealthy cosmopolitan family, Arthur Schopenhauer had his early education in several European countries including France and England. His mother, with whom he had a bad relationship all his life, was a novelist, and through her he met Goethe, Schlegel, and the Grimm brothers. He received his university education at Göttingen and then Berlin, where he started with medicine and then changed to philosophy. In 1813 he received a doctorate from the University of Jena for a dissertation on the principle of sufficient reason.

Schopenhauer was appointed to teach philosophy at Berlin, where Hegel was at the height of his powers, but few attended his lectures, so he gave up. He settled in Frankfurt and lived off his fortune, enjoying a somewhat epicurean life, having affairs and writing books. His major work was *The World As Will and Representation* (1818; second revised and enlarged edition, 1844). Sources of his ideas included Kant, Platonism, and Eastern thought, including Buddhism and the Hindu Upanishads.

Essentially gloomy and pessimistic, Schopenhauer was quick to quarrel and could be violent. He was a gifted writer and a master of invective. Targets of his savage comments included Fichte, Schelling, Hegel, religion, women, and Jews. Though not well known for much of his lifetime, in his closing years he was hailed as a champion of romanticism, and his idiosyncratic philosophy had considerable effect on a number of individuals, including Leo Tolstoy, Thomas Hardy, Richard Wagner, Sigmund Freud, Friedrich Nietzsche, and Ludwig Wittgenstein.

The will. The two key elements of Schopenhauer's thought are his pessimism and his emphasis on the will. Accepting Kant's two spheres of the phenomenal and the noumenal, he stated that the phenomenal world, the sphere of ordinary experience, is the world as "representation," where the principle of sufficient reason operates. Kant had said that the noumenal world is inaccessible to us. But Schopenhauer disagreed; we do have access to our own inner experience, and we find that the thing-in-itself in us is our will. Since plurality only applies in the phenomenal world of space and time, there cannot be a plurality of essences of things-in-themselves. So if we find that will is the essence of ourselves, then will must be the basic noumenon that underlies all things. So will is the fundamental reality; everything is an expression of will.

Will as we experience it in ourselves is the will to be, the will to live. It is the will to be that objectifies itself in my body, the phenomenal aspect of me. All other aspects, including my mind or reason, are also expressions of will. Will therefore is foundational and prior to intellect or reason. In the same way, the world itself is the expression of will, the will to be. This is the key to all nature, animate and inanimate. It drives living creatures to reproduce and preserve the species; it is the power that turns the magnetic needle toward the pole.

Though all things possess and express will, they do not do so to the same extent; Schopenhauer saw a hierarchy of will. In humans the will is conscious; in animals it is less so; in inanimate nature it is unconscious. Though the expression of will varies and conflicts in its various outworkings, both in the individual and between individuals, it is at root one.

Pessimism. Schopenhauer's view of the nature of the will is very gloomy. The world around us, he said, is full of horrors; human nature is intrinsically evil. This is inevitable, he believed, because each manifestation of the will to live or exist must assert itself at the expense of all others. As a consequence, as Buddha said, all is suffering. The will is constantly striving, never achieving, never satiated. It is a tortured will, always in conflict, always thirsting. It causes us to be self-centered and aggressive, to hate and devour one another, thus increasing the suffering that is already the hallmark of life in the world; it holds us in eternal penal servitude.

Some escape from the torment of will can be gained through aesthetic contemplation. Here for a moment the conflict of our insatiable will is forgotten and we taste in part unity with the world around us as we experience not so much other objects as the Platonic ideas that lie behind them. But this respite can only be temporary. The only way of finding final salvation from the torment of will is to follow the Four Noble Truths of Buddhism and find relief by the total elimination of desire. We must silence the voice of the will, cease from willing, and live a life of resignation and asceticism. Only "the saint" can do this; Schopenhauer certainly didn't manage it himself. Only saints are able to reach the point where they have so denied the will to live that they cease from aggressive self-centered striving and live at one with other humans and the world around them.

TO THINK THROUGH

It is pretty easy to see how Schopenhauer's personality shaped his philosophy. With others it is not so easy, though we have encountered enough variety in our survey so far to establish that there must be substantial factors other than rational ones that caused philosophers to think as they did. Speculate on the nonrational factors that influenced Kant, Marx, and Comte. It will certainly be worth bearing this issue in mind when we come to Kierkegaard and Nietzsche, but it could also be relevant to others we will be looking at.

For Further Study

Janaway, C. *Schopenhauer*. Oxford: Oxford University Press, 1994.

We now turn to four very different figures who sought to respond from a Christian standpoint to what they saw as the excessive stress on the powers of reason. Each in his own way sought to break the stranglehold of reason, not just on religion, but on life in general. There is much more to us, they said, than our intellects. This "much more" they defined in different ways. Schleiermacher saw it in terms of feeling. Coleridge posited a higher reason. Newman analyzed a nonrational element of knowing. And Kierkegaard explored what it is to be a passionate existing individual.

FRIEDRICH SCHLEIERMACHER

Breslau, Prussia (1768–1834). Son of a Reformed chaplain in the Prussian army, Schleiermacher was reared in the devotional and experiential atmosphere of the pietistic Moravians. Dissatisfied, however, with the Moravians' answers to his intellectual questioning, he left seminary to study philosophy at Halle, where he became especially involved with Plato and Kant. He was ordained in 1790 and spent the next years teaching and pastoring. His first and most celebrated book was *On Religion: Speeches to Its Cultured Despisers* (1799). In 1804 Schleiermacher was appointed professor of theology at Halle. In 1810 he became professor of theology and philosophy at the new university at Berlin, where he was contemporary with Hegel. He was vigorously involved in both academic, practical, and political affairs, sometimes running considerable risks as an enthusiastic patriot. He was a popular preacher and an indefatigable worker. He was eventually appointed rector of Berlin University.

Sometimes referred to as the father of modern theology, Schleiermacher did much to set the pattern for the development of nineteenth-century German theological thinking and thus of liberal theology at large. He was essentially a bridge builder and was very involved in developing unity between German Protestant denominations. His *Speeches* built bridges to those who felt that Christianity had nothing to say in the current culture. Above all, he sought to build bridges between the best insights of the extreme rationalism of the German Age of Enlightenment, romanticism, idealism, and Christianity. Quite apart from his achievements in the area of philosophical theology, Schleiermacher's translation of most of Plato's works became a classic, and he is also credited with being the first German to develop a philosophy of hermeneutics.

Feeling. In the *Speeches*, Schleiermacher drew on his Moravian background and his reading of Kant to argue that the essence of Christianity was not rational in the sense of intellectual. He was writing for those who believed that Christianity had been intellectually discredited by the rationalists but who themselves had moved on from rationalism to romanticism. To such Schleiermacher announced that Christianity was not a philosophy or a metaphysical or scientific system. It was not even primarily ethics or aesthetics. Instead, it was primarily a feeling; we relate to God, not through our mind, but through our feeling. And the religious feeling is basically one of dependence.

We are social creatures, said Schleiermacher. In our relationships we are dependent on one another. In our relationship with God, we recognize and express our dependence on what is infinite and absolute. In a sense, the feeling of dependence is an awareness of our finitude in the presence of infinity. This is something we all experience, he said, whether we are overtly religious or not. In this way he was able to claim that even the cultured despisers of religion to whom he was writing were in fact religious. They only think they aren't, because they have a wrong concept of what religion is.

Although Schleiermacher called on his readers to find the essence of Christianity within them, in their "inward emotions and dispositions," his "feeling of absolute dependence" seems to be something deeper than a conscious emotion. Like our relationship of dependence or interdependence with other people, it is more a "given" of which we gradually become aware. It is something we experience immediately, intuitively, something that is very deep in the heart of our being.

Schleiermacher saw this realm of feeling as a distinct third realm to be set alongside that of the intellect and of practical action. In accordance with Kantian theory, he said that the two realms, of intellect and feeling, are to be kept completely separate; we don't apply the principles of rational thought to this vital core of religion. Indeed, it needs no argument or evidence; it is experienced and known immediately without the intervention of the intellect. This is not to say that the intellect has no place in religion; later, when we explore ideas and build theological systems, as Schleiermacher did, it has a significant role to play. But our basic experience and knowledge of God is not via the intellect.

Though claiming that the feeling of dependence lies at the heart of all religions, Schleiermacher saw it most clearly in Christianity, where he linked it with our relationship with Christ. Individual believers are consciously dependent on Christ as their Redeemer; it is Christ who is the center and object of their immediate awareness of the infinite. In keeping with his stress on the centrality of feeling, Schleiermacher saw the uniqueness of Christ focused in his God-consciousness, which, in his case, was the very presence of God in him.

Theology.

Seeking to keep faith with his basic premise that Christianity is primarily not a matter of either the intellect or doctrine, Schleiermacher accepted that we can't build a Christian theology by starting with revealed doctrinal truth. Indeed, he accepted the conclusion of Kant's first *Critique*, that we can't even build it on God. The best we can do is build it on our experience of God. In saying this, Schleiermacher was taking a highly significant step that resulted in most nineteenth- and twentieth-century theologians (though not most ordinary Christians) approaching Christianity in a way that was radically different from the whole Christian tradition up to that point. The New Testament writers, the early church, Augustine, and the medieval tradition had all explored and developed theology on the understanding that they were recipients of divine truth revealed and communicated in love and grace by the supernatural action of God himself. They saw their task as to receive, digest, and pass on this God-given, "from above" teaching. From Schleiermacher onward, most theologians were to take as the data of their studies human experiences and ideas about God. The direction was to be essentially "from below." Theology became a study of human awareness of God, human religious experience, and human concepts of the supernatural and all that it might entail. Thus Schleiermacher was able to say specifically that when he spoke of the attributes of God, he was not saying anything about God himself. Rather, he was bringing out aspects of human experience, of the divine consciousness we all feel.

Schleiermacher would not have agreed, but it is possible to see the post-Kantian shift to theology "from below" as the final step in removing God from the central place he had occupied in the Christian and medieval worldviews. Post-Newtonian science was dispensing with the need for God in the running of the world. Feuerbach was seeking to remove all traces of him from our social and community consciousness. And now theology itself was following the trend. No longer is its subject matter the study of God or of God-given truth. There has been a Copernican revolution. From theocentricity we have turned to anthropocentricity. Theology is focused on humans. It has become the study of human ideas, human feelings, and human consciousness.

Hermeneutics.
In his contributions to hermeneutics, especially in his later writings, Schleiermacher highlighted the subjective role of both the writer and interpreter. The understanding of a text does not depend solely on a correct understanding of the meaning of the words. The interpreter needs to get beyond the text to the mind of its author, to share a "lived experience." In this way she or he can begin to understand parts of the text, and that understanding then helps to enrich further the awareness of the author's mind, and so on in an ongoing and developing process.

Like most post-Kantians, Schleiermacher has both wholeheartedly accepted and effectively neutralized Kant's great world-changing insight into the distinction between the phenomenal and noumenal spheres. He has accepted that religion belongs to the sphere of the noumenal and thus that it is independent of the rational intellect. He has accepted, in effect, that we can say nothing about God. But rather than simply remaining silent, Schleiermacher claims to have found a key that unlocks Kant's closed door. Indeed, he has not only unlocked it, but in his voluminous theological works, he has found it possible to pass through it complete with all the considerable powers of his intellect and find much on the other side that he can bring back and tell us. Clearly he believed that what he was presenting was in fact Christian truth and not mere summaries of psychological analysis; it was actually possible to extract truths about God from our experiences of him. But to assume this presupposes that our religious experiences are in fact experiences of God. And we can only presuppose this by breaking with Kant's principle and allowing that we do know something about God, that is, that he does give us experiences of himself. And once we have conceded that we can know one truth about God, why may we not know a lot more? Similarly, once we have conceded that God does take the initiative and communicate with us in the heart of our inner experience, why can't we allow that he takes the initiative and communicates with us in other ways, perhaps even through incarnation and revelation?

TO THINK THROUGH

Is our basic experience and knowledge of God through the intellect, or through feeling, or through something else?

For Further Study

Sorrentino, S., ed. *Schleiermacher's Philosophy and the Philosophical Tradition.* Lewiston, N.Y.: Edwin Mellen, 1992.

THIRTY-FIVE

IF REASON WON'T WORK, LET'S TRY SOMETHING ELSE

ANTI-RATIONALISM OUTSIDE OF GERMANY

In this chapter we continue our survey of those who reacted against rationalism. Leaving Germany, we travel to England, America, and Denmark to look at the varied ideas of Samuel Taylor Coleridge, John Henry Newman, Søren Kierkegaard, and the Transcendentalists.

SAMUEL TAYLOR COLERIDGE

Ottery St. Mary, Devon, England (1772–1834). Samuel Taylor Coleridge was primarily a romantic poet, but he regarded himself as a philosopher and spent his life seeking to develop a satisfying philosophical system. Historically his most significant contribution to philosophy was the part he played in the spreading of the ideas of the romantic and idealist German thinkers to Britain and America. It seems likely that he coined the term *existentialist*. He lived a somewhat chaotic life; he enthusiastically supported the ideas of the French Revolutionaries, he had a broken marriage, he constantly fell out with his friends, and he was addicted to opium.

Educated in the empirical philosophy of the Britain of his day, Coleridge renounced orthodox Christianity for Unitarianism during his student days at Cambridge, though he later turned back to a somewhat more orthodox position. After a visit to Germany in 1798–1799, he began studying German romanticism and idealism. He recognized in them an approach to philosophy that reconciled the demands of both "head and heart." He was particularly influenced by Kant, Fichte, Schelling, and Schlegel, with his romanticism and deep faith. Though accepting many of their insights, Coleridge still felt the need to work out a system of "ideal realism" that was to cover all aspects of what it means to be human. His notes for this, not published until the mid-twentieth century, ran to five volumes. They show the breadth of his reading and depth of his understanding and at times demonstrate the chaos of his thinking.

A life, not a set of doctrines.

The best-known prose works Coleridge did publish were *Confessions of an Enquiring Spirit* (1825) and *Aids to Reflection* (1840). A key theme in them was that Christianity was not a set of doctrines but a life. It is to be experienced, not theorized over. He attacked belief in the "dictation" theory of the inspiration of the Scriptures. He also attacked those who produce arguments for their divine origin. We don't need to produce evidences of inspiration, he said; the Bible finds us. "Evidences of Christianity," he declared, "I am weary of the word. Make a man feel his want of it."

Understanding and reason.

Coleridge made a significant distinction between "understanding" and "reason," based on Kant's split universe. "Understanding" was his word for what most people would see as ordinary reason. That is, it is the thinking and reasoning we use in ordinary living and in scientific investigation. It explores the realm of Kant's phenomena. What Coleridge called "reason" was something quite different. It was, in effect, the faculty by which we explore the realm of the noumena. It is thus a higher reason, taking us far beyond what understanding can tell us. It is this reason that comprehends the moral, the aesthetic, and the religious. It is the means by which our spirits communicate with the divine spirit. Since religion is the sphere of reason, understanding can have no place in it; hence Coleridge's virulent opposition to those who sought to produce "evidences" of the truth of Christianity or to systematize doctrine into dogma. Whenever understanding touches spiritual reality, it inevitably corrupts it.

JOHN HENRY NEWMAN

London (1801–1890). The son of a banker, John Henry Newman experienced an evangelical conversion at age fifteen. He entered Oxford at sixteen and was ordained as an Anglican minister in 1824. After two years of university teaching, he became vicar of the Oxford University Church, where he exercised a very influential ministry, not least through his printed sermons. He became the intellectual leader of a group of Oxford men who were deeply concerned about the state of the Church of England, the attenuation of its position as the state church, and the inroads of secularism and liberal theology. This group, essentially conservative in theology and Anglo-Catholic in churchmanship, was known as the Oxford Movement or the Tractarians, from its practice of publishing frequent polemical and apologetic *Tracts for the Times.*

By the early 1840s Newman had become discouraged at the lack of response by the Anglican hierarchy to the Oxford Movement. Additionally, his historical studies persuaded him that his previous conviction that the Church of England was able to take a valid middle position between the errors of Protestantism and those of Catholicism was a mistake. As a consequence, in 1845 he became a Roman Catholic, and he received Catholic ordination in 1847. He founded an oratory in Birmingham and stayed there the rest of his life. For the most part Catholics were suspicious of his "modernism," but he was made a cardinal in 1889, and his theological contribution to Catholicism was increasingly recognized from the mid twentieth century onward.

Epistemology: The "illative sense." Newman's most significant philosophical work was *An Essay in Aid of a Grammar of Assent* (1870). He rejected the rationalistic assumption that we should proportion the strength of all our beliefs according to the strength of the evidence that supports them. That principle may apply in the formal reasoning of math and parts of science, but it doesn't apply in what Newman called "concrete" informal reasoning, that is, the way our minds discern truth in situations where the evidence is not conclusive, but we still have to make a responsible judgment. It may be a moral choice or a practical decision, a judgment about a historical event, an assessment of a work of art, or a religious commitment. Science also has to use this informal reasoning, for instance, when scientists have to assume there is an external world for them to observe or that their observations are trustworthy. Newman called this power of judging and concluding the "illative sense" (from the late Latin word for inferring or concluding). It is, said Newman, something we all acquire and develop through our varying experiences; it enables us to make a judgment, often in very complex situations, about which we can be certain, even though technically it is only in the realm of probability. Newman used "certitude" in this context rather than "certainty," which he reserved for propositions that could be definitively established. Certitude is more personal, our "closing with the truth." This is "assent," effectively a commitment to a truth. Newman distinguished "notional assent" from "real assent." The first is merely intellectual, operating in the dry and sterile world of abstract truth. The latter is personal, a matter of commitment, supremely in religion a commitment to God in a personal relationship.

Theology. Although Newman's insights into the illative sense take us into the realm of the subjective and intuitive, Newman remained implacably opposed to all theology that failed to accept the objectivity of divine revelation. Doctrinal truth was for him foundational. Against the rationalists who sought to reshape Christianity according to what they saw as acceptable to reason, he argued that unaided human reason cannot give us spiritual reality. Rather than allowing our reason to be the judge of religious truth, says Newman, we must let religious truth be the judge of our reason. He accused the rationalists of a basic misunderstanding of human nature. It is not true to say simply that we are rational animals; there is much more to us than our reason; we are seeing, feeling, contemplating, and acting animals. A specific mistake of rationalism is its desire to remove the element of mystery from religion; but, said Newman, the very concept of God demands reverence and awe at something far greater than us.

TO THINK THROUGH

Is Newman's claim that we don't need to proportion the strength of our beliefs according to the strength of the evidence that supports them valid?

SØREN KIERKEGAARD

Copenhagen (1813–1855). Søren Kierkegaard came from a pietistic and scholarly home. He was educated at Copenhagen University for ministry in the Danish Lutheran Church and, apart from two brief stays in Berlin, he spent his whole life in Copenhagen. His mother and five out of six of his siblings died before Kierkegaard was twenty-one. He had a bad relationship with his guilt-ridden but demanding father, which may have been in part the cause of his own sense of worthlessness, expressed by his strategy to make his fiancée break off their engagement and, at the same time, his resignation from his pastorate. For the next twelve years until his death, he wrote prodigiously, publishing twenty-five books and writing some thirty thousand pages of papers and journals. He used a variety of pseudonyms. Kierkegaard's style is elegant, easy to read, and often very personal. He saw himself as a man with a mission, to stir up the nominal Christians of what he saw as the degenerate, self-satisfied, rationalistic, Hegel-dominated Lutheran church of his day to realize the truly radical nature of Christianity.

Kierkegaard was both profoundly influenced by Hegel and profoundly repelled by the application of his philosophy to Christianity. He revolted against his virtual pantheism and his rationalism and the way he made Christ so different from the Christ of traditional Christianity. Most of his dogmatic claims were in conscious contrast to what he saw as Hegel's teaching.

Some of Kierkegaard's chief books are *Either/Or* (1843), *Fear and Trembling* (1843), *Philosophical Fragments* (1844), *Concluding Unscientific Postscript to Philosophical Fragments* (1846), and *The Sickness unto Death* (1849).

Though scarcely recognized outside his home country during his lifetime, Kierkegaard's influence in the twentieth century was huge, particularly through existentialism and postmodernism, but also in psychology, theology, and philosophy in general. Philosophers and theologians who have acknowledged a debt to him include Heidegger, Sartre, Derrida, Wittgenstein, Barth, Bultmann, and Tillich.

Interpreting Kierkegaard.

The interpretation of Kierkegaard has spawned something of a scholarly industry. Since, in attacking the Hegelian system, Kierkegaard was rejecting not just Hegel but the concept of a philosophical system itself, it is hazardous to try to systematize his work. Quite apart from his use of pseudonyms and his insistence that the pseudonymous writers are not necessarily expressing his own views, he made use of humor, sarcasm and irony, story and imagination, and a range of autobiographical devices and contemporary allusions. All these things mean that it is possible to interpret him in a number of different ways. Indeed, there is a divergence of interpretation among those who have particularly expressed their indebtedness to him. It may in fact be that there is no one "correct" way of understanding Kierkegaard. He himself accepted that there were alternative ways of reading his work, and as someone who insisted on the centrality of paradox, he may well be happy for mutually inconsistent readings of his message to stand side by side in the twenty-first century.

God.

God is transcendent. He is in no way a part of the world, nor is the world part of him. He wholly transcends it. He is absolutely qualitatively other than the world and human beings. His existence cannot be rationally demonstrated. It is spiritually offensive to try to find God through our reason.

Reason and revelation.

Since we cannot find God by reason, revelation is essential. The key to revelation is the historic Christ described in the New Testament. The key to encountering Christ is faith, which is a nonrational leap that involves the person and the will, not reason.

The existing individual. Of paramount importance is the existing individual. Kierkegaard chose the words "That individual" to be put on his gravestone. The state and the church of his day, not to mention Hegel, submerged the individual and denied his or her freedom and personhood. But the fact is, said Kierkegaard, we are individuals; we each stand individually before God. We cannot escape our individuality or its implications. Freedom and choice, and personal responsibility for our choices, are key elements of our existence; they are what it means to be human. The conformists are barely human; the truly "existing" individuals are the ones who are committed, making authentic choices along the pathway toward a chosen end, supremely God. Kierkegaard likened truly existing with riding a wild stallion; the conformists are like those who fall asleep in the hay wagon.

Kierkegaard wrote of three stages on the way to true existence, though these are probably not to be seen as necessarily consecutive. The first is the awakening of the aesthetic consciousness. But that in itself does not satisfy and leads only to despair. The second stage, which some may choose to go on to, is the ethical stage, the way of moral goodness. This in its turn leads to despair because it shows us our sin and guilt. The third stage of the journey is the religious stage, where in our sinfulness and despair we leap out in faith to God, passionately committing ourselves to a personal relationship with him. This commitment is continually repeated and is lived out in obedience.

"Truth is subjectivity." Kierkegaard didn't deny that there is such a thing as objective truth; indeed, he accepted the objective truths of the historic Christ and God's revelation. What appalled him was the cold detached speculative approach of philosophers and theologians and even ordinary Christians who could talk about God and about Christ and not feel the power of the truth they were confronting. Whatever this detached rational attitude grasped, it could not be, for Kierkegaard, real living dynamic and personal truth; so for him it was precisely untruth. He graphically described the two approaches. The objective thinker contemplates the world slowly, indecisively, uncommittedly, in the hope of finding God. But the subjective thinker can't wait. His passion, says Kierkegaard, drives him forward. He leaps out to the truth, grasping it, entering into a relationship with it, even without pausing to define it. Of course, he may be mistaken; that is the risk of faith. But it is better to be mistaken than to take the objective way and never enter into any subjective relationship. "Inwardness," "passion," "faith," "spirit," "personal," and "subjectivity" all fit together as key elements in Kierkegaard's protest at the rationalistic impersonal objective detachment of his day.

Kierkegaard's understanding of true existence and of subjectivity were both taken up by subsequent existentialists and developed in a way that makes our act of choosing the source of our true existence and our subjective choice the source of truth. But Kierkegaard would not have accepted either of these developments. Nor would he have accepted the parody of his position that makes him advocate a totally groundless blind leap of faith. Each of these concepts needs to be understood in the context of Kierkegaard's underlying (though at times rather shaky) belief in the reality of God. A leap of faith is conceivable because there is a God to catch us even if, when we leap, we have no assurance that he will do so. Similarly, Kierkegaard could not say that our choosing is the ground of our existing, since he believed God was that ground. Nor could he say that we create truth by our subjective act, since he was sure that truth was not to be created but rather experienced.

The significance of Christ.

There are two places where we might look for truth, says Kierkegaard: in Socrates, typifying philosophy, especially Hegelian philosophy, or in Christ. In radical opposition to the Hegelian reductionist Christology, Kierkegaard stated three contrasts between Socrates and Christ.

- Socrates could only draw out truth that was already there. Christ gave a new revelation—himself—something we could never find on our own.
- Socrates assumed that if we know the truth, we will do it. Christ knows we cannot do this, so he comes as Savior as well as teacher.
- Socrates deliberately directed attention away from himself toward the truth. Christ requires faith in himself as the truth.

The antisupernaturalistic rationalist presuppositions of German liberal theology had led to savage attacks on the historicity of Christ. Kierkegaard, having rejected those presuppositions, was convinced of Christ's historicity and of his divinity and humanity. In keeping with his anti-rationalism, he refused to even begin to reconcile these two concepts. They present us, he said, with a scandal, a paradox, and we have no option but to accept the scandal and the paradox. Where Hegel sought to move from thesis and antithesis on to synthesis, Kierkegaard simply dug in his heels and stayed where he was.

In keeping with his stress on subjectivity, however, Kierkegaard stated that there was no value in merely accepting the historical facts about Christ. To do so would be to remain detached, having a mere intellectual knowledge of the truth. What we have to do is each personally take our subjective leap of faith and encounter Christ now.

TO THINK THROUGH

Many look on Kierkegaard as the father of existentialism. Yet Sartre was later to claim that the essence of existentialism is atheistic humanism, which fits oddly with Kierkegaard's passionate Christianity. Is Kierkegaard's worldview theocentric? Or does it contain the seeds of atheism?

Schleiermacher, Newman, and Kierkegaard all reacted against rationalism. The results were very different, perhaps illustrating the different character and settings of the three men. Could their insights be combined?

For Further Study

Gardiner, P. *Kierkegaard*. Oxford: Oxford University Press, 1988.

Hannay, A. *Kierkegaard*. London: Routledge, 1982.

TRANSCENDENTALISM

For the most part, Americans adopted the scientific worldview with even more enthusiasm than the Europeans. But, probably inevitably, there were reactions. The most significant one was New England transcendentalism. Though as a movement it had no more than fifty adherents, it caught the imagination of many in the middle decades of the nineteenth century. Names particularly associated with the movement are **Henry David Thoreau** (1817–1862), **Theodore Parker** (1810–1860), and Ralph Waldo Emerson.

Almost all the Transcendentalists were Unitarians, many of them Unitarian ministers. Unitarianism had been particularly committed to a commonsense scientific worldview and found the rejection of the miraculous by science hard to reconcile with its religious approach. The discovery of Coleridge, with his romanticism, commitment to nature, and useful distinction between understanding and reason, laid a foundation on which the Transcendentalists were able to develop a generally nonsupernatural form of Unitarian Christianity in which the transcendent is separated from the world of science and ordinary understanding, and apprehended and embraced through a higher intuitive reason. Coleridge thus transmitted post-Kantian romanticism to the Transcendentalists. Though many of them were very aware of early-nineteenth-century post-Kantians, scholars generally feel that the direct influence of Hegelianism on the movement was slight.

Thoreau spent most of his life at Concord, Massachusetts, seeking to live in "back to nature" simplicity, in protest of the complexity of industrialization and urbanization. Parker was well read in German idealism and translated the work of Schelling among others. He had reservations, however, about the pantheistic implications of Hegelian thought, and unlike most of his colleagues who left Unitarian ministry, he remained a minister throughout his life.

Ralph Waldo Emerson. Boston (1803–1882).

Emerson was educated at Harvard and trained for the Unitarian ministry. However, he resigned as a minister in 1832 and traveled to Europe, where he met Coleridge, Wordsworth, and Carlyle. On returning to the United States, he spent most of the rest of his life at Concord. Though in some senses withdrawing from the world, he was an active campaigner on social issues, including the abolition of slavery, and exercised considerable influence through his lectures and writings, which included essays and poetry. Among those influenced by his writings were Nietzsche, James, and Dewey.

Emerson was opposed to philosophical systems. Each individual must find his or her reality and principles for living by communing with nature and especially by looking within. Any experience, however apparently insignificant, can lead us to the transcendent. In particular, Emerson rejected any form of dualism. God, whom he also called "the Over-Soul," is not different from nature or from human beings. Humanity and nature are divine, though in a lesser way than God. Emerson's confidence in the presence of the divine in each individual led to a stress on self-reliance; in this he both expressed and furthered a key element of the nineteenth-century American spirit.

Though elements of romanticism and a "back to nature" attitude have reappeared from time to time in American thought, transcendentalism as a movement was short lived. Its rejection of the traditional concept of the supernatural and its seeming pantheism made it unacceptable to more orthodox Christian thinkers. At the same time, its basically religious thrust made it unacceptable to those who were seeking to develop a truly "scientific" worldview. By the end of the nineteenth century, science-dominated thinkers in America were developing a very different philosophy, whose criterion was practical usefulness and which had small place for the romantic or the transcendent.

THIRTY-SIX

EVERYTHING IS TO BE
EXPLAINED NATURALISTICALLY

BENTHAM, MILL, SPENCER, AND MACH

In this chapter we return to those whose worldview
was dominated by the approach of science. Utilitarians
Jeremy Bentham and John Stuart Mill applied naturalistic
presuppositions in their worldview. Herbert Spencer
applied the concept of evolution. And Ernst Mach prepared the way for logical positivism in his strongly
anti-metaphysical scientific approach.

DESPITE THE RADICAL CHALLENGES BEING MADE BY SOME
to the stress on the centrality of reason, the nineteenth century continued to
see one vindication after another of the rationalistic approach of the scientific
worldview. Though the century saw a substantial growth in the number of professing Christians, from 23 to 34 percent of the world's population (208 million to 558 million), the attempts to establish a "scientific" worldview based
on the powers of human reason and excluding God continued unabated. In
Victorian England two contrasting systems were developed by John Stuart Mill
and Herbert Spencer. Since Mill owed much to the influence of Jeremy Bentham, we will look at his system of thought first.

JEREMY BENTHAM

London (1748–1832). After studying at Oxford University from age twelve,
Jeremy Bentham trained as a lawyer with the intention of following his father
and grandfather in practicing law in London. However, he became dissatisfied

with the legal system as it was and, as a result, devoted his energies to reforming it rather than practicing it. His major work was *An Introduction to the Principles of Morals and Legislation* (1789). He was the founder of the utilitarian school. With his fellow utilitarians, he was seen as something of a radical; his reforming vision extended to universal suffrage and the abolition of the monarchy. He had broad interests outside of Britain, and he was the first person to use the word *international*. He offered to draw up a constitution for Jefferson and the United States and also for new states in South America. He was a friend of Catherine of Russia and was made a citizen of France in 1792. He requested that after his death his body should be made into an "auto-icon" and preserved as a monument to the founder of utilitarianism. The request was complied with, and Bentham may be seen in a glass case in the college he founded, University College in London.

Utilitarianism.
Bentham rejected a number of approaches to the basis of morality, including that of "moral sense," the law of nature, right reason, the fitness of things, the social contract, and an emotive approach in terms of approval and disapproval. In their place he argued a utilitarian theory in terms of happiness. The link between pleasure or happiness and goodness had been recognized throughout the modern period both by those who saw it as an expression of God's purposes and by those who sought to provide a nontheistic basis of morality. Hume in particular had identified value with utility. Bentham's contribution was to make this link a foundational principle. Pleasure, he said, is the only good. Pain is the only evil. All our actions are motivated by the desire for pleasure or the avoidance of pain. This doesn't have to be self-centered; it allows for altruism in that we may get pleasure from another's enjoyment, not just from our own. Bentham's principle of utility laid down that the basis of moral behavior should be the maximization of utility, which is defined as the greatest happiness of the greatest number. Bentham accepted that this basic principle could not be established by rational proof; it is to be accepted as a foundational first principle.

Calculating happiness.
As a means of developing right policy and so right legislation, Bentham developed what he called a "felicific calculus," a means of calculating the relative pleasure value, and so rightness, of specific actions. Factors to be considered include duration, fecundity, the number of people affected, and the extent to which they are affected. Legislation based on a system of rewards and punishments can then be formulated accordingly.

JOHN STUART MILL

London (1806–1873). John Stuart Mill's father, James Mill, was a Scottish economist and philosopher who was a leading member of the group that gathered around Bentham and furthered his radicalism. As a result, John Stuart Mill was surrounded with radical and utilitarian ideas from his birth. His rigorous education was organized by his father, with the help of Bentham (who lived next door), in accordance with their innovative theories. It included Greek from age three and all the principles of Benthamite philosophy. But, as Mill describes in his autobiography, his relationship with his father lacked affection and joy, and at twenty he went through a mental crisis, linked with a breakdown, in which he felt he had nothing left to live for. He came through this crisis by turning to poetry, especially Wordsworth, Coleridge, and Goethe. This experience moderated his philosophical position. Four years later he was introduced to the ideas of Saint-Simon and Comte, which also had a significant influence on him.

Mill spent much of his life working for the East India Company until its dissolution in 1858. His interests and activities ranged over social and political issues, economics, psychology, history, botany, and literature. For three years beginning in 1865 he was a Liberal member of the British parliament, vigorously supporting women's suffrage.

Mill was a gifted writer with a fine style. Among his most significant works are *System of Logic* (1843), *Principles of Political Economy* (1848), *Utilitarianism* (1861/3), *On Liberty* (1860), *Examination of Sir William Hamilton's Philosophy* (1865), and *Autobiography* (1867).

Mill's agenda was to develop the best of the insights of his Benthamite upbringing but at the same time to soften and broaden them, incorporating some of the insights he had learned from romanticism. His philosophy can be summarized under four topics.

1. Radical empiricism.

Though Mill wasn't keen on the label, his *System of Logic* argued for radical empiricism. He vigorously rejected any form of intuitionism with its claim that we can build our understanding of the world on intuitively or divinely given principles that are independent of sense experience. Nothing, said Mill, can be known apart from experience; everything is to be explained naturalistically. Where some empiricists had allowed that some propositions, especially those of mathematics and logic, were not dependent for their validity on things in the world around us and so were *a priori*, Mill rigidly extended his empiricism to every area of human thought. If the propositions of math and logic were *a priori*, says Mill, they could tell us nothing "real"; they would be merely analytic or tautologous. But the fact is they do contain real significance. Thus all our reasoning is *a posteriori*, arising from empirical observation.

Mill was well aware of the basic flaw in empiricism, that it is unable to give us certainty. Since it always operates through observation, it is always fallible. In particular, science has to operate by means of induction, using the enumeration of specific experiences to justify making universal generalizations. These generalizations, Mill accepted, can never be finally established beyond any possibility of doubt. They include not just simple matters of fact, but such essential principles as the uniformity of nature and causal laws. Similarly, we can never show beyond any possibility of doubt that we are justified in using the principle of induction to make generalizations. Nevertheless, says Mill, induction is a valid means of obtaining knowledge, especially if we develop and refine it into what he called "eliminative induction," a process of scientific method that involves the forming, testing, and eliminating of hypotheses, and which, by its ongoing success, continues to raise our confidence in its validity. Like Comte, Mill accepted in theory that all areas of human knowledge operate in the same way; the principles of induction that apply to physics and chemistry should apply equally to the social sciences. But he admitted that in practice the issues in social science were much too complex for us to be able to apply them.

2. Knowledge of the external world and of God.

As an empiricist Mill believed in the reality of the external world, but he accepted that the only things we can know are our experiences, and since these are states of consciousness, we can't produce a justification for moving from a belief in our states of consciousness to belief in objects outside of us that cause those states. Even when we let an experience, say the sound of a dog barking, cause us to conclude that a real dog exists, we have in fact only moved from a concept or idea of barking to a concept of an independently existing dog. We have not moved and cannot move from a concept to an external reality. Nevertheless, Mill was prepared to postulate something beyond the strict limits of our consciousness, at any rate in ordinary life and in science. He called this "permanent possibilities of sensation," which somehow continue even if we are not experiencing them, and so in some way constitute an external world. Similarly, he conceded that mind, "the thread of consciousness," may be more than a mere succession of experiences. Rather more reluctantly, he conceded the possibility of the existence of God as the intelligent designer of the world.

3. Utilitarianism.

Mill adopted Bentham's basic utilitarian principle, stating it as, "Actions are right in proportion as they tend to promote happiness, wrong as they tend to produce the reverse of happiness." However, in the light of extensive criticism, he refined Bentham's concept of happiness, emphasizing the significance of its quality and not just its quantity. Better to be a human being dissatisfied than a pig satisfied, better to be a Socrates dissatisfied than a fool satisfied. The higher forms of happiness are the ones we should be especially concerned to foster. Mill was also careful to insist that the happiness envisaged is communal, not individual. It is the greatest (and highest) happiness of the greatest number.

Mill defended the utilitarian principle by appealing to empirical fact. People, he said, do in fact seek pleasure and only pleasure. This, of course, is open to challenge simply as an empirical fact, whether or not the concept of pleasure is defined in individual or universal terms. It is also, like all naturalistic theories of ethics, open to the objection, "Even if we grant as an empirical fact that everyone seeks only pleasure, we can still ask whether or not they ought to seek only pleasure."

4. Social and political theory.

Mill used the principle of utility to critique all social, political, and religious institutions. Anything that doesn't promote the greatest happiness of the greatest number was to be challenged and reformed. He rejected Bentham's simplistic method of calculating happiness and conceded that there was considerable room for debate. But he argued, for example, for personal freedom and the encouragement of individuality, believing that they would in the long term produce benefits that would be enjoyed by all. For this reason social and religious institutions that curtail individual liberty should be reformed; freedom of belief, association, and expression must all be safeguarded. Private ownership of the means of production, on the other hand, will not on balance be a good thing in that it will mean poverty for the many, and so it should be discouraged.

One specific area in which Mill pressed home his concept of personal freedom was that of women's liberation. If we accept that freedom is good for men, then we must accept that it is good for women too. If it is objected that freedom for women is not appropriate because men and women are different by nature, we must be prepared to test this hypothesis by giving women access to everything to which men have had access for as long as men have had that access.

TO THINK THROUGH

Is it right to assume that human happiness is a valid basis for morals?

For Further Study

Skorupski, J. *John Stuart Mill*. London: Routledge, 1989.

HERBERT SPENCER

Derby, England (1820–1903). After a somewhat disturbed childhood and education, Herbert Spencer settled in London and earned his living by journalism and writing. His magnum opus, which took more than thirty years to write, was *System of Synthetic Philosophy* (1862–1893). His most widely read book was *First Principles* (1862). His work was very popular toward the end of the nineteenth century, fitting as it did current concepts of progress and evolutionary theory, but the twentieth century saw a rapid loss of interest in his approach.

Evolutionary theory. Evolutionary theory didn't originate with **Charles Darwin** (1809–1882). A number of theories had been put forward and discussed well before the publication of *Origin of Species* (1859). The particular form of evolutionism that Spencer followed was in fact pre-Darwinian. It was put forward by **Jean-Baptiste Lamarck** (1744–1829) and included an element that allowed beneficial developments during the lifetime of an organism to be inherited by its offspring. Where Darwin's theory in its use of "chance" or "random" variations seemed to challenge the popular determinism of the nineteenth-century scientific worldview, Lamarck's theory seemed to allow for a more purposive process. Darwin in his writing in fact acknowledged his indebtedness to Spencer in a number of areas, though he personally was unwilling to apply evolutionary theory outside the field of biology.

Spencer had no such inhibitions and took the concept of evolution and sought to make it a principle that applied to all aspects of human society. He defined it in terms of a progressive and beneficial movement from simplicity to complexity, from "an indefinite incoherent homogeneity to a definite coherent heterogeneity." He in practice equated evolution with progress, which he described as "a beneficent necessity." Evolution takes place in all systems—

physical, biological, psychological, historical, ethical, and social—though at different rates. Over all, the progress is upward, though Spencer recognized there can be periods of reversal, or "dissolution." Since evolution involves constant change, human nature and human institutions must be constantly changing. Thus nothing is to be seen as fixed, not even beliefs or moral principles. Goodness is to be defined in terms of beneficial adjustment to the stage of evolution that has been reached; when another stage is reached, the nature of goodness will change.

Social evolution.

Despite his admission that there may be reversals in the evolutionary process, Spencer seemed to believe that the story of human social evolution was one of uninterrupted upward progress, from the "naked houseless savage" to all the refinements of nineteenth-century industrialized society. Societies that have reached a higher stage of evolution rightly cause less-evolved societies to dwindle through war or by driving them into "unfavourable habitats" or simply by spreading industrialization and so eradicating "barbarism."

The eradication of the weak by the strong is applied by Spencer not just to groups but to individuals. Since this was for him an inherent part of the evolutionary process, we should not, he argued, interfere with it. Government protectionism, even of the vulnerable members of society, is to be resisted, since in the end it will be harmful, allowing "the multiplication of those worse fitted for existence" and, as a result, leaving less room for those "best fitted for existence." Spencer applied this principle in his opposition to any form of government regulation of trade or imposition of social welfare measures, a factor that considerably enhanced his reputation in America, where he was feted as a champion of *laissez-faire* and capitalism—not, however, by everyone. William James, with more perspicacity than most, summed up his system as "wooden, as if knocked together out of cracked hemlock boards."

TO THINK THROUGH

If "goodness" is to be defined in terms of the evolutionary process, and if human social evolution is always upward, would Spencer have to admit that if there were a nuclear war in which all survivors become zombies, he would have to call it a good thing?

What has Christianity to say about "the survival of the fittest"?

Britain was by no means the only place where the worldview of science was claiming to provide the norm for the whole of life. Comte's positivism was alive and well on the Continent, and Ernst Mach, among others, was advocating a strong form of empiricism that was to contribute to the rise of logical positivism in the early twentieth century.

ERNST MACH

Turas, Czech Republic (1838–1916). Ernst Mach (pronounced like Bach) was an outstanding Austrian physicist who taught at Graz, Prague, and Vienna. He was nominated several times for the Nobel Prize. His philosophy of science was forthright and influential, and he is seen as a forerunner of logical positivism. An ardent empiricist, he was strongly opposed to any "metaphysical" entities that we are not able to experience directly. As a result, he argued against Newton's concepts of absolute space and time and against the existence of subatomic particles. He was also very reluctant to accept the theory of relativity. His skepticism here, however, needs to be set alongside his general skepticism; since we can only experience our "sensations," we have no substantive grounds for believing in any external objects, such as chairs and tables. And in the same way, all our scientific theories, which Mach insisted were descriptive rather than explanatory, are merely aids to future predictions; they are not to be taken as saying anything about any underlying reality.

THIRTY-SEVEN

ANOTHER WAY TO LIVE WITHIN LIMITS

PHENOMENOLOGY

In this chapter we explore the Continental philosophical tradition of phenomenology, which took the content of our minds as its data and built on it a distinctive approach to philosophy that was to have significant influence in the twentieth century.

$\mathbf{I}$N THINKERS LIKE MILL AND MACH, THE REASON-centered tradition enshrined in the scientific worldview and expressed especially in empiricism and positivism continued both in Britain and on the Continent throughout the nineteenth century. However, on the Continent it was the alternative traditions that either rejected the authority of reason or followed Kant in severely curtailing its influence, that were most active and were to have the greatest effect on the development of philosophy through the twentieth century. We have already looked at the German idealists. Their views spread throughout Europe and helped produce transcendentalism in America and a brief flowering of idealism in Britain toward the end of the century. As a movement, however, idealism faded fairly rapidly, and its direct impact in the twentieth century was small.

Others, like Schleiermacher, Schopenhauer, Kierkegaard, and Nietzsche, sought to offer alternatives to the narrow definition of human beings as rational animals. All of these were to influence twentieth-century thought, though none of them gave direct rise to a "school" of philosophical thinking. But an approach to philosophy that arose on the Continent toward the end of the nineteenth century became an established school and fed directly into the rise of existentialism, the great twentieth-century approach to philosophy that was to challenge—and in the end topple—the dominance of the rationalism of the scientific worldview. That approach was phenomenology. Rather than taking the approach of science as the paradigm for all of life, phenomenology chose to accept Kant's split universe and to leave the approach of science to those dealing with things scientific. Rather than make the mind or the human person function like a scientific machine, it said, we should accept it for what it is and build our understanding of who we are from what we find we are, not from what science tries to make us.

To lead us into this way of doing philosophy, we will look briefly at the approach of Wilhelm Dilthey.

WILHELM DILTHEY

Biebrich, Germany (1833–1911). Educated in theology, history, and philosophy at Heidelberg and Berlin, Wilhelm Dilthey (pronounced *dit*-eye) held chairs in a number of universities, finally settling in Berlin from 1882. He was one of a group of German "Neo-Kantians" who were active in the last decades of the nineteenth century and up to the First World War. Their aim was both to get back to Kant and to go beyond him in applying his insights to contemporary issues. Dilthey's special interest was history, and he did much to define the limits of historical knowledge as Kant had defined the limits of rational knowledge. Additionally he had a significant impact on the development of sociology and hermeneutics.

In opposition to positivists like Comte and empiricists like Mill and Spencer, Dilthey argued for a radical distinction between the natural sciences, such as physics, and the human or cultural sciences, such as philosophy, art, history, law, religion, psychology, and sociology. In the natural sciences we seek explanations; in the human sciences we seek "understanding" (Ger. *Verstehen*). Dilthey's definition of understanding developed during his life, but in its essence it is grasping the spirit or life of the subject or its authors, rather than seeking rational causal explanations in the detached external objective way that is applicable in natural science. We are able to do this because there is at least some degree of continuity of experience between ourselves and those we are seeking to understand. We are thus able to enter in and share their lived experiences.

THE PHENOMENOLOGICAL MOVEMENT

Like many philosophical terms, the word *phenomenology* and its cognate forms can be used in a range of ways. Basically it means the study of phenomena, just as *biology* means the study of living things (Gk. *bios*, "life") and *theology* means the study of God (Gk. *theos*, "God"). Philosophically, phenomena (Gk. for "appearances") are the "appearances" we experience, for example, the sensory data you have at this moment of a book; philosophically you may not be able to be sure there is a real independently existing book before you, but you probably find it very hard to doubt that you are experiencing a booky phenomenon. Phenomenology, then, is the study of our experiences. It leaves on one side the deep philosophical question "How does my experience of a book relate to "reality," an actual book in an external world?" And instead, it limits itself to studying and analyzing our experiences. Though it started with mental experiences, the movement later extended the principles developed to examine other forms of experience.

FRANZ BRENTANO

Marienberg, Germany (1838–1917). After studies at Würzburg, Munich, Berlin, and Münster, Franz Brentano was ordained in the Roman Catholic Church in 1864. He was appointed professor of philosophy at the Catholic University of Würzburg, but he resigned from his chair and his priesthood and left the Catholic Church in 1873 over the issue of papal infallibility. He became professor of philosophy at Vienna and then settled in Florence. Shortly before Italy entered the First World War, he moved to Zurich, where, despite the onset of blindness, he continued writing until he died. His interests ranged over a number of fields, including ontology, philosophical theology, the history of philosophy (especially Aristotle), ethics, epistemology, and the philosophy of language. But his most significant contributions were in psychology and the development of phenomenology. Brentano was an influential teacher; among his students were Sigmund Freud, Edmund Husserl, and Alexius Meinong.

The phenomenology of mind. To make any progress in our philosophizing, said Brentano, we need to reject groundless speculation and deal only with things that are evident or at the very least highly probable. An immediately evident thought, he says, gives us an "Archimedean point" for all our thinking. This applies to science, and it also applies when we are dealing with ontology, the study of what is. There are two main types of possible existences

whose status and nature philosophy seeks to explore—the experiences we each have in our own minds and the external realities that lie behind those experiences. In the first of these two, we are dealing with the immediate content of our own minds or consciousness, something that is clearly evident. This investigation of the contents of our consciousness he called the "phenomenology of mind."

Mental phenomena and intentionality.

On examination, Brentano said, we find two classes of phenomena in our consciousness. There are "physical phenomena," such as color, sound, shape, warmth or cold, and "similar images" that we produce through our imagination. Then, second, he said, there are "mental phenomena," in which he included judgments, emotions, and different mental operations like hoping, fearing, liking, worrying, and so on. Brentano set himself to analyze the distinctive feature of mental phenomena. The key feature, he decided, of these mental phenomena was intentionality, a concept he borrowed from the scholastics. Every mental act contains an object, an intended or intentional object, to which it is directed. Thus, if I have a desire, it is a desire for an object, say food or drink. If I'm sad, it is because I'm sad about something. If I worry, I worry about something. The object doesn't have to exist; I may desire the perfect ice cream or worry about something that never happens. So Brentano is careful to say that intentionality is not an actual relation between the mind and an object but rather "relationlike."

Brentano carefully ("microscopically") analyzed mental phenomena into three classes. First are presentations, which are direct and immediate. Second, there are judgments; this is where the intellect is involved, accepting or rejecting the object. The third class contains emotive phenomena, where our emotions and our will are involved. The second class provides the basis for knowledge of truth, and the third provides the basis for moral judgment.

EDMUND HUSSERL

Prossnits, Czech Republic (1859–1938). Edmund Husserl (pronounced *hood-ser*) studied science, math, philosophy, and psychology at Leipzig, Berlin, Vienna (where he attended the lectures of Brentano), and Halle. From 1887 he taught at Halle, moving to Göttingen in 1901 and to Freiburg in 1916. He retired from teaching in 1929. Academically he started as a mathematician, but he became increasingly involved in logical and philosophical issues. His first book was *The Philosophy of Arithmetic* (1891); his second was *Logical Investigations* (1900–1901). Later came *The Idea of Phenomenology* (1907) and *Ideas*

(1913), in which he set out and defended his system of phenomenology. As the key figure in the development of phenomenology, Husserl had considerable influence on the development of twentieth-century thought, especially existentialism. Among those specifically influenced by him are Sartre, Merleau-Ponty, and Heidegger, who studied under him at Freiburg.

Brentano's pioneering work in the phenomenology of mind had been taken up by a number of his students and followers, including **Alexius Meinong (1853–1920)**, who taught at Graz, where he established a laboratory for experimental psychology. Meinong further analyzed the object to which a mental phenomenon or mental act could be directed, paying special attention to what is happening when it is directed to nonexistent objects like a golden mountain or an impossible object like a round square.

Husserl built his phenomenology on the foundation of Brentano's work, accepting as basic Brentano's principle that intentionality is the key feature of mental phenomena or states of mind. But he developed it in ways that were distinctively his own. Even more than Brentano, he went into fine details analyzing and classifying the content of our consciousness and the relations between its various parts. But the broad principles of his system can be summarized under five points.

1. Phenomenology.

The task of the phenomenologist is to analyze and describe the various sorts of mental intentional acts (such as perceiving, believing, imagining, or predicating) and the various objects of those acts (such as beliefs, the perception of a cat, a golden mountain, or mathematical entities).

2. The significance of consciousness.

These objects, the content of our minds or consciousness, don't have to correspond to anything in the world to make them significant for the phenomenologist. My dream, my fear of something that never happens, and my concept of a unicorn are just as much objects in my consciousness as the table I'm working at or the sounds I hear. This is what distinguishes the phenomenologist from the scientist, says Husserl; the scientist is only concerned with things in the world, not with the content of consciousness.

3. Accepting data.

Whether examining the acts of consciousness or the objects that are the content of consciousness, the phenomenologist must consciously lay aside all preconceptions that are instilled within him or her by the ordinary way of seeing things, by the scientific worldview, and by common sense, and simply examine things as they are. For example, I shouldn't dismiss the act of my dreaming or the content of my dream with "That's just a dream," nor should I dismiss the thought of a square circle with "That's impossible." Rather, I should be truly empirical and accept them as data to be analyzed every bit as much as the scientist accepts physical data and analyzes them. Husserl went into considerable detail over this process of clearing away all the baggage that might prevent us from examining impartially the content of our minds, using concepts like "reduction" and "bracketing" (bracketing out and ignoring aspects that the phenomenologist thinks are irrelevant) and "epoche" (suspension of judgment).

4. Consciousness and reality.
Husserl raises the question of how real the contents of our consciousness are. They are certainly real to us, but does that give them any status independent of our minds? This was a particularly relevant issue for Husserl in that he came to philosophy via math and, like the Pythagoreans, was fascinated by the question of the ontological status of mathematical concepts. Toward the end of his life, Brentano had moved to a "reist" position (Latin: *res*, "thing"), in which he saw the objects in our minds as having real existence, as opposed to being just ideas. Husserl moved in the opposite direction. From insisting in *Ideas* that the objects of consciousness are real, he changed in later life to thinking of them as ideas, thus to some extent merging his thinking with the tradition of German idealism.

5. The aim of phenomenology.
The phenomenologist's aim in analyzing the contents of our consciousness is to draw out their essences or essential features and thereby gain a clearer picture of how we as human beings function and by what principles our minds work. I might, for instance, set myself to examine doubting or worrying. Through looking at various processes of doubt or worry and at various things I doubt or worry about, I come to a clearer understanding of what is happening when I doubt or worry and of the status of my doubts and worries. This in turn gives me a clearer understanding of myself, of others, and thus of the world at large.

TO THINK THROUGH

What do you think about bracketing? Some say that it is a very useful tool; looking at something in isolation from its context and ignoring wider issues can be very fruitful. Others suggest it can be a profound mistake, a mistake that has characterized the reductionist thinking of the last hundred years or so. It encourages examination of a phenomenon or issue apart from its essential context, enabling the development of concepts, such as the will, without facing the prior questions like "Does this thing actually exist?" or "How does it fit with all other phenomena?" It thus leads to the abandoning of a holistic worldview in favor of developing a collection of isolated bits of knowledge. Others would say that it is an inevitable result of the increasing specialization brought about by the huge increase in knowledge and areas of study; to study anything, we have to bracket out most other things. So what do you think? Is it inevitable? And if bracketing is as dangerous as some people think, how might we avoid those dangers?

DEVELOPMENTS OF PHENOMENOLOGY

The phenomenological approach gave rise to a considerable "school," largely in Germany, but also spread through Europe and to the United States. As might be expected, there were divisions within the school, but each member sought to remain faithful to the basic vision of analyzing the contents of our minds and thus of our world. Two successors of Husserl especially worthy of note are Scheler and Merleau-Ponty.

The German **Max Scheler** (1874–1928, pronounced *shay*-ler) continued the work of Husserl by applying phenomenological principles to ethics, culture, and religion. He set himself to apply the phenomenological method of analysis to knowing, values, personality, religion, and anthropology. In his study of values, he categorized them in a rising hierarchy as:

Sensory values: pleasure—pain
Values of vital feeling: noble—base

Mental or spiritual values: beautiful—ugly, right—wrong,
true—false

Religious (sometimes called spiritual) values: holy—unholy

These values, which we discern through our feelings rather than our reason, are objective and known *a priori*. Morality, for Scheler, is the social application of these objective values; goodness consists of following the higher values rather than the lower.

The French philosopher **Maurice Merleau-Ponty** (1908–1961) was chiefly responsible for propagating phenomenology in France. He was a personal friend of Sartre and is generally also looked on as a father of existentialism. Central to his thought is a phenomenological approach to the role of the body. He strongly repudiated any Cartesian body-mind dualism along with the opposing of subjectivity and objectivity. He saw the body as neither subject nor object, but rather as the expression of our being-in-the-world, and sought to explore the essence of its relationship with the experienced world, both in perception and in action. In his study of perception, Merleau-Ponty pointed out that fallacious perceptions do not in fact lead us to skepticism, as most earlier philosophers had believed. Rather, we reject the fallacious perception in order to adopt an alternative one; thus our confidence in perception itself remains constant.

TO THINK THROUGH

Can we objectively examine the acts or contents of our consciousness?

For Further Study

Hammond, M., J. Howarth, and R. Keat. *Understanding Phenomenology.* Oxford: Blackwell, 1991.

THIRTY-EIGHT

GOD IS DEAD

THE PHILOSOPHY OF NIETZSCHE

In this chapter we look at another philosophy that had a profound effect on the twentieth century, both historically, through Hitler and others, and ideologically, through its impact on philosophy and the social sciences.

PHENOMENOLOGY LED DIRECTLY INTO EXISTENTIALISM, a movement that sought to face the human condition as we find it, without imposing any preconditions on our approach. Existentialism was also profoundly influenced by the writings of Nietzsche, who went much further than the phenomenologists in rejecting preconceived ideas, and who has become something of an icon in the late twentieth and early twenty-first centuries.

FRIEDRICH NIETZSCHE

Röcken, Saxony, Germany (1844–1900). Nietzsche (pronounced *nee*-che) was the son and grandson of Lutheran ministers. When he was five, his father died insane as a result of a brain injury, and he was brought up in a household of four adult female relatives and his sister. From his childhood he had a deep love of literature and music. His mother wanted him to train for the Christian ministry, and he started studying theology at Bonn. But he abandoned theology in favor of classics and continued his studies at Leipzig. Formative influences on him in this period were Greek mythology, Kant, Schopenhauer, and Richard Wagner.

Despite his lack of formal academic qualifications, Nietzsche was appointed professor of classical philology at Basel University at age twenty-four. From then until the onset of insanity in 1889 he produced a stream of books critiquing most aspects of Western civilization and seeking to propose an alternative philosophy, a "philosophy of the future," on which a new world could be built after the collapse of our current culture. His work attracted little attention at the time, but in the last decade of the nineteenth century a number of artists and literary people began to take notice of it, and his influence in the twentieth century and into the twenty-first has been profound. He was a forerunner of existentialism and postmodernism; Nazism and fascism hailed him as a hero; and even those who disagreed most strongly with him were willing to accept the validity of some of his critiques and insights.

Nietzsche's writing style was graphic and innovative. In many ways he wrote as a poet or a prophet rather than as a philosopher. Particularly in his later works, he chose to use aphorisms in place of coherent argument. He saw himself as the destroyer of all philosophical systems and especially Christianity, but he didn't attempt to destroy them in the time-honored way of rationally demonstrating their falsehood and proposing something better. Instead, he used his vivid imagination and considerable literary skills to attack caricatures and score points and to present graphic images and make enigmatic suggestions.

As a person Nietzsche was a sad figure. His teaching role at Basel didn't work out, and after ten unhappy years there, he accepted a pension and retired. He had few friends and lived a lonely life. He moved frequently. He went for long solitary walks. He suffered ill health, including migraines, eye trouble, syphilis, and a form of psychosis. His interest in Greek mythology at times became almost obsessive, as when he declared himself to be Dionysus, the Greek god of fruitfulness, drama, ecstasy, and orgy.

Besides the thirteen books Nietzsche published himself, often at his own expense, his copious notebooks were preserved by his sister, and some have been published. Among his best-known works are *The Birth of Tragedy* (1872), *Untimely Meditations* (1873–1876), *The Gay Science* (1882; second edition, 1887), *Thus Spake Zarathustra* (1883–1885), *Beyond Good and Evil* (1886), and *On the Genealogy of Morals* (1887).

As with Kierkegaard, Nietzsche's style has made a number of differing interpretations of his work possible. We will look at it in three main sections: the problem, the wrong answers, and Nietzsche's answer.

THE PROBLEM

In Nietzsche's own words, the problem is "God is dead." This is not to say that God was ever alive. But Nietzsche meant more than just "There is no God." Despite the fact that he lived at a time when Christianity was growing worldwide at an unprecedented rate, Nietzsche, from his limited German viewpoint, appears to have believed that religion, especially Christianity, was in terminal decline and very soon would cease to exist altogether. So "God is dead" meant also that those who had based their worldview on the myth that God was alive would no longer be able to do so, with catastrophic results. Perhaps a third meaning underlying the proclamation "God is dead" is a call to dispense with God, to get rid of him from our lives, and, in Nietzsche's eyes, to become truly human.

Because God is dead, all "horizons" have been wiped away. There is no up or down, no fixed points, no standards, no truth, no values, no morals, no meaning, no rationality. Every foundation that human life had been built on is gone. We are confronted with "the advent of nihilism" (from Lat. *nihil*, "nothing").

Nietzsche was by no means the first atheist thinker. But he was the first atheist thinker to face the full implications of atheism. Marx was an atheist, but in Russell's phrase, he "retained a cosmic optimism which only theism could justify"; he believed he could establish an alternative worldview that would work. Many nineteenth-century scientists similarly thought that our scientific understanding of the world could function without any reference to God and still make sense. Even the liberal theologians were doing their best to remove all the supernatural elements from Christianity in the fond belief that they could do that and still retain an ethic and a philosophy that would work. Nietzsche saw further than any of them and realized that if we lose God we lose everything. We lose the basis for morals, values, truth, meaning, and everything that makes life human.

THE WRONG ANSWERS

Confronted with the loss of everything, what are we to do? Before he can present his answer, Nietzsche seeks to demolish a range of possible answers.

Schopenhauer. Nietzsche was deeply influenced through reading Schopenhauer, and he accepted his basic philosophy. But he rejected his response of hopeless resignation.

Wagner. For a time Nietzsche was hopeful that Wagner was on the track of an answer through the arts, especially through the merging of music and the Greek concept of tragedy. But he became disillusioned with Wagner, partly because he felt he was not sufficiently radical, and partly because of personal disagreements.

Christianity. Quite apart from rejecting Christianity's basic belief in God, Nietzsche vigorously attacked Christian values and morality, things that liberal theologians like D. F. Strauss and many a nineteenth-century atheist thought well worth retaining. In particular he attacked humility, grace, forgiveness, pity, love, compassion, and practically all the virtues seen in Jesus, whom he described as an "idiot." He enjoyed contrasting himself with Jesus.

Philosophers. Philosophers have tried to interpret the world, said Marx. Nietzsche agreed, and like Marx, he saw himself rejecting all their interpretations. Like Kierkegaard, he attacked "all systematizers." There can be no such thing as "pure reason"; all philosophies are subjective perspectives on the world, and none of them contains any absolute truth. All that the philosophers are doing is trying to make others see things the way they see them, as an attempt to gain power. Reason itself is but the product of our drives and desires and passions. Any hope of ever attaining absolute truth, certain knowledge, or fixed moral principles must be totally abandoned.

"The herd." If God is dead, then any meaning and values must be rooted in humanity. But Nietzsche had no time for humanity at large or for any form of democracy. The huge majority of people, whom he called "the common herd," were weak and inauthentic, practicing the Christian virtues Nietzsche so despised. In keeping with evolutionary (non-Darwinian) theory, Nietzsche believed in the elimination of the weak lest they should hinder the progress of the strong.

Scientists. Despite his own naturalistic worldview, in his early period Nietzsche was inclined to blame science for many of the failings of nineteenth-century culture. He looked back with fondness to the Greek prescientific period, where myth and art, not science, were the basis of culture. Later he showed much more support for the scientific enterprise while still attacking the superficiality of many scientific thinkers and especially their lack of commitment to values and their belief that they were dealing with ultimate reality.

Socrates. Nietzsche saw Socrates as the one who had stressed the priority of reason over against the higher values of earlier Greek culture, such as art, beauty, and the sense of the tragic. In a wider sense, he saw him as typifying any philosophy or religion that urged the subordination of our natural desires and feelings to reason, moral or social values, or religious principles. As such he represented the wrong pathway that much of human history has followed.

NIETZSCHE'S ANSWER

Creativity and authenticity. Values, meaning, and so on cannot be rooted in God because God is dead. So unless we are to give way to pessimism and despair, we must create them for ourselves. Here is the pride and glory of the human race, to take the place of God and become the creator. "What would there be to create if there were–Gods" who have already done all the creating, he asked. But there are no gods, and so now we can truly show our greatness by becoming the creator. Then we will be truly human, truly authentic, truly ourselves.

The new morals, values, meaning, and truth that we create will be totally unlike the old. What the old called "virtues" we may call "vices"; what they rejected as evil or false we will praise as good and true. In a sense Nietzsche urged that all individuals should do this. But he accepted that this would lead to conflict and chaos and totally unlivable relativism. So in practice it will only be done by a few or by one individual, the *Übermensch*, or Superman, who will then impose his values, truth, and authentic self-expression on "the herd," who become the "dung" spread thickly so that the one flower may grow.

Human creativity is not limited to meaning, values, and truth. It extends also to the external world. In attacking belief in the independent existence of a world beyond our experiences, Nietzsche saw each of us creatively imposing our particular ordering upon our perceptions.

Superman. Superman was, for Nietzsche, the true expression of what it is to be human. He is a law to himself, supremely alive, asserting his boundless vitality and surging powers, a man truly himself, limited by no external restraints, free to create and to impose his creations on others. Any specific culture in any age can produce its Superman, and each will be different, showing its creativity in different ways and imposing different values. However, despite his insistence that his power to create values is unlimited, Nietzsche seemed to assume that Superman would always choose to express the values that Nietzsche himself thought important, such as generosity (the counterpart to resentment) and self-discipline.

Superman on the stage of history has his counterpart in the psychology of the individual. To be a real person I must rise above all that expresses the values of the herd in me and assert my will to exercise power over all that is weak or belongs to "slave morality."

The will to power.

Nietzsche adopted his stress on the centrality of will from Schopenhauer in conscious opposition to those who put reason at the heart of their systems. But where Schopenhauer saw will as the source of all the world's problems, Nietzsche saw it as the key to his answer. It is the will to power that is the source of living and the key to life. Here we meet Dionysus, exuberant and uninhibited, giving expression to unbridled natural feelings and desires.

Nietzsche seems also to have accepted Schopenhauer's view that will is not limited to humans; the world and nature itself are also driven by will, a universal force, manifested in its raw form in the desire to live by destroying others or to survive by asserting power. In Nero the will to power was expressed by his desire to burn Rome. In a more sublimated form (and Nietzsche was the first to use the concept of "sublimation" in this sense), the great poets have expressed their will to power both by mastering their creative thoughts and expressing them in their work and through the influence those works have had over others. We are all driven by the will to power; it controls all our actions. In his attack on Christianity, Nietzsche claimed that even the Christian actions that seem most loving and unselfish are in fact at root an expression of the will to power. They are simply a self-centered way of manipulating others for our own ends.

Eternal recurrence.

Nietzsche believed in endless cycles of repeating events. Everything that is happening today has already happened in the past, not just once, but an infinite number of times. And every event will recur and be endlessly repeated in the future. Scholars have struggled to understand just what he meant by this theory, and some have tried to remove the difficulty by suggesting that he was not speaking of a historical process (as he seems to be doing) so much as a psychological one or a moral one; the choices I make today, for instance, have all been made many times before and will be made many times in the future.

Master morality and slave morality.
Traditional morality, based principally on the teaching of Jesus, has seen what Nietzsche called "slave morality" as virtuous. Those who practice meekness, compassion, grace—the marks of a slave mentality—are good; those who assert themselves over others—the mark of a master mentality—are evil. For Nietzsche slave morality was unhealthy, a failure to be what we truly are. Humility, love, and the like are masks of our weaknesses, covering up our failures by diverting attention to those of others. Master morality, by contrast, rightly accepts that the expression of the master's life and the satisfaction of his desires are necessarily good. This is true moral health and is right and good; therefore any other approach to morality is bad. Slave morality, said Nietzsche, focuses on negative aspects like lack of pride or self-assertiveness; master mentality delights in just these things. Slave morality is typical of the herd, master morality of the Superman. Above all, slave morality is typified by Christians.

Religion.
Assuming that there was no God and no life after death, Nietzsche concluded that the only way to assess anything was the extent to which it benefited the individual in this life. As a result, he saw Christianity's ideals of self-control and self-denial as "crimes against life," against the free and authentic expression of the true nature of the individual. But this didn't apply to all religions. In particular, the religion of Dionysus, with its encouragement of free expression of the self and satisfaction of one's desires, was the kind of religion Nietzsche was happy to commend. In doing this he wasn't making any claims about the truth, in the traditional sense of the word, of Dionysian religion. The traditional issue of the truth or falsity of any religion didn't arise for Nietzsche in that he had abandoned the traditional concept of truth. But since for him it was "the value for life" that constituted truth, then insofar as Dionysian religion affirmed and enriched the individual's life, for that individual it was true.

TO THINK THROUGH

Why do you think Nietzsche is so popular today?

Is Nietzsche right in saying that the death of God liberates the human individual?

In his "death of God" passage, after proclaiming the collapse of all standards and the loss of all meaning and truth, Nietzsche acknowledged that his contemporaries were unable to accept what he was saying. "I've come too soon," he said. "It takes time for great events to make their impact. It will take time for people to realize the full implications of the death of God, the greatest event in human history." Well over one hundred years later, despite the realization of Nietzsche's vision by postmodernism, the vast majority of people still haven't gotten the message. They still believe we can dispense with God and keep all the things that are of greatest value. Why do you think this is so?

For Further Study

R. Schacht. *Making Sense of Nietzsche*. Urbana, Ill.: University of Illinois Press, 1995.

THIRTY-NINE

THE BIGGER PICTURE

BRITISH IDEALISM AND THE WIDER WORLD

We come in this chapter to the end of our survey of responses and reactions that arose following Hume's radical challenge to the modern vision. Before we turn to the final section of this book, with its theme of the death of philosophy, we will look at a last flowering of idealism at the close of the Victorian era; and then, taking our cue from its call to look at the bigger picture, we will spend a moment reminding ourselves that world philosophy is bigger than Western philosophy.

THROUGHOUT THE NINETEENTH CENTURY, THE SUCCESS story of science continued unabated, expressed in technological advance, industrialization, and urbanization. Though most scientists believed in God, the commitment to explain everything without reference to God remained one of the scientific worldview's central principles. By the end of the century, the general acceptance of Darwin's concept of evolution was largely countering the teleological way of viewing the world, which went back to Aristotle and beyond. Things no longer had meaning or purpose. No God was needed to oversee the processes of nature or the story of the world. Everything that happened was purposeless and meaningless, the product of pure, random chance.

The scientific worldview was to dominate in the early part of the twentieth century in the philosophies of the pragmatists, empiricists, and positivists. Nevertheless, as we have seen, there were influential reactions against the dominance of the scientific approach throughout the nineteenth century and into the first few years of the twentieth. In Britain this reaction was expressed in the brief philosophical dominance of a form of idealism.

BRITISH IDEALISM

Though throughout the modern period British philosophy has been dominated by empiricism, for a few decades at the end of the Victorian era and into the early twentieth century idealism held center stage, so much so that it was able to claim that empiricism finally had been discredited. This idealism was a development of Hegelianism; three key figures were T. H. Green, F. H. Bradley, and Bernard Bosanquet. Empiricism was impossible, they said. Though it claimed to build a system in accordance with observation and reason, neither reason nor observation could establish its basic presuppositions. Its great mistake was to focus on bits of reality and ignore the whole. Rather, we should start with the whole, with reality itself, and only then seek to understand the parts.

Thomas Hill Green. Birkin, Yorkshire, England (1836–1882). Educated at Oxford, Green became professor of moral philosophy there in 1878. He criticized empiricism for being based on assumptions that were empirically unprovable, such as the existence of a continuing subject that has empirical experiences. As a theory of human knowledge, he said, it can only lead to skepticism.

In place of empiricism, Green proposed a form of idealism close to Hegel's. Sense experience, he said, is inadequate to tell us what things really are. The key to making sense of the world is mind. Everything in the world is to be seen as a complex network of relations; these relationships make things what they are, and mind is what apprehends and, in the Kantian sense, constitutes these relationships. Supremely, the world is constituted by an infinite eternal Mind, God. Human minds are able to know reality because they participate in the eternal Mind.

Francis Herbert Bradley. London (1846–1924). The son of an evangelical minister, Bradley was educated at Oxford, where he spent the rest of his secluded life, having no teaching responsibilities but studying and writing philosophy. By the turn of the century, he had become the leading figure in British philosophy. But his reputation waned rapidly, especially after his death, when he was viewed by most as the last representative of speculative idealist metaphysics.

Bradley first attracted attention through his *Ethical Studies* (1876), in which he attacked both utilitarianism and Kant's ethical theory and argued that we can only make sense of ethics by viewing the individual in the context of an organic living community made up of spiritual and, in the last analysis, religious beings.

Bradley's best-known work was *Appearance and Reality* (1893). In it he started by examining and rejecting worldviews based on common sense, popular science, and popular religion. They all lead us into contradictions and thus fail, he said, to give us a holistic harmonious explanation of everything that is. They are, in fact, only operating in the sphere of "appearance"; they use reason to abstract bits of reality from the whole and so see them in a distorted way. They see the world primarily as diversity, a lot of different things side by side, rather than holistically, in harmonious unity. What we need to do is get behind all appearances, with their inherent problems and contradictions, to the unity or "reality" that lies behind them. This reality must be contradiction-free, containing everything that is in a harmonious whole. Bradley called this reality "the Absolute" and went on to develop a complex analysis of it.

It was this type of speculative analysis of a supposed entity lying behind the experiences we have of the world that provoked a scornful reaction from people like G. E. Moore and Bertrand Russell, who, though trained in idealism, turned against it and successfully reinstated the British empirical tradition. But Bradley was not in fact postulating a new entity distinct from all the usual items of experience. Rather, he was saying that if we want to make sense of the world, we must start with the world as a whole, as "the Absolute," rather than starting with the bits and seeking to make sense of them. We might think of a jigsaw puzzle with thousands of pieces scattered before us. As long as we just look at the pieces, the diversity, we will have problems; each doesn't fit the one next to it; the pieces don't make sense. But then we look at the picture on the box, and suddenly the whole thing makes sense. We can understand the pieces because they are parts of a consistent, unified whole.

In keeping with his Kantian heritage, Bradley stressed that the Absolute was not to be grasped by the use of our reason or intellect. Rather, we encounter it through feeling, an immediate intuitive awareness, in which there is no distinction between the experiencing and what is experienced. Reason has a place in our subsequent description and analysis of that experience, but the experience itself transcends reason. In the nature of things, reason's description and analysis will always fall short of reality.

Reality is manifested in the objects in the world around us. Bradley developed a system of levels or degrees of reality; inert matter is lower on the scale than living matter; humans are higher than animals. The same scale applies to truth; the more spiritual a thing is, the truer it is. Both error and evil arise because our ideas and actions fall short of full reality.

Bernard Bosanquet. Alnwick, England (1848–1923). Bosanquet (pronounced bow-za-*ket*) was educated at Oxford, where he taught for eleven years

and then left in order to concentrate on charity work in London. From 1903 to 1908 he was professor of moral philosophy at St. Andrews, Scotland. He then returned to London. The two main philosophical influences on his thinking were Plato and Hegel. He collaborated with F. H. Bradley but adopted a more positive approach than his. He wrote widely on a range of subjects, including aesthetics, social theory, and political philosophy, as well as epistemology and metaphysics.

Like Bradley, Bosanquet believed that the only way to escape from the contradictions that arise from ordinary thought and experience was to postulate that they arise because in them we are dealing only with parts, not the whole, which is reality, the Absolute. In the Absolute there are no contradictions.

Bosanquet assessed the value of an object by its ability to satisfy desires. Thus the Absolute, which satisfies all desires, is of greatest value. Further, as we partake more and more in the Absolute, through what Bosanquet called the religious consciousness, we acquire greater value and attain greater satisfaction.

He applied this concept to his social theory. Just as Bradley stressed the significance of the community for ethics, Bosanquet rejected classical individualism for an understanding of the person as a social entity, who can only be understood and can only function satisfactorily in a wider social and cultural context. The social whole gives significance to the individual, not the other way around.

TO THINK THROUGH

What do you think about Bradley's concept that the Absolute is apprehended in an immediate intuitive awareness rather than by reason?

Do you think we should start with the jigsaw pieces or with the picture on the box?

Up until the twentieth century it was almost inevitable that when philosophers tried to conceive of "the whole" or "ultimate reality" they produced something that looked like God. Empiricists, for the most part, were committed to providing explanations that were able to dispense with God. Does this mean that someone who believes in God has to reject empiricism in favor of idealism? Is it possible to combine the strengths of both approaches?

INTO THE TWENTIETH CENTURY

For most people the dawn of the twentieth century was greeted with excitement and hope. The future was bright. The human race had at last come of age and had become lords and possessors of nature. Reason, science, technology, medicine, and the like, coupled with progress in education and social care, were improving the quality of human life and opening doors of opportunity. Things could only get better; the human race could only go from strength to strength.

Yet for most people the twentieth century ended in disillusionment. Hopes had been dashed. Science had not brought the expected utopia. Reason and knowledge had failed to meet the deepest needs of humanity. The dawn of the year 2000 was greeted with cynicism rather than hope.

Philosophy gave voice to the general loss of hope. We could debate which way around it was. Did the disillusionment of the century cause the negative philosophies? Or did the negative philosophies cause the disillusionment? My own view is that it happened both ways. The loss of hope had a number of sources, but a key one was the failure of philosophy to answer the questions raised by the human condition. Faced with the horrors of war and of Auschwitz, people cried "Why?" and "Where do we go from here?" And the philosophers answered, "Let's examine the meaning of the words," or "Despair and suicide," or "Any answer is as good as any other," or "It's all meaningless."

But it is also probably true that the prevailing mood of the day determined which philosophical concepts caught the public imagination and became popular. Some philosophers in the twentieth century did offer positive answers, but their voices were drowned in the cries of despair.

Before we turn to the story of the twentieth century, we will pause to look at two philosophical approaches outside the Western tradition. Sadly, rather than being willing to learn from other traditions, the West has generally sought to impose its worldview on everyone else, insisting on the philosophical McDonaldization of all the world. At worst, it deliberately destroyed the records of alternative worldviews, as the Spaniards destroyed what remained of Aztec philosophy. At best, it recognized, with a degree of wistfulness, positive elements in other cultures, whether in terms of "the noble savage" in the Pacific islands or the richness of the sense of community in African culture. But such recognition did little to break the power of Western savagery and self-centered individualism.

PHILOSOPHY IN SUB-SAHARAN AFRICA

North Africa, of course, has produced many philosophies and has had a large influence on the story of Western thought. The huge area of the rest of Africa has through the centuries developed a range of cultures, doubtless with world-views that differed in detail among themselves. But, with the exception of Ethiopia, we have no written records. We do, however, have many oral traditions. Researchers have tried to gather these and have found a number of recurring themes. Though it is not possible to say how far back in time these themes go, it is tempting to think that they go back a very long way. Just as, we assume, African lifestyle changed comparatively little until the impact of twentieth-century westernization, so it is possible that their traditional beliefs are not far removed from those of their ancestors who were alive when the story of Western philosophy was just beginning.

God. African traditional thought is essentially religious. The sense of the divine pervades the whole world; the spiritual element of life is very real and powerful; nature itself is primarily spiritual. This is expressed in a number of animistic beliefs, in nature spirits, and in deified heroes and ancestors. But, as in the ancient Near East, the existence of spirits does not preclude the existence of one supreme God. Every African tradition that has been researched appears to have a concept of one God who is over all the other spirits or deities. John Mbiti, in *Concepts of God in Africa*, wrote:

> Every African people recognizes one God. According to the cosmology of some, there are, besides him, other divinities and spiritual beings, some of whom are closely associated with him. These divinities are mainly the personification of God's activities, natural phenomena and objects, or deified national heroes, and some are said to have been created as such by God. . . . But even where other spiritual beings are recognized, people do not lose sight of the one supreme God who is regarded in a class of his own.

Attributes of this God vary, but according to Mbiti, in most traditions he is seen as creator, self-existent, all-wise, all-powerful, transcendent, infinite, eternal, morally good, and concerned for the well-being of the world.

The individual and the community. The traditional African worldview is thus essentially God-centered, frequently in a more immediate and dynamic way than the Western tradition has been. The African concept of the individual and the community arises from this. While the Western tradition in the modern period made the individual the center of the universe, African thought is nearer to the medieval or ancient traditions that gave the individual a much humbler position. The tribe or community is of much greater significance than the individual; indeed, the individual only gains significance as he or she fulfills a meaningful role in that community. It is in this sense that dead ancestors can still be seen as an integral part of the current community.

Epistemology. Some study has been done on African epistemology, but as yet it is only limited in scope. What has been done, however, would indicate a strongly realist epistemology. What is personally experienced is to be accepted as true. This does not, of course, imply a materialist worldview, as it has done for many in the West. For the African, spiritual realities are to be personally experienced every bit as much as physical realities.

TO THINK THROUGH

What elements do you think the West needs to learn from the traditional African worldview?

LATIN AMERICAN PHILOSOPHY

Limited though it is, our understanding of traditional African culture can be built on contemporary beliefs preserved in tribal traditions, despite the lack of written records. Sadly, almost all the written records of Latin American worldviews were lost or destroyed over five hundred years ago, and very little oral tradition has survived intact. However, some understanding of the culture and worldviews of the great Maya, Aztec, and Inca civilizations that flourished in Latin America before Europeans arrived has been gained through extensive archaeological research.

The worldview of each of these civilizations, like that of traditional Africa, was strongly religious. They too were polytheistic in the sense that they recognized and worshiped many deities, but they also tended toward monotheism in that they recognized one supreme deity who was identified with the sun.

Again, in contrast to the West's post-Cartesian commitment to the separation of mind or spirit and matter, Latin American worldviews stressed the unity and holistic nature of the universe. Even the gods are not of a different nature from us and from things in the world. Out of this arose a sense of oneness with and respect for nature that has been the hallmark of many non-Western peoples and from which we, in our technology-dominated age, need to learn.

TO THINK THROUGH

When did you last see the Milky Way? I have talked to many people who have never even seen it once, thanks to street lights and all that our culture provides to do away with nighttime and protect us from the real world. Can you really get a true focus on life if you are surrounded with artificiality? Isn't it time we broke free and got back to the real world?

THE DEATH
OF
PHILOSOPHY

PART SIX

FORTY

THE DEATH OF PHILOSOPHY

In this chapter we take a deep breath and prepare to enter the most tragic century in the history of philosophy.

THE KEY THEME IN THE STORY OF MODERN PHILOSOPHY has been the search for truth or the search for how we can know that what we believe is true. This was the agenda set by Descartes. Indeed, it was the agenda set before Descartes by the rejection of the medieval worldview, which had held its well-formulated answer to the question. The loss of God as the basis for truth set modernism the task of finding an alternative epistemological basis for our knowledge, just as the loss of God as the creator and holy one and the *telos* set modernism the task of finding an alternative basis for the external world and ethics and meaning.

The epistemological answers offered through the modern period varied, but some elements kept reappearing. One was that there is such a thing as truth that we as human beings can know. Another was that the ideal model for truth was one that gave us certainty. To establish something as true, we need to produce practical evidence or rational arguments that make it impossible to disbelieve that truth. The pattern here was mathematics, where everything was assumed to move in logically watertight ways, such that everyone had to accept the validity of the conclusions. A third element was a tendency to limit the search for the basis of truth to ourselves and the content of our minds. A fourth element was the assumption that somehow science was the key to the answer.

DISILLUSIONED WITH TRUTH

We now live in a century that is said to have abandoned this search for truth. Not one of the answers proposed throughout the modern period has worked. Increasingly, the conclusion has been drawn that the sort of truth that was being sought is either nonexistent or unattainable. Most would assume that unattainability and nonexistence are the same thing. As a result, we must learn to live without that sort of truth. And, since we can't live without some concept of truth, we must develop some alternative concept. Accordingly, a number of alternatives have been put forward, ranging from pragmatism to full-blooded relativism.

As with truth, so with the other areas of human life that have been the focus of philosophical exploration through the centuries. Nietzsche was right; the sponge has wiped away the entire horizon. Epistemological relativism was in fact just about the last form of relativism to pervade Western society; ethical, social, cultural, and aesthetic fixed points had long before been wiped away. The hope that reason could provide a basis for morality, for society, or for any other aspect of human life had proved facile.

The disillusionment with the quest for rationally established truth or principles for human life, and the willingness to settle for less, grew steadily throughout the nineteenth century. It is illustrated by the rise of pragmatism and the recognition by the scientist-philosopher Peirce and others that not even the statements of science could claim such a status. But the early twentieth century saw one last vigorous attempt to escape disillusionment. Like pragmatism, it started with science. But unlike pragmatism, it saw science as a route to definitive truth, either in the facts that it establishes or in the principles that underlie it. After all, science was universally recognized as benefiting the human race in thousands of ways. It was hugely successful, claiming to be knowledge of truth. Surely it must contain the key to truth.

Thus Bertrand Russell in effect spent his whole philosophical life seeking to pin down sure and certain truth. He was convinced that it existed; that is, he was sure that the statements of mathematics were valid and thus true and that most of the statements of the scientists were completely dependable. But as a philosopher he was determined to find out how or why they were true. He deliberately rejected any "metaphysical" answer. He was an atheist, and so he was unable to accept God as the basis for truth. Therefore, all his life Russell sought to find an alternative answer, one that did not require the adopting of any presuppositions or any primary step of faith. At first he was convinced that the kind of truth he was looking for was to be found in math, and he worked incredibly hard to establish the logical basis of math. But although his achievements there were Herculean, he failed to establish math as a discipline in which truth could be logically and definitively established.

In the middle part of his life Russell worked hard at seeking the basis for truth in science. What is it that makes the facts discovered by the scientists true? How do we justify our belief in them? He tried a number of answers to this question, but in the last purely philosophical book he wrote, *Human Knowledge, Its Scope and Limits* (1948), he ended his search by admitting failure. Starting from his atheistic naturalistic position, he was unable to establish a firm basis for our belief in the statements of the scientists. Both science itself and our belief in its statements are based on assumptions that cannot be proved, he said; we have to accept them by faith. We can never be sure that science or any of its claims are true. The only reason for putting our faith in science as opposed to any other worldview, such as Christianity, is that, in Russell's opinion, it is more likely to be true than its rivals.

So ended Russell's search for truth. In the final phase of his life, after *Human Knowledge, Its Scope and Limits*, he wrote no more purely philosophical books.

RELIANCE ON SCIENCE

One of Russell's students was Ludwig Wittgenstein, who had a major influence on the development of logical positivism, a philosophical approach that arose in the 1920s. It was based firmly on the scientific worldview and made dogmatic claims about the nature of meaning and truth, limiting them to what could be scientifically verified. As a philosophical movement, its considerable weaknesses were being exposed before the middle of the century, but its influence continued for some time after that.

In a sense logical positivism was simply an attempt at a scholarly presentation of what almost everyone in the early and mid twentieth century believed, that science had the truth and that the scientific test for truth, having shown by its huge success that it worked, was to be applied to all other areas of life. If a thing was scientific, it was true or at least potentially true. If it was unscientific, it was false or meaningless. This presupposed, of course, not only that the scientific way of establishing truth was valid, but that it was the only way of establishing truth and that there was only one sort of truth, scientific truth.

This second presupposition was to be challenged by the work of the later Wittgenstein. But for a time it had a devastating effect. Philosophy down through the ages had sought to answer the big questions of life, not just about truth, but about how we should live, why we are here, who we are, and so on. Logical positivism dismissed all answers to these questions. But it didn't do so in order to produce its own alternative answers. Instead, it pronounced the questions invalid. Science, it said, cannot provide the answer to these sorts of questions. Therefore, there can be no answer; the questions are meaningless. In effect, philosophers through the centuries have been wasting their time.

Logical positivism didn't last as a philosophy or perhaps rather as an anti-philosophy. But the immediate effect of the failure of Russell and logical positivism to establish a philosophical basis for the scientific enterprise had a significant effect on the empiricist philosophers who immediately followed them. They abandoned the search for truth or the attempt at justification of our acceptance of scientific truth and narrowed their interest to the analysis of language. This in itself was no insignificant task, and it has had fascinating and positive results. But, in effect, it was an admission of failure, just as the work of the postmodernists is an admission of failure. We have tried, they were in fact saying, to establish a firm basis for science, knowledge, and truth and thus for all of human ideas and philosophy. And we admit that we have failed, so, in effect, the whole Enlightenment project has failed. This doesn't make any difference at all either to science or ordinary life. Both carry on as before, largely unconcerned that we can't justify what they are doing. So instead of seeking to provide a foundation for them, we will simply accept that the foundation exists, and we will focus instead on what science and ordinary language have built on that foundation.

The focus thus turned to the analysis of the language and meaning we use when we are involved in science or in ordinary life. Though Russell was himself part of the cause of this shift of emphasis, he saw this focusing on language as a tragic abandoning of philosophy's "grave and important task" pursued "throughout the ages" of seeking to understand the reality that is the world.

UNANSWERABLE QUESTIONS

At the same time as those in the empirical tradition were denying philosophy the right to seek to answer the big questions, a very different philosophical tradition was insisting on facing them. As we have seen with Kierkegaard, existentialism scorned those whose horizons were so narrow that they couldn't see beyond the scientific worldview. Science turns us into things, objects, machines, they said. But we are not things, objects, or machines. We are conscious existing human persons. We experience, we hurt, we choose, we fear, we live, we die. The issue is not the boiling point of water but what it is to be human, to exist, to find our place in Being, to cope with alienation, dread, despair, and death.

The tragedy of the great figures in twentieth-century existentialism is that though they asked the big questions, they were unable to find the answers. The human condition cries out for meaning and truth, but the heavens are silent. No answer comes. Meaninglessness, anxiety, alienation, and death continue to mock us. We can assert our human authenticity, but we cannot give the answer. The reason for this is straightforward. Existentialism, explained Sartre, is a humanism—humankind seeking to manage without God. We as humans are alone in a world we find absurd, alone in the midst of a monstrous silence. If there were a God, things would be different. We would have a foundation for our personhood. We would have answers to our questions. There would be up and down; there would be clear horizons. But there is no God. Sartre was quite candid. The existentialist, he said, finds it very troublesome that God doesn't exist. If there is no God, we have no possibility of finding values, meaning, goodness, or moral principles by which we should live. He found this profoundly troublesome, but as an atheist he had no alternative.

So, just as the empirical tradition effectively killed philosophy by pronouncing its questions meaningless, so existentialism killed it by pronouncing its questions answerless. There is no way out of the maze. As Albert Camus famously put it, there is only one philosophical question, and that is suicide.

The main impact of reductionist empiricism and atheistic existentialism was felt in the first two-thirds of the twentieth century. Toward the end of the century, a further iconoclastic anti-philosophy arose, declaring dogmatically that philosophy, as it had been traditionally understood, was dead. Postmodernism, said French philosopher Jean-François Lyotard, is to be seen as the abolition of all metanarratives. All explanatory structures are to be destroyed. There are no explanations.

You will have noticed the overwhelmingly negative feel of these twentieth-century movements. Traditional philosophical questions are meaningless. The world is absurd. There are no answers. The human condition is one of alienation and despair. We are without God and without hope. Science itself is a god who has failed. Even the term *postmodern* is a negative, the rejection of the modern without putting anything in its place. God is dead. Philosophy is dead. And we may as well accept that the human race is dead.

Quite apart from the specific philosophical movements, much of the general feel of the twentieth century, especially in the second half, reflected a negative rather than creative outlook. It has been a time of disillusionment, with politicians, with science and education as the answers to all our ills, even with human nature itself. We have failed to stop wars or to prevent prejudice, exploitation, injustice, or crime. There is growing pessimism about the human condition and a decreasing sense of hope for the future. All these things are the expression of the ever receding tide, leaving more and more bare rocks exposed, interspersed with isolated rock pools where each person seeks to find his or her own answer to our desperate need for the fullness of the ocean.

PIERCING THE GLOOM

If this leaves you feeling pretty gloomy, let me share with you three things before we plunge into the story of the century. The first is that, like the confident statements that God is dead, the claims that philosophy is dead are open to refutation. Logical positivism abolished metaphysics. But metaphysical philosophy enjoyed a revival toward the end of the twentieth century. Lyotard abolished metanarratives. But the huge majority of people still believe in them and live by them. Sartre courageously faced a universe without God, but if the reports are correct, the majority of professional philosophers at the end of the century still believed in him. Though hugely influential, the gurus of postmodernism are in fact very much in the minority, arguably the remnant of the pro-Marxist student movements of the middle of the century, disillusioned by the collapse of the Marxist metanarrative and unable to think of anything to put in its place.

Second, I disagree with the view that we should reject out of hand the wisdom of the past. We have a rich heritage of philosophical ideas behind us from which we can draw as we face the future. We have the opportunity to seek to replace the nihilism and chaos that some would see as the result of the twentieth century with something positive that will take us through the twenty-first. And we certainly have a lot to draw on. Even some of the more obscure ideas of the past could be adapted and applied to our current situation. And there is plenty to be learned from the mistakes of the past. For all its faults, even the story of the modern period has a great deal to teach us.

Although, with the postmodernists, I am very happy to reject many aspects of the agenda of the modern period with its naively optimistic assumption that it could manage without God, I still feel we have benefited greatly from the discussions and discoveries of the past five hundred years. And though I have reservations, especially in the light of technological exploitation, I accept that the scientific worldview has been enormously fruitful and will continue to be so. The issue is not to free ourselves from the modern or scientific worldview altogether, any more than it is to free ourselves from the medieval worldview altogether. Rather, it is to refuse to let it be our master. Like everything else in the world, it has its place, and our task is to enable it to fulfill its right role as it fits into the greater whole that makes up reality in our universe.

And the third thing goes back to my basic reason for writing this book. The destruction and death of philosophy in the twentieth century has put before us the challenge of finding a philosophy for the twenty-first century that will be universally acceptable and that will truly fit both the human condition and the realities of the universe. This is no time for petty relativisms. If all philosophers can offer is a discordant and fragmented answer to the questions of the human race, then we may as well let philosophy die. The challenge is to produce something much bigger. And I believe we can do it.

TO THINK THROUGH

What would you say to someone who assumes that the modern period's failure to find an adequate basis for truth and the whole of life proves that no such basis can be found?

Is science a master or a slave? What should it be?

Does philosophy have a right to answer the big questions?

Do you feel we have much to learn from the past? What sort of things might we learn?

IT'S THE RESULTS THAT MATTER

PRAGMATISM

In this chapter we explore the pragmatism of four American thinkers—Charles Sanders Peirce, William James, Josiah Royce, and John Dewey—who analyzed meaning in terms of results and stressed that any worthwhile philosophizing must have practical applications.

PHILOSOPHICAL MOVEMENTS IGNORE NEAT TIME LINES. Pragmatism started in the nineteenth century, but it is nevertheless a thoroughly twentieth-century approach to philosophy. It was a distinctively American movement, doubtless reflecting the American mind-set and experience of the time. Like existentialism and positivism, it helped prepare the way for the relativism of the later part of the century. Peirce and James were the two main exponents of pragmatism. Their approach was attacked, not always fairly, by Russell and Moore, but the basic insights of the movement have been widely accepted and further developed by Royce, Dewey, and others.

CHARLES SANDERS PEIRCE

Cambridge, Massachusetts (1839–1914). Son of Benjamin Peirce, a leading American mathematician of the day, Charles was educated at Harvard and the Lawrence Scientific School, where he studied chemistry. For some thirty years he worked for the United States Coast and Geodetic Survey, and by the time he retired in 1891, he was recognized as one of America's top scientists. He maintained an interest in philosophy all his working life, publishing a number of papers and lecturing (in his spare time) at several universities and colleges. After his retirement he devoted himself to philosophy. Major philosophical influences on him were Kant and, increasingly, Scottish realism. He published numerous essays and articles. He had an unattractive personality and a low opinion of the abilities of others compared with his own. He died in poverty.

Pragmatism. Peirce was the founder of American pragmatism (Gk. *pragma*, "action, deed"). He described himself as a "laboratory philosopher"; it was his work as a scientist that shaped his pragmatic theory. Whatever the philosophers may argue, he said, there is only one approach to the world that will work in science, and that is the "realist" one that assumes that there are real objects whose existence is independent of us and whose nature can be explored by careful investigation.

What Peirce called his "pragmatist principle" was designed to clarify the meaning of ideas and concepts, particularly in the context of a laboratory hypothesis, rather than as a test of truth.

To ascertain the meaning of an intellectual conception, we should consider what practical consequences might conceivably result by necessity from the truth of that conception; and the sum of these consequences will constitute the entire meaning of the conception.

You have an idea, a hypothesis, a belief, or a theory, and you wish to explore its meaning. Think up a list of things that will happen if that idea is true or that belief is implemented. That list gives you the meaning you require. You don't need to engage in some metaphysical exploration of the meaning of the belief; the key to its meaning is in its potential consequences. We might, for example, have a concept of the United States of Europe. To clarify that concept, Peirce would say, we need to look at the practical consequences that would result from setting up such a thing. These would be in all sorts of areas: political, commercial, monetary, legislative, linguistic, and so on. When we have listed all these consequences, we have done all we need to do to understand the concept of a United States of Europe. We don't need to explore the meaning of the words used or investigate some *a priori* concept of statehood or anything of the sort. The practical consequences determine the meaning.

Truth. A particular application of the pragmatist principle gives us a way of defining truth. In the context of Peirce's "laboratory" background, we are able to define truth in terms of the results of the thorough testing of a hypothesis. If that testing confirms the hypothesis, then we are justified in assuming it to be true. So truth is to be defined in terms of the eventual agreement of all careful investigators. A proposition is true if it is "ultimately agreed to by all who investigate." Peirce goes a step further and adds that "the object" thus investigated and established by universal agreement is "the real."

Though Peirce talks of "ultimate" agreement, he in fact envisaged the process of investigation or inquiry as an ongoing one. At a given point, we may feel that we have enough confirmation to adopt a hypothesis as our working truth. But it is always possible that at a later date a new piece of evidence will turn up that appears to run counter to our conclusion and so makes it necessary to start the process over again.

One way the pragmatist principle can be used, said Peirce, is to identify "empty" metaphysical statements. If a hypothesis turns out to be untestable—that is, if there are no conceivable consequences that could flow from it—then we are justified in dismissing it. In this he prefigured the verification principle of the logical positivists.

The logic of relations.
Peirce developed a logic of relations. From a scientific viewpoint, he said, there are only three types of meaningful relations.

1. Relations that involve one individual or object. These he called "monadic" (from the Gk. *monos*, "alone"), or "one-place" relations. An example would be "The rose is red."
2. Relations that involve two individuals or objects. These are "dyadic" (from the Gk. *duo*, "two"), or two-place relations. An example would be "John loves Mary."
3. Relations that involve three individuals or objects. These are "triadic" (from the Gk. *treis, tria*, "three"), or three-place relations. An example would be "John gives Mary a rose."

Everything can be described in or reduced to one of these three types, said Peirce; there is no need to devise four- (or more) place relations.

Linked with this schema, Peirce classified everything in three ontological categories:

1. Linked with monadic relation is the category of "firstness" or "quality," which contains the objects of sensation or feeling. It is the domain of science. All objects in this category have phenomenal qualities such as redness.

2. Linked with dyadic relation is the category of "secondness" or "relation," which contains other individuals, minds, or wills. This is the domain of psychology, and the key concept is relationship.
3. Linked with triadic relation is the category of "thirdness" or "representation," which contains thought, rationality, generalizations and abstractions, and ultimately the mind of God. This is the domain of theology.

Peirce developed his concept of the logic of relations and the ontological categories through his lifetime. Of special interest was the category of thirdness in that it applies to the task of understanding and explaining, particularly in a scientific context. The observer sees a relation between two objects, say a hammer breaking glass, and seeks to establish the laws and patterns that govern the relationship between them, thus making a triadic relationship of hammer-glass-law/pattern.

Science and truth. Peirce was one of the first people to counter the almost universal belief of his day that what science was discovering was certain, secure, and final truth about the world around us. The statements of the scientists are not infallible, he said. All their discoveries, even their foundational principles, are fallible. What they actually do is adopt a theory that, though tested, cannot be proved, and use it as long as it works satisfactorily. But if and when it proves unsatisfactory, they drop it and try another. He coined the word "fallibilism" to describe this process. What applies in science also applies in all other areas. No belief in ordinary living or even about our own experience or inner thoughts (such as Descartes's *cogito*) can be infallible; there is always the possibility we may be wrong. This, however, doesn't have to lead to skepticism, provided we are always holding our beliefs open to the process of inquiry and continuing confirmation through their consequences.

WILLIAM JAMES

New York City (1842–1910). James's father was a religious philosopher who followed the spiritualism of the Swedish theologian-philosopher **Emanuel Swedenborg** (1688–1772). After early education in England and Europe, William trained at Harvard Medical School. In 1872 he was appointed to teach anatomy and physiology at Harvard, where he developed his interest in psychology and philosophy and was subsequently appointed professor of psychology (1887) and then of philosophy (1897). He was a highly sensitive person, subject to depression and a range of psychosomatic conditions. This may well have fueled his interest in psychology, a field of study that was then in its infancy. Perhaps as a result of his father's influence, he also had a special interest in psychic phenomena. He had a very attractive and readable writing style; his best-known books were *The Principles of Psychology* (1890), *The Will to Believe and Other Essays in Popular Philosophy* (1897), *The Varieties of Religious Experience* (1902), *Pragmatism* (1907), and *The Meaning of Truth* (1909).

James adopted Peirce's pragmatist principle, or maxim, and applied it especially to truth. Like Peirce he rejected the concept that we can know only our own experiences. Rather, he said, we directly observe objects in the world. The traditional concept locks up each of us in our own world and leads to skepticism. But the fact is we all share a common world. A number of people observing an object will be found to share a common experience and will thus provide an external basis for our shared beliefs.

In testing a belief for truth, there are some situations in which we can verify it directly. I can, for example, find out if my food is salty by tasting it. But most beliefs don't allow such a direct verification, so we need to verify them through their results. James was perhaps less careful than he might have been in publishing his views in this area, and he seems to have been widely understood as rejecting the objective nature of truth in favor of a definition in terms of what happens to work. But there is, of course, a great deal of difference between "What works is true" and "What is true will work." James was not advocating the first; he was advocating the second, but only in the sense that the consequences of a theory or proposition need to be taken into account when we are seeking to establish its meaning or its truth.

The will to believe.
The criterion of shared common observations and experience is sufficient to establish beliefs in most areas, especially the scientific. But in some areas, such as belief in free will or God, or the belief that we can make a difference in the world, it is insufficient. It is in these areas that James spoke of "the will to believe." In these kinds of areas we are "forced" by the pressure of circumstances to make a decision that will have significant consequences for our future. But there is no possibility of definitively establishing the truth or the right course of action. So, said James, we are justified in adopting the belief that is the most psychologically useful to us and will produce the most positive moral results or richer consequences. For most people this will mean adopting a positive belief in each of the three examples cited above.

Religious experience. In *The Varieties of Religious Experience*, James gave priority to personal religious experience over institutionalized religion. He fully accepted the validity of religious experience as a satisfactory basis for moral conduct and as a healthy psychological phenomenon. A conversion experience, for instance, is a positive step toward psychological integration. James analyzed a number of features of religious experience, including a felt encounter with and surrender to something greater than us and beyond this world resulting in joy and elation and subsequent positive moral and personal development. He classified two types of experience, both of which were valid, that of the "healthy minded" and that of "sick souls." Sick souls are likely to have a deeper experience after tribulation and distress. The healthy-minded reach their experience more directly. James's wide-ranging examination of the many varieties of religious experience led him to conclude that they all are encounters with the same existing reality that appears to be personal, good, and great but finite.

Psychology. In *Principles of Psychology*, James explored psychology especially from a philosophical viewpoint. The book was immensely influential and established him as a major psychologist. In it he applied his basic pragmatism in a functional approach to his understanding of mental activity. A defining characteristic of mind is "the pursuance of future ends." We can understand what mind is by studying what it does, the consequences that arise from its presence. James also applied what he called his "radical empiricism" to psychology in that he insisted that research into mind must be empirical and so consist of thorough and exhaustive introspective observation.

James developed the idea of mind as a flow or stream of consciousness, each moment arising from the previous moment, continually recreated by the brain and in turn affecting our brain states. It is the key to free will in that it is able to select from the data presented to it which elements will be allowed to affect action. James also analyzed the individual person into the "I" and the "Me." The Me is made up of the material Me, the social Me, and the spiritual Me. The I holds these aspects of Me together through thought and especially through recollection. Emotions are the feeling or experiencing of a specific bodily state; the bodily state is the basis of the emotion, not the other way around.

Neutral monism. Later in life James coined the term *neutral monist* to describe his philosophical position. He was a monist as opposed to a dualist; that is, he believed that there was only one basic stuff of the universe, not two (such as Descartes's mind and matter). And he was neutral in that he refused to say whether this one stuff was mental or material.

JOSIAH ROYCE

Grass Valley, California (1855–1916). Born in a gold rush mining camp, Royce studied at Berkeley and then spent a year in Germany studying German idealism, by which he was strongly influenced. He earned a Ph.D. at Johns Hopkins University and, with help from William James, secured a temporary teaching post as James's substitute at Harvard. Three years later he was made an assistant professor there, and in 1892 he became professor of the history of philosophy. He and James worked closely as colleagues and friends, and they engaged in continual debate over their opposing philosophical beliefs.

While he remained faithful to idealism, Royce, especially later in his career, sought to ground his philosophy in the more practical and social world and so, in a sense, seek to merge neo-Kantianism with some of the insights of the American pragmatic school. One of the titles he gave to his position was "absolute pragmatism." Equally, he tempered idealism to make room for democratic individualism, a key element of late-nineteenth-century America. He described the Absolute in terms of both thought and experience; it contains all human minds in an interactive network. In ethical and social areas, he made loyalty and community key concepts. He wrote extensively. Two of his best-known works are *The Religious Aspects of Philosophy* (1885) and *The World and the Individual* (1901). His interests included religion, literature, and history as well as metaphysics.

JOHN DEWEY

Burlington, Vermont (1859–1952). After studying at the University of Vermont and Johns Hopkins University, where he wrote a thesis on Kant's psychology, Dewey taught at the University of Michigan (1884–1894). In 1894 he became chairman of the new department of philosophy, psychology, and education at Chicago and was responsible for establishing the Laboratory School, embodying his relatively liberal educational theories. He moved to Columbia University in New York in 1904. From his early Hegelianism, he moved on to develop what he called "pragmatic instrumentalism." Toward the end of his life, his interest moved to religion, art, and politics. He was a prolific writer of articles and books; his collected works (apart from his correspondence) fill thirty-seven volumes. Some of his best-known books are *Democracy and Education* (1916), *Human Nature and Conduct* (1922), *Experience and Nature* (1925), and *The Quest for Certainty* (1929).

Pragmatic instrumentalism.

Basic to all Dewey's philosophy, and therefore to his social and educational work, was the conviction that the value of any philosophy is assessed in terms of its practical usefulness in the community. Dewey criticized philosophers who spent their time exploring obscure issues, however long their philosophical pedigree. He saw no point, for instance, in producing an argument that shows that we cannot have any true knowledge. Rather, we need to build a philosophy that helps support and further the tremendous advances in knowledge and practical living that have come through the sciences. For Dewey thoughts or ideas were always to be linked inseparably with action. Philosophers throughout history have made the mistake, said Dewey, of adopting a "spectator theory of knowledge." But in fact the thinker, including the scientific thinker, is not a detached observer or spectator gathering mere facts, but someone who is involved, an agent, someone whose life is affected by what she or he is investigating. Knowledge can never be an end in itself; it is only ever of value if it enables us to survive or to enrich life. It is thus an "instrument"; it is functional, never merely factual. Its purpose is to affect and improve life, not to build up irrelevant information.

The process of inquiry.

Dewey took over and developed Peirce's stress on the importance of investigation or inquiry, applying it not just to scientific inquiry and problem situations in ordinary life, but to ethics and social issues. He outlined the standard process from the arising of a problem to its resolution in some detail. Normally, as with riding a bike, we do things without invoking a process of thought. Thought comes in when something goes wrong, when there is a problem to be solved, when action is thwarted. First, it formulates the problem, the question that requires an answer. Next, it begins to formulate "hypotheses" that serve as guides to our observations, which may help us to find an answer. Then comes the process, highlighted by Peirce, of working out what consequences will follow from any given hypothesis if it is valid. The final stage is to test (either in action or in theory) the hypothesis and see if the consequences follow. If they do, then we have found the solution to the problem and can be said to have established what action we need to take or to have arrived at the "true" answer to the problem.

Truth.

In a celebrated discussion, Bertrand Russell accused Dewey and the pragmatists of failing to make the vital distinction between the criteria we use to discover if a thing is true and the *meaning* of truth. Dewey, whose concept of meaning was, like Peirce's, wholly in terms of consequent action, saw Russell's stress on the meaning of truth as a typical bit of irrelevant philosophizing that had no practical significance. But he did in the end give ground to Russell and decide to talk in terms of establishing that hypotheses are "warrantedly assertible" rather than "true."

Moral and social philosophy.

Dewey's practical interest also motivated his approach to moral philosophy. He modeled thinking in the realm of values on thinking in the realm of science, using the same process of inquiry. His analysis of the human person followed a similar pattern. There are three elements in human nature: "Impulse" expresses the dynamic and active aspect of our nature; "habits" are the stable patterns that we develop to cope with our impulses and with external pressures; and "intelligence" is the functional activity of solving the problems that arise when habits are disturbed or upset. Dewey also extended this pattern to apply it to social issues, where again habits may be challenged or shaken by internal or external impulses, and where intelligence is required to follow through the process of finding a solution. Both at the personal and the social level, Dewey firmly rejected any "from the top down" type of solution that imposes a doctrinaire moral or social principle. All solutions, he said, need to be worked out "from the bottom up."

Education.

In his theory of education, Dewey

- Strongly opposed the concept of education as something imposed on an unwilling child.
- Believed that children have natural drives that should be harnessed in the process of education.
- Stressed the link between learning and doing.
- Pointed out the value of learning by doing.
- Saw education as a key aspect of life, not a preparation for life.
- Held up scientific inquiry as the model for all other forms of inquiry.
- Applied his principle that any worthwhile thinking arises in the context of problem solving.
- Was committed to starting where the children were at, with their problems, "from the bottom up."
- Majored on the need to develop thought habits and skills that could be applied in all sorts of situations.

TO THINK THROUGH

Does pragmatism represent a realistic acceptance of the limits of human reason, or is it an unjustifiable retreat from asking the big questions that have occupied earlier philosophers?

Can pragmatists claim that the principles of pragmatism are true or "warrantedly assertible"?

For Peirce to point out that science was not discovering facts about the world that can be taken as certain was a radical claim, undermining the huge confidence that most people had in science. Although most philosophers would now agree with Peirce's claim, it is still generally assumed that scientific "facts" are in some sense the paradigm of truth. Why do you think this confidence in science remains so firmly entrenched? Do you think it is valid?

Is James's case concerning "the will to believe" justifiable or just a bit of wishful thinking?

Are thoughts or ideas always to be linked with action? Must knowledge be practically beneficial? Is there a place for "spectator" knowledge?

For Further Study

Murphy, J. P. *Pragmatism: From Peirce to Davidson*. Boulder, Colo.: Westview Press, 1990.

FORTY-TWO

SEARCHING FOR CERTAINTY

FREGE AND RUSSELL

In this chapter we focus on Bertrand Russell, who spent his life trying to establish that, starting from atheistic presuppositions, there is at least something we can know for sure—yet ended up admitting that there was nothing.

MANY ORDINARY PEOPLE BELIEVE THE TWO GREATEST philosophers of the twentieth century were Bertrand Russell and Jean-Paul Sartre. Both were controversial figures who had a high public profile. They wrote prolifically and used the media to express their views on a whole range of subjects, generally with a left-wing bias. Both were prepared to accept the consequences of their beliefs even if it hurt. Though few took the trouble to examine their philosophies in detail, they both appealed strongly to the public imagination as what a true philosopher should be. And both were atheists.

Before studying Russell, we will look briefly at Gottlob Frege, whose work is generally linked with that of Russell, particularly in his earlier phase.

GOTTLOB FREGE

Wismar, Germany (1848–1925). Gottlob Frege (pronounced *fray*-guh) studied at Jena and then Göttingen and returned to Jena to be professor of mathematics. He is generally regarded as the father of twentieth-century logic and a key figure in the shift in interest away from epistemology toward logic and philosophical analysis.

The logical basis of mathematics.
Frege set out to demonstrate that the propositions of arithmetic were such that they could all be derived from the basic principles of logic. This would mean that we could have certainty in arithmetic; its statements would all be valid deductions from logically established first principles. To do this he devised a brilliant way of expressing arithmetic in logical notation. He did this in his 1879 *Begriffsschrift* (Concept Script). He failed, however, to demonstrate that arithmetical propositions could all be deduced from logical first principles. He thought he had done so, but Russell pointed out a fatal flaw in his argument, and he abandoned it.

Meaning.
Nevertheless, work that Frege did in philosophical logic had far-reaching effects in the twentieth century, largely as a result of Russell's interest in it and popularizing of it. Frege made many careful logical distinctions and analyses, for instance, between "argument" and "function" and between "concepts" and "objects." Perhaps his best-known piece of logical analysis was the distinguishing of the "sense" of an expression from its "reference" (or "denotation" or "meaning," *Bedeutung*). Here he was saying in effect that there are two ways a "naming" word or phrase can have a meaning. The "reference" is the straight application of the word to an object or something else. So "the U.S. president" or "my home" each refers directly to things in the world. But besides this familiar form of meaning, there is, said Frege, another form of meaning, the "sense" (*Sinn*). "The U.S. president" and "my home" are more than just labels; there is more to them than that. Each has "sense"; each carries meaning over and above its label value. Frege illustrated this using the planet Venus. Venus seen in the evening is called "the evening star." Seen in the morning, it is called "the morning star." If we operate, says Frege, only on the level of reference, to say, "The morning star is the same as the evening star," would be tautologous, the same as simply saying, "Venus is Venus." But it is not tautologous, because the "sense" of "the morning star" is different from the "sense" of "the evening star."

Another way of seeing the difference is to look at the kind of word or phrase that describes a clearly nonexistent object or person. It has puzzled many philosophers to think of ways words like *unicorn* can have meaning if there is no existing object to which they can refer; some have even ended up suggesting that though there are no actual unicorns, there must be a sort of Platonic-form unicorn somewhere for the word to have meaning. Frege's answer is simple. Neither "unicorn" nor "the present king of France" has a "reference," that is, an existing object to which it refers. But that doesn't stop it from having "sense." So that is how these words have meaning, though it is only part of the meaning that a phrase like "the U.S. president" has.

This analysis can also be usefully applied to an expression like "is good." It doesn't need to have a reference for it to be meaningful, said Frege, since it carries meaning in its "sense" component.

The objectivity of logic. Another emphasis of Frege that has been very influential is his view that the laws of logic are objective, independent of our minds. They are not something created by us as we think and imposed by our minds on our ideas. They would still apply even if no one ever grasped them and followed them.

Context. Similarly, Frege's innovative "context principle," that we shouldn't ask for the meaning of a word in isolation, but only in its context in a sentence, has become a foundational principle of philosophy and hermeneutics.

BERTRAND RUSSELL

Trelleck, Wales (1872–1970). Grandson of a British prime minister and godson of J. S. Mill, Bertrand Russell was born into a titled family. Both of his parents died by the time he was four, and he was brought up by his grandmother, Lady Russell, and given a private education. He studied math and philosophy at Cambridge, then became a fellow of Trinity College, Cambridge, in 1895 and a lecturer in philosophy in 1910, a post he lost in 1916 as a result of his pacifist activities. This didn't deter him, and in 1918 he was found guilty of libeling the British government and the American army and was sent to prison for six months. His most serious philosophical work had been completed by then, but he continued to live a colorful and active life, visiting Russia and living for a time in China, running a number of times unsuccessfully as a Labor candidate for Parliament, engaging in lecture tours of the United States, founding a progressive school, and writing both books and articles.

Russell modified his pacifism in the Second World War, spending most of that era in the United States, where his political and personal views aroused considerable opposition. After the war he settled back in England, writing, broadcasting, and vigorously supporting nuclear disarmament. He married four times. He was awarded the Nobel Prize for literature in 1950. Among his large output of books were *The Principles of Mathematics* (1903), *Principia Mathe-*

matica (with A. N. Whitehead, 1910–13), *The Problems of Philosophy* (1912), *An Enquiry into Meaning and Truth* (1940), *History of Western Philosophy* (1945), and *My Philosophical Development* (1959).

Russell started his philosophical career as an idealist, influenced largely by Bradley, though he didn't follow Bradley in his monism, stressing instead the diversity of things in the world, an emphasis he kept all his life. Another conviction he held all his life was that the scientific approach to knowledge was the best model for philosophical epistemology to follow. By 1898, largely under the influence of G. E. Moore, he abandoned idealism for realism.

The logical basis for mathematics.
Unaware that Frege had already done the same thing, Russell sought to show that math (not just arithmetic) could be shown to be built securely on a foundation of pure logic. Like Frege, he set about this by translating basic mathematical concepts, including number, into purely logical concepts. He published the results in *The Principles of Mathematics*. In *Principia Mathematica*, a much larger and more complex work, written jointly with Whitehead, he sought to build on this by definitively establishing mathematical principles on the basis of logic. There has been considerable debate over the extent to which he succeeded; not all the problems that arose were able to be solved (for example, problems associated with infinity), though Russell for a time was confident that a solution would be found. Now, however, it is generally held that Kurt Gödel's arguments, published in 1931, have shown that the project to establish all the truths of math on the basis of logic alone is impossible, and Russell accepted this.

Philosophical logic and the theory of descriptions.
Russell coined the phrase "philosophical logic" to describe his application of the logical principles that apply in math to broader philosophical issues. In his "theory of descriptions," he tackled the issue Frege was facing when he distinguished reference from sense in the meaning of naming words and phrases. Russell defined a description as a phrase that describes something or someone by a specific property, such as "the author of *Waverley*" or "the golden mountain" or "the present president of the United States." Phrases like these, as we have seen with "the present king of France," can cause puzzles in that they are meaningful, and so seem to denote something, yet we all know there is no present king of France or existing golden mountain to be denoted. Russell used his logical analysis to rephrase sentences containing such descriptions in a way that avoided the problem. Thus "the author of *Waverley* was Scott" he interpreted as:

There is an entity c such that the statement "x wrote *Waverley*" is true if x is c, and false otherwise; moreover c is Scott.

Similarly, "The golden mountain does not exist" is to be interpreted as:

There is no entity c such that "x is golden and mountainous" is true when x is c, but not otherwise.

This analysis, says Russell, avoids the problem of the apparent "existence" of nonexistent entities; it also allows us to predicate existence only of things designated by descriptions. On the basis of "The author of *Waverley* was Scott" we can say, "The author of *Waverley* exists," but we cannot say, "Scott exists."

Logical atomism.

Russell's commitment to logic found expression in his basic ontology, which he called "logical atomism." Ultimate reality is factual. But it is not one integrated factual whole. It is a vast number of facts, just as the world is made up of a vast number of atoms—hence the name "logical atomism." We encounter these facts in our empirical experience. Russell is here reacting against the view of the idealists that we can only understand the parts, that is, our individual experiences, with reference to the whole, that is, the Absolute. His response was that there is no whole to refer to. All we have is our isolated individual experiences—a vast number of them, each lasting only a moment, and each one independent of all the rest. The task of the philosopher, as logical analyst, is to examine the logical relations between these atomic data.

Empiricism and the scientific worldview.

In his approach to the general problems of philosophy, Russell was an empiricist, totally committed to the scientific worldview and the method of science. Beliefs are to be based on objective observations, which are able to give us "scientific truthfulness." This is possible in philosophy, he said, if we clear away unsupported theories and metaphysical speculations and put into practice the "powerful logical technique" he found in mathematics. He was fond of using Ockham's razor, which he paraphrased, "Whenever possible, substitute constructions out of known entities for inferences to unknown entities." Applying the clarity of logical mathematical analysis to philosophical problems can give us answers, he believed, that "have the quality of science rather than of philosophy."

Whatever his early hopes, by the time he wrote *Human Knowledge: Its Scope and Limits* in 1948, Russell was willing to accept that the scientific worldview, however successful its logical method, was itself founded on assumptions or "postulates" we are unable to establish by logical proof; we have to accept them in faith. They include assumptions about permanence, continuity, and causality. We cannot establish these by empirical observation, because they are themselves the basis for our trust in the validity of our empirical observations. On his Ockham's razor principle, Russell felt it was preferable to assume these postulates than to seek other explanations, such as the existence of some metaphysical principle or of God.

Besides conceding that the scientific worldview rests on a basis that is ultimately neither logical nor empirical, Russell was aware that, as a philosophical method, it was limited in its range of application. Not all the problems philosophers face could be approached this way. There is a "vast field," traditionally part of philosophy, in which he was aware his scientific approach would not work. This field includes values, ethics, politics, religion, and issues of how we should live. These things philosophy must leave on one side; it doesn't have the competence to make pronouncements about them. For instance, Russell said that philosophy can neither prove nor disprove religious beliefs. The human intellect, using science and logic, simply has to accept that it cannot find answers in these areas. Russell thus redefined philosophy, limiting it to the scientific and the logical or mathematical. In keeping with this, and no doubt reacting against his early idealism, he opposed any attempt to build a philosophical system in the traditional sense.

Ethics. If philosophy, as Russell claimed, has nothing to say in the areas of value, ethics, and the like, on what basis do we make moral or value decisions? Russell's answer was in terms of desire, emotion, attitudes, wishes, or feelings. When I say, "It is wrong to possess nuclear weapons," I am not making a statement that can be set alongside a "scientific" statement like "Britain and America possess nuclear weapons." In his early work, Russell went so far as to say the first statement was not a genuine statement at all; later he conceded it was a statement but only a statement about the speaker's feelings or attitudes, not about anything in the objective world.

TO THINK THROUGH

Is it possible to reconcile Russell's strong moral stances over pacifism and nuclear weapons with his philosophical approach to ethics?

Though strongly committed to the method of science, Russell seems to have held back from applying it in the more extreme ways that some of his students and contemporaries did. He never joined the logical positivists, he criticized the pragmatists, and he called the approach of the narrow linguistics philosophers "the metaphysics of savages." Yet it is often the more extreme views that get publicity and win followers; the influence of Russell's later philosophy has been small compared with that of Wittgenstein. Do you think philosophers should push their views to their full implications?

For Further Study

Slater, J. G. *Russell*. Oxford: Oxford University Press, 1994.

FORTY-THREE

SCIENCE AND SENSE

FROM LOGICAL POSITIVISM
TO KARL POPPER

In this chapter we trace some further stages in the decline of the philosophical dominance of the modern scientific worldview as we look at the rise and fall of logical positivism and Karl Popper's philosophy of science.

YOU SHOW ME GOD, AND I'LL BELIEVE IN HIM." BUT, OF course, God isn't quite the same as cousin Griselda's dog, which howls every time the president appears on the television. We can't see God or hear him in the same way. True, many people claim to have experienced him. The snag is that they describe their experiences in terms of feelings or faith or supernatural activity and not in terms of things that are empirically verifiable in a scientific sense. Thus they carry no weight with the scientifically minded skeptic.

I'm writing this late on a summer evening. It is already twilight. All day dozens of swallows have been flying around and around the huge oak tree outside my window, catching the many insects it harbors. One or two swallows remain, but as it gets darker, they'll give up and go away to roost. And then the bats will come, flying in the same air space, catching the insects in the dark.

Said a swallow to a bat, "How on earth do you see to catch the insects in the dark?"

"See?" said the bat. "I've never experienced seeing. Seeing is a meaningless concept."

"Then how do you catch the insects?" repeated the swallow.

"The usual way," said the bat. "By radar."

"Radar?" said the swallow. "I've never experienced radar. Radar is a meaningless concept."

The story of logical positivism is the story of an attempt to impose the early-twentieth-century scientific way of viewing the world in areas where it was simply inappropriate. It was assumed that the method that had proved intensely successful in many (though by no means all) areas of natural science could be applied not just to the human sciences, as others had sought to do, but to every other part of human life as well, and in particular to philosophy.

LOGICAL POSITIVISM

In the 1920s and 1930s a group of Austrian and German scientists, social scientists, mathematicians, and philosophers formed a discussion group at the University of Vienna called the Vienna Circle. They shared a common interest in science and its significance for philosophy and a common desire to break free from the influence of Kantian and Hegelian idealism, which was still in vogue on the Continent. Well-known names in the Circle were **Rudolf Carnap** (1891–1970), **Kurt Gödel** (1906–1978), **Otto Neurath** (1882–1945), **Friedrich Waismann** (1896–1959), and **Moritz Schlick** (1882–1936). Though Russell never identified himself with the movement, he had an indirect influence on its development in that the members of the circle were strongly influenced by Wittgenstein's *Tractatus*, and Wittgenstein had gained many of his ideas from studying with Russell from 1911 to 1914. The movement spread to Britain and the United States and was very influential up to the 1950s among empirically and analytically minded thinkers, after which it declined rapidly. The main person to publicize the views of the Circle in Britain was A. J. Ayer.

The elimination of metaphysics. Like Russell, the members of
the Circle, known from 1931 as logical positivists, were committed empiricists and were enthusiastic about the resources of science and logic for the whole of our philosophical understanding. As a result, they were implacably opposed to anything "metaphysical," that is, anything that couldn't be established on the principles of logic and science. They saw their task as eliminating all metaphysical elements and establishing a worldview that was built on the logic of science alone.

Verification. To do this they used the concept of verification. Assuming, as empiricists, that the only sources of knowledge are the items of our experience, they concluded that for any assertion to be meaningful it must either be analytic or such that it can be verified through some experience or observation. An analytic statement, as Kant had pointed out, is one whose truth or falsehood depends entirely on the terms it contains, such as "All bachelors are unmarried." To have meaning any nonanalytic statement must be verifiable; if it is unverifiable, it is meaningless. It is non-sense, that is, it makes no sense; it doesn't communicate. Though it appears to say something it in fact says nothing at all.

The verification principle.

To clarify their concept of verification, the logical positivists developed what they called the verification principle. At first it was stated in a "strong" form, requiring conclusive verification, either actual or potential. So, for the statement "This tree is fifty feet tall" to be meaningful, it must be at least possible to measure the tree definitively and so prove conclusively that it is fifty feet tall. This, however, was too strict a definition, since it was clear that most scientific principles could never be conclusively verified.

A modified form of the principle replaced conclusive verifiability with conclusive falsifiability. Though we can never establish that all metals expand when heated, it is conceivable that we might discover a metal that contracts when heated, thus conclusively falsifying the statement. Given that, it can be accepted as meaningful. However, this form of the verification principle proved to be inadequate, since, as philosophers well know, it is always possible to bring in skeptical arguments about dreaming or hallucinating or a malignant demon to challenge the concept of conclusive falsifiability. How do we know we aren't hallucinating when we observe the contraction of this special metal?

So the verification principle had to be pared down yet further, to a "weak" form that simply said that for a statement to be meaningful it must be possible to think of some empirical evidence that could have a bearing on its truth or falsity. This seems a workable principle, but it turned out to be inadequate for the purposes of the logical positivists. For instance, it is perfectly open to someone who believes that God exists—a "metaphysical" belief the logical positivists were particularly eager to dismiss as meaningless—to satisfy the criterion in terms, say, of a Damascus Road experience or an answer to prayer.

There was a further major problem with the verification principle in that, for all its usefulness in eliminating metaphysical statements, it turned out itself to be nothing short of a metaphysical statement, in that it cannot be empirically verified. Just as Russell had to accept that his whole scientific and logical edifice was built on "faith," so logical positivism was not able to exist without "metaphysics."

Quite apart from the philosophical weaknesses in the logical positivists' approach, its considerable popularity waned rapidly because of two additional features. The first was a growing dissatisfaction with such a reductionist worldview, coupled with a growing disillusionment with logic and science as the sole arbiters of all thought and knowledge. The second was the development of science itself and of the philosophical understanding of what science is actually doing. Elements of subnuclear physics, for example, did not appear to follow the standard scientific paradigm assumed by logical positivism, and by the 1960s philosophers of science were realizing that the traditional stress on the rationality of the scientific worldview was open to serious challenge.

Nevertheless, logical positivism had a powerful impact for a brief period. It was seen as a most effective tool for sweeping away the cobwebs of metaphysical beliefs, particularly by those who wished to undermine the hold of religion and traditional principles of morality. Among those who adopted and proclaimed it with missionary zeal was A. J. Ayer.

A. J. AYER

London (1910–1989). A. J. Ayer's father was Swiss and his mother was Belgian. He was educated at Eton and Oxford. Influenced by Russell and Wittgenstein's *Tractatus*, he went to Vienna in 1932 and spent a short time studying the ideas of the logical positivists. He returned to lecture at Oxford and published an enthusiastic and popular version of logical positivism in *Language, Truth and Logic* (1936). After war service in military intelligence, he became professor of the philosophy of mind and logic at London in 1946, and from 1959 he was professor of logic at Oxford. As time went by, he increasingly modified his acceptance of logical positivism without abandoning its original vision. He was a wholehearted empiricist, totally committed to the scientific worldview, full of faith in human reason, an enthusiastic atheist, politically left-wing, a popular broadcaster and public figure, and a great admirer of Russell. He was knighted in 1970. His best-known books are *Language, Truth and Logic* (1936; second edition, 1946), *The Foundations of Empirical Knowledge* (1940), and *The Problem of Knowledge* (1956).

The solution of all philosophical problems.

In *Language, Truth and Logic*, Ayer claimed to be using the insights of Hume, Russell, and the logical positivists to solve all the philosophical problems of the preceding two thousand years and more. He did this by proposing that everything be judged by the language and method of science. What did not pass that test was to be rejected, not as false, but as meaningless. In this way, he felt, all the traditional problems of philosophy can be shown to be pseudo-problems and so dismissed. On the grounds of the verification principle, he dismissed all the statements and concerns of metaphysics, theology, ethics, aesthetics, and other issues of value as meaningless; thus all the problems associated with them are unreal and can be ignored. Ayer conceded that moral statements and value judgments and the like do appear to be meaningful in that they do seem to communicate something. But in keeping with his definition, he still insisted they were meaningless; the appearance of meaning arises because these statements express our feelings or emotions. If I say, "Murder is wrong," I'm expressing my negative feelings about murder, no doubt with the hope that whoever hears me will also feel negative about murder. But I'm not actually saying anything meaningful.

The role of philosophy.

Ayer rejected the traditional role of philosophy as giving us understanding about the world or about reality and help on how to live. For him understanding about the world is given by science, not philosophy, and there is no further "reality" that lies behind scientific facts. Nor can philosophy involve itself in ethics or social or political theory, since statements in these areas, like those of metaphysics and theology, are meaningless. So philosophy's role has to be reduced to analysis and clarification. It analyzes concepts and definitions, and it clarifies our ordinary language and the terms of science. So it contributes nothing new to our knowledge; all it can do is help us better understand "scientific" knowledge.

TO THINK THROUGH

Logical positivism had a profound impact in the second quarter of the twentieth century. Many felt its case was unassailable. Why do you think this was so? Would any of your contemporaries accept logical positivism as a worldview? Why do you think it feels so alien to many people today?

Ludwig Wittgenstein dominates both ends of the story of logical positivism. His *Tractatus* was the handbook of the early positivists. But while they were enthusiastically applying his principles, he was already aware of their inadequacy. His later philosophy was to fill the vacuum left by logical positivism's collapse. But before we turn to Wittgenstein, we will look at two other significant figures in the empirical tradition up to the middle decades of the twentieth century, the Englishman G. E. Moore, and the Austrian Jew Karl Popper.

G. E. MOORE

London (1873–1958). Educated at Trinity College, Cambridge, G. E. Moore was fellow there from 1898 to 1904. After some years in Edinburgh, he returned to Cambridge as lecturer and then professor of philosophy from 1925. Like Russell, with whom he worked closely, he moved from philosophical idealism to realism and was a key figure in the development of the analytical philosophical approach. Also like Russell, he spent much of the Second World War in America.

Common sense. Moore was a great defender of common sense, arguing that where common sense and philosophical dogma clashed it was usually wisest to follow common sense, something that has been well tested and which we are experienced in applying.

The naturalistic fallacy. One of Moore's most influential books was *Principia Ethica* (1903), in which he attacked what he called "the naturalistic fallacy." It is a mistake, he said, to define ethical concepts like "good" in terms of something in the "natural" world, such as "the greatest happiness of the greatest number," or "what furthers the evolutionary process," or "what satisfies desire." "Goodness" cannot be reduced to any "natural" category. It is in a category of its own, which we access through intuition, as opposed to through reason or empirical observation.

KARL POPPER

Vienna (1902–1994). Popper's parents were Jews who became Lutherans. He studied at the University of Vienna, concentrating on math and physics. He was lecturer in philosophy at Christchurch, New Zealand, from 1937 to 1945. In 1945 he went to the London School of Economics, where he became professor of logic and scientific method in 1949. A keen supporter of left-wing politics in his youth, he later opposed the excesses of socialist and Marxist politics. His opposition to totalitarianism led him to attack some of the key ideas of Plato, Hegel, and Marx. He was committed to the scientific worldview but never joined the Vienna Circle or the logical positivists. He became a British subject in 1945. Among his writings are *Logic der Forschung* (1934), translated as *The Logic of Scientific Discovery* (1959; revised edition, 1968), *The Open Society and Its Enemies* (1945), and *The Poverty of Historicism* (1957).

Popper and logical positivism.
Like Russell and the logical positivists, Popper was fully committed to the centrality of science and its worldview. But he disagreed with the positivists' view that all nonscientific statements are meaningless. This was partly because he didn't share their approach to issues of meaning as such; but it was also because he didn't believe that any scientific statement was verifiable in any of the ways the positivists required. Thus he was willing to allow for the meaningfulness of ethical and metaphysical statements.

Science, induction, and knowledge.
Underlying Popper's *The Logic of Scientific Discovery* was a conviction that in the post-Einsteinian age we need a new understanding of how science operates. The old view, held since Bacon and beloved of the positivists, was that science was able, through careful observation, the forming of hypotheses, and experimental confirmation, to give us certain knowledge. Popper used the example of Newton to show that this was not so. When Newton advanced his theories, they explained the behavior of the planets perfectly except for some discrepancies in the behavior of Uranus. These discrepancies could be explained, however, by postulating the existence of an unknown planet in a specific location. Sure enough, Neptune was then discovered in that location. This was universally seen as establishing the truth of Newton's system. However, said Popper, Einstein is now accepted as showing that Newton's system wasn't true after all. Even such impressive confirmation was unable to establish it in any definitive way. Thus no scientific theory, says Popper, can ever be established; there are no grounds for having the confidence in scientific facts that people have felt for so long.

More specifically, induction as a method of finding truth is discredited; no amount of confirmatory observations can establish truth. Further, a large number of confirmations of a scientific hypothesis doesn't even increase the probability of that hypothesis being correct. Scientists for the most part had been willing to accept that induction can't definitively prove a hypothesis but had claimed that repeated confirmation made the truth of the hypothesis more likely. Popper, however, challenged this. Given that just one black swan exists, the truth of the hypothesis "All swans are white" is no more established by observing a million white swans than by observing ten.

Falsification.

Though we thus have to abandon any hope of the confirmation of hypotheses, refutation or falsification is still possible. The observation of one black swan will refute the hypothesis. Thus observations are to be seen as tests, with a view to falsification, instead of means of confirmation. The scientist starts with conjecture or intuition and then devises tests in an attempt to refute it; until it fails a test, the theory is allowed to stand as a working hypothesis. If there are other different conjectures that explain the data equally well and have not been refuted, choice between the conjectures becomes a matter of personal preference.

Popper also used his concepts of testing and refutation to attack what he called "pseudo-science," in which people claimed to be making "scientific" statements but failed to subject them to testing or refused to accept the refutation of a counter-instance. He argued that both Marxists and Freudians were guilty of this. Marxists were guilty because they refused to abandon Marxism, even though many of the predictions Marx had based on his theories have turned out to be false. The theories of Freud and Adler, though they claimed they were "scientific," were such that no significant testing of them had ever been done.

Popper applied his concept of the testing and falsification of theories to his social and political philosophy, arguing for an "open" society in which testing and rejecting of social and political theories could take place, as opposed to an authoritarian or totalitarian one, in which such activities were stifled. In *The Open Society and Its Enemies*, he particularly attacked the myth of a process of inevitable historical development as propagated by Hegel and applied by Marx. The mark of an open society is not democracy as such, but the opportunity to dismiss the rulers without bloodshed or violence.

TO THINK THROUGH

The scientific approach to knowledge has been extremely fruitful, whether or not we are to take it as the paradigm for all knowledge. But we have moved a long way from the Enlightenment concept of what scientists are doing when they make statements about the world around us. How would you describe what you think they are doing?

HOW LANGUAGE WORKS

THE TWO PHILOSOPHIES
OF WITTGENSTEIN

> In this chapter we examine the role of philosophy as understood by Ludwig Wittgenstein, who limited it to helping us understand what we are doing when we use language.

LUDWIG WITTGENSTEIN

Vienna (1889–1951). Ludwig Wittgenstein was brought up as a Roman Catholic in a wealthy and cultured home where Brahms and Mahler were regular visitors. He showed early ability in engineering rather than academics, and he studied engineering at Linz, Berlin, and Manchester. An interest in math and the recommendation of Frege led him to study under Russell at Cambridge in 1912; this in turn led him to work out his own answer to the problems of logic and philosophy. In 1913 he built himself a remote hut in Norway to work on this answer, but when war broke out in 1914, he joined the Austrian army. All through the war he continued to work at his philosophy and eventually published the results in 1921 in his *Tractatus Logico-Philosophicus*. The English translation was published 1922. This book immediately became foundational for the thinkers of the Vienna Circle and for logical positivism generally. Wittgenstein, however, did not join the Circle. Assuming that the *Tractatus* had provided the final answer to all philosophical problems, he gave up philosophy and became a primary school teacher in Austria until 1926. Realizing there was more philosophical work for him to do, he returned to Cambridge in 1929, eventually being appointed professor of philosophy there in 1939. During the Second World War he worked as a hospital porter and a laboratory assistant. He resigned as professor in 1947 and died of cancer in 1951.

Apart from the *Tractatus* Wittgenstein published nothing substantial in his lifetime. His *Philosophical Investigations* was published in 1953 after his death and has had a huge influence. Several collections of his notes have also been published since his death. Both the philosophy of the *Tractatus* and his later philosophy have had a wide and profound impact. Disciplines especially affected by his later ideas are philosophy, particularly linguistic philosophy, literary studies, and the social sciences, but applications of his ideas have been made in just about every other area, including theology, aesthetics, and politics. More than seven thousand books and articles have been published expounding and developing his ideas. Wittgenstein was an enigmatic figure; though apparently an atheist, he frequently wrote about God with considerable depth of feeling.

Wittgenstein's philosophy divides into two clear parts. His early philosophy is that of the *Tractatus*. His later work dates from the late 1920s, when he repudiated the views of the *Tractatus* and set to work developing a new approach. This is most clearly seen in the *Philosophical Investigations*. Though it is right to contrast the two philosophies, common elements link them. In both, Wittgenstein is exploring the significance of language for human thinking and life and seeking to establish the right uses of language. But his two answers to that quest are very different.

THE TRACTATUS

The picture theory of language.
The *Tractatus* set out to develop a theory of how language works and to define its limits. Wittgenstein agreed with Frege that sentences rather than isolated words convey meaning; words are only meaningful when they are functioning in a sentence. Apart from the statements of logic, which are tautologous, sentences are to be seen as attempts to picture facts. We use language to represent states of affairs in the world, and we choose language—that is, words specifically selected and arranged in a certain way—that corresponds to reality in the world. In other words, reality shapes our language. The cat sitting on the mat shapes "The cat is on the mat." If the cat is on the chair, reality shapes "The cat is on the chair." If the cat is under the chair, reality shapes "The cat is under the chair." Because reality

shapes the structure of our language, we can safely accept that by examining the structure of language, we can discover the structure of reality.

Wittgenstein didn't claim that all sentences express the structure of reality, since many sentences in ordinary language are imprecise or poorly constructed. But, like Russell, he believed that sentences could always be restated in a logically pure form. He called a sentence stated in this logical way an "elementary" sentence, and it was these he claimed accurately pictured reality. All elementary sentences help us picture reality, in his theory, even if they are false; their logic is such that they give a picture of potential as well as actual states of affairs.

Wittgenstein's picture theory of language was designed to analyze language about facts in the world around us. As such it was inapplicable to areas of discourse that weren't concerned with the kind of facts that interested the scientists. Thus language about ethics, religion, aesthetics, the self, or even about philosophy or meaning itself was excluded. While the logical positivists were eager to accept this conclusion, Wittgenstein found it profoundly disturbing. It made the things that were for him most important in life inaccessible to language. "Whereof we cannot speak, thereof we must be silent." In his second philosophy, developed from the late 1920s onward, he tackled the problem of developing an understanding of language that reinstated them.

THE LATER WITTGENSTEIN

Language in use. In his later period Wittgenstein made three key changes to his earlier thinking. In the first place, he rejected the picture theory of language and adopted an approach that saw the significance of language in its use. Language is not the expression of a formal static relationship between us and the world. Rather, our relationship with the world is alive and active; we constantly are doing things with words, using them as tools in all sorts of ways. We don't just make factual statements. We joke, command, complain, advise, express our feelings, request, encourage, and so on. All these are activities, part of living, forms of life. Our understanding of language, said Wittgenstein, must be rooted in this activity, in language actually being used, rather than in the introspective investigation of our mental processes or in some artificial philosophical laboratory where words are dissected and analyzed totally out of their life context.

Language games. Second, following from this, Wittgenstein rejected the idea that there is just one way of understanding what is happening when we use language. On the contrary, we use language in many different ways. "Scientific" fact statements are just one way of using language among many. Wittgenstein referred to the many different ways of using language as "language games." The metaphor of games was a very fruitful one. Just as there is a wide range of different games, from football to cards and from musical chairs to tiddlywinks, so there is a wide range of uses of language. And just as the way we play different games varies and follows different rules, so different uses of language operate in different ways and follow different principles. The rules of tennis don't apply in hunt-the-thimble. Nor do the rules of scientific discourse apply in ethical or theological discourse.

Even individual words don't have fixed meanings in that they can be used in a variety of ways. Sometimes it isn't even possible to find a core meaning, some sort of essential key definition. Wittgenstein pointed out that the word *game* is like that; there is no "essence" of game, no key feature that belongs to all games. We may think there is, but Wittgenstein challenges us to find it. Many games are competitive, but some are not. Many involve several players, but some need only one. Many are leisure-time pursuits, but others are deadly serious. And so on. All we can say is that there is a "family resemblance" among the various uses of the word, and that, for Wittgenstein, is all we need to say.

This lack of a fixed meaning or essence in at least some words or concepts is particularly significant when we come to look at words like "good" that have been debated by philosophers since Plato. Socrates seems to have assumed that there is a single fixed "essence" of goodness, something that ties together all its different uses and is therefore key to our understanding of it. Philosophers ever since have followed Socrates' lead and tried to analyze the essence of goodness. Wittgenstein, by contrast, tells us not to look for any such key essence of goodness but to look at the range of ways we use the term. This is what philosophers should be doing, seeing how we actually use words in all the varieties of ordinary language.

Language and life.

A third key difference between the later and the earlier Wittgenstein has echoes of Kant's Copernican revolution. Instead of reality shaping our language, as it does in the *Tractatus*, in the later Wittgenstein the emphasis is on the way our use of language structures our understanding of the world. It is our language that provides the structure for our understanding. In fact, we could put it even more strongly. Without language we couldn't think or experience anything. We have to have a word "table" to be able to think of or experience a table. Language is foundational to all of thought and life.

Further, rather than providing us with just one fixed structure for understanding the world, language offers us a wide range of structures. So our understanding of the world will depend on the structure we choose to use, the game we choose to play. If we choose to play the "scientific" game, we will see the world one way. If we choose to play the theology game, we will see it differently. And, according to Wittgenstein, it isn't possible to say that one game is more correct than another. Nor do we need to try and justify or explain why we play one game rather than another. All we should do, said Wittgenstein, is accept that we do play them. They are a part of life, and that alone is sufficient justification. Indeed, given Wittgenstein's theory, not only do we not need to justify one in preference to another, we simply couldn't do so if we tried, since there is no way we can step outside the pattern of language and its games to make an objective judgment.

However, Wittgenstein wouldn't have accepted that this opens the door to total relativism. Though we can choose to use language in a number of ways, we don't have freedom to invent the rules that govern any specific use of language. Language is a social thing; we don't shape its rules—we learn them from other people. There may be a certain amount of flexibility in the rules, but it is far from total. So our use of language is controlled by something outside of us. Language is public and shared; it can't be private and personal to the individual. Indeed, the root cause of philosophical problems is the failure to observe the established rules for the use of a term or concept. For example, we take a concept like the existence of God, which belongs to theological discourse, and try to treat it as though it belonged to scientific discourse, seeking to establish the existence of God as we would the existence of dinosaurs or the far side of the moon. The answer to such philosophical problems is to go back to the forms of life in which the specific terms or concepts are used and see how they are appropriately used and thus realize that the problem has arisen through inappropriate use.

Thus the conclusions of the later Wittgenstein about the role of philosophy are not all that far removed from his views in the *Tractatus*. In both periods he greatly limited the task of the philosopher. In no way is it to develop an explanatory system or to answer life's questions. Rather, it is to clear out of the way the pseudo-questions that the wrong use of philosophy has raised, through careful observation and description of how language is actually used.

TO THINK THROUGH

Like Russell and the logical positivists, Wittgenstein in both his early and late philosophies put very narrow limits on what philosophers are actually permitted to do. These limits mean in effect that almost all philosophers before Wittgenstein were engaged in illicit activity practically all the time. Is such radicalism justifiable?

The later Wittgenstein rejected his earlier view, that language pictures reality, for the view that language is a tool we use. Are the two incompatible? Can you think of a way in which we could accept his later insights into our use of language and still hold on to a belief that things in the real world at least play some part in the shaping of our language about them?

For Further Study

Fogelin, R. J. *Wittgenstein*. London: Routledge, 1995.

FORTY-FIVE

THREE MISTAKES OF THE MODERN PERIOD

This chapter is a kind of interlude, looking back and analyzing why the modern approach didn't work. In some ways it also prepares the ground for the next few chapters as we work our way toward postmodernism.

LOGICAL POSITIVISM AND THE MOVEMENTS ALLIED TO IT were the last major attempt to fulfill the Enlightenment or modern vision described by Descartes, of using reason, as expressed in the scientific worldview, to "discover a practical philosophy" that would make us "lords and possessors of nature." The story of philosophy in the rest of the twentieth century is effectively one of retreat. Philosophers had to accept, with Russell and Wittgenstein, that reason can't do what the moderns wanted it to do. If it has any role, it is a very limited one. At best it can analyze our language. It can't answer our questions or tell us how to live. Not surprisingly, such an admission has led both to a general disillusionment with philosophy and to an outburst of irrationalism.

Before we turn to other philosophical approaches to see how they responded to the failure of the Enlightenment program, let's look at what I see as the three great mistakes of the modern, or Enlightenment, period. I'll state them pretty strongly. You don't have to agree with them, but you may want to keep them in mind as we continue the story of the death of philosophy in the twentieth century.

THE COPERNICAN REVOLUTION

The first great mistake was the Copernican revolution. Though the term was first applied by Kant, the revolution in fact took place much earlier. It marked the shift from objectivity to subjectivity. Bacon, Locke, and Descartes insisted that human beings are the key to everything, that our reason is the test of reality. Kant put the individual mind at the center of the universe, where Locke and the others had put the individual reason.

This in fact was exactly the reverse of what Copernicus had done. He had taken planet Earth, until then seen as the center of the solar system, and given it a much more lowly role. For him, we ceased to be the center; something bigger and more important was the true center. But the Enlightenment did the opposite. It made us the center, the key to everything. Ultimately, I suggest, there are only two options: Either God is the key to all that is, or we are. The medieval period accepted the first. The modern period explored the second and found that it leads to the death of philosophy.

A new Copernican revolution is needed, a true Copernican revolution, reversing the tragic mistake of the Enlightenment and admitting we are not the center of the universe.

THE UNWILLINGNESS TO ACCEPT THE GIVEN

The second mistake of the modern period, linked to the first, was the unwillingness to accept the given. The story is told about Bertrand Russell that when, as a boy, he was being taught geometry, he refused to accept its basic axioms, since they couldn't be proved. When told that he had no option but to accept them, he grudgingly agreed to accept them provisionally in order to get on with the geometry lesson. Later in life, of course, he came to the realization that none of our basic axioms, whether in geometry, science, or life in general, could be proved, and that we have no option but to accept them as given. But his unwillingness to do so was typical of the Enlightenment mind-set.

A key issue in the modern period, for example, was the problem of perception and in particular the problem of illusion. As we have seen, the argument was this: I put a straight stick partly under water, and it appears bent. I seem to be seeing a bent stick. But what I am seeing is unreliable, because I in fact know the stick is still straight. If that perception is unreliable, how am I to know that all my other perceptions aren't unreliable? If I can be deceived once, I can be deceived all the time. Therefore I can't ever accept what is given in perception. All I can know is my inner experience, of a stick, a tree, or a table.

I can never allow myself to move from that experience to something outside of me, something in the real world, something given.

There are, of course, many answers to this kind of argument. People have been putting straight sticks in water from the dawn of time and have had no problem at all in coping with the result. Ask any of them. None of them will reply, "The fact that the stick looks bent leads me to conclude that none of my perceptions are reliable, so I have to abandon belief in the external world." Much more likely they will say, "Despite the effect being half in the water has on the appearance of the stick, I am still convinced that there is a real stick and that it really is straight. Maybe I don't understand why it appears bent, but I am prepared to accept that there is an explanation. The fact that I can't explain it makes no difference to the objective nature of the real world any more than the fact that I have only ever seen this side of the moon makes any difference to the real existence of the other side of the moon."

Descartes had another answer to the skepticism that the argument from illusion was thought to produce. He got it from the medieval period and in using it was actually going against the modern trend of finding all explanation inside ourselves. For this reason his answer was specifically rejected by later modernists. It was "God would not let me be deceived." In other words, the answer to skepticism about the world around us is God. He is the foundation for knowledge and truth about what is given and is also their guarantor.

It wasn't just in the area of perception that Enlightenment philosophers chose to question and reject what is given. They followed the same policy in the area of ethics. Socrates had assumed that there is such a thing as virtue or goodness, that it is a given. The task before us is not to create or to shape it. Rather, it is to explore and develop our understanding of it so that we can put it into practice. The modern period also started with the assumption that virtue was a given, but the demand that everything should be subject to human reason soon meant that the nature and givenness of virtue and even of the concept of morality were called in question. The outcome of this questioning has been the abandonment of virtue as a given and the retreat into moral relativism.

The same process can be seen in the attitude to God and his revelation of himself to us. The early modern period inherited the medieval legacy of confidence in a God who not only created the universe, but who loves it and gives it meaning and purpose, and who communicates with it. Science was seen as "thinking God's thoughts after him." Jesus and the Bible were accepted as specific ways in which God has revealed himself and his thoughts to us. But rather than continuing to accept these as given, the Enlightenment mind-set insisted that these too should be subject to human reason. And the dominance of the "scientific" worldview, with its assumption that everything must be explained without reference to the supernatural, soon challenged and removed all supernatural elements from God and his revelation, thus emptying them of their content.

This issue confronts us today in the area of meaning and language. Rightly we have come to realize that meaning is not totally objective. Just as two observers never see a table in exactly the same way—each will have a slightly different perspective on its shape and so on—so they will have different understandings of the meaning of *table*. Here, for example, is Tom. Next to his cradle was a solid oak table, strong, dependable, secure. As a child he sat on the table and had happy and positive experiences of tabledom. As a growing boy he continued to have positive experiences. Good meals were spread on the table. His weekly pocket money was lying there on the table when he came downstairs on Saturday morning. And so on. Alice, on the other hand, has had only negative experiences of tables. Her cradle was placed next to a rickety old table whose constant creaking terrified her. As a young child she fell off a table. Another table collapsed on her when she crawled underneath it. She sat at a table hour after hour struggling in vain to understand her schoolwork. And so on. So Tom's concept of *table* will be warm and positive; Alice's will be rejecting and negative.

The conclusion of many is that since Tom and Alice's experiences contribute something to their understanding of *table*, they therefore create the meaning of the word. There is no given. There is no objective meaning of *table*. Such a conclusion is, of course, perverse. Granted, Tom and Alice both bring their own understanding of tabledom to their interpretation of the word or concept. But that does not prevent there being an objective core. The table remains a given, however much they may add their subjective feelings. The basic meaning of the word remains a given, whatever they may add to it. In fact, we learn to compensate for our subjectivity: "To me the table is brown, but I know I have a bit of color blindness, so I can accept that it looks red to you." "I do actually have a phobia of rickety tables, but I can accept that this one is secure." "Looking from where I'm standing at the moment, the table looks rhomboid, but I accept that that is just my perspective and the table is actually rectangular."

In all these areas we have a choice among three positions. We can take the straightforward position, which can be called naive or common sense, according to the way we view it. It simply accepts the given and assumes that the given as we experience it is as it is. This, of course, is the position that philosophers have questioned; we would love to accept things as they appear to us, but, they say, we simply can't; the problems that arise are too great.

A second position is the skeptical or relativist position. If we have to reject the first position, then we must conclude that we are wholly controlled by our subjective experience; that is all we have to go on. I never see the object in the world; I only ever experience my visual perceptions. There are no such things as objective goodness, meaning, or value; there is only what I create.

But, of course, we don't have to swing to the extreme of the second position just because we reject the first. If we don't find Annabella at the North Pole, we don't have to conclude that she is at the South Pole. There is plenty of middle ground in between where we might find her. And there is, of course, a perfectly valid middle position between the first and second. It holds that my subjective input affects my experience of the world but doesn't control it. There are two factors at work. There is the given, something external to me, which I don't control. Rather, in a sense, it controls me. I'm subject to it. I can't change it or cause it to go away just by the exercise of my reason. The table continues to stand in the corner of the room whether I'm looking at it and thinking about it or not. It stays there even if I decide that it no longer exists. Truths and meanings and values and goodness remain unchanged whether I believe or accept them or not.

The other factor at work is my process of appropriation, of perception or understanding. To a large extent this is personal and subjective and therefore varies from one person to the next. But it is something that is added to the given, not something that replaces it. Tom and Alice both bring their subjective baggage to the table, but both put their baggage on the table. The table is still there even if there is so much baggage it is hard to see it.

Let's take the case of a text. In chapter 42 I gave some details of the life of Bertrand Russell. I made certain claims—that he was born in 1872, that he was sent to prison for libeling the British government and the American army, that he was married four times, and so on. It may be that you reacted subjectively to these various pieces of information. "Wow, that was ages ago." "Serves him right." "Poor fellow." Or whatever. It may also be that your reaction was quite different from mine or from that of the person next to you. But our reactions don't change the basic givenness of the text. That is something that is beyond and outside of us, beyond our control. We don't shape it; it shapes us. We may react in several ways to the fact that Russell was born in 1872, but we can't change the fact. Hermeneutics has rightly stressed the role of the reader in the understanding and the interpretation of a text. But the reader's role is only partial, not absolute.

I suggest that the unwillingness to accept the given is part of our unwillingness to accept that we are creatures. Nietzsche assumed incorrectly that if we were created we could not be creative. "What would there be to create if there were gods?" he declared. In order to assert human creativity, he rejected a creator God. But there is no inconsistency in accepting that we have been created with the ability to exercise creativity. What we don't have is the ability to create the world, ourselves, truth, meaning, or value. That has already been done. Certain things are given.

THE DEMAND FOR TOTAL RATIONAL CERTAINTY

I said there were three great mistakes of the modern period. The first was the Copernican revolution. The second was the unwillingness to accept the given. The third was the demand for total rational certainty. If the Enlightenment has shown anything, it has shown that reason is inadequate on its own to provide a sufficient basis for knowledge and living. Early modern thinkers simply assumed that reason was adequate but soon began to demonstrate its shortcomings. Russell set himself to produce a definitive proof that reason was adequate, at least in some areas, and had to admit failure. Recent philosophy has had to accept reason's many limitations and choose to work within them or to go outside of reason to find a foundation for life.

The fact is, of course, that we don't need definitive rational proof to accept a belief as true or to live in the world. The process of logical reasoning has a far less significant role to play in most of our living than that suggested by Enlightenment philosophers. They tended to take math as the paradigm of human mental activity and so assumed that all our thinking should ideally conform to the sort of mathematical proofs that appear to give irrefutable demonstration of the truth of the matter in question. But very few people actually function according to mathematical reasoning. I guess even mathematicians stop doing it when playing with the dog or deciding to get a drink out of the refrigerator.

Think of half a dozen things you have done so far today. To what extent were they accompanied by processes of reasoning? When you tipped your breakfast cereal into the bowl, did you question its existence? Did you work through the possibility that the text on the outside of the packet could be open to a number of interpretations and deconstructions, and that in fact it might mean that the packet contains arsenic? I doubt whether you reasoned at all. Rather, you lived. You accepted the given. You trusted the label on the packet. If challenged, you might have sought to produce some reasons for your action.

"I always eat this cereal, and it has never poisoned me yet." "Kellogg is a reputable cereal maker." And so on. But these reasons would be the basis of your justification of your action, not of your action. Though reason is doubtless a highly significant part of us, we don't live by reason alone.

So what do we live by? We touched on part of the answer to that question when we looked at things like the anti-rationalist reaction and phenomenology. And there's more to come in the next couple of chapters. There's a lot more to being human than met the logical positivist's eye.

TO THINK THROUGH

Well, do you agree with me? Or have I been too tough? Or have I picked up the wrong things? Should we throw out the whole modern approach? Or are there babies in the bath water?

FORTY-SIX

MUCH MORE THAN MACHINES

FROM DURKHEIM TO BUBER

In this chapter we turn back to Continental philosophy, with its tendency to focus more on the human condition in society, psychology, philosophy, and relationships.

THE TWENTIETH CENTURY SAW THE DEATH OF PHILOSOphy as it had been traditionally practiced for more than two millennia. So far we have traced this in the tradition that was largely dominated by empiricism and the scientific worldview, a tradition that was particularly strong in the English-speaking world. We now turn back to the Continent, where a diversity of thinkers each contributed to a process of development that led directly to the rise of postmodernism. Here the commitment to the strictly scientific worldview was less marked. Interest in the social or human sciences tended to be more dominant. Rather than seeking to reduce everything to the model of a scientific machine, the Continental tradition sought to accept and analyze the human condition as we experience it.

Philosophy traditionally has concerned itself with a very wide field of interest, including the analysis of the mind and our understanding of human behavior and social institutions. But by the twentieth century the subdivisions of philosophy were tending to develop into disciplines in their own right, just as the physical sciences had asserted their independence of philosophy in the early modern period. However, just as the scientific approach continued to interact with philosophy in the empirical tradition, social and psychological concerns exercised considerable influence on Continental philosophical thought. So, before we turn to the story of existentialism and twentieth-century Continental philosophy, we will look at three key figures, Émile Durkheim, Max Weber, and Sigmund Freud, who, while marking the coming of age of their disciplines, also had a profound effect on every area of twentieth-century thought, not least philosophy.

ÉMILE DURKHEIM

Épinal, France (1858–1917). Born into a rabbinical family and educated in Paris, Émile Durkheim started his career teaching philosophy. Later he was professor of social science at Bordeaux from 1887, and from 1902 he was professor of education and sociology at the Sorbonne, Paris. He sought to establish that sociology, the study of society, is a distinct science, to be studied in its own right. It is to be studied scientifically, using the positivistic approach of the rejection of metaphysical theory and focusing solely on observable social phenomena. Morality and religion are to be included among social phenomena. Durkheim exercised a strong influence on the development of sociology, but he also helped set the agenda for Continental philosophy's interest in human beings as essentially social creatures.

MAX WEBER

Berlin (1864–1920). Max Weber studied law at a number of universities and taught at Freiburg, Heidelberg, and Munich until he had to retire due to ill health in 1897. He started as an economist, but his greatest contribution to Western thought was in the area of social theory. He has exercised great influence on the development of twentieth-century social science, and his impact on many philosophers has also been substantial.

Understanding. Weber was a personal friend of Dilthey, and he adopted and developed his concept of understanding. In the human or social sciences, as opposed to the natural sciences, we exercise understanding, by which Weber meant grasping the full range of motives and intentions that lie behind human actions, including religious, moral, and political factors. However, unlike Dilthey, Weber didn't exclude the type of causal explanation that operates in the natural sciences from the social sciences; he accepted that both understanding and explanation have a part to play.

Reason, Fact, and Value. Weber also explored the nature and role of reason as it has developed in the West. He traced its role in rationalizing practices and institutions and its tendency to become a tool in this process. One of the effects of the development of reason is the irreversible separation of fact and value; art, science, and morality operate as separate areas according to their own logic and cannot interact with the others. As a result, social scientists must be value-free in their understanding and interpretation of the data.

TO THINK THROUGH

Is it possible in real life to separate fact and value?

SIGMUND FREUD

Freiberg, Czech Republic (1856–1939). Brought up by poor Jewish parents, Sigmund Freud studied medicine and developed a special interest in mental illness, especially psychoses and neuroses. Through observation and experiment, using his mentally ill patients and himself, he developed a complex analysis and understanding of the functioning of the human person that has dominated much twentieth-century thought. He coined the term *psychoanalysis* to describe both his theory of the mind and his method of mental analysis and therapy. Though his claim that his theories had been "scientifically" established and confirmed has been almost universally disputed, they have had immense influence not just in psychology and the social sciences but on certain aspects of philosophy. The Frankfurt school, for instance, took the validity of psychoanalysis as a given and used it in their philosophical and sociological critique, thus setting a trend for socially orientated twentieth-century philosophers later on. Freud spent most of his life in Vienna, but persecuted by the Nazis, he moved to London and died there from lung cancer in 1939.

Key elements of Freud's theories are that

- Outward behavior is controlled by the inner psyche.
- Our normal awareness of what is happening in our "inner" processes, such as thought, desire, and feeling, is naive and inadequate.
- In contrast to traditional Cartesianism, the inner person is to be seen as divided into two, the conscious and the unconscious.

- The unconscious is the key to who we are and how we function and in particular is the source of problematic behavior. Though we have no direct awareness or knowledge of it, it is the substantial part of our inner being and has a major input into every aspect of life. Freud was not the first to point out the significance of the unconscious. Others before him had posited its existence to explain the elements of human behavior that do not appear to be controlled by the conscious mind.

- Evidence for the existence of the unconscious and a clue to its contents can be found in dreams, when our conscious mind relaxes its control and the unconscious is able to surface.

- The unconscious is shaped by our experiences, especially those of childhood, and particularly by painful or traumatic experiences. We don't retain these experiences in our memory, partly because there are far too many of them but, more sinisterly, because we don't like them and so repress them out of the conscious into the unconscious.

- Quite apart from negative experiences repressed into the unconscious, Freud saw the inner person as a maelstrom of desires and dark powers that seek to control the life of the individual. He proposed this analysis in deliberate opposition to the optimistic view of human nature that many accepted in the nineteenth century and that in particular stressed the controlling role of reason in human behavior. The two strongest expressions of these irrational inner forces, said Freud, are aggression and sex.

- Since our inner drives, for the most part, make us want to behave in ways that are socially unacceptable, human life is characterized by continuous conflict between what our "id," or inner person, demands and what our "superego," a kind of socially and rationally determined conscience, allows. The clash between the id and the superego gives rise to shame and guilt. Given such a conflict, the "ego," the person, adopts a number of techniques to help it cope. Such "defense mechanisms" include repression, regression, projection, and sublimation.

- Though Freud largely used mentally ill and so "abnormal" patients as the basis for his investigations, he applied his findings to all human behavior, claiming that his theory was the key to all aspects of our understanding of human nature.

- Our sexual desires and drives play a dominant role throughout life. Freud notoriously analyzed the developments of infants and children in sexual terms, and though no one now accepts the details of his analysis, many twentieth-century thinkers were happy to recognize the centrality of sex in the shaping of the human person.

- Among the other drives that influence us are the pleasure principle and a drive toward death, the *thanatos* (Gk. meaning "death") principle.

- Freud extended his theory to produce explanations for the source of morality and religious beliefs. Morality arises from the internalization of the dictates of the superego.

- Freud developed techniques to enable the psychoanalyst to access the unconscious. These included the interpretation of dreams, the interpretation of data supplied or expressed in any way by the patient, and the technique of free association. As a result of using these techniques, he concluded that the most significant sources of human behavior were the problems encountered in the sexual development of the young child.

- The pressures of society and our Western civilization are a major factor in the development of anxiety and conflict and the defense mechanism of repression; thus the more "civilized" we become, the more we increase our problems.

From its earliest days, the psychoanalytic theory has given rise to both vigorous opposition and devoted discipleship. Those who oppose it point out that none of its theoretical claims have been satisfactorily established and that its psychotherapeutic value has turned out to be quite limited. On the other hand, many both inside and outside the field of psychology have hailed Freud's theory as of parallel significance to those of Newton or Darwin and have used it in a wide range of applications, especially in the social sciences. However, as the twentieth century progressed, the theory's supporters divided into a large number of opposing schools, demonstrating perhaps the unsatisfactory nature of any specific presentation of it. Counterbalancing this fragmentation and the general proliferation of theories in the psychotherapeutic industry, the last decades of the twentieth century saw an increasing tendency toward eclecticism and holism. Thus many of those who would still claim to be basically Freudian in their orientation would be willing to incorporate into their understanding of human nature elements lifted from other schools of thought, such as behaviorism and cognitive psychology, which have been the traditional enemies of psychoanalysis.

TO THINK THROUGH

You may love Freud or hate him, but you can't ignore him. What do you think about him? How much of his theory should we accept?

In the early years of the twentieth century, the dominance of the scientific worldview was such that very few chose to question it. Durkheim, Weber, and Freud all claimed to be applying a truly "scientific" approach in their studies of society and the human person, even though those in the more positivist tradition would have disputed the claim. But the tendency of the scientific worldview to reduce human beings to machines was already beginning to provoke a reaction. In different ways Henri Bergson and Martin Buber sought to break out of the scientific straitjacket and stress key elements of human life that took us beyond the world of science. In this they helped prepare the way for the rise of existentialism.

HENRI BERGSON

Paris (1859–1941). Henri Bergson's parents were Anglo-Polish. Educated at the École Normale Supérieure in Paris, he taught at Clermont-Ferrand from 1884. He was appointed professor at Collège de France in Paris in 1900, where he became a well-known figure, influencing artistic, literary, and social thought as well as philosophy. He wrote a celebrated study of laughter. He received various honors, including the Nobel Prize for literature, and was involved in the setting up of the United Nations Educational, Scientific and Cultural Organization (UNESCO). At first influenced by the philosophy of Herbert Spencer, he subsequently rejected it as too mechanistic. His best-known work was *Creative Evolution* (1907).

Rejection of the scientific worldview. Bergson's philosophy claims that the world is much richer than the mechanistic system assumed by the scientific worldview. The scientific view, he believed, is inadequate and reductionist and denies our freedom. But we know intuitively that we are free and that there is more to the world than a materialistic mechanistic system.

Time. Bergson developed a concept of time as duration (Fr. *durée*). While the scientist, as a necessary fiction, divides time into measurable units or isolated moments that each in effect lack length, time, as we intuitively experience it, is much more of a process. We don't experience time as isolated moments any more than we experience a musical tune as isolated notes. Rather, time, or duration, as Bergson termed it, is dynamic, continuous, flowing, qualitative, unitary, and such as to allow for spontaneous free acts.

The Life Force. Parallel to his view of duration, Bergson saw the nature of the world as basically dynamic rather than inert. In *Creative Evolution* he proposed a nonmechanistic approach to evolution. Behind the evolutionary process, he said, lies a creative force, which he called the life force (*élan vital*), inaccessible to science, but the source and cause of all evolutionary development.

Morals. In moral and social theory, Bergson again contrasted a closed systematized approach dominated by custom and the like, with an open, free, creative society with room for innovation and reform.

TO THINK THROUGH

The concept of a "life force" that lies behind everything has a long history and has resurfaced several times in the twentieth century, for instance, in the Gaia hypothesis and some New Age beliefs. What do you think about it? Is it a way of reintroducing God without making him personal? Does the scientific worldview have to reject it?

MARTIN BUBER

Vienna (1878–1965). Brought up by his grandfather, who was a Midrash scholar, Martin Buber was a keen supporter of Zionism, arguing for "peace and brotherhood" between Jews and Arabs and the formation of a joint Jewish-Arab state. He was professor of religion at Frankfurt am Main from 1923 to 1933 and professor of social philosophy at the Hebrew University from 1938. His most significant work was *I and Thou* (1923).

I-It. At the heart of Buber's thinking is the contrast between two types of relationship, the I-thou and the I-it. I-it can apply to any relationship; it is an attitude that treats the object or person we are relating to as an "it," an impersonal object governed by causal laws and the like. It is detached, uninvolved, typified by the scientific mind-set. If universally adopted, it destroys community and human authenticity.

I-Thou. I-thou, by contrast, is the authentic human relationship between the self and the other, characterized by love, self-giving, and appreciative understanding and acceptance of the other as a person. Key to it is involvement and reciprocity through dialogue. As we respond to and are transformed by each other in the I-thou relationship, we encounter reality and become more truly human. Moreover, the dialogue that arises from the I-thou relationship provides a basis for ethics and even aesthetics.

Though I-thou relationships are generally between persons, Buber allowed that we can have an I-thou relationship with an object, such as a tree, where we become "bound up" with an inanimate object, which thus has an existential impact on us. Buber sees the possibility of this experience in various aspects of nature and art.

God. The supreme I-thou relationship is between the individual and God. God is the ultimate Thou, who can never be reduced to an it, and who cannot be limited by our relationship with him. He is encountered by speaking with him, not by speaking about him, though we catch glimpses of him in our other I-thou relationships. We are unable to objectify that encounter, for that would be to turn God into an it. So, though the relationship is real, the one to whom we relate can never become an object of our thought.

Science. Science is the sphere of I-it relationships. Buber, like the existentialists, stressed the full expression of personhood seen in I-thou relationships much more than I-it relationships; but he by no means rejected the validity of science, provided it didn't claim more than its due. What he was strongly opposed to was the demand of science to reduce everything to its own terms, as seen in any form of positivism. This, in effect, is reducing us to the level of it-it, which was, for Buber, unacceptable.

TO THINK THROUGH

What do you think of the relative merits of seeing human beings as part of a "scientific" world or of seeing them as persons in social relationships with other persons?

Seeing God as a thou has had a profound effect on the development of much twentieth-century Christian theology and seems to take us to the heart of New Testament thought. But does having an I-thou relationship with God make thought or talk about God on an I-it level impossible? If not, how can the two work together?

FORTY-SEVEN

THE ENIGMA OF BEING

EXISTENTIALISM

In this chapter we look at the philosophies of five existentialist thinkers—Karl Jaspers, Gabriel Marcel, Martin Heidegger, Jean-Paul Sartre, and Simone de Beauvoir.

WE HAVE COME NOW TO WHAT MANY WOULD SEE AS THE most significant philosophical movement of the middle part of the twentieth century, existentialism. In many ways it wasn't a movement in the sense of a school of philosophy at all. It is perhaps best thought of as a way of viewing life rather than as an attempt to produce a philosophical system. Its roots are generally traced back to Nietzsche and Kierkegaard and even Pascal. But for the most part existentialists weren't interested in developing the specific philosophies of these three. Rather, they empathized with their mood and feel and applied them to the human condition of their day.

In a world without God, philosophy dies and life collapses into absurdity and hopelessness. There are perhaps three ways of trying to cope with this. One way is to ignore it or at least to try to ignore its implications. This is the way chosen by David Hume and by innumerable atheists and agnostics since. The second way is to face it and to seek to find some way of being truly human in spite of it. This is the way chosen by the existentialists. The third way is to accept it and, instead of resisting it, to side with it and live with it. This is the way of anarchy and postmodernism.

KARL JASPERS

Oldenburg, Germany (1883–1969). Karl Jaspers (pronounced *Yaspers*) was trained in medicine, psychology, and psychiatry. He started his working life as a psychiatrist and taught psychiatry at Heidelberg from 1916. He then served as professor of philosophy there from 1921 until he was removed by the Nazis in 1937. He was reinstated at Heidelberg in 1945, and in 1948 he became professor at Basel. He wrote many works; the best-known is his three-volume *Philosophy* (1932; English translation, 1967–1971).

Jaspers outlined three areas of philosophical concern. The first was the world as seen by science. Here we find a degree of relative truth but no answers to the basic questions of life. The second was existence, the part of being we each can possess and which is thus open to us to explore and develop. The third was the transcendent, ultimate Being, an enveloping presence we discover as the complement to our finitude and existence.

Existence. Jaspers disliked being called an existentialist. Nevertheless, his concept of existence is key to his philosophy and typical of the general existentialist approach. Existence is not something that can be defined or examined objectively. Rather, it is something we experience or live. Like Kierkegaard, Jaspers saw existence as the true fulfillment of what it is to be human and as something we could miss out on. It is possible for humans to be merely "there" (*Dasein*—a use different from Heidegger's); this is inauthenticity. By contrast, we can be committed to existence, working toward it, exercising our true freedom, fulfilling our potential, realizing our being, creating something unique, opening ourselves up to reality. We do this through the creative use of our freedom to make authentic choices, and we don't do it in isolation; we exist in community and in communication with others.

Existence is rich, deep, and mysterious, involving many paradoxes. It confronts us with death, guilt, chance, anxiety, freedom, and choice. All these things are vital parts of existence and must be faced, accepted, and lived. By using our freedom to make creative choices, we express and authenticate our humanness. Each choice shapes us; particularly in "limit situations" such as death, suffering, struggle, and guilt, each is momentous; each is accompanied by the anxiety of freedom and responsibility.

Transcendence. Our existence highlights our finitude, limits, and incompleteness and thus confronts us with transcendence. Though by its nature transcendence, or God, is beyond our grasp, we encounter it through "ciphers" and myths. A cipher, such as the face of another person, points beyond itself indirectly to the transcendent. A myth is a sacred story that carries with it the experience of the transcendent; like Kierkegaard, Jaspers believed that through it we are able to encounter transcendence in a unique way.

TO THINK THROUGH

Many thinkers in the empiricist tradition refused to admit that existentialists were doing philosophy at all. To what extent do you think it is the business of philosophy to investigate humanness, existence, and relationships?

GABRIEL MARCEL

Paris (1889–1973). Born into a wealthy family, Gabriel Marcel studied philosophy at the Sorbonne in Paris. At first attracted to idealism, he was convinced by his experiences in the First World War of idealism's inadequacy to face the tragedy inherent in human existence; and as a result, he developed an interest in existentialist themes and in Christianity. He became a Roman Catholic in 1929. He was a playwright and music critic as well as a philosopher, and he used the thirty plays he wrote to express his call to authentic human living. He coined the word *existentialism*, though, like most existentialists, he disliked having the term applied to himself. His works include *Being and Having* (1935) and *The Mystery of Being* (1951).

Living in the world.
Marcel's interest was in human beings in a broken world, with all its emptiness, superficiality, and lack of meaningful relationships. Like other existentialists, Marcel distinguished between two ways of relating to the world. The objective "scientific" way he called "primary reflection." It is essentially impersonal and detached. The way of "secondary reflection" explores the wonder and mystery of being with all its involvement and personal experience. Here we find personal relationships, love, hope, faith, and the like. Linked with this is Marcel's distinction between problems, which are external and impersonal, and mysteries, in which we face the realities of life with all their pain in a truly human and involved way.

Being.
Marcel saw embodied human life, our "being" as "given." This is the primary datum, and it is mysterious. It points us to God as the ground of that

being. But it is also always being "in jeopardy," being confronted with nonbeing, something that for him points us to the hope of life after death.

MARTIN HEIDEGGER

Messkirch, Baden, Germany (1889–1976). From a peasant background, Martin Heidegger first studied theology at a Jesuit seminary and then math and philosophy at Freiburg University, where he taught from 1915. He was influenced by the phenomenology of Husserl, who joined the staff at Freiburg in 1916. In 1923 Heidegger moved to Marburg. After five years as professor there, he was appointed professor of philosophy at Freiburg. He was an enthusiastic and outspoken supporter of Hitler and Nazism, and he used his position in the university to fire Jewish staff. After the war Heidegger was suspended from teaching. As a key figure in the development of existentialism (though he rejected the label), his influence has been widespread, reaching into theology, hermeneutics, and postmodernism. Those influenced by him include Bultmann, Sartre, Gadamer, Derrida, and Foucault. His *Sein und Zeit* (Being and Time, 1927) brought him fame and remains his best-known work. He wrote copiously, and his collected works run to a hundred volumes.

Being. Heidegger saw the question of "being" (*Sein*) as the great central question of all philosophy. He called *Being and Time* "a fundamental ontology," an investigation into being. His goal in it was to examine human being (*Dasein*) to discover what being in general is. After 1930 his interest was focused more specifically on being in general or being itself. In his long career his thought developed from something close to Husserl's phenomenology to something much nearer to postmodernism. But at each stage his interest was basically existentialist, a practical interest in how to live authentically, rather than a concern for abstract and irrelevant speculation.

Distinctive features of Heidegger's "early" existentialism are:

● **Rejection of dualism.** Heidegger vigorously rejected the primacy of dualism, including the distinction between subject and object, and between mind and experience. He saw the whole Cartesian tradition, down to and including Husserl, as presupposing a distinction between subject and object, whether it is my mind contemplating my body or Husserl's consciousness directed toward its objects. But in fact, Heidegger says, though that may be the way we function some of the time, it is not our foundational way of functioning.

● **"Primordial understanding."** Heidegger illustrated our foundational way of being or functioning by hammering. When we hammer, he said, we do not see ourselves as a subject, a hammerer, using an object, the hammer. We don't engage in any mental activity—we simply hammer. There may be times when we do relate to a hammer as subject to object, for instance, if we go into a shop to buy a new hammer and carefully inspect the hammers on display. But normally we simply hammer. So with our basic "primordial" living; we are, we do things, without a subject/object distinction. Many of the questions that have puzzled philosophers, such as the existence of the external world, or how our experience of the world can relate to the world as it really is, thus become irrelevant. They are created by this false subject/object distinction. We are not, says Heidegger, primarily beings that engage in objective contemplation, though we sometimes do, especially when problems arise. Rather, we are primarily living, existing, "coping" beings with a much more direct involvement in the world than that of the contemplative thinker.

● **Dasein.** Heidegger coined a distinctive meaning for this term. Its general meaning is "existence," but it literally means "being there." In the way Heidegger used it, it is generally translated as "being-in-the-world." It is not to be equated with our mind or consciousness, since both of these tend to be set over against the world of which we think or of which we are conscious. *Dasein* includes the world as well as the subject; we cannot separate the two. Further, though Heidegger often applied it in the context of an individual, *Dasein* is much more than my personal private existence; part of being-in-the-world is being in a social context with other people, a shared being.

● **Facticity.** Being-in-the-world involves facticity. We are "thrown" into our world. We do not choose it or make it; we are not asked whether we want it. What it is and what we are are given facts that we cannot change. What we have to do is accept it and go on from there.

● **Involvement.** The heart of being-in-the-world is not an intellectual process or empirical experience. Rather, it is involvement, doing things, especially creative things, appropriating what we find in our facticity, using hammers, being what we are. This involvement is in fact an involvement in being on a much larger scale than, say, hammering in a nail. Any single act only makes sense in a larger context, making a shed, building a house, earning our wages, living in the world. These are all part of what we are and what the world is, even though we generally don't stop to think about them in a subject/object way.

• **Inauthenticity and authenticity.** Our situation and especially other people tend to shape us, to make us what they want us to be, an inauthentic construct, what Heidegger called *Das Man*. By contrast, the authentic person is the one who creatively uses what is given in the present as the basis for decisive action that will shape the future, especially when confronted by death, anxiety, guilt, finitude, freedom, and the like.

• **Death.** The key moment of authentic self-awareness arises when we face the full reality of our finitude, especially as it is presented in death, the thing that forms a boundary to all our being. Heidegger in fact used the phrase "being-to-death" to express our finitude. Facing death is much more than being aware that we have to die. It is the experience of being alone, unsupported, facing nothingness, the final denial of being, and being able to accept that, to appropriate it, to allow it to be part of being.

• **Anxiety.** Quite apart from death, our being-in-the-world causes anxiety. Though we find ourselves shaped by the things and people around us, we are aware that we don't have to be; we can make authentic meaningful choices. But on what basis should we make them? Where do we find "meaning"? There are no God-guaranteed or rationally supported principles; everything is open. From this openness arises anxiety. We can, of course, escape anxiety by becoming inauthentic conformists. But if we are authentic, we choose openness, and as a result, we choose anxiety as our way of life.

• **Being and time.** Our being is in time. Time has a past, present, and future that correspond to our facticity, our inauthentic existence, and authenticity. Time is more than temporality; it is the expression or enactment of being, my taking on board the facticity of the past, my taking responsibility in the present and reaching out through resolute choice to the future.

The later Heidegger. In his later, post-1930, stage, Heidegger decided that his earlier stage had been too much influenced by traditional metaphysical understanding, and he set out to reshape his philosophy "without presuppositions." Perhaps the most significant shift was a realization that his earlier analysis of the human predicament was not universally valid. Other ages were not faced with the structureless situation that threw the Europeans of the twentieth century into meaninglessness and anxiety. The pre-Socratic Greeks, for example, had clear structures that gave them security; so did the medieval Christians. As a result, Heidegger's later thinking tended to be less specific and direct. His own explanation was that he was dealing with the broader concept of the search for Being itself, something much more elusive and mystical than *Dasein*, something he would not call God, but that seems to bear considerable resemblance to God. The choice, he said, is between "nihilism," which is the rejecting of Being, and a turning to Being and its call upon our being.

In his later period, Heidegger also developed a concept of language as both reflecting and shaping a specific culture. Not only do we shape language; language shapes us. Perhaps Heidegger's philosophy is a case in point. Those who try to read him find his fondness of coining new words or new uses of words frustrating. Yet the coining of a new concept like *Dasein* has in fact opened up for many a whole new way of seeing the world and living in the world. Heidegger himself has changed language, but as a result, language has changed the world.

TO THINK THROUGH

If we are searching for Being, is human "being" the place to start?

Do you agree with Heidegger's rejection of the subject/object distinction? To what extent do you find it helpful? In what ways could it be dangerous?

Inauthenticity, finitude, being-to-death, and anxiety are concepts that most philosophers through the centuries have ignored, perhaps assuming that they are the domain of religion. Why do you think they came so much to the fore in existentialist philosophy?

For Further Study

Pöggeler, O. *Martin Heidegger's Path of Thinking*. Atlantic Highlands, N.J.: Humanities Press, 1987.

JEAN-PAUL SARTRE

Paris (1905–1980). Born into a Calvinist family, Jean-Paul Sartre studied philosophy at the École Normale Supérieure in Paris. After a period of teaching philosophy at Le Havre, which he did not enjoy, he did further study at Berlin and Freiburg, where he encountered Husserl and Heidegger. He joined the French army in 1939; he was taken prisoner in 1940 and returned to occupied Paris in 1941. His experiences in the war affected him deeply, giving him a lasting concern for the oppressed. By 1945 his fame was such that he was able to refuse academic appointments and earn his living by writing. He was a social and political activist with marked sympathies with communism. He actively supported the Algerian struggle for independence and the French opposition to the American war in Vietnam. In 1964 he refused the Nobel Prize for literature.

Sartre was a gifted writer. He used his novels and plays to express his philosophical and social convictions. By the early 1940s his work was marking him out as the leading French left-wing intellectual, a reputation he kept for a generation. His first novel, *La Nausée* (Nausea) was published in 1938. His major philosophical work was *Being and Nothingness* (1943; English translation, 1956). His defense of existentialism in *Existentialism Is a Humanism* (1946; English translation, 1947) marked him as France's leading existentialist. In later years he worked at combining the insights of existentialism and Marxism.

"Man makes himself." Foundational to Sartre's philosophy is his conviction that we are what we make ourselves. There is no God to make or shape us. If we are going to be anything, the responsibility and the freedom to be it are solely ours. "Man makes himself," "existentialism is a humanism"—the courageous individual asserts her or his humanness in the face of a hostile world. Granted, there are limits on our freedom. Our facticity is such that we can't escape from this or that situation. But we don't have to submit to our situation; we are free to "negate" it, to imagine possibilities, to make creative choices, to change it, to transcend it.

Imagination. Sartre saw the use of imagination as the paradigm expression of human freedom. Following Husserl's phenomenological approach, Sartre analyzed the imagination as a distinctive mode of intentional consciousness. Our imagination is able to transcend the actual world so it can't be controlled by anything in the world; it is truly free. Moreover, all our perceptions of the world are attended by imagination. So even in our perceiving we are free; we have before us options and alternatives. Indeed, all acts of the consciousness are in some sense free.

L'en-soi and le pour-soi. In *Being and Nothingness*, Sartre distinguished consciousness from all other forms of being. Everything apart from consciousness is simply what it is in itself (*en-soi*). Such being is fixed, static, inert, already complete; it has no potential; it is not becoming; it simply is. As such it is meaningless, superfluous, absurd.

Consciousness, by contrast, has the ability to be conscious of itself and thus is being *pour-soi*, "for itself" or "for oneself." As such it is all that *en-soi* is not. It is open, free, fluid, lacking fixed structure, and incomplete. In addition, it is nonbeing. Sartre established this by a strange piece of reasoning. Everything, he says, must be *en-soi*, a thing in itself. But if consciousness is *pour-soi*, it can't be *en-soi*. So it can't be a thing. So it must be a nonthing, nothing, nothingness *(le néant)*. So to be human is to be nothing. Human consciousness is a kind of gap, a hole, a nothingness that lies at the heart of all things that are. Meaningless and empty though the things-in-themselves may seem, the human condition seems to surpass them in bleakness.

Some have sought to remove some of the bleakness by suggesting that this concept of nothingness lying at the heart of being is the same as Augustine's concept of evil as the privation of good, implying that the more you move away from good toward evil, the more you move from being to nonbeing. But Sartre seems to be saying something much more than Augustine. Where Augustine said that it is possible for humans to move from being toward nonbeing, Sartre is saying is that every human being is essentially nonbeing to start with; our desire and indeed our potential may be to move toward being, but such is the absurdity of the situation in which we find ourselves that there is no guarantee this will happen. We are, after all, a "useless passion."

Existence and essence.
For all objects in the world apart from ourselves, essence, said Sartre, precedes existence. That is, they have a fixed essence or nature that is foundational to them as existing objects. Human beings lack that fixed nature. We find ourselves existing, but we are not presented with a fixed essence. It isn't something given; we have to make it. For us, uniquely, existence precedes essence. We exist first and define ourselves afterward. There is, he said, no human nature as such, because there is no God to have the concept of it. We are nothing other than what we make of ourselves.

Freedom and authenticity.
The openness of our freedom and the fact that it is through the exercise of our freedom that we can become truly human is for Sartre both glorious and terrifying. It is glorious in that it opens up the tremendous possibility of becoming truly human and, like Nietzsche's Superman, even more than human. We have the potential to create both ourselves and our world.

But for all its glory, Sartre saw us as viewing this prospect with dread and anguish. It is terrifying because it shows us the awfulness of what we truly are. We hang on the brink of nothingness. We are without essence. We are absurd. All the objects of the universe have meaning; we alone are meaningless. We are incomplete with a yearning and a capacity for completeness that can never be satisfied. It is also terrifying because so much is at stake. My choice creates me, my meaning, my values, and all my world. And I have to make it alone. I have no one, nothing to guide me. In a number of passages, Sartre wrote almost longingly that if there were a God, we would not be alone, we would have some criteria by which to choose, we would know which way to go forward. But without God we are alone, "alone in the midst of a monstrous silence, alone and free, without recourse or excuse, irrevocably condemned, condemned to be free."

I can, of course, use my freedom wrongly. For Sartre this wouldn't be the wrong use of freedom in a traditional moral sense, such as to do a selfish act or harm someone else. Rather, it is using it to make inauthentic choices. I may, for example, run from the opportunity to make authentic creative choices and follow the crowd, do what someone else tells me to, conform, become an object, a thing-in-itself, in that I follow a predetermined essence. This is objectification, inauthenticity, or in Sartre's language, "bad faith."

Morality and community.

In theory this intense individualism and removal of all objective criteria that might affect my choice can only lead to total moral relativism: Whatever I choose must be totally spontaneous, affected by no external conditions at all. But in practice Sartre was unable to apply this concept consistently and fell back on a version of the Kantian categorical imperative, thus limiting not just the openness of our freedom, but the intense individualism of his basic philosophy.

Nevertheless, Sartre still remained a long way from a developed concept of community. In his analysis of human relationships, he contrasted what I am in my own eyes and what I am in the eyes of others. In my own eyes, I'm a free subject, a *pour-soi*, a human consciousness. But in the eyes of others, I become an object. What's more, when we are encountered by other people, we are somehow at their mercy. They "look at" us, and what they see becomes part of what we are. They penetrate into our being; we are at their mercy. Sartre allowed that this "being-for-others" can be a positive thing. I can regard the other not as a thing but as a person and choose to assert his or her freedom and humanness. But Sartre seemed to feel that most often it gives rise to conflict and frustration; the presence or "look" of the other means that neither of us can be truly ourselves. Each seeks to dominate or possess the other. "Hell is others."

In his later writings, as he sought to combine existentialism and Marxism, Sartre seems to have abandoned both his intense individualism and his stress on the complete openness of our choices in order to incorporate elements of Marx's theory, especially the concept of the dialectical movement of history toward a new and positive society.

TO THINK THROUGH

Like Nietzsche, Sartre believed that a universe without God must be meaningless and absurd. Is that an inevitable conclusion of atheism?

Sartre never knew his father. Both Nietzsche and Russell lost their fathers by the time they were four. Do you think there could be some connection between this loss and these philosophers' vehement atheism?

Sartre openly acknowledged his debt to Heidegger. When accused of being the disciple of a Nazi, Sartre argued that Heidegger's politics did not affect his philosophy. Russell and Sartre were both left-wing political and social activists, and yet their philosophical views were radically different. Should a philosophy apply to all areas of life?

Sartre insisted that existentialism is a humanism and is thus necessarily atheistic. Yet others have sought to combine existentialist concerns with a God-centered worldview. Do you think this can be done?

For Further Study

Caws, P. *Sartre*, London: Routledge, 1979.

SIMONE DE BEAUVOIR

Paris (1908–1986). Simone de Beauvoir studied at the Sorbonne, where she met Sartre and Merleau-Ponty. The three worked together in the development of existentialist thinking, de Beauvoir having a particularly close relationship with Sartre all her life. She saw her own philosophy as largely based on Sartre's ideas, though it is generally agreed that she influenced Sartre in some areas, tempering his extreme view of freedom and emphasizing the social elements of human existence. She was a key figure in the development of feminism. Unlike many existentialists, she happily accepted the existentialist label, though she refused to be called a feminist until she was in her sixties. Her best-known work was *Le Deuxième Sexe* (1949; English, *The Second Sex*, 1953). She also incorporated her ethical and philosophical ideas in novels, short stories, and essays.

Ethics. In *The Ethics of Ambiguity* (1947), de Beauvoir sought to develop an existentialist understanding of ethics, something Sartre had promised to do but never achieved. In a world where we live in relationships with others, she saw the necessity of limiting Sartre's concept of totally open freedom and argued for an ethic based on the realization of authenticity in the context of willing both our own freedom and the freedom of others. But, like Sartre, she was unwilling to introduce any form of external value or structure, such as consistency, into her concept of morality.

Feminism. In *The Second Sex*, de Beauvoir rejected current theories explaining the subordination of women by men in terms of biology, Freudian psychology, or Marxist economics. Rather, she said, the roots of inequality lie in social values and attitudes imposed by men and accepted by women. Using Sartre's terminology, she saw men as the *pour-soi* subject forcing women to be the "the other," the *en-soi* object.

TO THINK THROUGH

Is it really possible for someone who rejects fixed moral standards to argue coherently for values like the desirability of equality between the sexes?

Was existentialism just a mid-twentieth-century phenomenon, or does it have insights and ideas that are relevant today?

For Further Study

Oaklander, N. *Existentialist Philosophy*. Englewood Cliffs, N.J.: Prentice Hall, 1992.

FORTY-EIGHT

NEITHER LANGUAGE NOR SCIENCE HAS ALL THE ANSWERS

FROM RYLE TO FEYERABEND

In this chapter we look at nine thinkers who all operated in the English-speaking world in the mid to late twentieth century. The first seven—Gilbert Ryle, J. L. Austin, W. O. Quine, P. F. Strawson, Noam Chomsky, Michael Dummett, and John Searle—all found ways of developing the linguistic tradition; the last two—Thomas Kuhn and Paul Feyerabend—completed the process of the discrediting of the scientific worldview as the key to all else.

WHILE THE MAIN STREAM OF CONTINENTAL PHILOSOPHY was following the course that was to lead to postmodernism and anarchy, many philosophers in the English-speaking tradition were seeking to follow Wittgenstein's lead and find a role for philosophy through the analysis of language. For a time hopes were high that the method of analysis would have useful results in a whole range of areas. After all, it had shown its value, in the work of Frege and Russell, in analyzing math and descriptive statements. In the same way, it was to be an immensely valuable tool in developing an enriched understanding of how we use language, as analyzed, for example, in Austin's speech-act theory. But for the most part, these hopes were disappointed. It was gradually realized that as a tool there are few areas where clear and universally acceptable analyses can be obtained. The truth of the matter was that the promise that all philosophical problems would be solved and be seen to be solved by the careful and painstaking clarification of what we are doing when we use words was not fulfilled.

As a result, there were two parallel tendencies. As the century wore on, interest began to shift from the analysis of isolated concepts and statements to the realization, voiced by people like Kuhn and Quine, that a statement needs a wider context to give it meaning. At the same time, some of the aspects of traditional philosophy began to reappear, partly because language, being a reflection of life, inevitably confronts us with these issues. In place of the strong reductionism of the original analytic vision, exemplified by Ryle's attack on the concept of mind, philosophical interest began to widen. Several of the issues that had been rejected as irrelevant or meaningless by Russell and the logical positivists were reinstated. Strawson, for example, dared to talk about metaphysics, and Chomsky and Searle did much to counter Ryle's reductionism in their discussions of the nature of mind.

GILBERT RYLE

Brighton, England (1900–1976). Gilbert Ryle was educated at Oxford and spent all his teaching career there, serving as professor of "metaphysical philosophy" from 1945 to 1968. He was a keen exponent of the linguistic analysis approach inspired by the later Wittgenstein, and he was noted for his vigorous attack on the Cartesian "ghost in the machine" concept of the mind and his substitution of a largely behaviorist alternative in *Concept of Mind* (1949). The task of philosophy, for Ryle, is to dispel bogus philosophical problems by showing that they arise from the wrong application of language. The problems, for example, arising from traditional mind-body dualism can be solved by acknowledging that in this case language has misled us into making a "category mistake," that is, allowing our talk about our mind to postulate that it must be an existing entity. A category mistake is applying the logic of one type of word or discourse inappropriately to another, thus leading to absurdity.

TO THINK THROUGH

Russell and Ryle are just two examples of what I call the DOGMAS approach (Declare Observations Gainsaying My Approach Spurious). To some extent we are all guilty of it. We produce a theory that seems to work well in some area, and because it works well there, we assume it must be the answer in every other area as well. So we force it on every other area. But in certain areas it doesn't seem to fit. So rather than emend our theory to fit reality, we declare the areas that don't fit to be bogus; they are nonissues. Can you think of other examples of this, not least among the thinkers we have been studying?

J. L. AUSTIN

Lancaster, England (1911–1960). J. L. Austin was professor of philosophy at Oxford from 1952 and was the most significant advocate of ordinary language philosophy. He was noted for his patient and rigorous examination of the way language is used in order to understand the nature of philosophical concepts like knowledge, freedom, and perception. He saw this approach as the key role of philosophy, parallel to the careful observations and analyses of those working in the empirical sciences.

Speech-act theory. One of Austin's distinctive contributions to linguistic philosophy was the development of the "speech-act" theory, which has been influential in linguistics and hermeneutics. In *How to Do Things with Words* (1962), he pointed out that utterances can have a range of purposes, often intermingled. They may convey information, give instructions, express feelings, and so on. Austin was especially interested in performative utterances, or the performative element or force of statements, with which one is seeking to do something, rather than simply convey information. For example, when we say, "I promise," we are doing something other than making a factual statement. "It's raining," in addition to being a comment on the weather, may be a warning or a suggestion to take an umbrella. Austin suggested a threefold classification of utterances:

- Locutionary, conveying information: describing the weather.
- Illocutionary, doing something: suggesting the person we are addressing take an umbrella.
- Perlocutionary, achieving something: getting the person to take the umbrella.

Austin clarified the distinction between illocution and perlocution by saying that an illocutionary utterance usually has a "hereby" sense ("I hereby warn you"), while a perlocution does not. But he conceded that the distinction was difficult to define, and subsequent speech-act theory has focused on illocution.

 Theory of ideas. Austin also attacked the theory that had been at the heart of British empiricism since Locke, that all we can ever be aware of is sense-data rather than objects in the world. Language like "I have an experience" or "I have an idea" or "I perceive a sense-datum" misleads us, he said, into thinking that experiences, ideas, and sense-data have some sort of real existence.

TO THINK THROUGH

How often in ordinary life do we make purely descriptive statements like Russell's "The author of 'Waverley' is Scott"? Think of the things you have said so far today. How many of them contain performative elements?

How do Austin's insights tally with the biblical concept of a word doing things?

W. V. O. QUINE

Akron, Ohio (1908–2000). W. V. O. Quine was educated at Oberlin College and Harvard, where he did postgraduate work in the logic of Russell and Whitehead's *Principia Mathematica*. He was influenced by logical positivism during visits to Europe in the 1930s and continued to maintain a basically empiricist position, seeking to keep a close link between philosophy and the natural sciences. He became professor of philosophy at Harvard in 1948.

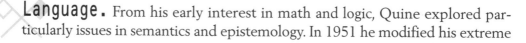 **Language.** From his early interest in math and logic, Quine explored particularly issues in semantics and epistemology. In 1951 he modified his extreme

empiricist position by rejecting "two dogmas of empiricism," the dichotomy between analytic and synthetic, and the insistence that only statements about immediate experiences are meaningful. Like Russell, he sought to clarify the logic of language to avoid words leading us into philosophical problems by appearing to describe nonexistent entities. Meaning is not to be derived from a statement as an isolated unit, but rather from a statement in its whole context, or system of statements, which Quine equated with the "whole of science." Alternatively, if we want to hold on to an interpretation of a specific statement, it is up to us to adjust the rest of the system so that it supports the meaning we require.

The indeterminacy of translation. In *Word and Object* (1960), Quine advanced an influential theory he called "the indeterminacy of translation." We can never be sure, he said, that our translation or interpretation of a statement or a language is the correct one; alternative translations will always be possible. This seems to imply an arbitrariness in all our reception of language that undermines any confidence in rational communication between one person and another, thus bringing the linguistic analysis tradition of philosophy to an admission of loss of meaning parallel to that in the postmodern tradition.

TO THINK THROUGH

Quine rejected the traditional analytic/synthetic distinction. Do you think "A bachelor is an unmarried man" is necessarily tautologous? In what circumstances could it be "synthetic" in that it conveys information?

P. F. STRAWSON

London (1919–). P. F. Strawson was educated at Oxford and spent his entire teaching career there, following Ryle as professor of metaphysical philosophy in 1968. Starting as an enthusiastic supporter of ordinary language philosophy, he retained throughout his life a stress on the validity of our normal way of viewing the world, as opposed to that of the scientist or philosopher.

Metaphysics. Strawson later broadened his interest to include a form of metaphysics in which he incorporated Kantian insights. He distinguished between

"descriptive" and "revisionary" metaphysics. The former, his own approach, describes "the actual structure of our thought about the world"; the latter seeks to impose a metaphysical structure on the world in the way that Descartes or Leibniz did. The subtitle of his book *Individuals* (1959) was *An Essay in Descriptive Metaphysics*. In it he examined the concept of a person and concluded that it is a "logically primitive concept" to which we can apply both bodily language and language about states of consciousness; it is equally a mistake to posit a Cartesian-type mind or person and to reduce the person to mere bodily terms.

NOAM CHOMSKY

Philadelphia (1928–). Educated at Pittsburgh, Noam Chomsky taught at the Massachusetts Institute of Technology from 1955. Besides being the most celebrated figure in the field of linguistic theory in the second half of the twentieth century, his left-wing political activism and opposition to American government policy especially in Vietnam made him a well-known figure. He had considerable influence on philosophical linguistic analysis and philosophy of mind.

Mind and innate abilities. Applying the insights of structuralism to linguistic theory and the functioning of the mind, Chomsky argued that just as fish swim and birds fly as a result of inherited biological structures, so humans have specific innate abilities or dispositions of the mind, which he called the language faculty, that enable them to master language. As evidence of this, Chomsky cited the speed with which children learn the intricacies of language. This led him to posit a universal grammar that we each know innately and into which we fit each experience of language. On a broader canvas, he argued that the wide range of complex cognitive abilities children develop cannot be sufficiently explained by a process of learning; they too must be the result of innate dispositions. As suggested by the title of the book in which he developed this theory, *Cartesian Linguistics* (1966), this supports a rationalist concept of the human person, and Chomsky has been vigorous in attacking empiricist theories such as those of Gilbert Ryle and, in particular, of behaviorist psychology. One of the results of his work has been the decline in influence of pure behaviorist theories in psychology and the rise of cognitive-behavioral or pure cognitive theories.

MICHAEL DUMMETT

London (1925–). Like Strawson, Michael Dummett was educated at Oxford and spent his whole teaching career there. He was professor of logic from 1979 to 1992. Two key influences on his philosophy were Frege and Wittgenstein. Strongly committed to the analytic tradition, he argued that true philosophy only started with Frege and the concern with language; all Western philosophy before then had been on the wrong track.

Realism and truth. Dummett used a verificationist approach to meaning to tackle the issue of realism, that is, whether or not we can know that something exists independently of us. The truth of a proposition, he said, is to be seen in terms of "verification conditions," things that we are normally able to apply. But with some propositions (about the future or counterfactual conditionals, for example), it is impossible for us to know what the verification conditions are, so we can't apply them. As a result, the propositions in question can't have a truth value that we are able to establish. This leaves two possibilities, that truth is in some way transcendent, independent of our ability to find verification conditions, or that there are some propositions that we have to accept as neither true nor false. The first option would commit us to a realist position; Dummett opted rather for the second and in so doing rejected the principle of bivalence, a traditional law of logic that states that every proposition is either true or false.

JOHN SEARLE

Denver, Colorado (1932–). After studying at Wisconsin and Oxford, John Searle taught for a time at Oxford before moving to Berkeley, where he taught from 1959 on. He was strongly influenced by J. L. Austin.

Speech-act theory. Searle developed the theory of speech acts, focusing especially on illocutionary acts such as promises, statements, commands, pledges, and apologies, arguing in *Speech Acts* (1969) that an adequate understanding of speech acts can throw light on a number of philosophical problems, especially in the area of reference and meaning. Later he analyzed illocutionary acts, placing them in five categories:

- Assertives; e.g., This is a book.
- Directives; e.g., Shut the window.
- Commissives; e.g., I promise I'll do it later.
- Expressives; e.g., Congratulations!
- Declarations; e.g., I name this ship *The John Searle*.

Mind and brain: The Chinese Room Argument.

Searle made major contributions to the philosophy of mind. He saw the mind as intentional, using Brentano's concept of mental acts containing an intended or intentional object, to which they are directed. Thus he rejected strongly materialistic or behavioristic concepts of mind. Rather, for him, consciousness is an intrinsic feature of mind. In this connection he devised his Chinese Room Argument in refutation of the widespread assumption that the mind/brain can be adequately viewed as a computer or, more specifically, that the mind is to be seen as the computer program run by the brain, which is a computer.

Imagine, he said, a computer program that produces appropriate Chinese responses to utterances in Chinese. According to the view he is attacking, the computer is doing all that the mind/brain of a conscious understanding Chinese conversationalist is doing. Then imagine yourself, with no knowledge of Chinese, locked in a room with two windows. In through one window come pieces of paper with marks on them. You follow instructions you have been given and match the marks on the papers with marks on other papers, which you then pass out through the second window. Unknown to you, the papers that come through the first window actually consist of a series of questions in Chinese, and the papers you hand out through the second window are the correct Chinese answers. You are doing, says Searle, precisely what the computer does, but in no way could you be said to be conscious of what you are doing or to understand Chinese. Therefore, what is happening in the human mind, says Searle, is something very different from what happens in a computer. Consciousness, he concludes, is a subjective, substantive biological phenomenon.

Realism and truth.

Searle also sought to defend two linked concepts—what he called external realism and the correspondence theory of truth. External realism, in contrast to, say, Dummett's anti-realist arguments, is the position that holds that there is a real world that exists independently of us. The correspondence theory of truth holds that a proposition is true if and only if it corresponds to an actual state of affairs in the external world.

TO THINK THROUGH

The Chinese Room Argument has generated a huge amount of discussion, but twenty years after putting it forward, Searle was able to say that nothing had been produced that invalidates it. What do you think?

As we have seen, after three centuries of growing dominance, the scientific worldview suffered considerable setbacks in the twentieth century. Some were in reaction to the things that it had produced, such as weapons of mass destruction. Some were the result of its failure to deliver on its promise of providing a better world, as witnessed by two world wars, and many other horrific conflicts. In an increasingly "green" age, science was seen as destructive of the environment in its fixation to make us "lords and possessors of nature." Many saw it as a tool of the powerful, a means of exploitation in a world where the rich grow richer and the poor continue to grow poorer. And most of us have reacted against its insistence on turning human beings into machines.

But the dominance of science was also challenged by a further, more philosophical factor, one we have already encountered in Peirce and Popper and the later Russell, and which can be traced back to Hume. Throughout the modern period science was seen as a discipline in which we discover and exploit facts about the world around us. Its huge success was seen as a vindication of its method. Whatever doubts philosophy may raise, science was seen as giving us facts of which we could be certain and on which we could base our lives. As such, it should be accepted as authoritative and paradigmatic for all other areas of human thought. But the work of Thomas Kuhn and others, such as Paul Feyerabend, provided a radical challenge to this view and helped topple the scientific approach from its position of dominance.

THOMAS KUHN

Cincinnati, Ohio (1922–1996). Thomas Kuhn was professor at Berkeley, Princeton, and the Massachusetts Institute of Technology. Educated in theoretical physics, he developed an interest in the history and philosophy of science; his work in this field has had significant repercussions in philosophy and the social sciences.

How science functions. In 1962 Kuhn published *The Structure of Scientific Revolutions*, in which he sought to show that the traditional image of the nature of scientific knowledge and of the whole scientific enterprise was mistaken. As a result of his historical and sociological research, he concluded that science neither establishes definitive facts about the world around us, nor does it proceed in the coherent rational way that has generally been supposed. What in fact happens is that a community of scientists who have been trained to see the world in a particular way and thus to practice science according to their belief system or "paradigm," work at fitting all the data from their observations and experiments into that paradigm. Some don't fit well, so these become the challenges and puzzles on which they concentrate. The resolving of these problems or anomalies is seen as success and progress. Paradigms continue to be used unquestioningly until the number of unsolved problems begins to mount up. This precipitates a crisis; some of the scientists begin to realize that the paradigm is at fault and search for a new one. One is found and adopted, not because it can be shown to be true, nor even because logical arguments can be adduced to show its superiority over any other one, but because it answers some of the problems inherent in the old paradigm. Not all will convert to the new one; in particular older scientists will be more conservative and try to keep the old one going. But the more radical and adventurous younger scientists will support the paradigm shift, and the new paradigm will eventually oust the old one and become accepted orthodoxy.

The new paradigm may well provide better answers to the current problems than the old one, but, said Kuhn, it will also bring with it a new crop of problems. So the change is not necessarily for the good. In fact, from the nature of the case, said Kuhn, there is no rational way of relating one paradigm to another to see which one is better. They are "incommensurable." We shouldn't think in terms of science gradually getting nearer and nearer to the ultimate goal of a "full, objective, true account of nature." Rather, we should see it as "evolution-towards-what-we-wish-to-know." Despite his views, Kuhn claimed that his position did not entail relativism, in that he believed in irreversible progress in scientific development.

PAUL FEYERABEND

Vienna (1924–1994). Like Kuhn, Paul Feyerabend was trained in theoretical physics and became a philosopher of science. He studied at Vienna and taught in a number of countries, including Britain, Germany, Switzerland, and especially the United States (Berkeley). He went well beyond Kuhn in his skepticism about the rationality of science. In contrast to the traditional concept of orderly rational progress, the story of science, he said, is one of "epistemological anarchism." Historically so far from advancing in a rational manner, the dominating factors in the story of science have been nonrational elements like politics, rhetoric, and propaganda. There is no rational justification for adopting the scientific worldview over any other, such as that of voodoo.

TO THINK THROUGH

Most philosophers of science have accepted the validity of Kuhn's case, even if they have not gone to the extreme of Feyerabend. But most ordinary people still have a tremendous confidence that science is discovering facts about the world around us. Do you think this confidence is justified?

Once there was a man who collected pearls. He had a large and varied collection. One day he was visited by a dealer who offered him the most incredible pearl he had ever seen. It was so fantastic that he agreed to let the dealer have his entire collection in exchange for it. Ten minutes after the dealer had driven away with his entire collection, the man realized his new pearl was a fake.

If Kuhn and Feyerabend are right, and most people accept that they are, the English-speaking empirical philosophical tradition has made two terrible mistakes. It abandoned the richness and variety of traditional philosophy and adopted instead a narrow and limited concept of what philosophy is all about, as dictated by the scientific worldview. But even more seriously, it has been taken in by the claims of the scientific worldview, which have turned out to be false. The need is desperate for a new beginning, building on a new and firm foundation.

FORTY-NINE

THINKING AGAIN OF GOD

TWENTIETH-CENTURY GOD-BASED PHILOSOPHIES

> In this chapter we look at five twentieth-century philosophies that gave God a significant place in their systems. They are those of George Santayana, A. N. Whitehead, Simone Weil, Pierre Teilhard de Chardin, and Jacques Maritain.

THE TWENTIETH CENTURY IS VIEWED BY SOME AS THE period when the "death of God" became a reality. "Man has come of age" was a favorite theme. We are at last grown up. We no longer need anyone to take care of us or to tell us what to believe and what to do. We can launch out on our own.

This view was not by any means shared by all, though those who held it tended to make the most noise and get the most attention. Indeed, there is something of a crusading anti-God spirit that goes beyond traditional philosophical detachment in many of their writings. The tone of Ayer's *Language, Truth and Logic,* for example, betrays a sense of triumph at having found a tool that will finally dispense with God and demonstrate once and for all that believers and theologians alike down through the centuries have been talking total nonsense. In a remarkable statement, Russell, who had regarded Whitehead as a brilliant thinker, commented that he couldn't comprehend a word of the God-centered system that was the culmination of his life's work. This is not to be seen so much as an indication of Russell's failing intellect as a dogged refusal even to think about the possibility of God. In a similar way, postmodern thinkers, in their elimination of metanarratives, refuse to countenance any way of viewing human life and the natural world in a larger context that has a place for God.

Yet all through the twentieth century a substantial proportion, if not the majority, of philosophers included at least some concept of God in their thinking. Some of these did so because they were Christians. They believed in God and the Christian revelation on personal and experiential grounds. They can be said to have started their philosophizing with the presupposition of theism, just as the anti-God philosophers started with a presupposition of atheism.

Others, however, like Maritain and Whitehead, can be seen as moving in the opposite direction. Starting with the challenge of having to produce a livable worldview, they developed systems that accepted the need for God, since without him we can't make sense of the world. The form they gave to this "God of the philosophers" may not have tallied at all points with the Christian God of revelation. But the basic fact remains that they were convinced that a philosophical understanding of the world must include a belief in God. And this conviction was as strong, if less vehemently expressed, as the determination of the anti-God philosophers to eliminate him altogether.

To illustrate the richness and diversity of God-based philosophies that were being put forward in the twentieth century, we will look briefly at the work of a Spaniard and an Englishman who both spent a significant part of their lives in America, and two men and a woman from France.

GEORGE SANTAYANA

Madrid (1863–1952). Born to Spanish Catholic parents, George Santayana had an unsettled childhood in Spain and then in America. After studying at Harvard (under William James) and Berlin, he taught philosophy at Harvard from 1889 to 1912. He then left America for Europe, living the rest of his life mainly in France and Italy. A poet and novelist as well as a philosopher, both by temperament and in his philosophy he stands in strong contrast to the mainstream of American philosophy, with his lack of involvement with science, his pessimism, and his attitude of resignation. Though he remained a Spanish citizen all his life, he considered himself an American philosopher.

Rejection of rationalism. Santayana rejected the demand for rational justification of a worldview and the skepticism that arises from it. We may be incapable of producing proofs for the validity of our beliefs, he said,

but we have to assume them as a matter of "animal faith"; our lives in the world demand beliefs about the world as the basis for our action; these beliefs are often expressed symbolically in poetry, beauty, and religion.

Critical realism.
Santayana's philosophy is an idiosyncratic blend of materialistic naturalism and Platonism, at times with a pragmatic flavoring, which offered an integrated system covering aesthetics, epistemology, ethics, and metaphysics. His naturalism stressed the givenness of the world; he was strongly opposed to the assumption made by most of his contemporaries that the world and its truth are constructed by or dependent on human beings. Santayana described his position as "critical realism"; reality exists independently of us, and we are able to experience it through our direct perception of essences.

Being.
Santayana posited four basic realms or categories of being: matter, spirit (or human consciousness), essence, and truth. Matter is the formless force of physical reality. Essences are the eternal forms in which matter is embodied; apart from this embodiment they cannot be actualized. Truth is "the total history and destiny of matter and spirit," the "enormously complex essence which they exemplify by existing." It is thus, for Santayana, objective and absolute. However, we are able to apprehend just small fragments of this total truth, generally only in a symbolic form. Thus truth for us is partial and largely pragmatic as we seek to cope effectively with the world.

Religion.
Santayana's naturalism didn't exclude a significant role for religion as the source of meaning and morality and a key element of personal identity. As with all beliefs, however, religious beliefs do not provide us with absolute truth.

ALFRED NORTH WHITEHEAD

Ramsgate, Kent, England (1861–1947). A. N. Whitehead's early work centered on mathematics and logic; in his middle period he was mainly interested in the philosophy of science, and in his later period he developed a unique metaphysical system. After studying at Cambridge, he taught there until 1910; one of his students was Bertrand Russell, and Whitehead and Russell worked together on *Principia Mathematica*, a project they thought would take a year, but which actually took them ten years. Whitehead moved to be professor of applied mathematics at London in 1910; and, in 1924, at the age of sixty-three, he went to Harvard to become professor of philosophy there until his retirement in 1938.

Process philosophy. Whitehead was impressed with current developments in physics and sought to develop a philosophy of science that fit with concepts of flux, energy and force, and relativity theory. This led him in his middle period to analyze scientific explanations in dynamic terms, according to his understanding of nature as overlapping series of events. Once he had moved to Harvard, he developed these ideas in a wider metaphysical system he called the "philosophy of organism" but which is generally known as process philosophy. Its best-known statement is in his book *Process and Reality* (1929).

Dynamic reality. In his description of the basic nature of things, Whitehead proposed a dynamic model of the nature of the world in place of what he felt was the static model that had dominated Western thinking since the Enlightenment. We should not think of the world, he said, primarily as made up of substances, or objects, inert things behaving mechanistically in Newtonian space and time. Nor should we divide between mind, as something active, and matter, as something passive. Reality is one. Mind is the product of nature, not something standing over against it. We should view everything that is as an organically interrelated interdependent system, in which events and process are primary. The basic units of the universe are events, not things. These events combine together to form processes, which are themselves part of one great cosmic process. The things we call objects, whether an electron, a human body, or what we call the mind, are the products of these events and processes.

God. Foundational to the total process is God, who orders the processes and thus causes things to be. But Whitehead didn't see God as transcendent in the traditional sense; his naturalism required that God, though eternal, should be inside the overall process and so share in it. He therefore rejected the "unmoved mover" concept of God in favor of a much more involved, or "Galilean" one. God is not the detached absolute; rather, he is intimately connected with the world in its process, affecting it and being affected by it. Whitehead posited two "natures" or poles of God. Seen in his "primordial nature," he orders the processes and so causes things to be, both as objects in the world and as the developing process of history. But in his "consequent nature," God shares in the process of becoming. All the events and series of processes are preserved in him; in this sense he too is in the process of becoming; he is the cosmic process. Whitehead didn't develop any details of this concept of God, but others have worked on his ideas and developed "process theology" in considerable detail. Most notable among them was **Charles Hartshorne** (1897–1994).

SIMONE WEIL

Paris (1909–1943). Born into a prosperous Jewish family, Simone Weil (pronounced *vay* or *vile*) studied philosophy at the École Normale Supérieure in Paris and then became a teacher. Converted to left-wing political views, she left teaching in the 1930s to become a factory worker in solidarity with the socially deprived. Following three deep mystical experiences, she became a Christian in 1938, though, in keeping with her identification with outsiders, she was never baptized. She used Platonic and Hindu concepts in her understanding and application of Christianity. She described Christianity as "the last marvelous expression of the Greek genius." She died at age thirty-four, largely as the result of starving herself in solidarity with the Jewish victims of Nazism.

Reason and mystery.

Weil's philosophical interests focused on epistemology, ethics, and social and political theory. In epistemology she stressed the limits of rational thought; pushed too far, rational thinking always leads to contradiction. As a result, we need to follow the mystic way, where the self becomes united with God. The essence of God's revelation is self-emptying, as shown in creation, which was a relinquishing of power, and especially in the incarnation and crucifixion. In the face of life's "affliction," we can only discover meaning by sharing in this process of renunciation. Beliefs and dogmas have a place, but they are to be seen as mysteries into which we enter rather than rational definitions of truth. In the last analysis, for Weil, action was always more meaningful than knowledge.

The human condition.

Weil attacked the dehumanizing results of capitalism, the oppressive role of the state, the dangers of increasing bureaucracy, and the soul-destroying results of developing technology. All of these things, she felt, oppress the individual and create an environment in which her or his needs for freedom, equality, security, truth and the like fail to be met. As a result, we are rootless, alienated, and psychologically fragmented.

PIERRE TEILHARD DE CHARDIN

Auvergne, France (1881–1955). Teilhard was a Jesuit priest and a paleontologist, who sought to reconcile his Christian beliefs with those of science, especially geology, biology, and evolutionary theory. His early education was in philosophy and math. After the First World War, he studied geology, biology, and paleontology, and he spent some years in successful and influential field research in China and other parts of Asia. Toward the close of his life he lived in America. He was a sensitive man who experienced personal suffering and loneliness. He was deeply influenced by his experiences in the First World War and hurt by the refusal of the Catholic hierarchy to accept his ideas. He wrote prolifically, but his more philosophical writings were not published until after his death. His best-known work is *The Phenomenon of Man* (1955; English translation, 1959).

Cosmic evolution.

Influenced by Bergson, Teilhard developed a concept of the evolution of the universe, from the "Alpha point" of creation toward ever higher forms of consciousness, culminating in an "Omega point" of union with God, which Teilhard identified as the full presence of Christ. This process is possible because, for Teilhard, there is no final distinction to be drawn between inorganic matter like rocks (the "lithosphere"), organic matter (the "biosphere"), and thinking conscious matter (the "noosphere"). All are to be seen as stages of the process. All that happens in the process is to be seen as the action of God, the disclosure and increasing manifestation of Spirit. No piece of matter is to be seen as merely inert because it is pregnant, at least potentially, with life through the presence of God. The process of development, however, is not automatic. We share in it and have moral and social responsibilities to further it, not just by the development of knowledge and consciousness, but by the expression of love and the drawing together of our fragmented world in the love of Christ.

JACQUES MARITAIN

Paris (1882–1973). Jacques Maritain studied at the Sorbonne and Heidelberg. The hopelessness of his science-dominated worldview drove him to make a suicide pact with his fiancée, Raïssa Oumansoff, a Russian Jewish poet. But attending the lectures of Bergson opened the way to an alternative worldview, and in 1906, two years after marrying, he and Raïssa became Catholics. A layman, Maritain was professor at the Institut Catholique in Paris, then at the Pontifical Institute for Medieval Studies in Toronto, and finally at Princeton University. He shared in the drafting of the United Nations' Universal Declaration of Human Rights. After retiring he returned to France. He wrote more than sixty books, some with his wife. He developed a comprehensive philosophical system, using the work of Aquinas as a base, and seeking to apply it in all parts of life including moral and social areas, politics, and art.

Reality and knowledge.
Maritain attacked the subjectivity of philosophy since Descartes. Objective reality, he said, can be known. It takes many forms, and we need to recognize that there are many ways of knowing. In *The Degrees of Knowledge* (1932; English translation, 1959), he distinguished conceptual knowledge from nonconceptual knowledge, obtained through things like intuition and mystical experience. These two classifications of knowledge may be further subdivided; each division has its own way of functioning. For example, scientific knowledge doesn't function in the same way as mathematical or metaphysical knowledge. In the nonconceptual area, we have moral awareness through an intuitive "knowledge by inclination"; then there's the kind of knowledge that arises from the subconscious part of us, or from the spiritual part of us; and in the sphere of aesthetics, we experience another direct form of knowledge.

God.
Maritain sought to update Aquinas's arguments for the existence of God and added a further one of his own, arguing from the existence of the personal human self to the existence of a divine person.

Maritain was a leading figure in the revival of interest in the work of Aquinas known as neo-Thomism. Another thinker who built on Aquinas's worldview, with a key role for God, was **Bernard Lonergan** (1904–1984), a Canadian Jesuit who taught in Montreal, Toronto, and Rome, and whose work has been developed by a number of disciples. He too focused on the issue of our knowledge of reality, arguing that we can have reliable knowledge through a process, which we all follow, of testing our experience. The stages of this process are experiencing (sense data or mental activity), understanding (what the experience might mean in the context of the whole of reality), judging (what it does mean), and then, in the light of this, deciding on action.

TO THINK THROUGH

We can see God in the light of the world or see the world in the light of God. Which do you think these philosophers did? Were they right in doing so?

FIFTY

THINGS AREN'T ALWAYS WHAT THEY SEEM

HERMENEUTICS AND THE FRANKFURT SCHOOL

In this chapter we turn back again to the story of twentieth-century Continental philosophy and its final descent into postmodernism. We will look first at the development of hermeneutics, which links with the interest in linguistic analysis in the English-speaking tradition. Then we will look briefly at the Frankfurt school, which has been noted for its left-wing political involvement. This interest in Marxism or left-wing politics has been shared by a number of the guru figures of recent philosophy and has served to increase their popularity among students, not least in the French universities where Marxism and student unrest tended at times to assume more importance than academic study.

HERMENEUTICS

Though hermeneutics (Gk. *hermeneuo*, "interpret") has been practiced for centuries by theologians seeking to interpret the Bible, it was only in the twentieth century that it became a central issue in philosophy. This was partly the result of the widespread interest in language both in the British analytic tradition and in the Continental phenomenological and structuralist traditions. But philosophical hermeneutics has not limited its interest to the interpretation of texts. It is not just the Bible or other written texts that need understanding and interpreting. The world itself, with all its data, needs it too. We too need interpreting; human existence challenges us to tease out the hidden meaning of life.

Social practices, history, all the story of humankind is in a sense a text that needs understanding and interpreting.

As we have seen, Dilthey in a sense set the agenda for philosophical hermeneutics by pointing out that in all the human or cultural sciences, such as philosophy, art, religion, psychology, history, and sociology, we don't seek the kind of causal explanations that we would expect in the natural sciences (see chapter 37). Rather, we seek the kind of understanding that grasps the spirit or life of the subject or its authors. We can do this because there is at least some degree of continuity of experience between ourselves and those we are seeking to understand. We are thus able to enter in and share their lived experiences, a practice that was recommended by Schleiermacher, who is often looked on as the forerunner of the current hermeneutical movement.

Philosophical hermeneutics thus concerns itself with any element of life that has meaning, effectively any aspect of human society, practice, language, and culture. Heidegger had a major impact on the development of philosophical hermeneutics, both because he saw human being as being that understands and interprets, but also because of his fusion of subject and object, seen in his concept of *Dasein*, which not only includes both the human subject and the "objective" world, but also stresses community and involvement. Two key figures in the development of philosophical hermeneutics are Hans-Georg Gadamer and Paul Ricoeur.

HANS-GEORG GADAMER

Marburg, Germany (1900–2002). Gadamer studied philosophy and classical philology at Marburg and taught at Marburg from 1929. He became professor at Leipzig in 1938, then at Frankfurt in 1947, and he was at Heidelberg from 1949 until retiring in 1968. His most influential work was *Wahrheit und Methode* (1960; English translation, *Truth and Method*, 1975).

Personal involvement. Strongly influenced by Heidegger, with whom he studied, Gadamer rejected the way of understanding or explanation used in the natural sciences as the model for our understanding in the human sciences. In the human sciences we cannot follow the "scientific" detached observer approach that seeks to establish an explanation and confirm it by observation or experiment. Rather, we gain understanding through a process of personal involvement in which we make an essential contribution. It was a major mistake of the Enlightenment, said Gadamer, to be "prejudiced against prejudice."

He used the example of a work of art as a paradigm. When we approach a work of art, the key thing is our experience of it, our living relationship with it, not our intellectual explanation of it or even our understanding of the ideas of the artist or our analysis of how it came to be. It is a mistake to assume that there is just one correct interpretation of a work of art. Gadamer criticized Schleiermacher and Dilthey for assuming that the key hermeneutic task was to get inside the author's mind to find the "right" understanding. The fact is, says Gadamer, that though seeking to understand the artist's "horizon" is important, we can never do this completely because we are conditioned by our own historical and personal perspective; we can never see the picture as the artist saw it.

Dialectic and the fusing of horizons. But our own perspective is an advantage rather than a problem. We don't have to purge ourselves of all our preconceptions and baggage before we can understand. Rather, we bring ourselves and all our ways of seeing things, our horizon, to the work of art, and they form a key part of the process of understanding. We engage in dialogue with the artist and with the work of art itself. We listen and look; we bring questions and insights to the work that are distinctively ours, that may never have occurred to the artist. Thus we probe its meaning and fuse our horizon with that of the artist in a kind of dialectic. We enrich the work with what we bring to it; we are changed by what it says to us. This is no one-time experience; it is a continuing dialogue; as the work changes us, so our approach to it changes, and so on.

What applies to works of art applies to all other "human" areas, to texts, to historical events and processes, and to social phenomena. Each individual and each historical and cultural viewpoint, will bring different insights and questions to a "text" and thus engage with it differently and draw new meaning from it. Gadamer denied that this approach lands us in relativism. True, we never arrive at a definitive understanding, but by grounding our interpretation in the text and remaining in continual dialogue with it, we are safeguarded from subjectivity.

Gadamer applied his theory in a number of hermeneutical investigations into philosophical works, including those of Heidegger, Hegel, and Plato. He particularly stressed the importance of the careful analysis of the author's and text's situation; for example, we cannot take an argument in a Socratic dialogue and isolate it from the dialogue or the milieu in which Plato composed it.

TO THINK THROUGH

How can we accept Gadamer's approach and yet avoid relativism?

PAUL RICOEUR

Valence, France (1913–). Ricoeur's philosophical training and original interest were largely in the history of philosophy, an area that has influenced all his subsequent work. In his mid twenties he met Gabriel Marcel and was deeply impressed by his ideas. He spent most of the Second World War as a prisoner of the Germans and used the opportunity to study Husserl and Heidegger. He was professor of the history of philosophy at Strasbourg from 1948 to 1957 and then moved to Paris to be professor first at the Sorbonne and then at Nanterre from 1966 until 1980. He was also linked to Chicago as a professor from 1960. His early publications were on Jaspers, Marcel, and Husserl. His other writings range over many fields, including the will, evil, social theory, ethics, memory, a number of thinkers ranging from Augustine to Freud, and language, including metaphor, narrative, and especially hermeneutics. A Protestant Christian, he had a lifelong concern for social justice, which he developed in his moral and political philosophy.

Building bridges.

Ricoeur's first major work, a Husserlian examination of the will, was written to refute Sartre's concept of absolute freedom in *Being and Nothingness*. His philosophical willingness to listen to a "text" was also expressed in his willingness to listen to a wide variety of philosophical views. Over against the arrogance shown by many of his contemporaries, he stressed the humility that is needed in a philosopher. Essentially a generous mediator, he saw part of his role as building bridges between those engaged in the "conflict of interpretations." He had a special skill of understanding and seeking to accommodate the views of various and opposing schools of thought. His desire to build bridges also extended to the distinction between the method of the natural sciences and the method of the human sciences, where he sought to show that there are parallels between the logic of scientific explanation and that of hermeneutical understanding. A basic aim in all his explorations was to reply to skepticism and relativism by showing that it is possible to identify meaning or meanings in the text or the concept he is investigating.

Hermeneutic of suspicion.

In hermeneutics Ricoeur distinguished between a hermeneutic of tradition and a hermeneutic of suspicion. The first, he said, is exemplified by Gadamer. The second is his own approach. He called it "subversive" in that it assumes that the text is not as innocent as it appears but is in fact driven by subconscious or ulterior motives, social pressures, class interests, or the like. Starting with the presupposition that no meanings are immediately given, the task of the interpreter is to unmask the hidden and distorted meanings that lie beneath the surface of the text or the ideology. But by what criterion do we decide what is the correct interpretation? There are no criteria, replied Ricoeur, since there is no one "correct" interpretation. Quite apart from different interpreters reaching different interpretations, a single interpreter will find a dialectic in the text, a "negative" and a "positive" hermeneutic. But though each interpretation will be different and will conflict with the others, each makes its own contribution, so each must be heard. Out of the dialectic will come meaning and so truth. Ricoeur applied this approach in his own studies of Freud, Nietzsche, and Foucault.

TO THINK THROUGH

Fame and fortune in the twentieth century seem to have come more to those philosophers who adopted extreme positions than to those few who sought to build bridges. If you were to make philosophy your career, which camp do you think you would join?

THE FRANKFURT SCHOOL

The Frankfurt School is a name given to a group of philosophers, social scientists, economists, critics, and intellectuals associated with the Institute for Social Research, set up in Frankfurt am Main in 1923. Its original vision was to develop an acceptable form of Marxism, in contrast to the forms practiced in Eastern Europe. Though it gradually moved away from this as its central aim and maintained no specific affiliation to any political party, it has continued to develop a basically left-wing interdisciplinary critique of society. During the period of the ascendancy of Nazism in Germany, the school transferred to the United States, returning to Frankfurt after the war. Significant names in the "first generation" of the school were **Max Horkheimer** (1895–1973), **Herbert Marcuse** (1898–1979), **Erich Fromm** (1900–1980), and **Theodor Adorno** (1903–1969). The best-known member of the "second generation" of the school is **Jürgen Habermas** (1929–). The school had considerable influence on the development of left-wing movements and student unrest in the 1960s.

Power and society. The members of the school developed a critique of society that highlighted its manipulative and oppressive structures. Starting

481

from a Hegelian view of the historical conditioning of ideas and society, they were essentially gloomy about the human condition and pessimistic about the possibility of Marx's predicted proletarian revolution. Ordinary people, they felt, were too deeply conditioned by "the system" even to realize they had a problem. Through science and technology, the pursuit of wealth, ideological systems, and the exploitation and manipulation exercised through the mass media, we have all been manipulated and enslaved without realizing what has happened. If we are to be liberated, it will have to be through enlightened leadership. The insights of social science and especially psychoanalysis were adopted by the school as a significant means of increasing self-understanding and providing a model for social change and liberation through increasing awareness of our hidden problems.

Instrumental reason. Horkheimer and Adorno diagnosed "instrumental reason" as the foundational source of society's malaise. This is reason as seen by the Enlightenment as a means to gain control over nature. It is thus essentially a tool to dominate and exploit, and this is precisely what it has done to the individual, resulting in social and cultural domination and totalitarianism.

Communicative rationality. Habermas modified this concept. Enlightenment reason, he argued, is not just negative in an instrumental controlling sense. It also has a positive element, which he analyzed as communicative rationality. It is communication, he argues, that provides us with the possibility of understanding and rational consensus, which in turn provides a criterion for assessing and critiquing society. Not surprisingly, his positive attitude to an aspect of Enlightenment rationalism has been attacked by those, like Richard Rorty and the postmodernists, who believe that all elements of Enlightenment rationality are to be abandoned. But Habermas has continued to develop his concept of communication, incorporating elements of speech-act theory, and seeking to counter postmodern relativism by arguing for the establishing of criteria for values, morals, and truth through "communicative action."

TO THINK THROUGH

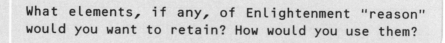

What elements, if any, of Enlightenment "reason" would you want to retain? How would you use them?

FIFTY-ONE

THE END OF THE ROAD

STRUCTURALISM, POSTSTRUCTURALISM, AND POSTMODERNISM

In this chapter we look at eight Frenchmen, a Swiss, a Belgian woman, and an American, all but one of whom have had close links with Paris. It may be no accident that most histories of philosophy see the Frenchman Descartes as the prophet of the modern period and trace the story of rationalism as something that particularly dominated French intellectual life. And it is in France that the wheel has turned full circle and the reaction against modernism has been so total.

STRUCTURALISM

Structuralism was an interdisciplinary movement emanating from France that peaked in popularity in the 1960s and 1970s and through poststructuralism fed into the development of postmodernism. It focused on the description of structures, tending to assume that particulars or individuals in relationships are more significant or more real than in isolation. Structures were seen as underlying these relationships and giving them shape. The task of the philosopher or sociologist or whatever is to uncover these hidden structures in order to explain the phenomena. Structures that were particularly explored were linguistic, social, aesthetic, literary, political, mathematical, and psychological. The movement lessened the significance of the individual person and thus of individual freedom and stressed the controlling influence of the structures.

Structuralists claimed there were features common to all structures, comprising structural laws that govern things as diverse as social practices, the structure of language, literary works, or religious beliefs. Structures were not seen as static, but as open to change. Names particularly associated with the structuralist movement are Ferdinand de Saussure, Claude Lévi-Strauss, Jacques Lacan, Louis Althusser, **Jean Piaget** (1896–1980, Swiss psychologist), and **Roland Barthes** (1915–1980, French writer and cultural critic). The work of Saussure in the structure of language has generally been seen as foundational for the movement, both in the sense that for the most part Saussure's work preceded that of those operating in other disciplines and in the sense that language is foundational to our understanding of all our other human institutions. The result of this priority of language has been that structuralism has readily led into relativism. The structures of the world around us are not to be seen as reflecting or expressing any objective reality or overarching truth about the world, but rather to be determined by the apparently arbitrary conventions of a given linguistic community.

FERDINAND DE SAUSSURE

Geneva (1857–1913). Ferdinand de Saussure was a linguist who studied at Geneva, Leipzig, Berlin, and Paris and then taught at Paris and Geneva. He was the founder of structural linguistics and so was at least partly responsible for the development of structuralism in its wider sense. He rejected the traditional approaches to the understanding of what language is, which had focused on the history or philology of words; he proposed instead a "scientific" understanding. Language, he suggested, is to be seen as an essentially arbitrary interrelated system. Its constituent parts, such as words, sounds, and meanings, cannot be understood in isolation, but only in relationship to each other. Thus, if I wish to understand the word *cat* or *good*, I neither trace the history or the etymology of the words, nor do I examine the isolated use of the words and their relationship to Felix or a virtuous person. Rather, I look at each word's place within a linguistic community, how it relates to other words and signs in that language. Picture a chess board with a game half played. Someone coming into the room and seeing the board doesn't need to know how the pieces got to where they are now. What matters is their current relationship with each other. Indeed, even the shape of the pieces doesn't really matter. If a pawn or a knight had been lost, it could quite easily be replaced by a button, which would serve just as well.

This gave rise to a key concept in Saussure that was to be taken up throughout the twentieth century. It is that of "difference." In language, he said, there are only differences. A word doesn't have a fixed positive meaning that it would retain if it is isolated from the language in which it operates. Rather, it has a meaning as it is different from or stands over against other words in use in the language in a differential relationship.

CLAUDE LÉVI-STRAUSS

Brussels (1908–). Born to middle-class Jewish parents, Claude Lévi-Strauss was brought up and educated in Paris. He studied law and philosophy and was for a few years a left-wing political activist, during which time he developed his interest in sociology and anthropology. He taught in Brazil, the United States, and France. He applied the approach of structuralism to social and anthropological issues like myth and ritual, totemism, kinship systems, and oral narrative, studying their hidden underlying structures rather than the details of the phenomena themselves, and finding meaning in relationships rather than in individuals.

JACQUES LACAN

Paris (1901–1981). Trained as a medical doctor, Jacques Lacan used the insights of structuralism, which Lévi-Strauss had applied to anthropology, to develop a new approach to psychoanalysis. His radicalism caused his exclusion from the International Psychoanalytic Association in 1960. His writing style was deliberately obscure and at times irrational, thus reflecting the nature of the unconscious itself. He viewed the unconscious, described by Freud as consisting of instincts and drives, as something that is structured "like a language," and thus open to much more precise analysis than Freud's approach permitted. But at the same time he rejected the Freudian concept of the ego or self, claiming it was a relic of Cartesianism and reducing it to a linguistic symbol.

LOUIS ALTHUSSER

Birmandries, Algeria (1918–1990). Louis Althusser's studies in Paris were interrupted by the Second World War, in which he was taken prisoner. He taught at the École Normale in Paris for all his professional career; among his students were Foucault and Derrida. He was a committed Marxist. He suffered from manic depression all his life and was confined to a psychiatric hospital after he murdered his wife in 1980. He applied the structuralist approach to a reinterpretation of Marx, using particularly his "scientific," as opposed to "humanistic," later works, notably *Capital*. In this Althusser claimed that his approach was truly "scientific" rather than ideological. His reinterpretation was severely criticized and appears to contain a number of inconsistencies. Indeed, later in life he conceded that it had been an "imaginary Marxism." Nevertheless, he exercised considerable influence on French intellectual life in the third quarter of the twentieth century.

POSTSTRUCTURALISM

Following the apparently successful application of Saussure's linguistic structuralism to other "sciences," such as anthropology, psychology, sociology, and literary criticism, in the years following the Second World War, it seemed to those in the structuralist tradition that they had at last found a tool that could be applied to all areas of human life. However, as happened with linguistic analysis, disillusionment set in, and some, like Foucault and Derrida, who were influenced by structuralism in their early days (though Foucault later denied it), became its strongest critics.

The case against structuralism centered on its claim to provide a system of knowledge or understanding that contained clearly defined basic concepts. Poststructuralists called into question the possibility or wisdom of defining such concepts and, more fundamentally, rejected the concept of an overarching system. The typical method of showing the inadequacy of structuralist approaches is deconstruction, whereby the kind of texts structuralists used are taken apart in order to demonstrate their failure to establish the system they are supposed to be building. This is done by seeking to show that the text at any given place is unable to communicate a specific meaning or establish a specific point. The text is in effect full of conflicts, contradictions, and ambiguities, and is thus unable to do what is claimed for it. Since the text of the deconstructor is as open to the application of the deconstructing method as any, the poststructuralists see no need to present their case in a coherent form. Traditional forms of philosophical argument are replaced by techniques like ridicule, innuendo, and exaggeration. These devices are all seen as legitimate tools in a situation where not only is every formerly accepted structure of morality or human behavior rejected, but even more seriously, a total veto is imposed on putting anything in their place.

GILLES DELEUZE

Paris (1925–1995). Gilles Deleuze taught philosophy at Lyon and then at Paris (Vincennes). He is regarded by many as the key figure in the development of poststructuralism. His early work sought for new and provocative readings of Spinoza, Hume, Proust, Kant, and Bergson. His *Nietzsche et la philosophie* (1962) was partly responsible for the considerable interest in the work of Nietzsche that arose in the latter part of the twentieth century. A number of his later works were written collaboratively with the "postpsychoanalyst" and political theorist **Félix Guattari** (1930–1992). Deleuze's friend Foucault regarded him as perhaps the greatest philosopher of the twentieth century. His iconoclastic anti-philosophy set the trend for much of postmodernism. It is dominated by a search for a way of escaping the abyss of chaos without having to resort to a solution that is in any way transcendent (and Deleuze included the subjective in the transcendent, in that it is human consciousness imposing order on the world). In this search he explored "differentiation" (the way things don't fit together) and the possibility that we may have to accept the abyss. Toward the end of his life, he summed up his concept of philosophy as "the art of forming, inventing, and fabricating concepts." Deleuze retired in 1987 and committed suicide in 1995.

MICHEL FOUCAULT

Poitiers, France (1926–1984). Michel Foucault studied at the École Normale Supérieure in Paris and had a number of teaching posts before becoming professor of the history of systems of thought at the Collège de France in 1970. Major influences on his thinking included Marxism, Nietzsche, and structuralism. He published books in a range of areas, including history, philosophy, linguistics, and psychoanalysis. His interest in history arose from a concern to understand how we have arrived at the place we are today. Among his best-known works are *Madness and Civilization* (1961; English translation, 1965), *The Order of Things* (1966; English translation, 1970), and *The Archaeology of Knowledge* (1969; English translation, 1972). His last writing project, a six-volume *History of Sexuality*, was left unfinished when he died in 1984, a victim of AIDS.

"Archaeologies of knowledge." Foucault didn't see himself as studying the history of ideas in the traditional sense. To make this clear he described his research as exploring archaeologies of knowledge, in which he sought to uncover the "systems of thought" that shaped attitudes and social practices, and by uncovering their "discontinuities," to demonstrate that they were nothing more than relatively arbitrary means of exercising power. In his survey of the treatment of madness, for example, he analyzed three historical

approaches, treating the insane as deviants, or as animals, or as suffering from an illness. Foucault didn't accept that any of these approaches is more enlightened or preferable than the others. His aim was simply to set one alongside the other and thus to show the arbitrariness of our current "system of thought."

Knowledge and power.

In the 1970s Foucault especially focused on the relationship between knowledge and power. Each implies the other, he said. There is no power relation without a corresponding field of knowledge. There is no knowledge that does not establish a relation of power. He applied his studies in the treatment and punishment of criminals to demonstrate the use of knowledge, especially as expressed in sciences such as medicine and psychology, to maintain social and political control or "domination." Knowledge, for Foucault, could not be objective or beneficial; it is essentially a means of manipulation and the exercise of power.

The self and freedom.

Submission to the domination that arises through the exercise of knowledge/power is not inevitable, said Foucault. We can resist it. In so doing, we refuse to be made what the knowledge/power system of our current culture or situation tells us we are, and so we become truly free. Foucault didn't suggest what patterns of alternative knowledge we might adopt in place of those we reject, and it may be that the only way the freedom he is advocating could be exercised is through anarchy.

TO THINK THROUGH

The assumption that reason and knowledge are inevitably used as expressions of power and domination is a common one in contemporary thought. Do you agree with it? If accepted widely, would it necessarily lead to chaos and anarchy? If we reject it, how do we counter it?

For Further Study

Foucault, M., and P. Rabinov, eds. *The Foucault Reader.* New York: Random House, 1984.

JACQUES DERRIDA

Algiers (1930–). Born into an Algerian Jewish family, Jacques Derrida studied phenomenology in Paris, where he taught at the École Normale Supérieure
and the Sorbonne. He has also taught at Johns Hopkins University and Yale.
Particular influences on his thought include Nietzsche, Heidegger, and Freud.
A leading figure among the deconstructionists, he wrote prolifically and had a
wide influence in a number of academic disciplines, including sociology, literary theory, linguistics, and psychology. From about 1980 Derrida's writings took
a more specifically political turn.

Deconstruction.
Derrida declined to give a definition of deconstruc-
tion, insisting that it was not a technique or a method. He regarded philosophical or literary texts as already containing the seeds of their own
destruction, in that any author unwittingly includes contradictions, blind
spots, elements of aporia (mentioning a problematic issue without resolving
it), unjustified assumptions, or the like. The deconstructionist, said Derrida,
is simply bringing these to the surface. In his own work, he used all sorts of
ways to do this, including many that would in another context be considered
irrational or unfair. But deconstructionists allow themselves the luxury of
being irrational and unfair, since rationality and fairness are two of the concepts they are seeking to deconstruct.

Logic and authority.
One of the key concepts Derrida was con-
cerned to undermine was the logic of identity, basically the laws of logical
thought that have dominated Western philosophy and thinking since Aristotle. Thought has, for example, taken it as axiomatic that A cannot be not-
A, or that what is, is. For Derrida these laws imply some reality outside of
us to which our thinking is subject. In that he can allow no source of meaning that stands outside the text, these laws must be shown to be invalid. In
a parallel way, Derrida argued against the traditional view that the spoken
word was to be valued more highly than the written word, in that the presence of the author helps fix the meaning of the words. This view too, he
said, expresses an invalid desire to resort to an authority outside of language.
The desire for a definitive and final interpretation must always be resisted;
every suggested interpretation must be "deferred" rather than being
accepted, in order to keep open all the "differences." Derrida combined the
French for "deferral" and "difference" to coin a term *différance* that described

the way we must constantly accept the contrast of different meanings of a text, refusing to earth it in any fixed point.

For Further Study

Norris, C. *Derrida*. Cambridge, Mass.: Harvard University Press, 1988.

POSTMODERNISM

JEAN-FRANÇOIS LYOTARD

Versailles (1925–1998). Jean-François Lyotard studied phenomenology with Merleau-Ponty. He began his philosophical career by teaching in secondary schools and ended it as professor at Paris (Saint-Denis) until his retirement in 1989. Up until the 1970s he was strongly committed to Marxism and to the theories of Freud and Lacan. His two best-known works are *The Postmodern Condition: A Report on Knowledge* (1979; English translation, 1984) and *The Differend* (1983; English translation, 1986).

Lyotard famously defined postmodernism as "incredulity towards metanarratives" or *grands récits*. A metanarrative is an overarching explanatory concept or system that seeks to give a coherent account of the world and of human life. It is, in fact, precisely what most philosophers through the ages have been seeking to produce. Such metanarratives, said Lyotard, have been used to control intellectual and social activity and to bolster political institutions. Postmodernism announces their abolition. There is nothing we can put in their place, he said. Instead, we accept a multitude of *petits récits*. These little narratives make no attempt to dominate or to claim truth or finality. They remain open and fluid, emphasizing their differences and mutual incompatibility. The task of the philosopher is to critique the metanarratives and all that has been built on them and to demonstrate their inadequacy. In his own critiques, Lyotard focused especially on the areas of art, literature, aesthetics, and politics.

Lyotard's concept of "the differend" stressed the incompatibility of different concepts or *petits récits* or language games. So far from seeking to build bridges between opposing ideas or interpretations or to find compromises, we must stress the contrasts and discrepancies, thus keeping the dialectic open.

JEAN BAUDRILLARD

Reims, France (1929–). Jean Baudrillard saw himself as "without a background." After study at Nanterre, Paris, he became a sociologist and worked in the Nanterre department of sociology. Like Lyotard, he started as a Marxist and developed a trenchant style of political and cultural negative critique. Though accepted as a leading figure in the postmodern movement, he typically stated, "Postmodernism doesn't have a meaning. . . . It's not even a concept. It's nothing at all."

LUCE IRIGARAY

Blaton, Belgium (1930–). After study in literature, linguistics, and philosophy in Paris, Luce Irigaray settled in France and became a practicing psychoanalyst in the Freudian and Lacanian tradition. Rejecting the term *feminist*, she saw herself as an exponent of sexual difference, urging the need to differentiate strongly between the sexes rather than to establish equality. Her most celebrated book was *Speculum of the Other Woman* (1974; English translation, 1985), in which she attacked the male domination of Western philosophy, focusing on figures like Plato, Hegel, and Freud. All claims, she said, to have produced a universal and objective worldview are totally vitiated by the fact that virtually every such attempt has been written by a male.

RICHARD RORTY

New York City (1931–). After study at Chicago and Yale, Richard Rorty taught at Wellesley College and Princeton. In 1982 he became professor of humanities at the University of Virginia. He was at first influenced both by pragmatism and by linguistic analysis. Later he developed his own distinctive version of skeptical postmodernism, which has led him to attack all forms of systematizing philosophy, especially the phenomenological and analytical traditions. Both these traditions, he said, have demonstrated their barrenness, in that there is no way of deciding between rival theories. Since all of us are limited to our own beliefs and have no external criteria by which to assess their truth, Rorty concluded that no belief can ever be established as true, and as a result, no belief is to be preferred to any other. Thus, he concluded, there is no place for epistemology in philosophy. Similarly, what has traditionally been regarded as moral philosophy is to be replaced by "literature and political experimentation."

TO THINK THROUGH

Can we live by "petits récits"?

For Further Study

Appignanesi, R., et al. *Introducing Postmodernism*. New York: Totem Books, 2001.

JOURNEY'S END?

> To make an end is to make a beginning.
> The end is where we start from.
>
> — T. S. Eliot
> *The Four Quartets*, "Little Gidding," Pt. 5

So it's up to you. This is no place to finish the story of philosophy. From here the journey's got to go on. And yours is the opportunity not just to take that journey, but to take a lead in showing others the way. To provide viable alternatives to despair and meaninglessness and relativism. To be part of the rebirth of philosophy.

Can it be done? I believe it can. The Enlightenment project to understand the world by putting us rather than God at the center has collapsed. In its place we need a God-centered approach that will work for the twenty-first century. It may take some doing, but it can be done. And you can do it.

T. S. Eliot based the climax of "Little Gidding" on the words of the late medieval mystic Julian of Norwich (b. 1343) in her *Revelations of Divine Love*:

> We shall not cease from exploration
> And the end of all our exploring
> Will be to arrive where we started
> And know the place for the first time. . . .
> Quick now, here, now, always—
> A condition of complete simplicity
> (Costing not less than everything)
> And all shall be well and
> All manner of things shall be well
> When the tongues of flame are in-folded
> Into the crowned knot of fire
> And the fire and the rose are one.

INDEX OF ICONS

GENERAL INDEX